De-industrialization and foreign trade

De-industrialization and foreign trade

R. E. ROWTHORN

Reader in Economics, University of Cambridge

J. R. WELLS

Lecturer in Economics, University of Cambridge
Fellow of King's College, Cambridge

The right of the University of Cambridge to print and sell all manner of books was granted by Henry VIII in 1534. The University has printed and published continuously since 1584.

CAMBRIDGE UNIVERSITY PRESS

Cambridge
New York New Rochelle Melbourne Sydney

Published by the Press Syndicate of the University of Cambridge
The Pitt Building, Trumpington Street, Cambridge CB2 1RP
32 East 57th Street, New York, NY 10022, USA
10 Stamford Road, Oakleigh, Melbourne 3166, Australia

First published 1987

Printed in Great Britain at The Bath Press, Avon

British Library cataloguing in publication data

Rowthorn, R. E.
De-industrialization and foreign trade.
1. Great Britain – Commerce 2. Great
Britain – Industries
I. Title II. Wells, John, 1947–
382′.0941 HF3506.5

Library of Congress cataloguing in publication data

Rowthorn, R. E.
De-industrialization and foreign trade.
Bibliography
Includes index.
1. Great Britain – Industries. 2. Great Britain –
Commerce. 3. Great Britain – Economic conditions –
1945– . I. Wells, J. R. (John R.) II. Title.
HC256.5.R683 1987 338.0941 87–6331

ISBN 0 521 26360 3 hard covers
ISBN 0 521 26947 4 paperback

BS

Contents

* may be skipped on first reading and read after Chapter 13.

Figures

Tables

Preface

When we first began this book in 1982, our aim was to produce a brief analysis of UK foreign trade since the Second World War. However, as our work progressed, our objectives gradually became more ambitious, and we have ended up covering a much wider variety of topics than we originally intended. Our initial concern with international trade has widened to include economic development and structural change, and the book now contains an extended discussion of economic structure, its evolution during the course of development and relationship to international trade. Moreover, our initial interest broadened out beyond the UK, and there is now a great deal of material dealing with other OECD countries.

The main difficulties we experienced in writing were associated with time and space. Both of us had many other commitments, and neither of us was able to devote himself single-mindedly to the task of completing the book. Moreover, for much of the time, we were located on opposite sides of the globe, and communication between us was limited. These factors help to explain why this book has taken so long to write. They also help to explain why there is a certain lack of uniformity in style. For practical reasons, we were forced to divide up the writing between us, and there was no opportunity to redraft the material so as to produce a common style. The drafting was done as follows:

Rowthorn – Chaps. 1, 5, 6, 7, 10, 11, 12 and 13 and Appendices 1, 2, 3, 4, 6, 7, 8, 9, 10, 11, 12 and 14.

Wells – The Introduction. Chaps. 2, 3, 4, 8 and 9 and Appendices 5 and 13.

We should like to thank the following for reading and commenting on various draft chapters: Andrew Glyn, Geoffrey Harcourt, Linda Hesselman, Robin Matthews, Pascal Petit, Jose Salazar and David Vines. In addition, we have also benefited from valuable discussions with Terry Barker, Richard Bending, Michael Landesmann and William Peterson. We are especially grateful to Diana Day for help with statistical preparation and to Mrs Indira Dholakia for typing out often grubby and near illegible hand-written drafts. We would also like to thank Lucia Hanmer for assistance with correcting the proofs and Beth Scott for preparing the Index.

R.E.R. and J.R.W.

Introduction

The aim of this book is to analyse the inter-relationships between manufacturing output, employment and trade, and to look at the effect of developments in each of these areas of the economy on the rest of economic life; the specific context chosen for this analysis is post-war British economic development. We have selected this topic not only because we believe these issues to be poorly understood at an analytical level, but also because of the present, parlous condition of the British economy and the crisis, looming up ahead of British society, as a result of the prospective decline in North Sea fuel production.

The event which originally stimulated this book was the sudden dramatic collapse, during the early years of Mrs Thatcher's first administration, of British manufacturing output and employment. This development gave rise to a rapid and substantial increase in unemployment, and, because of the associated loss of markets and industrial capacity, this sudden acceleration in the tempo of UK industrial decline has made the task of returning to acceptable levels of employment exceptionally difficult. However, even before the searing experience of the early 1980s, the seemingly inexorable rise in unemployment and Britain's relatively slow rate of economic growth gave rise to a debate concerning 'de-industrialization' in the UK – a debate which focussed on the role of weak industrial performance in Britain's poor overall economic record.

The facts of Britain's relative economic decline are well known. In the 1950s, Britain's standard of living was among the highest in Western Europe; it is now one of the lowest. Meanwhile, productivity in UK manufacturing industry grew much more slowly than in other advanced countries, and it is currently barely one-half (57%) the average for the rest of Western Europe (excluding Southern Europe).[1] In addition, the UK's departure from full employment began earlier (in the mid-1960s), and unemployment has generally been higher than in other advanced capitalist countries. Finally, after a temporary boost from North Sea oil, Britain's balance of payments is now weakening in a way which is all too reminiscent of much of her post-war history.

In our view, there is not the slightest doubt that the cause of Britain's relatively poor economic record lies in the thoroughly unsatisfactory performance of large parts of her manufacuring industry. When confronted with the challenge, posed by an increasingly integrated world economy, of growing competition in international markets for manufactures (both at home and abroad), large numbers of Britain's manufacturing enterprises failed to perform satisfactorily. They failed to invest and invest efficiently on a large enough scale; they failed to develop sufficient numbers of new products and they failed to raise productivity rapidly enough. All these factors resulted in an excessive loss of international market share and were the underlying cause of the persistent weakness in the UK's balance of payments in the post-war period. Poor industrial performance not only resulted in a slow rate of growth of manufacturing output, it also caused the output of other sectors of the economy, especially the services, to be held back.

At the present time, the main factor responsible for holding down the overall level of economic activity in the UK is British industry's inability to attract more customers to its products – either in the home market and/or in overseas markets: increased sales of British manufactured products could sustain a higher level of activity both by satisfying the increased domestic demand for manufactures, to which a higher level of activity would give rise,[2] as well as by financing any expansion-induced deterioration in the non-manufacturing balance of trade.

So far as the future is concerned, Britain could possibly get back to something like full employment without a really significant improvement in her comparative industrial performance – but only if people were prepared to accept virtually stationary levels of material consumption. However, the political consensus necessary for such a low growth strategy to be implemented has yet to emerge and may never do so; moreover, there probably needs to be a general shift towards 'Green' policies throughout the advanced capitalist world for such a strategy to be feasible in Britain. On the other hand, if attempts to return to full employment were to be combined with targets for increased levels of material consumption, these twin objectives could only be achieved if there were a significant improvement in Britain's comparative industrial performance. At a minimum, Britain would have to reproduce rates of growth of industrial output of the sort recorded in the period 1950 to 1973. However, given that the international economic environment over the coming decades will probably be less favourable than during that earlier Golden Age, and bearing in mind the need to make good the low levels of manufacturing investment which have characterized the Thatcher era, Britain's comparative industrial performance must improve significantly if the country is to achieve both full employment and rising material standards of living. However, such growth targets would require little short of a revolution in attitudes and behaviour – in industry, as well as in British society as a whole – if British industry is to have any chance of attaining the requisite increase in its share of domestic and foreign markets. Thus, we do not have the slightest hesitation in arguing that an improvement in Britain's comparative industrial performance is the key to achieving full employment and a sustained improvement in British material standards of living.

Many of those who share this view about the crucial role of manufacturing industry in the achievement of rapid economic growth have used a number of indicators to highlight the weaknesses of British industry – 'facts' about UK industrial performance which are now almost commonplace in discussions of this kind: for example, the steady decline in the share of manufacturing in total UK employment, the fact that the UK's manufacturing balance of trade has been subject to persistent adverse trends, and, finally, the fact that the UK now has large and growing deficits in trade in manufactures with many other advanced capitalist countries, in particular West Germany and Japan.

In our view, some of these ways of looking at the issue of weak industrial performance are both wrong and thoroughly misleading, and this is one of the reasons why we have written this book.[3]

So far as the 'facts' enumerated above are concerned, we shall be arguing, for instance, that the deterioration in the UK's manufacturing balance was, to a large degree, unavoidable, and would have occurred on much the same scale even if post-war British industrial development had been crowned with success. The reason for this is that the deterioration in the UK's manufacturing balance was, to a great extent, the consequence of improvements in the UK's non-manufacturing balance of trade – improvements of a kind which were largely independent of the country's industrial and economic performance as a whole. Nor are the manufacturing deficits which Britain is currently running with most other industrialized countries a sign of industrial weakness: given the greater triangularity of UK trade, resulting from OPEC's continued importance as a market for UK manufactured exports at a time of declining UK imports of oil from OPEC, Britain had little choice but to incur deficits in trade in manufactures with other advanced countries – unless she were to run large surpluses on her merchandise trade overall. Nor should the decline in manufacturing's share in total UK employment ('de-industrialization' in the employment sense) have been a cause for concern. Indeed, if British industry had been more dynamic and productivity growth faster, then the share of manufacturing in total employment would probably have fallen even further than it actually did.

In making these various points, we in no way wish to deny that British industry has become increasingly backward in the post-war period. However, its poor performance is not to be measured *either* by the deterioration in the manufacturing trade balance *nor* by the decline in manufacturing's share in total employment. If British industrial performance had been stronger, both manufacturing output and national income would now be higher, and unemployment would be lower. The manufacturing balance of trade would certainly be stronger – but not by very much, since autonomous factors would still have been responsible for an enormous improvement in the non-manufacturing balance. Manufacturing productivity would be higher; however, as a result, almost as many manufacturing jobs as were lost due to closures and lay-offs would have disappeared as a consequence of the automation and modernization which would have characterized industrial success. Thus, for much of the post-war period, Britain's economic problem was not, as Bacon and Eltis (1976) have argued, that there were 'too few producers' but rather that those who were employed in British manufacturing industry were working at too low a level of productivity.

In fact, the only true indicators of the diminished competitiveness and increasing backwardness of British manufacturing industry are as follows: the persistently low rate of growth of UK per capita income relative to that of other advanced capitalist countries; Britain's growing inability to combine full employment and external balance; and, finally, the seemingly inexorable rise in UK unemployment. In view of these unfavourable developments, we entirely concur with Singh's view (Singh, 1977) concerning the UK's paramount need to acquire an 'efficient' industrial sector: namely, one which is able to satisfy the full employment level of domestic demand for manufactures[4] (at a socially acceptable level and distribution of income), as well as finance any associated deficit in the non-manufacturing balance of trade.[5]

Structure of the book

This book is broadly divided into two parts: the first, which is both analytical and empirical in character, focusses on the interrelated questions of manufacturing output, employment and trade, whilst the second is devoted to our case study of the British economy.

1

The structure of employment and its evolution: the theory of de-industrialization

Introduction

This opening chapter is primarily concerned with employment in the manufacturing sector, with the factors which determine the share of this sector in total employment and govern its evolution through time. For the most part, attention is focussed on the advanced countries of the OECD, although some consideration is also given to the less developed economies. Our principal conclusion is that, in any given country at any given time, manufacturing's share of employment is determined by three main factors: first, the level of economic development reached by the country concerned; second, the phase of the business cycle in which the country finds itself; and third, the structure of its foreign trade.

The chapter begins with a general discussion of manufacturing employment and the factors which influence it. This discussion is largely analytical in character, although some empirical material is included. It is organized under three main headings, which correspond to the three main factors listed above: economic development, the business cycle and foreign trade. In the course of the discussion we consider at some length the question of 'de-industrialization'. This term has many different meanings, but throughout this present work we shall use it to denote a fall in the share of industry, especially manufacturing industry, in total employment. We show how de-industrialization can occur in a variety of ways.

There is what we call 'positive' de-industrialization, which is the normal result of sustained economic growth in a fully employed, and already highly developed, economy. It occurs because productivity growth in the manufacturing sector is so rapid that, despite increasing output, employment in this sector is reduced, either absolutely or as a share of total employment. However, this does not lead to unemployment, because new jobs are created in the service sector on a scale sufficient to absorb any workers displaced from manufacturing. Paradoxically, this kind of de-industrialization is a symptom of economic success. It is not a pathological phenomenon, as many believe, but is the normal result of industrial dynamism in an already highly developed economy. Throughout the process industry remains internationally competitive, per capita incomes rise and the economy remains close to full employment. For reasons we explain, positive de-industrialization occurs only in highly developed economies. It is not observed in less developed economies, where industrial dynamism is normally accompanied by a rising share of manufacturing in total employment.

At the opposite extreme is what we call 'negative' de-industrialization. This most certainly is a pathological phenomenon, which can affect economies at any stage of development. It is a product of economic failure and occurs when industry is in severe difficulties and the general performance of the economy is poor. Under these circumstances, labour shed from the manufacturing sector – because of falling output or higher productivity – will not be reabsorbed into the service sector. Unemployment will therefore rise. Thus, negative de-industrialization is associated with stagnant real incomes and rising unemployment.

There is also a third kind of de-industrialization, which is caused by changes in the structure of a country's foreign trade. It occurs when, for some reason, the pattern of net exports shifts away from manufactures towards other goods and services. Under certain conditions, such a shift will lead to a transfer of labour and resources from manufacturing to other sectors of the economy and, as a result, there will be a decline in the share of manufacturing in total employment. From a theoretical point of view, the distinction between these three different kinds of de-industrialization is, probably, the most important aspect of the present chapter.

The second part of the chapter is more empirical in character. Using data drawn from a number of advanced capitalist countries during the past thirty years, we test, by means of regression analysis, some of the ideas contained in the first part of the chapter. This allows us to quantify the relative importance of the main factors which affect the structure of employment. The results of the regression analysis are as follows. Comparing one advanced country with another, the post-war period has witnessed large and persistent differences in the share of manufacturing in total employment. These differences are mainly due to international differences in the pattern of trade specialization. Some advanced countries have a large and persistent trade surplus in manufactured goods, which is used to finance a roughly equal deficit in non-manufactures, such as services or primary products (food, fuels, materials, etc.). These countries have a relatively large manufacturing sector and, as a rule, the share of this sector in total employment is greater than average. In other advanced countries, however, the situation is just the opposite, and there is a large and persistent deficit in manufactures which is financed through the export of services or primary products. These other countries have a relatively small manufacturing sector and the share of this sector in total employment is normally well below average. In addition to such persistent differences *between* advanced countries, the post-war period has also witnessed major shifts in the structure of employment within the countries; in particular, manufacturing's share of total employment has fallen considerably in virtually all of these countries over the past twenty to thirty years. However, in only a few cases have such shifts in employment structure been due to shifts in the pattern of trade specialization (as we define it). For the most part, they have been the result of other factors, such as successful economic development, and more recently, recession.

Thus, whilst different patterns of trade specialization account for many of the persistent differences in employment structure *between* advanced countries, other factors account for most of the variations in employment structure *within* individual countries through time. However, as we shall see later on, in Chapters 5–12, the UK is an exception to this general rule. The UK has experienced a radical shift in its pattern of trade specialization during the post-war period, and this has had a major impact on the country's economic structure, especially on the structure of employment. No other advanced country has experienced quite such a large and sutained shift in trade specialization, and this helps to explain why the fall in UK manufacturing employment has been greater than elsewhere.

Economic development and the structure of employment

We shall begin by considering some of the more general aspects of economic structure and its evolution in the course of development. Economic structure has many different aspects, of course, but in what follows we shall be concerned mainly with the pattern of employment, with the proportions in which labour is allocated between different sectors of the economy. For the most part we shall confine our attention to what is officially called 'civil employment'. This definition covers all people, other than members of the armed forces, who are 'gainfully' occupied either as paid employees who work for others, or as employers or as self-employed workers. Full-time housewives are excluded, although domestic servants performing the same kind of work for a wage are included. The exclusion of full-time housewives is a serious omission but we have really no choice, since official statistics on employment provide no information on the activities of such women.[1]

Although there are significant differences between one country and another, virtually all countries which succeed in developing follow a broadly similar path. Their employment structure evolves in certain well-defined ways whose main characteristics are summarized in Fig. 1.1. In this diagram the economy is divided into three broad sectors: agriculture, industry and the services.[2] As the economy develops the distribution of employment between these sectors behaves as follows. First, the share of agriculture in total employment, which is initially very

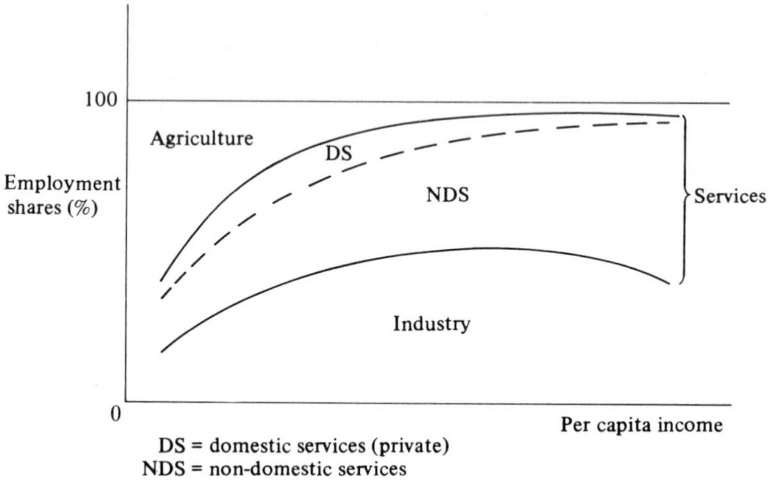

Fig. 1.1 Employment shares and economic development

large, undergoes a more or less continuous decline throughout the entire course of development. Eventually, at an advanced stage of development, the point is reached where agriculture employs no more than a tiny fraction of the total force. This is the point of economic 'maturity', beyond which any further reduction in agriculture's share can make little contribution to the growth of employment in other sectors. Second, there is a virtually continuous rise in the share of services in total employment. This share increases through all stages of development until the point is finally reached where the service sector accounts for well over 50% of total employment – a much higher proportion than that of agriculture and industry combined. The third major feature of development is the rise and subsequent decline in industry's share of employment. During the early and intermediate stages of development, this share normally increases. However, after a time, the share of industry stabilizes and then, at an advanced stage of development, goes into a prolonged decline.

On the basis of what happens to industrial employment we can distinguish two distinct phases in the development process: 'industrialization', which is the initial phase during which industry's share of employment rises, and 'de-industrialization', which is the subsequent phase during which this share declines. Let us now consider in detail what happens during these two phases and why one phase eventually gives way to the other.

Industrialization

When modern economic growth first gets under way in earnest, the share of agriculture in total employment falls rapidly and there is an enormous expansion in both the proportion and the number of people engaged in non-agricultural pursuits.[3] All kinds of new industries arise and there is a rapid growth of employment in manufacturing, construction and, sometimes, mining. This is accompanied by a parallel growth in the various commercial activities whose task is to service the rising industrial sector, amongst which the most important are transport, retail and wholesale distribution and finance. Moreover, the government begins to expand the range of its administrative activities to meet the needs of the new urban society created by industrialization. At the same time, there is some expansion in community services – health, education, social welfare and the like – although many of these services only really take off later in the development process, when the modern welfare state is more firmly established. In addition to the various commercial and community services just listed, economic development is also accompanied by the growth of certain other services. Some of these, like repair and maintenance, are directly linked to material production; whilst others, like hotels and restaurants, are more in the nature of consumer services. Finally, there is one more activity which is of immense importance in the earlier stages of development, but which is often neglected by economists and historians alike. And that is private domestic service.[4] When development first gets under way, there is a massive exodus of young people from the countryside into the towns. Many of these young people, especially the women, are taken on as servants in the houses of the new urban middle classes. The result is rapid growth in the number of domestic servants. The scale of this phenomenon can be gauged from the fact that even as late as 1891 over one-tenth of all employed workers in Britain were domestic servants (see Table 1.1.). This is by no means an atypical figure.[5]

We shall call the first stage of development just outlined the 'industrialization phase'. It is characterized by the fact that during this phase the share of industry in total employment rises strongly.[6]

Economic maturity and de-industrialization

As development proceeds, some of the trends we have described continue, but others are reversed. Agriculture continues to decline as a source of employment until eventually the point is reached where only a small percentage of the workforce can often produce enough food to feed the entire nation. A similar decline occurs in domestic service. After rising early in the development process, the number of domestic servants begins to fall as new job opportunities are created elsewhere in the economy and new labour-saving techniques are utilized in middle-class households. By contrast, employment in most other service activities continues to expand. There is a considerable growth in the number of people engaged in community services, especially health and education, as modern wel-

Table 1.1. *Sectoral distribution of the British labour force 1801–1981 (as a percentage of the total population)*

	(1) Agri-culture	(2) Industry	(3) Com-merce	(4) Private domestic service	(5) Armed forces	(6) Community and other services
1801	35.9	29.7	11.2	9.0	4.8	9.4
1811	33.0	30.2	11.6	9.2	6.2	9.8
1821	28.4	38.4	12.1	9.9	2.1	9.1
1831	24.6	40.8	12.4	9.8	1.9	10.5
1841	22.2	40.5	14.2	11.3	2.0	9.8
1851	21.7	42.9	15.8	10.1	1.4	8.1
1861	18.7	43.6	16.6	11.2	1.3	8.6
1871	15.1	43.1	19.6	11.9	1.2	9.1
1881	12.6	43.5	21.3	11.3	0.9	10.4
1891	10.5	43.9	22.6	11.2	0.9	10.9
1901	8.7	46.3	21.4	9.5	1.1	13.0
1911	8.3	46.4	21.5	8.5	1.2	14.1
1921	7.1	47.6	20.3	6.9	1.1	17.0
1931	6.0	45.3	22.7	7.7	0.9	17.4
1951	5.1	47.6	22.0	2.3	2.5	20.5
1961	3.7	47.7	23.4	1.6	1.3	22.3
1971	2.7	44.8	23.4	1.1	1.0	27.0
1981	2.3	37.5	25.4	0.4	1.0	33.4

Definitions: Industry = mining, manufacturing, construction, gas, electricity and water
Commerce = transport, distribution and finance

Sources: Cols. (1)–(3) for the years prior to 1951 are from Deane and Cole (1967), Table 30 and from 1951 onwards from the Census of Population. Col. (4) for 1851 onwards is estimated from data contained in the Census of Population; and prior to 1851 this column is estimated from data contained in Deane and Cole Table 30. Col. (5) is based on data contained in the Census of Population and in the official Army and Navy estimates. Col. (6) is merely the residual and covers all forms of employment not contained in Cols. (1)–(5); in later years it consists mainly of public administration, health and educational services

fare principles become more firmly established. Quantitatively, this kind of employment is often the most important area of service expansion in the later stages of development. However, there is also a spectacular growth, admittedly from a rather low base, in what are sometimes called producer services, such as accounting, consultancy and finance. By contrast, there is a more modest growth of employment in the main commercial services (transport and distribution), and in some cases their share of total employment stabilizes or even falls a little. Evidence on the behaviour of service employment in recent years in the advanced capitalist countries is given in Table 1.2, and more detailed information for the UK alone is contained in Table 1.3.

From Fig. 1.1 it is clear that the share of non-domestic services in total employment rises continuously in the course of development. However, the implications of this growth for the industrial sector depend on the employment situation in the other sectors of the economy, namely agriculture and domestic service. So long as there is plenty of labour still employed in agriculture and domestic service, the non-domestic services can increase their share of total employment at the expense of these other two sectors without affecting the share of industry. Indeed, for a time, the share of industry may actually rise along with that of the non-domestic services. However, as development proceeds, employment in agriculture and domestic service will eventually decline until the point is reached where only a small percentage of the workforce is employed in these sectors. From this point onwards, any significant increase in the share of non-domestic services *must* inevitably be at the expense of industry whose share *must*, as a matter of arithmetic, decline.[7] This can be seen clearly from Fig. 1.1. We shall call an economy which has reached this point 'mature', and we shall refer to the falling share of industry in total employment as 'de-industrialization'.

The de-industrialization which accompanies development in a mature economy is not, as many believe, the result of new and radically different economic forces. It is merely the logical culmination of two basic trends which have been at work ever since the era of modern economic growth began well over a century ago. These trends are: (1) the decline of agriculture as a source of employment and (2) the growth of the non-domestic services. As agriculture declines and the non-domestic services rise, it is only a matter of time before the share of industry in total employment begins to fall. At first, the non-domestic services grow at the expense of agriculture and later, when this is no longer possible, they grow at the expense of industry. This is the essence of the argument. The picture is complicated somewhat by the behaviour of domestic service in the course of development. Viewed in historical terms, domestic service acts as a staging-post between agriculture and the non-domestic services, at first absorbing labour from agriculture and then later releasing labour to non-agricultural activities as the economy develops. But this is a mere detail, which does not affect the main thrust of the argument: de-industrialization occurs when agriculture is no longer a major employer of labour, and when further expansion in the non-domestic services must necessarily be at the expense of industry.

Note that we are talking here about relative shares and not absolute numbers. What happens to the absolute number employed in any particular sector depends on what happens to the behaviour of employment in the economy as a whole. In the USA, for example, the number of people employed in the industrial sector has increased by 4.5 million over the past thirty years, from 23 million in 1953 to 28.5 million in 1982. Yet, because of an even greater expansion in the non-domestic services, the share of industry in total employment has

Table 1.2. *Percentage share of various services in civil employment for selected countries, 1963–80*

	1963	1973	1980	Change 1963–73	Change 1973–80
Japan					
Transport and distribution	n.a.	27.0	28.8	n.a.	+1.8
Finance	n.a.	3.0	3.5	n.a.	+0.5
Community, social and personal services	n.a.	19.1	21.7	n.a.	+2.6
Total services	42.3	49.1	54.0	+6.8	+4.9
Canada					
Transport and distribution	24.9	24.9	24.5	0.0	−0.4
Finance	4.2	5.0	5.7	+0.8	+0.7
Community, social and personal services	26.6.	33.2	35.8	+6.6	+2.6
Total services	55.7	63.1	66.0	+7.4	+2.9
USA					
Transport and distribution	27.5	28.0	28.5	+0.5	+0.5
Finance	7.8	9.2	9.1	+1.4	−0.1
Community, social and personal services	27.1	29.5	33.1	+2.4	+3.6
Total services	62.4	66.7	70.7	+4.3	+4.0
Germany					
Transport and distribution	19.9	20.6	20.3	+0.7	+0.3
Finance	5.6	5.9	5.9	+0.3	0.0
Community, social and personal services	16.7	19.4	23.3	+2.7	+3.9
Total services	42.2	45.9	49.5	+3.7	+3.6
Netherlands					
Transport and distribution	23.8	24.8	25.3	+1.0	+0.5
Finance	n.a.	6.2	7.7	n.a.	+1.5
Community, social and personal services	25.6	26.1	29.1	+6.7	+3.0
Total services	49.4	57.1	62.1	+7.7	+5.0
Norway					
Transport and distribution	n.a.	26.2	26.0	n.a.	−0.2
Finance	n.a.	4.0	5.8	n.a.	+1.8
Community, social and personal services	n.a.	24.5	30.0	n.a.	+5.5
Total services	n.a.	54.7	61.8	n.a.	+7.1
Sweden					
Transport and distribution	n.a.	21.0	20.7	n.a.	−0.3
Finance	n.a.	5.3	6.7	n.a.	+1.4
Community, social and personal services	n.a.	29.7	34.8	n.a.	+5.1
Total services	n.a.	56.0	62.2	n.a.	+6.2

Table 1.2. (*contd.*)

	1963	1973	1980	Change 1963–73	Change 1973–80
UK					
Transport and distribution	24.5	23.2	23.8	−1.3	+0.6
Finance	4.1	5.4	6.4	+1.3	+1.0
Community, social and personal services	20.7	25.9	59.2	+5.2	+4.7
Total services	49.3	54.5	59.2	+5.2	+4.7

Definitions: transport + distribution = ISIC divisions 6 and 7 (and therefore includes hotels and restaurants); finance = ISIC division 8; community, social and personal services = ISIC division 9

Source: OECD, *Labour Force Statistics*

Table 1.3. *Employees in employment in Great Britain 1959–1981*[a]

	Thousands						% change
	1959	1966	1970	1973	1978	1981	1959–81
Agriculture, forestry, fishing	746	565	454	421	373	371	−50.3
Production industries	10449	11002	10247	9698	9023	7686	−26.4
of which:							
Mining and quarrying	822	566	407	361	351	334	−59.4
Manufacturing	7902	8408	8164	7664	7117	5924	−25.0
Construction	1350	1604	1294	1338	1225	1090	−19.3
Gas, electricity and water	376	424	382	335	330	338	−10.1
Private services	6917	7682	7428	7796	8222	8498	+22.9
of which:							
Transport and communications[b]	1633	1589	1549	1501	1462	1419	−13.1
Insurance, banking, etc.	631	808	943	1043	1182	1309	+107.4
Professional and scientific[c]	289	355	382	415	463	494	+70.9
Distribution	2597	2857	2617	2691	2724	2718	+4.7
Leisure services[d]	1019	1136	1076	1185	1303	1375	+34.9
Other private services	748	928	861	961	1088	1183	+58.2
Public services	2871	3538	3865	4267	4637	4593	+60.0
of which:							
Educational[e]	881	1218	1412	1620	1820	1692	+92.1
Medical and dental[e]	735	930	1007	1104	1263	1386	+88.6
National government	517	562	565	583	612	587	+13.5
Local government	738	828	881	960	942	928	+25.7
Grand total	20983	22787	21993	22182	22253	21148	+0.8

Source: HMSO *Employment Gazette*

Notes: [a] excludes employers and self-employed, HM forces and private domestic service

[b] includes nationalized industries

[c] excludes educational, medical and dental services and religious organizations

[d] religious organizations, cinemas, theatres, radio, sport, betting and gambling, hotels, restaurants, public houses, clubs, catering, hairdressing and manicure

[e] includes the private sector

fallen from 36.7% to 28.5% over the same period. Thus, a fall in the *share* of industrial employment does not automatically involve a reduction in the absolute number of people employed in industry, although this is certainly what has happened in most European countries in recent years (see chapter 10).

Note also that we are talking here about long-term trends in the pattern of employment and not merely about cyclical changes and the effects of economic recession. Although the present recession has certainly exacerbated the trend towards de-industrialization in Western countries, there are clearly longer-term factors at work which are causing the pattern of employment to shift away from industry, and from manufacturing in particular, towards the services. This shift towards the service sector predates the current recession and, indeed, the share of services in total employment has been rising for at least a century in most advanced capitalist countries. Moreover, the share of industry has been falling for the past twenty or thirty years in some of them. This is all illustrated in the graphs in Appendix 1 which show how the structure of employment has evolved over the past century in the main capitalist countries.[8] For lack of information, these diagrams do not distinguish between domestic service and the non-domestic services, both of which are placed under the heading 'services'. Even so, the general picture is unambiguous and the basic trends are clearly visible.

Explanation

Let us now consider some of the forces which account for the major structural changes just described. In general terms the shift out of agriculture is fairly straightforward to explain. It is the obvious result of rapid technical change in agricultural combined with a relatively slow growth of demand for food. In poor countries expenditure on food absorbs a high proportion of total income. However, as per capita income rises in the course of development, the relative importance of food expenditure undergoes a continuous decline. Known as Engel's Law, this particular statistical regularity has been confirmed by numerous studies concerning many countries and many periods of time. In a closed economy, Engel's Law would automatically imply a relatively slow growth in the output of food. In an open economy, with the possibility of food exports, the link between domestic demand and production is less rigid. However, even under these conditions, domestic demand is usually the predominant factor, and the output of food normally rises less rapidly than GDP even in countries which are specialist food exporters. On the supply side, labour productivity in agriculture is increased through a whole range of innovations. The concentration of land holdings and spread of capitalist property relations leads to the elimination of low productivity forms of land tenure and labour organization, whilst at the same time there is a continuous extension of mechanization and scientific methods of production. As a result of these demand and supply side factors, labour productivity in agriculture often rises much faster than output, and the absolute number of people employed in agriculture falls dramatically (see Table 1.5). In relative terms, the decline in agricultural employment is even more dramatic, for the fall in the absolute numbers occurs at a time when population and total employment are increasing.

Another major structural change is the shift in employment away from industry towards the services which occurs during the later stages of development. At one time this shift was explained primarily in terms of demand. In the initial phase of economic development, the pattern of demand shifts away from food towards industrial products, especially manufactured goods. From this well-established fact it was argued, by analogy, that in the later stages of development the pattern of demand shifts once again, this time from industrial products towards services.[9] And it is this shift in the pattern of demand which supposedly explains why service employment grows so rapidly at the expense of industry in advanced economies. However, in recent years, this line of argument has been severely criticized as more information on the service sector has become available and the theoretical questions involved have been explored more thoroughly.

One of the most telling criticisms concerns the question of output in the service sector. Although output is often difficult to measure in this sector and the results are sometimes difficult to interpret, virtually all attempts to measure the output of services in real terms arrive at the same result. Over the long term, the real output of services does not seem to rise significantly faster than the output of manufactured goods or industrial products in general. Some evidence on this point is given in Tables 1.4 and 1.5.[10] These tables also show what has happened to productivity in services and industry, and it is here that we find an explanation for why the pattern of employment has been shifting towards the services. In every country, in every time period, output per worker has been rising faster in industry than in the services, sometimes by an enormous margin. Even allowing for possible measurement error and difficulties of interpretation, there is little doubt that the apparent difference in productivity growth between the two sectors is genuine. The implications of this difference are obvious.[11] If output in the two sectors is growing at much the same rate, but productivity is rising faster in industry than in the services, then the pattern of employment will gradually shift away from industry towards the services. Because of their slower productivity growth, the services will have to absorb an even greater fraction of total employment to keep their output rising in line with that of industry.[12] This is merely an example of a more general principle. With a *given* pattern of output, differential productivity growth will always cause

Table 1.4. *Employment, productivity and output in manufacturing and market services since the mid-1960s*

	Average annual compound growth rates					
	Output per worker		Employment		Output	
	Manu-facturing	Market services	Manu-facturing	Market services	Manu-facturing	Market services
Japan (1970–80)	6.7	3.0	0.1	2.4	6.8	5.4
Belgium (1963–78)	5.4	1.5	−2.2	1.9	3.2	3.4
Germany (1963–78)	4.7	3.7	−0.7	0.4	4.0	4.1
Netherlands (1970–80)	4.5	2.6	−1.9	1.0	2.6	3.6
Italy (1970–80)	3.6	1.8	0.3	1.9	3.9	3.7
Sweden (1963–80)	3.4	2.2	−0.5	1.0	2.9	3.2
UK (1963–78)	2.9	2.2	−0.9	0.5	2.1	2.7
Norway (1963–78)	2.6	2.2	0.5	1.5	3.1	3.8
USA (1963–78)	2.4	0.7	1.3	3.5	3.7	4.2
Unweighted average	4.0	2.2	−0.4	1.6	3.6	3.8

Source: OECD *National Accounts*. Output is real value-added at constant prices originating in the sector concerned. Market services are those which are directly purchased by individual consumers. Most public services are excluded.

the pattern of employment to shift away from the most dynamic sectors towards those in which productivity is rising more slowly.

Thus, the fast growth in service employment in Western countries is explained, not by an especially fast growth in the output of services, but by relatively slow growth of productivity in the services as compared to other sectors of the economy. Just why service productivity should have grown so slowly is not fully understood, and there is some dispute as to whether or not past trends will continue into the future. Looking ahead, it seems likely that vigorous efforts will be made to raise productivity in the services, especially in areas like health and administration. Where this is not possible, efforts will be made to restrain employment growth by holding down the level of services provided. However, these efforts are unlikely to be completely successful and, over the long run, the share of services in total employment will probably continue to rise in the advanced economies. As a result, the share of industry will continue to fall.

Table 1.5. *Employment, productivity and output by sector 1870–1978 for selected countries average annual compound growth rates*

	Employment			Output per person employed			Output			
	Agriculture	Industry	Services	Agriculture	Industry	Services	Agriculture	Industry	Services	(GDP)
1870–1950										
France[a]	−0.8	0.2	0.7	1.4	1.4	0.7	0.6	1.6	1.4	(1.2)
Germany[b]	−0.1	1.4	1.5	0.2	1.3	0.7	0.1	2.7	2.2	(2.1)
Italy	0.1	0.7	1.2	0.5	1.4	0.6	0.6	2.1	1.8	(1.5)
Japan[c]	0.1	1.7	1.9	0.7	1.7	0.5	0.8	3.4	2.4	(1.9)
UK	−1.1	0.9	1.3	1.4	1.2	0.2	0.3	2.1	1.5	(1.6)
USA[d]	−0.3	2.3	2.6	1.3	1.6	1.1	1.0	3.9	3.7	(3.2)
Unweighted average	−0.4	1.2	1.5	0.9	1.4	0.6	0.5	2.6	2.1	(1.9)
1950–1978										
France	−3.6	0.5	1.8	5.6	4.9	2.8	1.8	5.4	4.7	(4.7)
Germany	−3.8	0.8	1.9	6.1	5.2	3.0	2.1	6.0	4.9	(5.3)
Japan	−3.5	3.3	3.7	6.2	8.6	3.3	2.5	12.0	7.1	(8.6)
Netherlands	−2.2	−0.1	1.9	5.4	5.4	2.3	3.1	5.3	4.2	(4.4)
UK	−2.0	−0.3	1.0	4.4	2.7	1.4	2.3	2.4	2.5	(2.4)
USA	−2.9	1.3	2.3	4.7	2.1	1.5	1.7	3.4	3.8	(3.6)
Unweighted average	−3.0	0.9	2.1	5.4	4.8	2.4	2.2	5.7	4.5	(4.8)

Note: [a] 1896–1949, [b] 1871–1950, [c] 1906–1950, [d] 1889–1948
Source: Maddison (1982), Tables 5.11 and 5.13, A6, A7 and A8

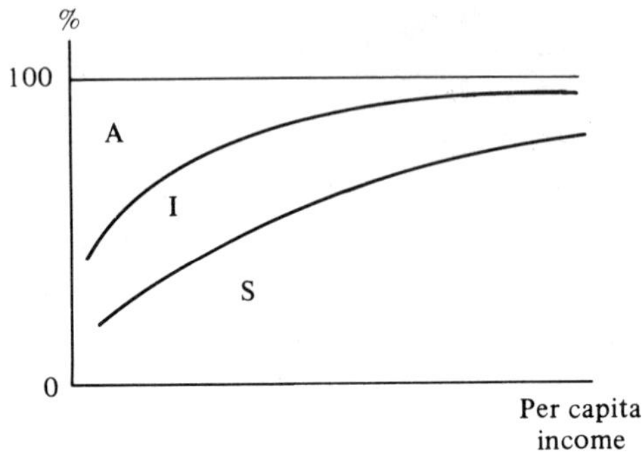

Fig. 1.2a Employment shares

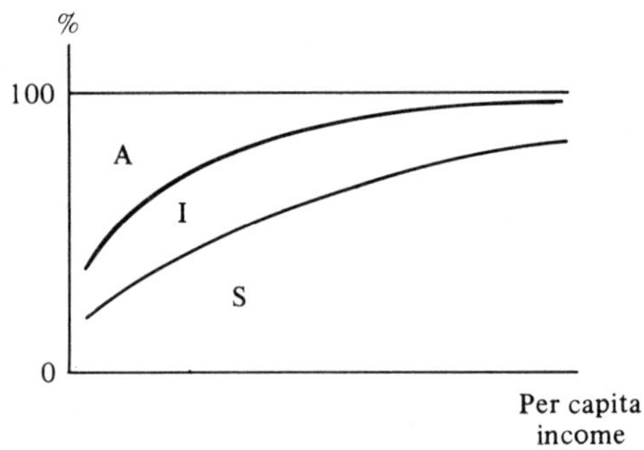

Fig. 1.2b Output and expenditure shares (current prices)

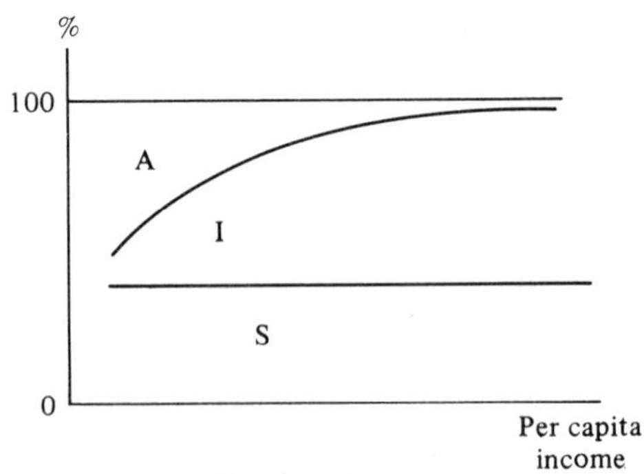

Fig. 1.2c Output and expenditure shares (constant prices)

A = agriculture, I = industry, S = services

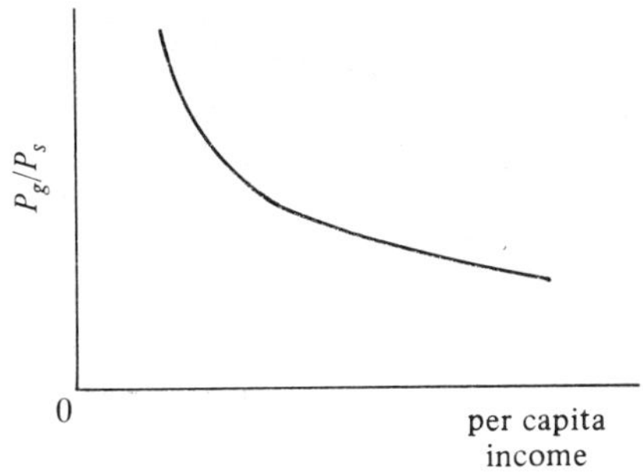

Fig. 1.2d Relative prices (goods/services)
P_g, P_s = Price of goods, services

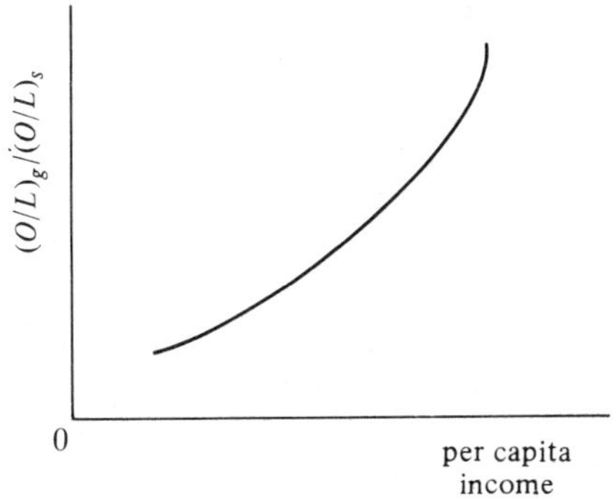

Fig. 1.2e Relative productivity (goods/services)
$(O/L)_{g,s}$ = Output per person of goods, services

Constant and current prices

To round off the discussion we shall now consider briefly the question of measurement. This will help to summarize the preceding argument and also correct some common misapprehensions about the behaviour of demand, and its influence on employment, during the course of development. Propositions about the role of demand are often based of the use of output and expenditure data measured at current prices. (Appendix 3 contains a review of some of the empirical data in support of assertions made in this section.) These data indicate a virtually continuous fall in the share of agriculture in total output and expenditure, and a virtually continuous rise in the share of services. In the case of industry, they indicate a curvilinear path. When development first gets under way, there is a marked rise in the share of industry, especially manufacturing, in total output and expenditure measured at current prices. After a time the share of industry stabilizes and then finally at an advanced stage of development this share begins to fall. These changes are summarized in Figure 1.2b. As we have seen above, similar changes occur in the structure of employment. The share of agriculture in total employment falls more or less continuously in the course of development, and there is a continuous rise in the share of services. Moreover, industry's share of employment at first rises and then later, at an advanced stage of development when the economy is 'mature', begins to fall. These changes are summarized in Fig. 1.2a.[13] Comparing Figs. 1.2a and 1.2b we notice a striking similarity. Expenditure at current prices, output at current prices and employment all undergo a virtually identical structural transformation in the course of development. It is this similarity which accounts for the widely held view that demand is the driving force responsible for the major structural shifts just described. In particular, the fact that services account for an ever-growing share of output and expenditure, measured at current prices, is taken as evidence that in relative terms demand shifts away from goods towards services in the course of development. This in turn is supposed to explain why there is a continuous rise in the share of services in total employment. Likewise, in highly developed economies, the falling share of industry in output and expenditure, measured at current prices, is taken as evidence that in relative terms demand is shifting away from industrial products towards non-industrial products (i.e. services). And this, in turn, is supposed to explain the falling share of industry in total employment.

Although at first sight plausible, the above argument contains a crucial weakness. It relies heavily on current price shares to indicate what is happening to the structure of expenditure and output. Moreover, these shares are subject to a particular kind of bias, which in the present context can render them virtually useless. Current price shares may change through the course of time for one of two reasons. On the one hand, the real quantities involved may change in a disproportionate fashion through the course of time. For example, the amount of steel produced or purchased may rise more rapidly than the amount of copper. In this case, there will be a genuine alteration in the structure of output or expenditure, and this alteration will be captured by the resulting change in current price shares. On the other hand, current price shares may change simply because of an alteration in relative prices, without any change at all in relative quantities. For example, the share of steel in output or expenditure, measured at current prices, may rise by a considerable amount simply because steel has risen a great deal in price as compared to other items. Under these circumstances, it would be quite misleading to use the current price share of steel in output or expenditure as an index of structural change. This merely illustrates the more general point that current price shares are only suitable for analysing structural change when relative prices remain reasonably constant. If relative prices vary a great deal, current price shares can create the illusion of structural change where none exists, and disguise structural change when it does exist. This warning should be obvious, but is frequently ignored. To analyse properly the influence of demand on economic structure we must eliminate, as far as possible, the bias caused by relative price changes, and focus exclusively on the behaviour of real quantities. The standard procedure for achieving this objective is to measure output and expenditure using so-called 'constant' prices. In the case of intertemporal comparisons, these are normally the prices obtaining in some given base year, whilst for interspatial comparisons they are normally the prices obtaining in some actual or hypothetical country or region.[14] When constant price data is used to calculate shares in output and expenditure, the results are not always easy to interpret, but they are free from the bias caused by relative price differences, and their variations – or lack of variation – do indicate something real about intertemporal or interspatial variations in economic structure.

Figure 1.2c shows, in stylized form, what normally happens to constant price shares in output and expenditure in the course of development. Comparing this diagram to Fig. 1.2b, which is based on current price shares, we can see both similarities and differences. Consider first the similarities. Both diagrams indicate a continuous fall in the share of agriculture in output and expenditure as per capita income rises. Both diagrams indicate a marked rise in the share of industry in output and expenditure, so we move from low to medium levels of per capita income. In these two cases, therefore, the shifts in economic structure indicated by current price data are perfectly genuine. Consider next the differences. Current price data on output and expenditure indicate a continuous increase in the share of services as per capita income rises; and, in already highly developed economies, they indicate a definite fall in the share of industry (especially manufacturing industry). However, when constant price data are used the picture is quite different. There is virtually no trace of a permanent shift towards the services at any stage in development, nor of a shift away from industry in the later stages of development. If cyclical variations are ignored, the share of services in output and expenditure measured at constant prices seems to be more or less independent of per capita income, being much the same at all stages of development. Moreover, in highly developed economies, the share of industry in output and expenditure appears to stabilize; apart from cyclical variations, there is not much sign of the fall indicated by current price data.

Thus, in two cases of great importance in the present work, constant and current price shares behave quite differently. The explanation for this divergence is surprisingly simple. It is the result of large and systematic variations in relative prices which occur in the course of development. And these, in turn, are the result of the uneven productivity growth described in the previous sector. As a general rule, the growth rate of labour productivity is much lower in the service sector than in the rest of the economy, whilst in the industrial sector, especially manufacturing, the growth rate of productivity is comparatively high. As a result, services become comparatively more expensive to produce and their relative price increases continuously. This, in turn, pushes up the current price share of services in output and expenditure, and makes it rise continuously in the course of development. Conversely, industrial products become comparatively cheaper to produce and their relative price falls. In advanced economies – though not at early stages of development – this is sufficient to cause a gradual fall in the current price share of industrial products in output and expenditure. Thus, two of the shifts in demand apparently indicated by current price data are merely a statistical illusion, arising from relative price changes. In real terms, there is no shift in demand from goods to services in the course of development, nor in advanced economies is there any marked shift in demand away from industrial products.

As far as advanced economies are concerned, the discussion can be summarized as follows. In such economies, the long-term growth rate of output is normally about the same for industrial products as for services. The same is true for expenditure. Thus, in real terms, there is no structural shift in output or expenditure from industry to services. However, labour productivity rises consistently faster in industry than services. Thus, to keep output rising at the same rate in the two sectors requires a continuous shift in the pattern of employment; in relative terms, labour must be continuously transferred from the industrial sector into the services. Moreover, differential productivity growth causes relative prices to change, making services ever more expensive in comparison to industrial products. Since, in real terms, output in the two sectors is growing at the same rate, the result of these price changes is an increase in the share of services in total output, measured at current prices, and a reduction in the share of industry. The same is true for expenditure. In real terms, expenditure on services and industrial products grows at about the same rate. However, because services are becoming relatively more expensive, the result is an increase in the share of services in total expenditure, measured at current prices, and a fall in the share of industry. Thus, although as a general rule the real structure of output and expenditure remains roughly constant in advanced economies (as between industry and services), differential productivity growth leads to a continuous shift away from industry in the structure both of employment and of output and expenditure measured at current prices. This form of 'de-industrialization' is not primarily due to a shift in demand from industry to services, but is mainly due to the superior dynamism of industry, especially manufacturing industry, as manifested in its above-average productivity growth.

Note that we are talking here about long-run forces which are at work in all advanced economies. We are ignoring the effect of cyclical factors which may exert a powerful influence on the structure of economic activity. These effects are considered below. We are also ignoring the role of trade specialization. Different countries specialize in different ways, and changes in the structure of foreign trade may influence the internal structure of an economy at all stages of development. Such trade-induced shifts in economic structure are superimposed on the long-run trends described here. As we shall see below, such shifts are not usually very important in advanced economies and do not, as a rule, have much effect on the industry–service ratio. However, as we shall also see, the UK is an exception to this general rule.

The business cycle

Superimposed on the long-run trends we have just described there are also cyclical factors to consider.[15] When an economy goes into recession, the share of manufacturing in total employment normally falls, as does the share of industry as a whole. There are a number of reasons for this. Investment in buildings and equipment declines during a recession, thereby reducing the demand for a wide variety of industrial products. If the recession is prolonged, this decline in investment may lead to a substantial reduction in industrial employment.

The effects of a recession on service employment are, however, more complex. Reduced industrial output and lower real incomes will mean a reduced demand for certain kinds of services, especially for those provided by the private sector, whose activities are, for the most part, directly linked to the production of material goods. This, in itself, will tend to reduce employment in the private services. However, there is another factor working in the opposite direction. Certain private services may act as a sponge which absorbs excess labour during a recession. Start-up costs are very low in many service occupations, and people unable to find industrial employment may set up in business on their own as shopkeepers, self-employed cleaners and the like; or they may accept low-paid service jobs which, in better times, they would have refused. Thus, although recession may reduce employment in some private services, it may also induce additional employment in others.

Employment in the public services is also subject to opposing forces. On the one hand, as the tax base contracts during recession, there will be financial pressures to cut expenditure, and this may lead to a reduction in the level of services provided by the government. However, the scope for such economies may be limited by political factors, and the resulting fall in employment may be quite small. Moreover, the government may deliberately create employment in certain public services, to provide work for the unemployed; and the recession itself will place new demands on the police and the prison, legal and welfare services, with the result that employment in some of these areas may actually increase.

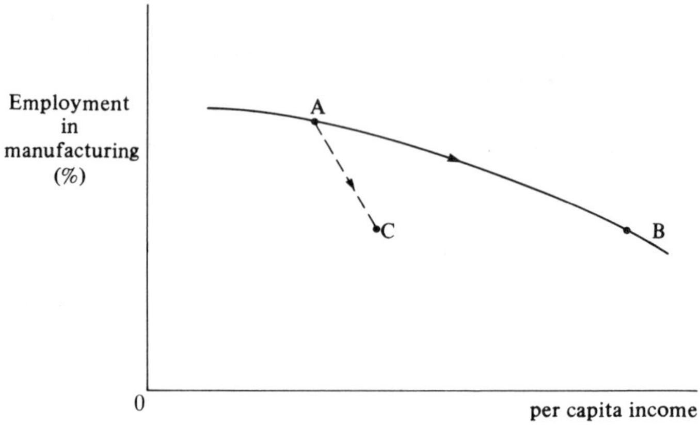

Fig. 1.3 Two kinds of de-industrialization

Taking all of these various factors into account, it is clear why the share of industry in total employment should fall below its trend value during a recession, while that of services should rise.[16] Note that we are talking here about relative shares and not absolute numbers.

Two kinds of de-industrialization

We have considered what happens to industry's share in total employment during the course of development and examined how this share is affected by economic recession. Our discussion suggests there are two ways in which an economy may 'de-industrialize'.

On the one hand, the economy may grow rapidly, maintain full employment and trace out the path shown in Fig. 1.3. Beyond a certain point, once the employment structure is mature, the normal process of growth itself will cause a shift in employment away from manufacturing and other 'production' industries towards the services. However, this will not lead to unemployment, because labour displaced from the industrial sector, by automation or other labour-saving methods, will be absorbed into the service sector. This is the kind of 'positive' de-industrialization which is likely to occur in Japan in the coming decades.

On the other hand, the economy may experience a severe recession in which real incomes and industrial output stagnate. In this case, the labour, displaced from manufacturing and other production industries, will fail to be absorbed into the service sector, and unemployment will rise. This is the kind of 'negative' de-industrialization which has occurred in the UK during recent years.

These are just two extreme possibilities, of course, and many intermediate combinations are possible. The contrast between these two extremes is pictured in Fig. 1.3. The diagram shows what happens through the course of time to two mature economies which start from the same point, A. At this initial point there is full employment in both economies, per capita incomes are identical and the same proportion of their total workforce is employed in manufacturing industry. One of the two economies is extremely dynamic. Its real income rises very fast, unemployment remains low and manufacturing employment follows the continuous line shown in the diagram. By contrast, the other economy is almost stagnant, real income increases very slowly, the level of economic activity falls well below its full potential, unemployment rises, and manufacturing employment falls. The path of this economy is shown by the broken line. Comparing the two economies we can see that, after a given period of time, the dynamic economy has reached the point B, where manufacturing's share of employment is well below its initial level, but real incomes have risen a great deal and the economy is close to full employment. By contrast, in the stagnant economy at point C, the share of manufacturing's total employment has fallen just as much as in the dynamic economy. However, real income has hardly risen, the economy is operating well below its full potential and unemployment is very high.

This example shows how, in itself, a reduction in manufacturing's share of employment tells us nothing about the success or failure of a country's manufacturing sector or of the economy as a whole. De-industrialization may be the result of either success or failure. An economy may de-industrialize because it has an extremely dynamic and successful manufacturing sector or, conversely, because its manufacturing sector is in severe difficulties. In each case, manufacturing's share of employment will decline. Two kinds of de-industrialization can be distinguished only by observing the behaviour of per capita incomes and unemployment through the course of time. Positive de-industrialization is associated with full employment and rising real incomes, whilst negative de-industrialization is associated with stagnant real incomes and rising unemployment.

In practice, of course, intermediate cases are possible, and an economy may combine aspects of both kinds of de-industrialization. An example of this is Belgium, which in recent years has combined rising real incomes with rising unemployment. As a result the country has de-industrialized at an extraordinary speed. Between 1973 and 1982, real income per head of population rose by 17% and real wages by 14%. Yet, over the same period, manufacturing employment fell by over a quarter, and unemployment rose from around 3% of the workforce in 1973 to 13% in 1982.

Foreign trade and the structure of employment

Having analysed the effects of economic growth and recession on the structure of employment, we shall now consider the effects of foreign trade. Foreign trade can influence the structure of employment, and its evolution through time, in two ways: first, through its macro-economic influence on the level of activity and the rate of economic growth; and, second, through its micro-economic influence on the structure of demand facing domestic producers.

Macro-economic effects

Let us begin by examining briefly the macro-economic effects of foreign trade. This is most easily done by means of examples. Consider, first of all, a mature economy which is in the midst of recession, manufacturing output is severely depressed, unemployment is high and there is a great deal of excess capacity. There is also a balance of payments constraint, so that output cannot increase because the result would be an unacceptable trade deficit. Now suppose that for some reason or other there is a dramatic improvement in trade performance, which removes the balance of payments constraint on growth. Should it wish to – which is by no means certain[17] – the government can now pursue an expansionary policy and promote a rapid economic recovery. If it does so, the result will be a large rise in manufacturing output, more people will be employed in the manufacturing sector and the share of this sector in total employment will amost certainly rise. However, this last effect may be only a transitory phenomenon. After a time, if the boom continues, the structure of employment will start to change. Since the economy is already mature, there will be a gradual shift in employment away from industry towards the services. The manufacturing sector, where productivity is increasing relatively fast, may begin to shed labour, and this labour will be absorbed into the service sector, where productivity is increasing more slowly. Thus, after rising during the initial phase of cyclical recovery, the share of manufacturing in total employment will later fall back again, as the longer-term consequences of sustained economic growth take effect.

Thus, in a mature economy, the short- and long-term implications of improved trade performance may be very different. Whereas a strong trade performance may increase manufacturing's share of employment in the short term, it may well have quite the opposite effect in the long term. The point is that, in a mature economy, sustained growth eventually leads to a shift in the structure of employment away from industry towards the services. So, if an improved trade performance results in sustained growth, its long-term effect will be to reduce the share of manufacturing in employment.[18]

Let us now consider the example of a country whose economic performance is successful: the rate of economic growth is quite fast and the country is close to full employment. Suppose that, for some reason, this country's trade performance deteriorates to the point where fast growth is no longer possible. As a result, investment declines and there is a reduction in the growth rate of manufacturing output. The government may respond to this situation by implementing various schemes to preserve employment in the manufacturing sector. For a time, these measures may succeed in limiting the fall in manufacturing employment and in preventing the emergence of open unemployment. However, if the country's trade performance continues to deteriorate, the economic situation will get worse and pressure on government finances will intensify. Sooner or later, austerity measures will become inevitable and the job protection programme may be curtailed. At this point manufacturing employment will start to fall, if it has not already done so, and unemployment will mount. The result will be a depressed economy, characterized by stagnant or falling output, rising unemployment and a falling share of manufacturing in total employment. This is an example of the 'negative' kind of de-industrialization described earlier in this chapter.

These are just two examples of the macro-economic channels through which trade performance can influence the structure of employment. However, they do bring out the central point that, *in a mature economy*, de-industrialization can be associated with either a strong or a weak trade performance. This point is frequently neglected by those who see de-industrialization only in its negative aspect, as the outcome of economic failure, which is either caused, or exacerbated, by a weak trade performance. In a mature economy, de-industrialization may also be the product of economic success, of sustained economic growth accompanied by a strong trade performance.

Structural effects of foreign trade

So far we have discussed foreign trade only in macro-economic terms. However, there are also the more narrowly defined, structural aspects to consider, which are often completely ignored in discussions about the impact of foreign trade on employment structure. As we shall demonstrate in subsequent chapters, the advanced countries exhibit very different patterns of trade specialization. Some have a large and persistent trade surplus in manufactures, which is used to finance a roughly equal deficit in non-manufactures, such as services or primary products (food, fuels, materials, etc.). In others, however, the situation is quite the reverse, and there is a large and persistent deficit in manufacturing trade, which is financed through the export of non-manufactures. Finally, there are some advanced countries which are comparatively unspecialized (as we define the term), having a rough balance on both manufacturing and non-manufacturing trade alike.[19] Thus, imports and exports of manufactures are approximately equal, and the same is true of non-manufactures.

Successful economies are to be found in each of the categories just described. Of course, for any given country, at any given time, some patterns of trade specialization are more appropriate than others. In deciding which pattern to adopt, a well-designed trade policy must take into account a variety of factors, such as the size and location of a country, its material resources and the skills of its people, as well as current prospective developments in international trade. However, at this point, we are not concerned with the question of trade policy, and in the following discussion we shall take a country's pattern of trade specialization as given, without enquiring whether or not it is appropriate. Having said this, let us now consider how a country's internal economic structure is affected by its pattern of trade specialization.

Normally speaking, a country which has an export surplus in some particular good or service will devote more of its resources to the production of this item than would otherwise be the case. Some of these resources will be utilized in the sector directly producing the export in question, whilst others will be utilized elsewhere in the economy, in sectors which indirectly contribute to the production of this export item. For example, suppose an economy has an export surplus in manufactures: then it will devote more resources to producing manufactures than would be the case in an otherwise similar[20] economy specializing in the export of non-manufactures (i.e. services or primary products). Some of these additional resources will be used in the manufacturing sector itself, whilst others will be used in sectors which supply the manufacturing sector, such as transport, banking and construction. Thus, because of interdependence between the various sectors, the impact of trade specialization runs right through the economy and is not just confined to the sector directly producing the exports concerned. However, this is really just a qualification which does not affect the general principle. An economy, which has an export surplus in a certain good or service, will normally employ more of its resources and labour force in the sector directly producing this item than would otherwise be the case. In particular, an economy with an export surplus in manufactures will normally have a larger manufacturing sector than would an otherwise similar economy specializing in some other direction.[21] As a general statement this is obvious.

To illustrate how important it is in practice, Fig. 1.4 compares the historical experience of two extreme cases: Norway and the area which is now West Germany. Over the past century, these two countries have developed at a similar pace, in terms of per capita income and economic efficiency, but West Germany has always had a far more industrialized economy than Norway, employing a much greater fraction of its workforce in manufacturing (up to half as much again) and a much lower fraction in the services. This difference in employment

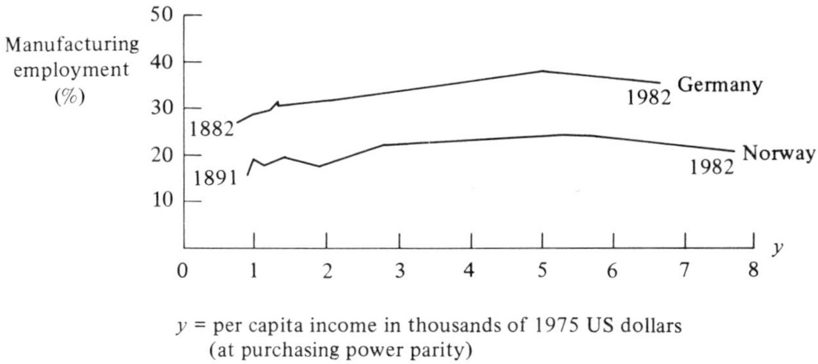

Fig. 1.4 Manufacturing employment in Germany and Norway

structure is explained mainly by the different patterns of trade specialization adopted by the two countries. As a major net exporter of manufactured goods, West Germany has always needed a much larger manufacturing sector than Norway, which has always been in surplus in its trade in non-manufactured goods and services (notably in shipping and oil) and in deficit in manufacturing trade.[22] West Germany and Norway are two extreme examples, but they do indicate the extent to which trade specialization influences the structure of employment in the advanced countries.

As we shall see below, trade specialization is the most important single factor explaining variations in employment structure from one advanced country to another. In some cases it can also help to explain why the structure of employment varies *within* individual countries through the course of time. For example, if a country's net exports of manufactures increase then, other things being equal, the manufacturing sector will expand, more people will be employed in this sector, and its share of total employment will rise. If net manufactured exports fall, the opposite will occur and the share of manufacturing will decline. This is an obvious point which requires no elaboration. However, there is one qualification. As stated, the argument takes as fixed the volume of GDP and is concerned only with variations in the composition of this given output. In reality, of course, a shift in trade specialization may also affect the macro-economic performance of a country, causing both the level of economic activity and rate of growth to change. To obtain a complete picture of what happens to domestic employment when the pattern of specialization alters, these macro-economic effects should also be taken into account. Again, this is an obvious point, which is discussed at greater length in Chapter 4. One example will serve to illustrate its significance.

Consider an economy which is operating well below its full potential, with a considerable amount of unemployed labour and excess productive capacity. This may be because the economy is facing an 'inflation barrier', such that economic expansion will lead to unacceptable inflationary pressures; or because it is facing a foreign exchange constraint, such that expansion will lead to an unacceptable balance of payments deficit. Suppose that a major source of indigenous oil is now discovered, whose costs of production are negligible. This discovery will strengthen the balance of payments and thereby relax any foreign exchange constraint which may be inhibiting expansion. It will also increase the resources available to meet competing claims on national income, thereby reducing inflationary pressures and increasing the scope for non-inflationary growth. Thus, *provided the government utilizes this new opportunity*, the discovery of oil will allow it to follow more expansionary policies, and the result will be an increase in the level of domestic activity and rate of growth. Such an expansion will increase the home demand for manufactured goods and this, in itself, will be of benefit to domestic producers. On the other hand, because of the increased supply of indigenous oil, the country's balance of trade in oil will improve and, as a result, the balance of trade in other items will almost certainly deteriorate. In particular, net manufactured exports will probably fall and this, in itself, will tend to harm domestic manufacturing producers. What finally happens to domestic manufacturing output depends on the relative strength of these two opposing forces. If the discovery of oil prompts a major expansion of economic activity, domestic manufacturing output will increase, despite the fall in net manufactured exports. On the other hand, if economic expansion is weak, the loss of net exports will be the paramount factor and manufacturing output will decline. Thus, the final impact of oil on manufacturing output and employment depends on the relative strength of the macro-economic effect (i.e. greater domestic demand) and the specialization effect (i.e. the reduction in net manufactured exports). All of this should be reasonably obvious, and the example has been included only for the sake of completeness.[23]

Summary: the determinants of manufacturing employment

We have presented a complex picture of employment structure and its evolution through time. This picture can be summarized as follows. There are certain fundamental forces, in the realm of demand and productivity, which cause the share of industry in total employment to rise during the early stages of economic development and then to fall later on, once the stage of economic maturity has been reached. Superimposed on this long-term behaviour are fluctuations of a more cyclical nature, resulting from the fact that the share of industry in output and employment rises in booms and falls in slumps. These are all phenomena which could be observed in a closed economy. In an open economy, there is also the influence of foreign trade to consider. This affects the structure of employment in two ways. First, it has macro-economic effects, which derive from the fact that foreign trade can influence both the level of activity at which an economy operates and its long-term rate of growth. An economy with a strong trade performance will normally operate at a higher level of activity and grow faster than would an otherwise similar economy with a poor trade performance. As a result, its current employment structure will be different, and this employment structure may evolve in a different fashion through the course of time. In addition to these macro-economic effects of foreign trade, there are also the 'pure specialization' effects to consider. These derive from the fact that different patterns of trade specialization are associated with different patterns of output and employment. Other things being equal, an economy which is a net exporter of manufactures will be more industrialized and will employ more of its workforce in the manufacturing sector than will an economy which is a net importer of manufactures. These are the principal conclusions arising from the preceding discussion.

An empirical test of the theory: regression analysis

Let us now apply some of the above ideas to the actual experience of advanced capitalist countries during the post-war period. This is not an easy task, because the inter-relationships involved are complex, and in order to do the job properly a complete model of post-war development would be required. To construct such a model is beyond our capabilities and would probably be a pointless exercise, anyway. Instead, we shall employ a simple uni-directional model, in which the structure of employment is determined by a number of independent variables whose values are taken as given. To be specific, we shall assume that

$$M = f(Y, U, B_m)$$

where M is the share of manufacturing in total employment; Y is a measure of real per capita income, indicating the stage of development reached by the economy in question; U is the rate of unemployment, indicating the stage in the economic cycle at which the country finds itself; and B_m is the ratio of net manufactured exports to GDP, indicating the nature and extent of the country's pattern of trade specialization. This choice of variables follows directly from our previous discussion.

The above equation is still too general for empirical use and a more exact specification is required. In line with conventional practice in this field, we shall employ a logarithmic equation of the following type:[24]

$$M + a + b \log Y + c(\log Y)^2 + dU + eB_m$$

From our previous discussion, we should expect that $b > 0$ and $c < 0$, indicating that the share of manufacturing in total employment at first rises and then falls during the course of development; that $d < 0$, indicating that manufacturing's share declines as the level of activity falls; and that $e > 0$, indicating that the more an economy specializes in net manufactured exports, the higher is the share of manufacturing in total employment.

Table 1.6 shows the results obtained when the coefficients of the above equation are estimated, using data drawn from the advanced capitalist countries between 1953 and 1978.[25] Japan has been excluded from the sample of countries because it is clearly a special case and its inclusion would simply cloud the picture.[26] The results given in Table 1.6 are grouped into two parts: those based on observations drawn from a number of countries in the same year, and those obtained when observations from all years and all countries are pooled together. Looking at these results, a number of points clearly stand out.

The first point concerns the correlation coefficients obtained when all three explanatory variables are included in the regression (equations (1) to (7)). These are all extremely high. In the case of individual years, it is perhaps not surprising that correlation coefficients are so high, because so few observations are involved. However, when all 67 observations are pooled together in equation (7), the value of R^2 is still equal to 0.811. This is an impressive result, which indicates just how great is the explanatory power of the three variables we have chosen.

Turning now to the individual variables, there is clear evidence of a curvilinear relationship between the manufacturing share M and real income Y. In every single equation, where it appears, the estimated coefficient of $\log Y$ is positive and that of $(\log Y)^2$ is negative, indicating that M first of all rises as Y increases and then, after a certain point, starts to fall. Moreover, in all cases where the relevant coefficients are statistically significant,[27] the value of Y at which M starts to fall lies within the fairly narrow range US \$3,300 to US \$4,300 (at 1975 prices). This suggests an average turning-point of around \$3,800, which is roughly the level of per capita income achieved by the UK in the early 1960s.

Looking at the coefficient on U, we find considerable variation from one equation to the next. In the first two years, 1953 and 1958, this coefficient has the wrong sign and only in later years is it negative, as it ought to be. When all observations are pooled together in equation (7), the coefficient on U is equal to -0.57, indicating that an increase of one percentage point in the unemployment rate is associated with a fall of 0.57 percentage points in manufacturing's share of total employment. This is a plausible figure and is consistent with the employment functions used by some economic forecasters for the UK economy.[28]

Finally, there are the estimated coefficients of B_m to consider. These are striking, both for their high degree of statistical significance and their uniformity from one equation to another. The highest estimate for a single year is 0.79

and the lowest is 0.63. When all years are combined in the main equations (7) and (8), the figure is 0.69. If correct, this last figure implies that, *ceteris paribus*, an increase in net manufactured exports equal to 1% of GDP will cause the share of manufacturing in total employment to rise by 0.69 percentage points.

Since the present book is primarily concerned with the question of foreign trade, it is desirable to have an independent check on the accuracy of this estimate. To provide a rough check, we have examined the input–output table for the UK in 1975. The details of our calculations are given in Appendix 4. These calculations indicate that, *ceteris paribus*, a rise in net manufactured exports equal to 1% GDP will cause the share of manufacturing in total employment to rise by between 0.62 and 0.78 percentage points.[29] These estimates are virtually identical to those obtained from the regression analysis, and they confirm the accuracy of the latter.

Let us now consider our regression results in more depth. The total variation in M over the sample as a whole is of two kinds: (a) *between* one country and another at any given point in time and (b) changes *within* individual countries over the course of time. It is clear from equations (1) to (6) that B_m is easily the most important variable explaining variations in M between one country and another. This impression is confirmed by equation (12), which uses dummy variables (the 'time dummies') to eliminate much of the intertemporal variation in M. What remains after the cross-section variations is M between one country and another. According to this equation, B_m is easily the most important variable accounting for such international differences; by comparison, the other variables Y and U are of secondary importance. On the other hand, B_m does not explain much of the intertemporal variation in M. Equation (13) uses dummy variables (the 'country dummies') to eliminate persistent international differences in the value of M, thereby focussing attention on intertemporal variations in M. According to this equation, Y and U are easily the most important variables accounting for such intertemporal variations in M; by comparison, B_m is of only secondary importance.

These conclusions are not really very surprising, given what we know about the variables concerned. Throughout the post-war period, there have been large and persistent differences in patterns of trade specialization between one country and another (see chapters 3 and 8 for further details). Some countries have been massive net exporters of manufactures, whilst others have been equally massive net importers of manufactures. Such huge international differences in patterns of trade are reflected in the structure of employment. On the other hand, in the case of individual countries net export ratios have, as a rule, remained reasonably stable through the course of time; countries that were originally net exporters or importers of manufactures have, in general, remained

Table 1.6. *The share of manufacturing in total employment: regression results (estimated coefficients)*

	No. of observations	Constant	log *Y*	(log *Y*)^2	*U*	*X*	R^2	*DW*	Turning-point
All countries (single years)									
(1) 1953	9	−2,252.1	627.10	−38.12	1.53	0.68	.924	1.77	$3,738
		(−3.06)	(3.07)	(−3.04)	(1.74)	(5.06)			
(2) 1958	10	−3,255.8	809.85	−49.45	0.93	0.76	.890	1.57	$3,317
		(−2.18)	(2.19)	(−2.17)	(1.01)	(5.64)			
(3) 1963	12	−1,935.1	471.81	−28.29	−0.71	0.70	.777	1.96	$4,189
		(−1.15)	(1.16)	(−1.15)	(−0.98)	(4.46)			
(4) 1968	12	−499.8	127.75	−7.43	−1.19	0.75	.848	1.95	$4,742
		(−0.31)	(0.33)	(−0.33)	(−1.83)	(5.67)			
(5) 1973	12	−109.6	38.45	−2.58	−0.82	0.71	.918	1.79	$1,741
		(−0.05)	(0.08)	(−0.10)	(−1.82)	(6.96)			
(6) 1978	12	−2,682.5	627.10	−36.26	−0.43	0.63	.773	2.03	$5,699
		(−1.08)	(1.10)	(−1.11)	(−1.06)	(3.72)			
All countries (all years together 1953–78)									
(7)	67	−687.7	173.68	−10.49	−0.57	0.69	.811	2.41	$3,944
		(−4.53)	(4.76)	(−4.78)	(−3.65)	(13.78)			
(8)	67	27.9				0.69	.603	1.88	
		(73.79)				(9.93)			
(9)	67	−870.5	220.00	−13.43			.205	2.99	$3,614
		(−3.20)	(3.36)	(−3.42)					
(10)	67	31.6			−0.83		.111	2.19	
		(27.17)			(−2.86)				
(11)	67	−667.2	171.26	−10.49	−0.45		.231	2.37	$3,517
		(−2.20)	(2.36)	(−2.40)	(−1.46)				
Auxiliary equations (1953–78)									
(12) with time dummies	67	−698.1	174.22	−10.42	−0.57	0.71	.818	2.46	$4,272
		(−4.16)	(4.31)	(−4.28)	(−3.01)	(13.43)			
(13) with country dummies	67	−546.9	141.28	−8.59	−0.58	0.35	.948	2.23	$3,722
		(−5.69)	(6.11)	(−6.17)	(−4.82)	(3.08)			

Errata: Table 1.6 pp 34–5

R. E. Rowthorn and J. R. Wells
De-Industrialization and Foreign Trade
0521 263603 hard cover
0521 269474 paperback

Page 34: The column headed X should be headed B_m
The column headed DW should be deleted
Page 35: Should read as follows:

Notes: The countries used in the above regressions were as follows: Canada, USA, Australia, Austria, Belgium, France, Germany, Italy, Netherlands, Norway, Sweden and the UK. The coefficients in lines (1)–(11) were estimated by ordinary least squares, starting from the equation:

$$M = a + b \log Y + c(\log Y)^2 + dU + eB_m$$

where: M = manufacturing employment as a percentage of civilian employment;
Y = GDP per capita measured in 1975 US dollars using purchasing power parity exchange rates;
U = percentage unemployment as defined by the OECD;
B_m = net manufactured exports as a percentage of GDP, averaged over a five-year period.

The coefficients in line (12) were estimated starting from the basic equation:

$$M = a + b \log Y + c(\log Y)^2 + dU + eB_m + \sum_{i \neq 1978} f_i D_i$$

where D_i is a dummy variable whose value is equal to 1 for year i and to zero for other years. There is a separate dummy variable for each individual year, except for 1978 which has no dummy.

The coefficients in (13) were estimated starting from the basic equation:

$$M = a + b \log Y + c(\log Y)^2 + dU + eB_m + \sum_{j \neq UK} g_j E_j$$

where E_j is a dummy variable whose value is equal to 1 for country j and zero for other countries. There is a separate dummy variable for each individual country, except for the UK which has no dummy.

The turning-point is the value of Y at which M reaches a maximum: this occurs when $\log Y = -b/2c$. The t-values are given in brackets.

so, and in only a few countries has there been a major shift in the structure of foreign trade.

Hence, the large changes in employment structure, which have occurred during the past thirty years, have not in general been caused by shifts in the pattern of trade specialization. They are the result of other factors, such as economic growth and, more recently, crisis and recession. The UK, however, is an exception to this general rule. As we shall see in chapters 5–12, there has been a massive and sustained shift in the structure of UK trade, quite without equal in the advanced countries, and this has certainly had a significant effect on the share of the manufacturing sector in UK employment.

Conclusions

This concludes our discussion of the structure of employment and its evolution. The above regression analysis has confirmed the analysis presented earlier in the chapter. It has established empirically that: (1) the share of manufacturing in total employment follows a curvilinear path during the course of development, first of all rising and then falling back again at very high levels of per capita income; (2) the share of manufacturing falls below its trend value during recessions; and (3) a country's pattern of trade specialization is a major influence on its employment structure: countries with a high ratio of net manufactured exports to GDP have a much larger fraction of their labour force employed in manufacturing than do otherwise similar countries which are net importers of manufactured goods. Later in this book we shall use these findings to help explain what has happened to manufacturing employment in the UK since the Second World War.

2

Economic development and the structure of foreign trade

Introduction

In Chapter 1, we showed that amongst the advanced capitalist countries in our sample, differences in foreign trade structure are by far the most important determinant of differences in internal economic structure; in particular, we demonstrated that differences in the ratio of net manufactured exports to GDP are much the most important factor accounting for differences in the share of manufacturing in total employment.

In that discussion, the structure of foreign trade and the level of economic development were treated as if they were independent variables. This was an unavoidable aspect of the regression analysis. However, this is not necessarily a reasonable assumption to make, because the level of development and the structure of foreign trade might well be systematically related in some way or other. The aim of this chapter is to determine whether such a relationship exists, and, if so, what it looks like.

Most people would probably accept that there is, indeed, a relationship between the level of development and the structure of foreign trade. They would point to the fact that most poor countries are primary producers, whilst many, though by no means all, advanced countries are specialist manufacturing exporters.[1] This observation leads most people to conclude that successful economic development is usually accompanied by a shift in foreign trade structure away from relying on primary product exports and towards a greater degree of dependence on net manufactured exports. This view is frequently based upon the very compelling historical experience of the UK and Japan, both of whom were primary producers during the early stages of their development but who both subsequently transformed themselves into two of the greatest manufacturing specialists the world has ever seen.

The view which we wish to put forward on the relationship between economic development and the structure of foreign trade is as follows: during the early and intermediate stages of development, most countries experience a deterioration in their balance of trade in primary products (food, raw materials and fuel) relative to GDP (measured at constant prices).[2] As a result, the non-manufacturing balance as a whole, which includes the balance in non-government services in addition to that in primary products, is also likely to deteriorate relative to GDP (measured at current prices). However, whether or not this happens depends partly on the behaviour of relative primary product prices, since changes in the latter may mask the underlying adverse trends at constant prices. The behaviour of the non-manufacturing balance also depends on what happens to the balance in non-government services: however, on this issue, valid generalizations are difficult to make. Nevertheless, during the early and intermediate stages of development, many, though by no means all, countries experience a deterioration in their non-manufacturing balance relative to GDP, measured at current prices.

Many advanced countries, on the other hand, appear to experience an improvement in their balance of trade in food and raw materials relative to GDP (measured at constant prices). This development appears to be relatively autonomous with respect to each country's industrial and economic performance overall. However, favourable trends in trade in food and raw materials do not necessarily result in an improvement in the non-manufacturing balance as a whole. Whether they do so or not depends partly on the evolution of the fuel balance, partly on the behaviour of relative primary product prices and partly on what happens to the non-government service balance. However, the behaviour of all three of these factors is such that it is difficult to make valid generalizations concerning any of them. As a result, favourable trends in trade in food and raw materials in a number of advanced countries have not been reflected in a general improvement in the non-manufacturing balance as a whole – though in some countries, of course, they have been.

Thus, during the course of development many, though by no means all, countries experience, first of all, a deterioration in their non-manufacturing balance relative to GDP (measured at current prices) and then, subsequently, an improvement. This has important implications for the evolution of the manufacturing balance, as well as for a country's internal economic structure.

This chapter is organized as follows: it begins by examining what happens, at each stage of development, to domestic demand, production and international trade in each of the main areas of non-manufacturing activity (food, raw materials, fuel and non-government services). It then goes on to describe how changes in domestic demand and production impinge on the trade balance and also how the latter is affected by factors such as resource endowments and economic policy, as well as by external shocks, such as changes in relative prices. The chapter concludes by analysing the implications of changes in the non-manufacturing balance for the evolution of the manufacturing balance. Although this book is mainly concerned with developments in advanced countries, a substantial discussion of what happens to the structure of foreign trade during early and intermediate stages of development is included for the sake of completeness.

Food and economic development: demand, production and trade

General

During the course of development, most countries undergo what we shall call the 'gastronomic transition'. This is a stage of development during which the demand for food, first of all, increases very rapidly and then, subsequently, stabilizes. Domestic food production, on the other hand, usually lags behind the growth of food demand during the latter's explosive phase, and this gives rise to a deterioration in the food balance of trade; however, once food demand stabilizes, a much better balance emerges between demand and production, with beneficial effects on the food balance of trade. We use the term 'gastronomic transition' to refer to the whole of this process. Only countries with an exceptionally favourable endowment of agricultural resources which are properly exploited can hope to avoid a deterioration in their food balance of trade during the early and intermediate stages of development. However, once countries have reached an advanced stage of development, the 'gastronomic transition' has normally been completed, and steady inprovements in the food balance of trade are a source of reduced pressure on the external balance.

Demand for food

The total domestic demand for food, measured in terms of grain equivalents, follows an S-shaped path during the course of economic development (see Figs. 2.1 and 2.2). It rises rapidly during the early and intermediate stages of development and then virtually stabilizes, once higher stages of development have been reached. The main factors responsible for this pattern are as follows.

Early and intermediate stages of development

During early and intermediate stages of development the demand for food undergoes enormous changes, both of a quantitative and of a qualitative kind. The total demand for food calories increases rapidly, and there are major changes in the composition of the diet. Taken together, these quantitative and qualitative changes give rise to a major increase in the total demand for food, measured in terms of grain equivalents.

There are two reasons why the total demand for food calories rises so rapidly: first, rapid population growth and, second, a rise in mean per capita calorie intakes. The reason why population growth is so rapid at this stage of development is that countries are in the midst of their 'demographic transition' from

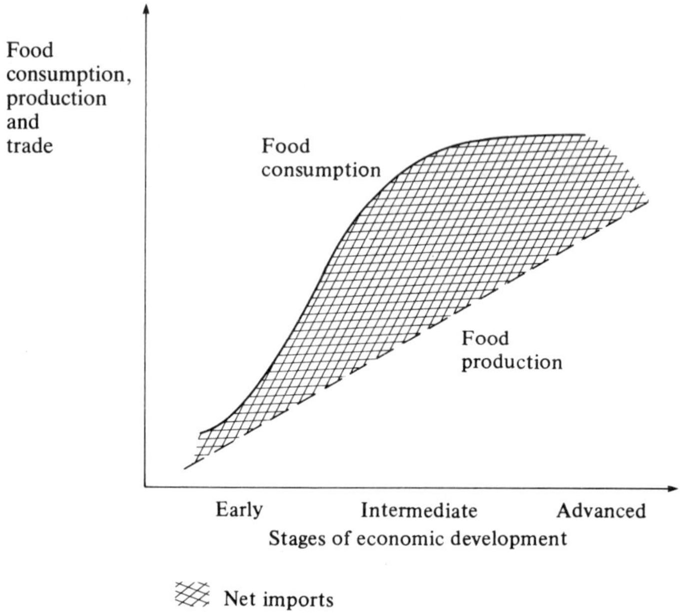

Fig. 2.1 The gastronomic transition: net food importer

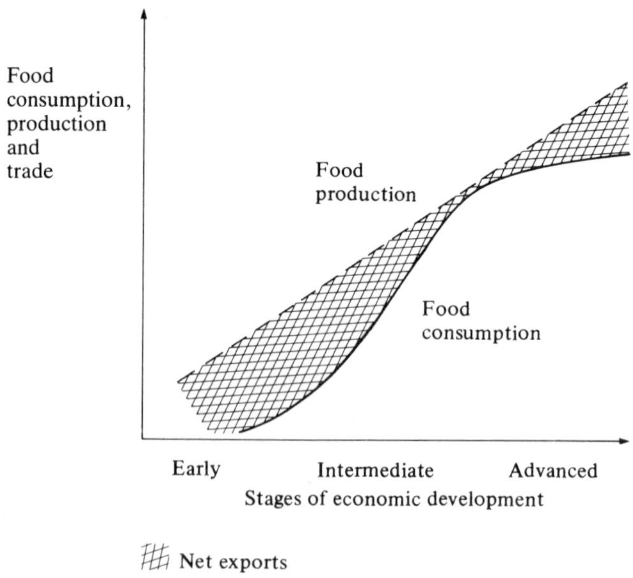

Fig. 2.2 The gastronomic transition: net food exporter

high rates of fertility and mortality to low rates.[3] Because fertility decline usually lags behind mortality decline, the 'demographic transition' is normally accompanied by an exceptionally rapid rate of population growth, and this is a powerful factor serving to augment the total demand for food calories.

In addition, the early and intermediate stages of development are also marked by a significant rise in mean per capita calorie intakes. The main factor responsible for this is that calorie-deficient households (i.e. those failing to meet their calorie requirements) devote quite a substantial proportion of any increase in real income to closing the calorie 'gap' (i.e. to eliminating the difference between calorie intakes and requirements). Although in most capitalist countries the intermediate stages of development are marked by an increase in relative income inequality,[4] most poor households do appear to experience at least some increase in absolute real income during this stage of development.[5] It is part of this increase which is devoted to closing the calorie 'gap', and this is the main factor responsible for the rise in mean per capita calorie intakes which takes place during the early and intermediate stages of development.

However, the qualitative shifts in food demand taking place at this stage of development are mainly the result of changes in demand by better-off, calorie-sufficient households (i.e. those meeting their calorie requirements). Such households have a high income-elasticity of demand for changes in the composition of their diet. This qualitative change normally consists of a shift away from a diet dominated by one or more starchy staples, such as root crops and 'inferior' cereals, to one consisting, to a much greater degree, of 'superior' foodstuffs:[6] 'superior' cereals (particularly wheat) and foodstuffs which are rich in animal proteins (e.g. meat, milk, butter, cheese and eggs). Thus, as income rises, a steadily diminishing proportion of dietary calories, proteins and other nutrients are supplied by 'inferior' cereals and root crops, whilst an increasing proportion are obtained from what might be called the 'wheat–meat' diet.

The other main factor responsible for the qualitative shifts in food demand taking place at this stage of development are changes in food habits, arising from the process of successful development itself. Urbanization, for example, is a major contributory factor to changes in food habits, because urban households are attracted to foodstuffs which are easier to process than the traditional starchy staples consumed in rural areas. Other consequences of successful economic development, such as improved transportation, better refrigeration and greater efficiency in wholesale and retail distribution also contribute to changes in food habits, due to the fact that they lead to lower prices and improvements in the quality and availability of meat and dairy products, as well as fresh fruit and vegetables.

The qualitative change in food demand, represented by the shift to the 'meat–wheat' diet, represents an enormous, hidden increase in the demand for food,

Table 2.1. *Japan and Italy: per capita food availability (kgs/head/year) and calorie intakes, 1934–77*

	Japan			Italy		
	1934–38	1960–62	1975–77	1934–38	1960–63	1975–77
Cereals[a]	157.7	149.1	132.2	160.4	134.2	130.5
Potatoes & roots	40.3	39.4	24.2	36.6	50.3	36.8
Pulses, nuts & seeds	33.0	30.2	22.1	22.5	10.8	10.0
Sugar	13.3	15.8	25.5	7.9	23.1	30.1
Meat	2.2	6.4	25.5	20.1	30.7	63.9
Eggs	2.3	6.0	15.8	7.3	9.3	11.0
Milk & dairy products	3.3	27.2	33.4	42.9	70.8	88.7
Fish & shellfish	9.9	32.3	44.1	6.3	7.3	9.3
Vegetables	70.0	88.9	108.4	55.8	138.6	151.5
Fruit	15.3	26.5	69.5	29.8	88.7	126.4
Edible oils & fats	0.9	4.8	12.1	11.7	16.8	23.2
Total daily calories (Kcals)	2199	2392	2707	2603	2831	3200

Note:

[a] of which:	1934–38	1960–62	1975–77
Rice	135.0	116.0	90.7
Wheat	8.6	25.9	32.1

Source: FAO, *Food Balance Sheets*

measured in terms of grain equivalents. The reason for this is that animals are relatively inefficient converters of the vegetable proteins which they consume. This important point is often neglected. For example, it takes 16 kilograms of grain and soya to obtain 1 kilogram of beef; for pork the ratio is 6; for turkey 4; for chicken 3 and for eggs 3.[7] Of course, these various sources of animal protein have a somewhat higher proportion of *utilizable* protein per kilogram of food weight than the vegetable proteins which can be obtained from grains and soya. However, even after taking this factor into account, the resource cost (in terms of grain equivalents) of animal protein is considerably higher than that of vegetable protein. Thus, the qualitative shift in consumption from traditional diets dominated by starchy staples to those which are rich in animal proteins represents a very significant hidden increase in the demand for food, measured in terms of grain equivalents.

These quantitative and qualitative changes in food demand, taking place during the early and intermediate stages of development, can be illustrated using recent data from Japan and Italy (see Table 2.1). Both countries have only recently emerged from the intermediate stages of development, and thus their data on food consumption are considerably more reliable than equivalent estimates for the first industrial nations.

Table 2.1 shows that, between the mid-1930s and the mid-1970s, both Japan and Italy registered considerable increases in their total demand for food calories. Japanese mean per capita calorie intakes rose by 23% (and the country's population by 75%); in Italy, there was a similar increase in per capita calorie intakes, and the country's population rose by 115%.

Both countries also registered major changes in the composition of their diets. In the case of Japan, the traditional diet consisted mainly of rice, potatoes, soya products and vegetables, with other foodstuffs being consumed in insignificant quantities. However, between the mid-1930s and the mid-1970s, Japanese per capita intakes of rice and potatoes both declined. Meanwhile, the country registered truly dramatic increases in per capita intakes of non-traditional foodstuffs: a tenfold rise in the consumption of wheat, elevenfold for meat, sevenfold in the case of eggs, a doubling for sugar and so on. Despite these dramatic changes, the traditional Japanese diet was not completely swept aside and, even in the mid-1970s, Japanese per capita intakes of the 'wheat–meat' diet were still considerably lower than those in Western Europe and North America.

In the period between the mid-1930s and mid-1970s, Italy also registered a reduction in per capita intakes of two of its traditional starchy staples: potatoes and maize. At the same time, post-war increases in Italian per capita intakes of foodstuffs such as sugar, meat, eggs, milk, dairy products and inedible fats and oils were almost as dramatic as those recorded in Japan, despite the fact that Italy's traditional diet was considerably closer than Japan's to the high-income 'wheat–meat' diet.

Higher stages of development

In advanced countries, the total demand for food, measured in terms of grain equivalents, shows a tendency to level off (see Figs. 2.1 and 2.2). The main factors responsible for this are that the total demand for food calories, as well as the composition of the diet, both tend to stabilize: thus, once higher stages of development are reached, both quantitative and qualitative changes in food demand are much less pronounced. The reasons why the total demand for food calories tends to stabilize are twofold: first, population growth slows down and second, mean per capita calorie intakes tend to level off.

Population growth in many advanced countries has now slowed to the point where it is only just positive.[8] Indeed, if fertility continues to remain below replacement levels,[9] population growth in many developed countries will be negative at some not too distant point in the future – though previous predictions of population decline (e.g. those made in the 1930s) have, it is true, proved to be incorrect.

The second reason why the total demand for food calories tends to stabilize in advanced countries is that mean per capita calorie intakes cease to grow and, in many developed countries, even appear to decline – though there are a number of glaring exceptions.[10] The principal factor behind this development is the decline in occupation-related calorie requirements, resulting from continuous increases in the relative importance of non-manual types of employment; an additional factor must be the growing awareness of the threat which obesity poses to good health.

So far as qualitative changes in food demand in advanced countries are concerned, whilst the composition of food demand continues to change, such changes are much more modest compared with those taking place during the early and intermediate stages of development.

Domestic food production

General

The rate of growth of domestic food production usually varies very little during the course of development. However, during the early and intermediate stages of development, the growth of food output tends to lag behind the growth of demand, and the resulting deterioration in the food balance of trade can pose a major threat to the maintenance of external balance. In advanced countries, on the other hand, domestic food production tends to increase relative to demand, and the resulting improvement in national food self-sufficiency is a source of reduced pressure on the external balance.

Early and intermediate stages of development

During the early and intermediate stages of development, the performance of domestic agriculture usually proves to be unsatisfactory relative to the huge changes taking place on the demand side; however, in absolute terms, agriculture's performance is often perfectly adequate. There are normally a number of factors responsible for preventing domestic agriculture from making a more satisfactory response to changes on the demand side.

First, the nature of land tenure arrangements as well as the 'semi-feudal' relations of production prevailing in 'traditional' agriculture often impede the spread of improved techniques of production. A second factor inhibiting the growth of agricultural production is the heavy concentration, at this stage of development, of resources of all kinds: financial, administrative, entrepreneurial and technological, on the urban–industrial sector. This situation is often exacerbated by policies which are designed to foster rapid capital accumulation in the urban–industrial sector but which leave agriculture de-capitalized and drained of the resources necessary to make a more satisfactory response to demand side changes.

Higher stages of development

In advanced countries, domestic agricultural output increases steadily and there might even be a slight acceleration in the sector's growth rate. This steady increase in output is based on apparently inexorable increases in yields in all areas of farming. What we observe is, in effect, the 'industrialization' of agriculture, with steady increases in fixed capital per person employed, as well as the continuous application of the fruits of scientific and technological progress. Traditional patterns of land tenure and archaic social relations of production have long since ceased to constitute an impediment to the spread of new techniques, whilst government policy (in the form of trade protection and financial incentives) usually provides an exceptionally conducive environment to increases in agricultural output. However, even in the absence of such incentives, most advanced countries would still have experienced a very considerable increase in agricultural production simply on account of steady improvements in yields in all areas of farming.[11]

The balance of trade in food during the 'gastronomic transition'

During the early and intermediate stages of development, when the growth of food demand tends to outstrip the growth of domestic production, many countries experience a reduction in domestic food self-sufficiency (i.e. in the ratio of domestic food output to consumption). As a result, either food imports increase and/or food exports decline, and the balance of trade in food deteriorates. In the case of net food-importing countries (see Fig. 2.1), this phase of the 'gastronomic transition' is marked by an increase in the volume of net food imports, both in absolute terms and, possibly, also as a proportion of GDP (measured at constant prices). These developments can be observed quite clearly during Japan's recently experienced 'gastronomic transition' (see Table 2.2). In the case of net food-exporting countries (see Fig. 2.2), if domestic production fails to respond adequately to changes on the demand side, this phase of the 'gastronomic transition' may also be marked by a deterioration in the food balance of trade, with the volume of net food exports declining, both absolutely and as a proportion of GDP (measured at constant prices).[12] Indeed, a traditional net food-exporting country may even develop a deficit in food trade during this stage of the 'gastronomic transition'.

However, once a more advanced stage of development has been reached, most countries have normally completed the 'gastronomic transition'. The growth of domestic food production outstrips the growth of demand, and, as a result, there is a marked improvement in national food self-sufficiency (see Table 2.3). Food imports decline and/or food exports increase, and the balance of trade

Table 2.2. *Japan: food trade data (at constant 1975 prices)*

	Imports US $b	Exports US $b	Net imports US $b	As a % of GDP
1961	1.71	0.65	1.06	0.69
1965	3.58	0.78	2.80	1.28
1970	5.84	1.08	4.76	1.22
1975	7.78	0.72	7.06	1.42
1980	10.04	0.89	9.15	1.48
1984	12.15	0.94	11.21	1.56

Notes: Data for export and import values for 1975 from UN, *Yearbook of International Trade Statistics*, extrapolated to other years using index numbers on food export and import volumes in OECD, *Historical Statistics of Foreign Trade*, updated with OECD, *Main Economic Indicators*. Data on GDP at constant 1975 purchasers' prices from OECD, *National Accounts*, updated with OECD, *Quarterly National Accounts*.

Table 2.3. *Self-sufficiency (%) in selected agricultural products for several OECD countries*

	North America	West Germany	UK	France
Cereals				
1956–60	121	77	50	110
1979–80	167	89	83	173
Sugar				
1956–60	43	92	24	118
1979–80	53	125	46	200
Butter				
1956–60	n.a.	94	8	106
1979–80	n.a.	130	47	119
Total meat				
1956–60	99	86	62	101
1979–80	100	89	75	100

Sources: Data for North America from FAO, *The State of Food and Agriculture*, various issues. Data for West Germany, UK and France from EC (1975), updated with EC (1982).

in food improves.[13] As a result, net food-importing countries experience a decline in the volume of their net food imports, both absolutely (see Fig. 2.1) and as a proportion of GDP (measured at constant prices) (see Table 2.4). Moreover, some traditional net food-importing countries even become net exporters at higher stages of development.[14]

So far as net food-exporting countries are concerned they should, in theory,

Table 2.4. *West Germany and Austria: net food imports by volume (1975 = 100) and as a % of GDP (at constant prices)*

	West Germany		Austria	
	Net food imports		Net food imports	
	By volume	As a % of GDP	By volume	As a % of GDP
1961–62	80.0	2.0	71.1	1.2
1965–66	87.7	1.9	107.0	1.6
1970–71	103.5	1.7	84.7	1.0
1975–76	104.8	1.5	103.7	1.0
1980–81	92.3	1.2	94.1	0.8
1983–84	87.1	1.1	61.9	0.5

Sources and notes: Index numbers of net food imports at 1975 prices computed as follows: exports and imports at 1975 prices computed from export and import values for 1975 from UN, *Yearbook of International Trade Statistics*, extrapolated using index numbers on food import and export volumes from OECD *Historical Statistics of Foreign Trade*, updated with OECD *Main Economic Indicators*. GDP at constant prices calculated from OECD, *National Accounts* and OECD, *Quarterly National Accounts*.

experience an increase in the volume of their net food exports and, thus, an improvement in their food balance of trade at higher stages of development (see Fig. 2.2). However, whether or not they do so depends on the strength of their agricultural resource endowment, as well as on the extent to which they decide to specialize in exporting food.

Note, finally, that there is little reason to expect any systematic relationship amongst advanced countries between the size of improvements in food balance of trade and industrial and economic performance as a whole. The reasons for this are twofold. First, on the demand side, since changes in both the level and composition of food demand are relatively minor at this stage of development, they are not very sensitive to differences in industrial and economic performance as a whole. Secondly, differences in the rate of growth of agricultural output between advanced countries are much less marked than differences in industrial performance.[15,16] Thus, changes in the food balance of trade in advanced countries must be considered to be largely autonomous with respect to each country's industrial and economic performance as a whole.

Trade in food and economic development: conclusions

During the course of economic development, most countries are forced to undergo the 'gastronomic transition', as a result of which their food balance of trade first of all deteriorates and then, subsequently, improves. During the course of this process, countries make the transition from a situation in which their population is relatively small, mean per capita calorie intakes are low and the diet is dominated by a few traditional, starchy staples to one in which the population is considerably larger, mean per capita calorie intakes are higher and the mass of the population are consuming the 'meat–wheat' diet. The growth of domestic food production usually lags behind the expansion of demand during the latter's explosive phase and, as a result, the food balance of trade deteriorates during the early and intermediate stages of developments. However, at higher stages of development, the demand for food more or less stabilizes, and a much better balance emerges between demand and production, with beneficial effects on the food balance of trade. We use the term 'gastronomic transition' to refer to the whole of this process.

However, what happens to the food balance of trade during the course of development is also affected by economic policy, which may either accentuate or modify the developments described above. For example, although much of mid-Victorian Britain's increased dependence on food imports was the result of a rapid growth in domestic demand, the country's growing resort to overseas suppliers was undoubtedly accentuated by the Repeal of the Corn Laws. On the other hand, many of today's developing countries could undoubtedly reverse their growing dependence on imported foodstuffs if only they could improve domestic agricultural performance.

In addition, the relationship between economic development and changes in the food balance of trade (measured at constant prices) just described may well be masked when current price data are used, on account of changes in the relative price of food. For example, in the case of a net food-importing country, a decline in the relative price of food may obscure the adverse impact of the early phases of the 'gastronomic transition' on the external balance. Such changes in relative prices are usually the consequence of external factors, over which individual countries have little direct control.

Finally, it must be stressed that the relationship between economic development and the balance of trade in food, sketched out above, is not uniformly applicable to all countries. Those who are especially well endowed with natural resources are an obvious exception. So long as they devote sufficient efforts to exploiting their natural inheritance, changes in domestic food demand may have hardly any impact whatsoever on their overall degree of food self-sufficiency. In cases such as this, the food balance of trade may remain virtually unchanged as a proportion of GDP (measured at constant prices) throughout the entire development process.

Nevertheless, the great majority of countries are forced to undertake the 'gastronomic transition' and, therefore, have little choice but to come to terms with the threat it poses to the maintenance of external balance.

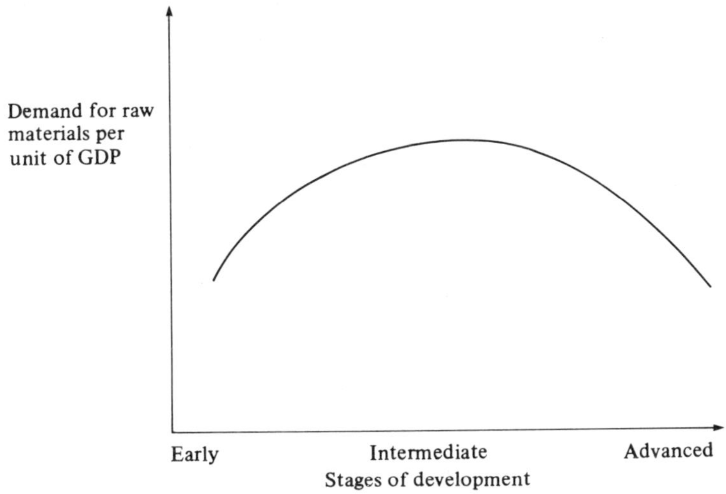

Fig. 2.3 The raw material coefficient at different stages of development

Raw materials and economic development: demand, production and trade

General

The raw material coefficient (defined as the input of raw materials per unit of GDP) rises during the early and intermediate stages of development and then, subsequently, once higher stages of development have been reached, goes into a steady decline (see Fig. 2.3). However, the level of domestic production of raw materials is not systematically related to the overall level of economic development and is much more likely to be determined by external factors, in particular by developments in world markets. It follows, therefore, that changes on the demand side, namely the rise and subsequent decline in the raw material coefficient, are the dominant factors accounting for changes in the raw materials balance of trade during the course of development: namely, for the fact that it deteriorates, as a proportion of GDP (measured at constant prices), during the early and intermediate stages of development, and then improves, relative to GDP, once higher stages of development have been reached. Of course, not all countries can be expected to conform to this pattern, on account of differences in resource endowment as well as in economic policy. Furthermore, when current price data are used, changes in the relative price of raw materials might well mask the relationship between the raw materials balance of trade and economic development (measured at constant prices) just described.

Demand for raw materials

Early and intermediate stages of development

The reasons for the rise in the raw material coefficient during the early and intermediate stages of development (see Fig. 2.3) are quite straightforward. Easily the most important factor is the rapid increase in the share of manufacturing in total GDP, since, per unit of output, manufacturing is by far the most raw material-intensive of all the main branches of economic activity. Furthermore, a substantial proportion of total manufacturing output at this stage of development consists of basic manufactures:[17] processed foods, beverages, tobacco products, textiles, clothes, shoes and leather products. Even within the context of manufacturing industry, basic manufactures of this sort have a particularly high input of raw materials per unit of output.

Higher stages of development

In advanced countries, the raw material coefficient ceases to rise and goes into a steady decline (see Fig. 2.3). The reasons for this are not to be found in any change in the relative importance of manufacturing in total GDP; as has already been shown in Chapter 1, in most advanced countries manufacturing output appears to grow at roughly the same rate as total GDP (measured at constant prices). Thus, the reasons for the decline in the raw material coefficient at higher stages of development must be sought elsewhere.

The principal cause appears to lie in a decline in the input of raw materials per unit of manufacturing output.[18] There are three main factors responsible for this. First, changes in the composition of manufacturing output: the decline in the relative importance of sectors producing basic manufactures, which have an above-average input of raw materials per unit output, and the shift to more technology- and knowledge-intensive branches of manufacturing production.[19] A second factor contributing to the decline in the raw material coefficient are steady advances in materials-saving technical progress (including the re-cycling of waste materials); this seems to be an inherent feature of manufacturing production processes. The third and final factor contributing to the decline in the input of raw materials per unit of manufacturing output has been the development of synthetic (oil-based) domestic substitutes[20] for a number of imported raw materials.

It should be noted that all advanced countries appear to experience a declining raw material coefficient, regardless of their overall industrial and economic performance. Indeed, the coefficient is likely to fall somewhat faster in industrially more successful countries, because of the greater speed with which they are able to transform their industrial structures and introduce materials-saving technology. However, even though the raw material coefficient may decline more rapidly in such countries, their consumption of raw materials is likely to continue to rise in absolute terms.

Domestic output of raw materials

By contrast with the evolution of the demand for raw materials per unit of GDP, valid generalizations concerning the production of raw materials at different stages of development are virtually impossible to make. Countries obviously vary enormously, both in terms of their natural resources endowment, as well as in the intensity with which they exploit their resources at different stages of development. Furthermore, the level of domestic production of raw materials, many of which are internationally traded, is more likely to be determined by developments in world markets than by the rate of growth of domestic demand – except, that is, for non-traded materials, such as those used in the construction industry. Thus, except in countries which are exceptionally well endowed with raw materials and where the output of materials is a significant proportion of GDP, the level of materials production is unlikely to vary systematically with the overall level of economic development.[21]

Trade in raw materials and economic development

The fact that the raw material coefficient rises and then falls during the course of development, whereas the domestic production of materials is not systematically related to the level of development, has obvious implications for the balance of trade in raw materials.

Consider, first of all, the case of a net raw material-importing country. During the early and intermediate stages of development, the rise in the raw material coefficient is likely to result in either an increase in imports and/or a decline in exports of raw materials relative to GDP (measured at constant prices). As a result, the deficit in raw materials trade is likely to increase relative to GDP (measured at constant prices).[22] Subsequently, at more advanced stages of development, the decline in the raw material coefficent is likely to result in either a fall in imports of raw materials and/or a rise in exports, and the deficit in raw materials trade is likely to diminish as a proportion of GDP (measured at constant prices) (see Table 2.5).

All advanced countries who are net raw material-importers are likely to experience a reduction in their dependence on net raw material imports, regardless of their overall industrial and economic performance. However, industrially more successful countries may continue to experience an absolute rise in the volume of their net raw material imports.[23]

Net raw material-exporting countries may also experience a deterioration in their raw materials balance of trade (relative to GDP) during the early and

Table 2.5. *West Germany: trade in raw materials (at constant 1975 prices)*

	Exports		Imports		Balance of trade	
	At 1975 US $b	As a % of GDP	At 1975 US $b	As a % of GDP	At 1975 US $b	As a % of GDP
1961–62	0.6	0.2	4.4	1.7	−3.8	−1.5
1967–68	1.3	0.4	5.6	1.7	−4.3	−1.3
1971–72	2.0	0.5	7.3	1.8	−5.3	−1.3
1975	2.4	0.6	7.5	1.8	−5.1	−1.2
1977–78	2.9	0.6	8.4	1.8	−5.5	−1.2
1981–82	3.4	0.7	8.8	1.8	−5.4	−1.1
1983–84	3.7	0.7	9.4	1.9	−5.7	−1.1

Japan: Trade in raw materials (at constant 1975 prices)

	Exports		Imports		Balance of trade	
	At 1975 US $b	As a % of GDP	At 1975 US $b	As a % of GDP	At 1975 US $b	As a% of GDP
1961–62	0.2	0.1	4.2	2.6	−3.9	−2.5
1967–68	0.4	0.1	7.5	2.6	−7.1	−2.4
1971–72	0.8	0.2	10.4	2.4	−9.6	−2.2
1975	0.8	0.2	10.3	2.1	−9.5	−1.9
1977–78	1.0	0.2	11.3	2.0	−10.3	−1.8
1981–82	0.9	0.1	11.2	1.7	−10.4	−1.6
1983–84	0.9	0.1	11.7	1.7	−10.7	−1.5

Sources and notes: Import and export values for 1975 from UN *Yearbook of International Trade Statistics.* Extrapolated using raw materials import and export volume indices from OECD *Historical Foreign Trade Statistics*, updated with OECD *Main Economic Indicators.* GDP statistics from OECD *National Accounts*, updated with OECD *Quarterly National Accounts*.

intermediate stages of development – but not necessarily so. Given that their raw material endowment is superior to that of net-raw material-importing countries, they may well be able to match the rise in the raw material coefficient with an increase in domestic production.[24] Similarly, when net raw material-exporting countries reach a more advanced stage of development, they may not necessarily experience an increase in net exports. Whether or not they do so depends partly on the strength of their resource endowment and partly on the extent to which they decide to specialize in exporting raw materials.

Trade in raw materials: conclusions

To summarize: during the course of economic development many countries, especially those which are net raw material-importers, experience, first of all, a deterioration in their balance of trade in raw materials relative to GDP (measured at constant prices) and then, subsequently, an improvement. Of course, not all countries conform to this pattern. Some are so favourably endowed with raw materials that the rise and subsequent decline in the raw material coefficient has no impact whatsoever on their balance of trade in materials. Similarly, economic policy may also affect the evolution of the materials balance; for example, countries with roughly similar endowments may exploit their resources with differing degrees of intensity. Finally, when current price data are used, changes in the relative price of materials might well mask the relationship between the raw materials balance of trade and economic development (measured at constant prices) just described.

Fuel and economic development: demand, production and trade

Introduction

The way the balance of trade in fuel behaves during the course of economic development is similar to that for raw materials.

Demand for fuel

General

The fuel-intensity of GDP (i.e. the input of fuel per unit of GDP) varies considerably amongst countries at a similar stage of development; nevertheless, it generally rises during the early and intermediate stages of development and then goes into a steady decline once higher stages of development have been reached (see Fig. 2.4).[25]

Early and intermediate stages of development

The main factor responsible for the rise in the fuel-intensity of GDP during the early and intermediate stages of development is the adoption of more fuel-intensive patterns of production and consumption: urbanization, rapid industrialization and the development of the transportation infrastructure are the principal contributory factors. The effect of such changes in production and consumption on fuel demand was undoubtedly accentuated, in the decades prior to the oil price rises of the 1970s, by the availability of cheap and abundant supplies of oil energy. Nevertheless, even in the post-OPEC era of higher relative fuel costs, the early and intermediate stages of development will probably continue to be characterized by a rise in the fuel-intensity of GDP.[26]

The existence of such a pattern is confirmed by the empirical evidence which is available.[27] In Japan, Italy and Spain, the fuel-intensity of GDP rose quite rapidly during the post-war period, when all three countries were passing through

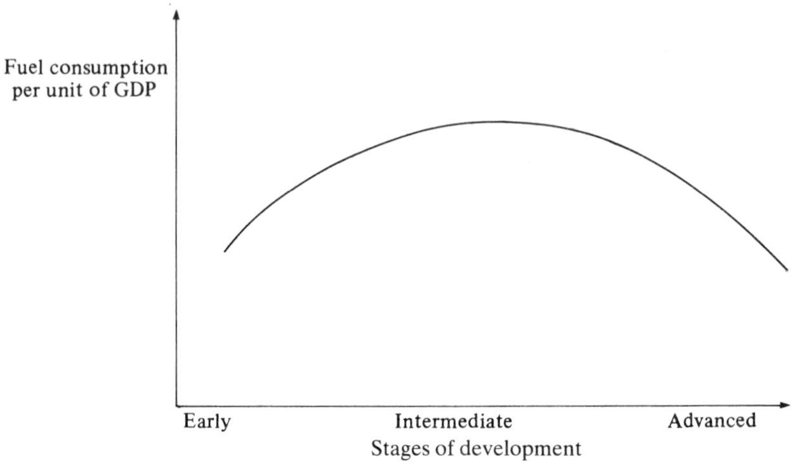

Fig. 2.4 The fuel-intensity of GDP at different stages of development

the intermediate stages of development.[28] In addition, estimates of the commercial fuel coefficient (i.e. the change in the consumption of commercial fuel divided by the change in GDP)[29] for a number of newly industrializing countries are generally greater than unity.[30]

Higher stages of development

At an advanced stage of development, most countries appear to experience a decline in the fuel-intensity of GDP, though there are some notable exceptions. There are two main factors responsible for this. First, steady increases in fuel efficiency – in industry, transportation and the home; and second, shifts in the structure of industrial production towards sectors which are relatively less fuel-intensive per unit of output.[31]

In a number of the more mature industrial countries (e.g. West Germany and the UK), the fuel-intensity of GDP has been declining for at least the past thirty years.[32] However, in the most recently industrialized of the advanced economies (Japan and Italy), this decline only appears to have started in the mid-1970s – coinciding with the rise in the real price of fuel.

There seems little doubt that higher real fuel prices in the post-OPEC era will depress the level of fuel consumption per unit of GDP at all stages of economic development.[33] Nevertheless, the basic picture on the demand side will probably remain much the same: namely, that the fuel-intensity of GDP will continue to rise during the early and intermediate stages of development, but then decline once higher stages of development are reached.

Domestic production of fuel

Countries obviously vary enormously, both in terms of their natural endowment of fossil fuels, as well as in their capacity to generate hydro-electrical energy. Moreover, except for countries which are exceptionally well endowed in fuel resources, there is little reason to expect any systematic relationship between economic development and the level of domestic fuel output. Certainly, the early stages of modern economic growth in Western Europe were accompanied by a massive expansion of domestic fuel production; however, in recent years, the intensity with which domestic fuel resources have been exploited has had more to do with the relative price of fuel than with the general level of economic development. Thus, during the pre-OPEC era of cheap and abundant oil energy, most Western European countries engaged in an extremely rapid run-down of domestic coal production,[34] although it is probably true to say that, in the post-OPEC era, greater emphasis is being placed on the development of domestic fuel resources (including nuclear energy).

Thus, valid generalizations concerning the relationship between economic development and the level of domestic fuel production are difficult to make.[35,36]

Trade in fuel and economic development

Early and intermediate stages of development

The rapid increase in the fuel-intensity of GDP, taking place during the early and intermediate stages of development, is bound to give rise to a deterioration in the balance of trade in fuel as a proportion of GDP (measured at constant prices), unless there is a corresponding expansion of domestic fuel production. If consumption runs ahead of production, then either imports increase and/or exports decline relative to GDP, and the balance of trade in fuel deteriorates. Japan and France were two notable examples of such a development in the post-war period. In both countries, the entire increase in fuel consumption in the period 1950–80 was satisfied by an increase in net imports.[37]

By contrast, countries which are favourably endowed with domestic fuel resources may experience no deterioration whatsoever in their balance of trade in fuel during the early and intermediate stages of development and may even witness an improvement.

Higher stages of development

If developments on the demand side were the only relevant factor, then we should normally expect to see an improvement in the balance of trade in fuel relative to GDP (measured at constant prices) at higher stages of development. However, the run-down of coal production in virtually all advanced countries in the post-war period meant that almost all of them experienced a significant deterioration in their fuel balance.

Meanwhile, higher fuel prices in the post-OPEC era, by encouraging economies in consumption as well as increases in domestic production, ought to have resulted in an improvement in the balance of trade in fuel (relative to GDP) in many advanced countries. However, it is too early to judge whether there has been a general trend in this direction.

In any case, in the post-OPEC era, the effect on the fuel balance (measured at current prices) of favourable trends in fuel export and import volumes is likely to be swamped by changes in the relative price of fuel.

Trade in fuel and economic development: conclusions

Because the fuel-intensity of GDP rises and then declines during the course of development, countries who are poorly endowed with fuel resources are likely to experience, first of all, a deterioration in their fuel balance of trade relative to GDP (measured at constant prices) and, subsequently, an improvement. However, this picture is obviously affected by changes in the intensity with which even poorly endowed countries exploit their domestic fuel resources – largely in response to changes in relative prices.

Of course, countries who are exceptionally well endowed with fuel resources may find their fuel balance completely unaffected by changes in the fuel-intensity of GDP – although even many OPEC countries have, at times, found their fuel surpluses severely constrained by the unquenchable thirst for energy arising from their domestic development efforts.

However, in the future, changes in the relative price of fuel are likely to be a much more important determinant of changes in the fuel balance (measured at current prices) than changes on the demand side, described above.

Non-government services and economic development: demand, production and trade

General

Valid generalizations concerning the behavious of the non-government service balance during the course of economic development are difficult to make. In some countries, the early and intermediate stages of development are marked by a deterioration in this balance, while in others they are marked by an improvement. Advanced countries exhibit a similar degree of variation in experience.

Early and intermediate stages of development

During the early and intermediate stages of development, most late-industrializing countries are likely to experience large and possibly growing debits in certain kinds of service activities. This is partly a consequence of their relative economic backwardness and partly due to the fact that many areas of international service trade are dominated by business interests in the advanced countries. The activities in which late-industrializing countries are particularly likely to incur large and growing debits are transport, insurance, royalty payments and tourism. The reasons for this are fairly obvious. A large proportion of the seaborne trade of many developing countries is carried in foreign-owned vessels,[38] for the simple reason that most poor countries do not possess a very highly developed merchant marine of their own.[39] Similarly, a large proportion of the re-insurance business of developing countries is likely to be placed with foreign insurers because of the small size of the domestic insurance market.[40] In addition, late-industrializing countries are highly dependent on technological transfers from more advanced countries and, as a result, have rapidly growing debits on their 'royalties' account. Finally, although mean per capita income is low during the early and intermediate stages of development, its distribution is usually very uneven. As a result the elites of many developing countries, whose cultural life is usually highly imitative of developments in more advanced countries, have the resources to be able to indulge their high propensity for foreign travel.

Thus, in areas such as transport, insurance, royalty payments and tourism, most late-industrializing countries are likely to have large and rapidly growing debits during the early and intermediate stages of development. If there are insufficient compensating strengths in other areas, not only is the non-government service account as a whole likely to be in deficit,[41] but successful development is likely to cause it to deteriorate.

However, a number of relatively poor countries are so strong in areas such as tourism and workers' remittances that their non-government service account as a whole is in surplus. Hitherto, geographical proximity to high income markets[42] has been the main determinant of which of the low-wage countries possessing the requisite natural and historical advantages have been able to exploit their comparative strength in tourism (e.g. Mexico, Southern Europe, North Africa). Proximity to high-income, labour-scarce economies has also been a common characteristic of recent, large-scale labour-exporting countries (e.g. Portugal, Yugoslavia, Egypt and Pakistan). Thus, many poor countries are actually in surplus on their non-government service account, and their services balance may even improve during the course of development as a result of favourable shifts in external demand.

Thus, it is difficult to generalize concerning the behaviour of the non-government service balance during the early and intermediate stages of development.

Higher stages of development

In advanced countries, there is normally an improvement in the balance of trade in those sorts of service activities in which countries are usually weak during earlier stages of development. This occurs despite the fact that, in most reasonably open economies, the income-elasticity of demand for virtually all internationally traded services is quite high.

For example, most countries normally expand their national merchant marine, as well as their national airline, during the course of successful development and, as a result, there is usually a considerable measure of import-substitution in transportation services. Similarly, the balance of trade in technology payments usually improves as countries become less dependent on imported technology and start to develop their own technology exports. In addition, advanced countries develop the capacity to produce a whole new range of service exports in areas such as finance, education, medicine and consultancy, some of which are a by-product of their industrial prowess.

If these were the only factors at work, then we would normally expect most advanced countries to experience a steady improvement in their non-government service balance. However, in many advanced countries, rapidly growing receipts in certain areas of service trade are more than offset by increased debits in others, notably in tourism and private transfers. For example, residents of those advanced countries, having a relatively cold climate and a strong rate of exchange, have a high propensity to take their holidays in warmer climates; meanwhile, the appearance, during the course of the post-war boom, of labour shortages in many advanced countries resulted in substantial labour immigration and the appearance of growing debits on the workers' remittances account. In Holland, for example, adverse trends in both tourism and workers' remittances gave rise to a really significant deterioration in a previously strong non-government service balance, whilst, in West Germany, despite the growth of new service exports, rapid increases in tourist expenditure and workers' remittances have resulted in a substantial deterioration in the overall service balance.[43]

Trade in non-government services and economic development: Conclusions

Valid generalizations concerning the behaviour of the non-government service balance as a whole during the course of economic development are difficult to make. Most late-industrializing countries are in deficit in their non-government service balance, and successful development usually results in a further deterioration; meanwhile, others are in surplus and experiencing steady improvements. Advanced countries exhibit a similar degree of variation in experience. Furthermore, the behaviour of the non-government service balance in any particular advanced country may be quite independent of its industrial and economic performance as a whole. For example, a country with the appropriate natural and/or historic advantages may experience a more rapid growth of tourist receipts and a slower growth of tourist debits than a country with an equally successful industrial performance but which lacks the specific advantages necessary for success in international trade in tourism.

Conclusions and implications

The aim of this chapter has been to try to see whether any relationship exists between economic development and the structure of foreign trade. Our discussion suggests that, during the early and intermediate stages of development, most countries experience a deterioration in their balance of trade in food and raw materials relative to GDP (measured at constant prices).[44] In addition, the fuel balance of trade may also deteriorate. Thus, during the early and intermediate stages of development, many countries experience a deteriorating balance in all three areas of primary product trade – food, raw materials and fuel – measured at constant prices.

Of course, economic policy can obviously affect this outcome, either accentuating these trends or attenuating them. The former is probably somewhat more likely, given the often extreme degree of zeal with which governments at this stage of development usually embrace the goal of rapid industrialization, together with their concomitant neglect of the primary sector. In addition, changes in relative primary product prices can also accentuate or mask the underlying trends at constant prices. However, such changes in relative prices are generally spasmodic and short-lived and tend to be interspersed by comparatively long periods of rather stable relative prices (Cuddy, 1976). Thus, except for relatively short periods of time, changes in relative primary product prices are unlikely to mask the underlying trends at constant prices.

In most late-industrializing countries, such adverse trends in primary product trade are likely to give rise to a deterioration in the non-manufacturing balance as a whole. However, whether or not this happens depends, in addition, on the behaviour of the non-government service balance and, on this question, it is difficult to make valid generalizations. However, as far as most countries are concerned, the non-government service balance, whether positive or negative, is usually so small relative to GDP that even if it registers an improvement this will usually not be large enough to compensate for adverse trends in primary product trade. As a result, where late-industrializing countries do experience unfavourable trends in primary product trade these normally give rise to a deterioration in the non-manufacturing balance as a whole.

What are the implications of this? If successful economic development is not to be inhibited by a shortage of foreign exchange, then the deterioration in the non-manufacturing balance has to be accompanied by *either* an increase in net capital inflow *and/or* an improvement in the manufacturing balance. However, although a country may be able to resort to foreign savings in order to ease the strains imposed by the 'gastronomic transition' and the other developments described above, some improvement in the manufacturing balance is, nevertheless, essential if countries are to avoid the risk of falling into the 'Debt Trap'. Thus, during the early and intermediate stages of development, some improvement in the manufacturing balance is necessary in order for countries to be able to reconcile continued economic progress with the maintenance of external balance.

The manufacturing balance of trade can be strengthened via *either* manufactured 'export-led' growth (i.e. increasing the ratio of manufactured exports to GDP) *and/or* import-substitution industrialization (i.e. reducing the share of manufactured imports in GDP). On a priori grounds neither strategy is necessarily more advantageous than the other; which strategy (or combination of strategies) a country adopts ought to depend on specific domestic considerations, as well as on the prevailing international situation.

However, improving the manufacturing balance of trade is by no means the only policy option available to late-industrializing countries trying to tackle the challenge to the maintenance of growth and extenal balance posed by the rapid growth of demand for primary products; in particular, the fact that the demand for primary products is so income-elastic at this stage of development suggests that such countries ought to devote more attention to fostering the development of their primary sector.

Once countries reach an advanced stage of development, our analysis suggests that many of them experience an improvement in their balance of trade in food and raw materials relative to GDP (measured at constant prices). However, whether these favourable trends in food and raw materials trade are reflected in an improvement in the non-manufacturing balance as a whole (measured at current prices) depends on a number of factors.

The first of these concerns what happens to the balance of trade in fuel and, on this issue, it is difficult to generalize. Certainly, the fuel-intensity of GDP tends to decline in advanced countries, and post-OPEC rises in fuel prices have undoubtedly accentuated this trend. Furthermore, post-OPEC fuel price increases have certainly stimulated an increase in domestic fuel production (including nuclear energy). However, even if trends in fuel trade volumes in advanced countries are favourable, large increases in the relative price of fuel might well erase, in net fuel-importing countries at least, any savings accruing from improvements in trade in food and raw materials. Thus, favourable trends in trade in food and raw materials may not necessarily result in an improvement of the primary product balance as a whole (measured at current prices).

Furthermore, even if there is an improvement in the primary product balance, this does not guarantee that the non-manufacturing balance, as a whole, will improve. Whether or not it does so depends on the behaviour of the non-government service balance and, as with trade in fuel, generalizations are difficult to make. Certainly, all advanced countries experience a growth in the volume of their non-government service exports. However, many advanced countries have also registered a rapid growth of certain kinds of service imports (especially foreign holidays and workers' remittances). Thus, any gains accruing from trade in food and raw materials are offset, in certain advanced countries, by a deterioration in the non-government service balance, leaving the non-manufacturing balance, as a whole, virtually unchanged.

Thus, although there is a very pronounced trend amongst a number of advanced countries towards an improvement in the balance of trade in food and raw materials (measured both at constant and current prices), it is difficult to generalize as far as the behaviour of the non-manufacturing balance as a whole is concerned. This is because neither the balance of trade in fuel nor that in non-government services appear to behave in any well-defined way, whilst, in many net fuel-importing countries, post-OPEC fuel price rises have completely offset the positive effects on the non-manufacturing balance of favourable developments in trade in food and raw materials.

Nevertheless, favourable trends in trade in food and raw materials have, in some advanced countries, given rise to an improvement in their non-manufacturing balance as a whole. Furthermore, as was argued earlier, this improvement may be largely autonomous with respect to each country's overall industrial and economic performance. Following an autonomous movement in its non-manufacturing balance, a country can allow its manufacturing balance to deteriorate by an equivalent amount – without this necessarily endangering the maintenance of growth and external balance.[45] If the manufacturing balance deteriorates in response to an autonomous improvement in the non-manufacturing balance, this is by no means a sign of poor industrial performance. So long as full employment, external balance and a satisfactory rate of economic growth can be maintained, there is no reason to treat such a deterioration in the manufacturing balance as a cause for alarm. This is particularly obvious in the case of a country which manages to maintain or even increase its share of world manufactured exports and allows all of the adjustment to the improvement in non-manufacturing trade to take the form of an increase import-penetration in manufactures. However, adjustment could take the form of a fall in the manufacturing export-coefficient and/or increased import-penetration without this necessarily being a sign of industrial failure.

To conclude, it is difficult to make valid generalizations concerning the behaviour of the non-manufacturing balance as a whole in advanced countries. Nevertheless, countries who experience an improvement in their non-manufacturing balance of a relatively autonomous kind can afford to allow their manufacturing balance to deteriorate by an equivalent amount, without this necessarily being interpreted as a sign of industrial failure.

3

Trade and industry in developed economies

Introduction

In the last chapter we analysed the relationship between trade structure and economic development. Wherever possible, an attempt was made to identify general trends and to stress similarities between countries rather than differences. The main aim of this chapter is to examine the empirical evidence on foreign trade structure for a sample of thirteen OECD countries for the period 1952–82.

The most striking feature of the data is that the developed countries exhibit an enormous degree of diversity, not only as regards the overall structure of their foreign trade but also in so far as some countries have experienced virtual constancy in their trade structure, whilst others have experienced major changes. Even so, the empirical evidence does confirm some of the general trends identified in Chapter 2.

One of our principal conclusions is that most advanced countries experienced very little change in their trade structure in the post-war period; however, a small number of countries did experience quite major changes. So far as the latter group is concerned, a high proportion of such changes in trade structure can be accounted for by developments in non-manufacturing trade of a kind which were relatively autonomous with respect to each country's industrial and economic performance as a whole. A further point is that there is little in the data to suggest the existence of a unique route, in terms of trade structure, to the attainment of successful development; in particular, it is simply not true to suggest that every country must become a specialist manufacturing exporter, in order to attain a high level of economic development. Even so, as we shall seek to explain in the second part of this chapter, successful industrialization (in the sense of developing the capacity to produce a high per capita output of manufactures) is, for the vast majority of countries, both specialist manufacturing exporters and non-manufacturing specialists alike, a *sine qua non* for successful economic development.

Data base and typology

In order to analyse the foreign trade structure of each of the thirteen countries in our sample, we have collected annual time-series data for the period 1952–82 on trade in goods and non-government services, as well as GDP.[1] In order to handle such a large volume of information, the data are organized as follows.

First, for each country, we present: (i) the non-manufacturing balance of trade[2] and (ii) the manufacturing balance of trade,[3] both as a percentage of GDP (at current purchasers' values) (see Tables 3.1 and 3.2).

Second, information from a number of countries was pooled, as follows:

(1) *Workshop economies* (highly dependent on net manufactured exports): West Germany, Japan and Belgium (including Luxembourg).

(2) *Emerging workshop economies* (becoming increasingly dependent on net manufactured exports): Italy and Sweden.

(3) *Unspecialized economies* (manufacturing and non-manufacturing balances both small relative to GDP): USA and France.

(4) *Non-manufacturing specialists*

Primary producers (net exporters of primary products): Australia and Canada.

Diversified non-manufacturing specialists (specializing in services, as well as in certain primary products): Norway and the Netherlands (data for these two countries are presented separately).

(5) *Others:* The UK and Austria do not fit into this typology.

Countries were then sub-divided into two categories: those whose foreign trade structure remained relatively constant during the period 1952–82 and those whose trade structure underwent a significant change. Data for the former group of countries are presented in Fig. 3.1 and for the latter in Fig. 3.2

Trade structure in advanced countries: principal results

The first point to note about Figs. 3.1 and 3.2 is that, as far as trade structure is concerned, the advanced countries in our sample have exhibited an enormous degree of diversity in the post-war period. Moreover, many of these differences must have existed during earlier stages of development, as well.

At one extreme, in terms of trade structure, can be found the 'workshop economies' (West Germany, Japan and Belgium), which normally have had manufacturing surpluses of between +8% and +9% of GDP. At the other extreme lie Australia and Norway, which normally have had manufacturing deficits of between −7% and −9% of GDP (see data in Tables 3.1 and 3.2). The rest of the OECD countries in our sample lie at various points between these two extremes in terms of foreign trade structure.

The second point to note is that countries which have been economically successful in the post-war period can be found in both groups identified in Figs. 3.1 and 3.2: namely in the group whose foreign trade structure was virtually

Table 3.1. *Balance of trade in non-manufactured goods and services at a % of GDP (at current purchasers' values)*

Years	UK	Belgium	West Germany	Japan	Italy	Sweden
1952	−10.8	n.a.	−6.8	−8.4	−3.8	+0.2
1953	−10.5	−9.1	−5.6	−8.6	−2.4	+1.7
1954	−10.1	−9.0	−6.2	−7.6	−1.4	+0.9
1955	−10.8	−7.6	−6.3	−7.1	−7.1	+0.3
1956	−9.9	−8.4	−6.7	−8.4	−2.0	+0.2
1957	−9.6	−8.1	−7.2	−9.6	−1.9	+0.3
1958	−7.6	−5.8	−6.2	−5.7	−0.6	−0.1
1959	−7.7	−6.9	−6.4	−6.0	−0.5	−0.0
1960	−7.9	−7.3	−6.7	−6.6	−1.7	+0.2
1961	−6.8	−7.1	−6.6	−7.1	−1.1	+0.1
1962	−6.5	−6.4	−7.0	−6.0	−0.8	−0.4
1963	−6.5	−6.3	−6.5	−6.6	−2.0	−0.5
1964	−6.7	−7.1	−6.7	−6.5	−1.5	−0.3
1965	−6.0	−6.7	−7.1	−6.2	−1.1	−0.6
1966	−5.3	−6.7	−7.1	−6.2	−1.4	−1.2
1967	−5.0	−6.3	−6.6	−6.4	−1.9	−1.1
1968	−4.8	−7.1	−6.6	−5.9	−1.8	−1.4
1969	−4.3	−6.4	−6.9	−5.6	−2.2	−1.4
1970	−3.9	−6.6	−7.0	−6.0	−2.8	−2.1
1971	−3.7	−6.3	−7.1	−5.6	−2.8	−2.0
1972	−3.4	−5.9	−7.0	−5.3	−3.0	−1.7
1973	−4.5	−6.0	−7.5	−6.3	−4.7	−1.4
1974	−7.3	−7.8	−8.5	−9.8	−8.4	−3.6
1975	−5.2	−7.3	−8.2	−8.9	−6.6	−3.2
1976	−5.0	−8.6	−8.6	−8.9	−7.3	−3.7
1977	−3.4	−7.6	−8.3	−8.0	−5.9	−4.4
1978	−2.2	−7.6	−7.6	−6.1	−4.9	−3.3
1979	−1.3	−8.7	−8.0	−8.4	−5.2	−3.8
1980	−0.1	−10.2	−9.0	−10.4	−7.2	−4.0
1981	+1.0	−9.6	−9.8	−9.7	−7.7	−3.9
1982	+1.1	−10.3	−8.5	−9.5	−6.9	−3.8

constant as well as in the group which experienced marked changes in trade structure. For example, West Germany, whose post-war economic performance was exceptionally strong, experienced virtually no change in its dependence on net manufactured exports; on the other hand, Sweden and Italy, whose economic records were also pretty successful, both experienced major changes in trade structure.

Furthermore, economically successful countries can be found not only amongst the countries who have been in surplus in trade in manufactures but also amongst those who have been in deficit. For example, West Germany and Japan, which were among the most successful OECD economies in the post-war period, are the world's principal specialist manufacturing exporters. However, Norway and

Table 3.1 (*contd*)

Years	France	US	Austria	Canada	Australia	Netherlands	Norway
1952	−4.9	−0.6	−6.9	+3.6	+8.8	+4.2	+8.1
1953	−4.1	−0.8	−4.5	+3.0	+12.4	+3.4	+6.6
1954	−3.7	−0.7	−3.2	+2.1	+8.1	+1.4	+6.8
1955	−3.3	−0.7	−5.2	+1.8	+7.2	+2.5	+6.7
1956	−4.8	−0.4	−3.5	+1.7	+8.3	−0.1	+9.0
1957	−5.2	−0.3	−3.4	+1.4	+10.3	+3.9	+10.3
1958	−4.2	−0.6	−1.5	+1.8	+4.6	+2.4	+8.9
1959	−3.0	−0.6	−0.8	+1.6	+6.8	+3.5	+8.7
1960	−3.0	−0.3	−1.2	+1.8	+4.9	+4.7	+6.9
1961	−2.6	−0.2	+0.2	+2.6	+7.0	+4.5	+7.0
1962	−2.0	−0.4	+1.0	+2.9	+6.8	+4.8	+6.7
1963	−2.1	−0.3	+0.9	+3.1	+7.8	+4.1	+7.3
1964	−2.0	−0.1	+1.4	+3.9	+7.5	+2.7	+7.4
1965	−1.5	−0.1	+1.3	+3.5	+5.9	+3.3	+7.7
1966	−1.5	−0.1	+0.6	+3.9	+5.9	+2.4	+6.5
1967	−0.5	−0.2	+1.0	+3.8	+6.2	+2.2	+6.9
1968	−1.5	−0.4	+0.9	+3.5	+5.0	+2.5	+7.9
1969	−2.0	−0.3	+1.2	+2.7	+5.6	+2.6	+7.4
1970	−2.0	−0.2	+1.2	+3.5	+6.0	+3.0	+6.2
1971	−1.6	−0.3	+1.8	+3.5	+5.9	+3.6	+5.8
1972	−1.3	−0.3	+2.4	+3.6	+6.7	+4.2	+6.2
1973	−1.6	+0.0	+1.4	+4.6	+7.0	+4.2	+6.3
1974	−4.0	−0.8	−1.2	+4.8	+5.1	+3.6	+4.1
1975	−3.5	−0.7	−0.7	+3.6	+6.8	+4.9	+2.7
1976	−3.8	−1.1	−1.1	+3.3	+6.2	+3.5	+2.5
1977	−3.6	−1.6	−1.7	+3.3	+5.9	+2.6	+1.2
1978	−2.4	−1.3	+0.0	+3.2	+4.5	+3.0	+1.8
1979	−2.8	−1.7	−0.4	+5.1	+6.0	+1.0	+7.9
1980	−4.0	−1.7	−1.6	+4.4	+5.6	+1.4	+12.0
1981	−2.8	−1.6	−0.9	+4.8	+4.7	+3.9	+14.2
1982	−3.5	−1.2	+0.6	+4.8	+6.0	+3.6	+13.7

Source: See Appendix 5.

Canada, whose economic performance was also pretty strong, have consistently been in deficit in manufacturing trade.

Thus, there appears to be no unique route, either in terms of the structure of foreign trade or its constancy, to the achievement of successful economic development. Which trade structure is appropriate obviously varies from country to country and depends to a large extent on each country's specific situation. For example, it makes no sense whatsoever for a country which is particularly well endowed with natural resources to become a specialist manufacturing exporter. This observation is amply borne out by the large number of net manufacturing importers in our sample. Not only have these countries achieved a high level of development, but, with the exception of Australia, they recorded some of the most successful post-war economic performances in our sample.

Table 3.2. *Balance of trade in manufactures as a % of GDP (at current purchasers' values)*

Years	UK	Belgium	West Germany	Japan	Italy	Sweden
1952	+9.1	n.a.	+7.5	+5.2	+1.5	−0.6
1953	+9.0	+8.6	+7.6	+3.9	+1.0	−1.2
1954	+8.4	+8.2	+8.1	+5.1	+1.0	−1.6
1955	+7.8	+9.7	+8.0	+6.2	+1.5	−1.6
1956	+8.1	+10.2	+9.1	+6.4	+1.7	−1.1
1957	+8.4	+9.3	+9.9	+5.5	+2.1	−1.1
1958	+8.1	+9.0	+9.0	+6.0	+2.6	−0.7
1959	+7.5	+8.9	+8.5	+6.5	+2.8	−0.2
1960	+6.5	+8.9	+8.4	+6.3	+1.9	−1.0
1961	+6.6	+7.1	+8.4	+4.8	+2.7	+0.2
1962	+6.6	+7.2	+7.6	+5.3	+2.1	+0.4
1963	+6.5	+6.6	+8.1	+5.1	+1.3	+0.7
1964	+5.3	+7.4	+7.8	+5.3	+3.0	+0.4
1965	+5.5	+8.6	+7.0	+6.9	+4.9	−0.5
1966	+5.4	+6.5	+7.9	+7.0	+4.8	+0.6
1967	+4.0	+6.7	+9.3	+5.9	+4.4	+0.9
1968	+4.2	+7.4	+9.2	+6.3	+5.4	+1.1
1969	+4.9	+8.0	+8.6	+6.5	+5.0	+0.9
1970	+4.8	+8.8	+7.7	+6.6	+4.2	+1.4
1971	+5.2	+6.1	+7.5	+7.8	+5.1	+2.8
1972	+3.4	+8.3	+7.4	+7.0	+5.4	+2.8
1973	+2.0	+8.3	+8.8	+6.0	+3.9	+4.1
1974	+2.4	+9.7	+11.5	+8.6	+4.9	+3.4
1975	+3.5	+7.1	+9.6	+8.6	+4.9	+2.8
1976	+3.9	+6.4	+9.8	+9.4	+7.2	+3.0
1977	+4.1	+5.3	+9.4	+9.5	+8.6	+3.2
1978	+3.0	+4.7	+8.7	+8.0	+9.0	+5.0
1979	+1.4	+4.7	+8.2	+7.5	+8.0	+4.5
1980	+2.5	+5.0	+8.1	+9.4	+5.5	+3.8
1981	+1.9	+6.1	+9.5	+10.4	+7.5	+5.4
1982	+0.9	+5.7	+10.5	+10.1	+7.4	+5.2

Thus, it is simply not true to suggest that every country must become a specialist manufacturing exporter in order to attain a high level of development.

A further point to note about Figs. 3.1 and 3.2 is that, taking the period 1952–82 as a whole, most countries experienced very little change in trade structure – i.e. in their overall non-manufacturing or manufacturing balance. This degree of continuity is all the more surprising in view of the fact that virtually all the countries in our sample registered significant improvements in trade in food and raw materials, taking the period 1952–82 as a whole (see Table 3.3). The only exceptions were: in trade in food: Australia, Canada, the Netherlands and Italy;[4] and in trade in raw materials: Australia, Sweden, Norway and Austria.[5,6]

Table 3.2 (*contd*)

Years	France	US	Austria	Canada	Australia	Netherlands	Norway
1952	+3.9	+1.8	+3.0	−2.6	−12.1	+0.6	−9.0
1953	+3.8	+2.0	+5.0	−4.1	−6.9	−0.4	−11.2
1954	+3.9	+1.8	+3.2	−3.1	−9.4	−1.8	−12.2
1955	+3.9	+1.5	+1.3	−3.7	−10.0	−2.9	−10.8
1956	+2.8	+1.7	+2.4	−5.1	−7.6	−5.1	−8.9
1957	+3.0	+1.8	+2.7	−4.5	−6.9	−5.2	−9.0
1958	+3.5	+1.5	+1.3	−3.8	−7.0	−1.4	−11.6
1959	+4.9	+1.0	+0.7	−4.2	−6.7	−1.2	−9.6
1960	+4.7	+1.2	−0.3	−3.6	−8.8	−2.8	−8.4
1961	+4.0	+1.2	−0.8	−3.8	−6.8	−4.6	−9.5
1962	+3.1	+1.2	−0.3	−3.6	−7.4	−4.4	−9.0
1963	+2.5	+1.1	−0.7	−3.1	−7.3	−3.9	−8.8
1964	+2.0	+1.1	−0.8	−3.1	−8.3	−4.0	−7.3
1965	+2.5	+0.9	+2.5	−3.9	−8.8	−3.8	−8.3
1966	+1.9	+0.6	−2.2	−3.5	−7.4	−4.2	−7.9
1967	+1.7	+0.6	−1.5	−3.3	−7.5	−3.0	−7.5
1968	+1.3	+0.4	−1.1	−2.4	−7.6	−2.8	−5.6
1969	+0.6	+0.4	−0.2	−2.9	−6.6	−2.8	−4.8
1970	+1.6	+0.4	−1.1	−1.1	−6.6	−4.4	−7.3
1971	+1.8	+0.0	−2.2	−2.1	−5.9	−2.9	−8.5
1972	+1.6	−0.3	−3.0	−3.3	−4.1	−1.4	−5.0
1973	+1.5	+0.0	−2.9	−4.0	−4.7	−0.8	−5.9
1974	+1.8	+0.6	−0.4	−5.3	−7.1	+0.6	−5.4
1975	+3.1	+1.3	−0.0	−5.3	−5.7	−0.5	−7.2
1976	+1.9	+0.7	−2.2	−4.1	−5.9	−0.0	−10.2
1977	+2.6	+0.2	−4.2	−3.7	−6.5	−1.6	−11.1
1978	+2.2	−0.5	−1.9	−3.1	−6.9	−2.2	−4.3
1979	+2.5	+0.0	−1.6	−4.5	−6.7	−1.6	−5.5
1980	+1.5	+0.6	−2.5	−3.1	−6.1	−0.9	−6.2
1981	+2.0	+0.5	−0.3	−3.6	−7.6	+1.0	−6.8
1982	+0.8	−0.2	+0.4	−1.0	−9.2	−0.5	−8.0

Source: See Appendix 5

Why were these gains in trade in food and raw materials not reflected in more widespread improvements in the non-manufacturing balance as a whole? The main reason appears to lie in the fact that, following the oil price rises of the 1970s, countries lacking indigenous supplies of oil and natural gas experienced large adverse movements in their fuel balance; these more than offset the positive effect on the non-manufacturing balance of improvements in trade in food and raw materials (see Table 3.3).

In the case of the relatively few countries which did experience major changes in trade structure (Norway, Austria, Sweden, Italy and the UK [see Fig. 3.2]), a large proportion of such changes can be attributed to developments in non-manufacturing trade of a kind which were relatively autonomous with respect to each country's industrial and economic performance, as a whole.

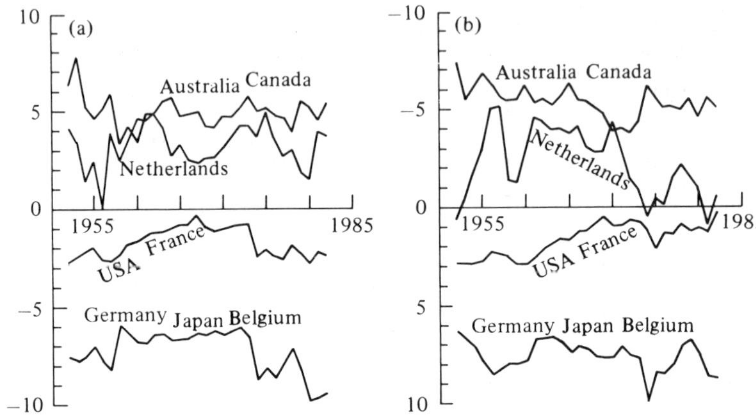

Fig. 3.1 Developed countries whose trade structure was reasonably constant, 1952–82
(a) Non-manufacturing balance as a % of GDP
(b) Manufacturing balance as a % of GDP

For example, the substantial improvement in Norway's non-manufacturing balance, which was mainly concentrated in the late 1970s and early 1980s, was entirely due to the discovery and successful exploitation of off-shore oil and gas reserves. In the case of Austria, the principal factor was the rapid growth of West European (especially West German) tourist expenditure. Thus, in both cases, improvements in non-manufacturing trade were largely autonomous with respect to each country's own industrial and economic performance, as a whole.

Sweden and Italy, on the other hand, both experienced a substantial deterioration in their non-manufacturing balance. In both cases, this was partly the product of successful development (a deteriorating food balance in the case of Italy and deteriorating fuel balances in the case of both countries) and partly due to adverse price movements, originating outside their economies: falling timber prices in the case of Sweden and higher fuel prices in the case of both countries. Finally, if we turn to the UK, which registered by far the largest change in non-manufacturing trade of all the countries in our sample, whilst some of the improvement was certainly the consequence of poor industrial and economic performance, much the greater part was due to developments in non-manufacturing trade of a relatively autonomous kind.[7]

Thus, in the case of the relatively few countries which did experience large changes in trade structure in the post-war period, a large proportion of such changes can be ascribed to developments in non-manufacturing trade of a kind which were relatively autonomous with respect to each country's own industrial and economic performance as a whole.

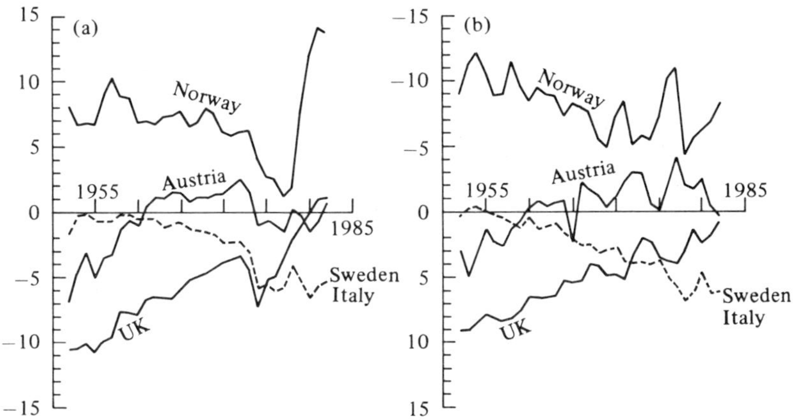

Fig. 3.2 Developed countries whose trade structure changed, 1952–82
(a) Non-manufacturing balance as a % of GDP
(b) Manufacturing balance as a % of GDP

Furthermore, in those countries where large and persistent changes in non-manufacturing trade did take place, they were usually accompanied by roughly equal, offsetting changes in manufacturing trade (cf. Fig. 3.2(a) and 3.2(b)). This implies that most countries were normally roughly in balance in trade in goods and non-government services as a whole.[8]

Manufacturing industry: the engine of economic growth

In arguing that successful economic development is possible under a great variety of foreign trade structures and that even non-manufacturing specialists can attain a high level of economic development, we in no way wish to call into question the fact that, for the vast majority of countries, successful industrialization (in the sense of developing the capacity to produce a high per capita output of manufactures) is an essential condition for the attainment of a high level of development.[9] And this is true even in the case of countries who remain in deficit in manufacturing trade throughout the entire course of the development process and, hence, remain dependent on foreign suppliers (on a net basis) to satisfy at least part of their domestic requirements for manufactures.

The reason why a high per capita output of manufactures is so essential for the attainment of a high level of development is quite straightforward. As we have already seen in Chapter 1, the demand for manufactures is quite income-elastic; as a consequence, a high level of per capita income gives rise to a high per capita domestic demand for manufactures. Thus, in order to be able to attain a high level of development, there must be an adequate per capita supply of manufactures, taking into account both domestic production as well as imports

Table 3.3. *Changes in non-manufacturing trade, 1952/5–1981/2 (as a % of GDP)*

	(1) Food, beverages and tobacco	(2) Raw materials	(3) Food and raw materials = (1) + (2)	(4) Fuel	(5) Primary products = (3) + (4)	(6) Non-government services	(7) Non-manufactures as a whole = (5) + (6)
West Germany	+1.7	+2.2	+3.9	−4.7	−0.8	−2.2	−3.0
Japan	+0.7	+2.5	+3.2	−4.7	−1.5	−0.3	−1.6
Belgium	+2.8	+1.5	+4.3	−6.8	−2.5	+1.1	−1.4
US	+0.7	+0.8	+1.5	−2.2	−0.7	−0.0	−0.7
France	+1.9	+1.4	+3.3	−3.5	−0.2	+1.1	+0.8
Netherlands	−1.1	+4.2	+3.1	+1.3	+4.4	−3.4	+1.0
Canada	−1.2	+0.0	−1.2	+2.9	+1.7	+0.4	+2.0
Australia	−1.3	−4.8	−6.1	+1.9	−4.2	+0.4	−3.8
UK	+4.8	+4.3	+9.1	+1.8	+10.9	+0.6	+11.6
Austria	+3.1	−1.5	+1.6	−2.4	−0.8	+5.6	+4.8
Sweden	+0.9	−4.0	−3.1	−1.6	−4.7	+0.2	−4.5
Italy	−1.2	+0.8	−0.4	−5.3	−5.7	+0.7	−5.1
Norway	+0.4	−3.2	−2.8	+15.1	+12.3	−5.4	+7.0

Source: See Appendix 5

less exports. However, countries also have to maintain external balance. The only way most countries can meet both of these objectives – namely the need to satisfy the domestic demand for manufactures, as well as to maintain external balance – is to produce a high proportion of their manufacturing requirements themselves. This is the reason why a high per capita output of manufactures is so essential to successful development, even in the case of countries which, throughout the entire course of the development process, remain in deficit in manufacturing trade. The only exceptions to this rule are a number of economically rather small countries, possessing truly exceptional advantages in the production and export of non-manufactures.[10]

Manufacturing: the engine of growth in 'workshop' economies

This proposition will be readily accepted in the case of fairly densely populated countries, whose natural resource endowment is relatively modest. In fact, countries such as this constitute the vast majority of large nations in the world today. Because of their modest resource endowment, countries in this kind of situation are unable to generate an export surplus in primary product trade. As a result, unless they have truly exceptional advantages in trade in non-government services, they are likely to be in deficit in non-manufacturing trade as a whole.

In this situation, there are two reasons why successful industrialization (in the sense of developing the capacity to produce a high per capita output of manufactures) is an essential condition for attaining a high level of development. First, because it enables the 'workshop' economy to satisfy its income-elastic domestic demand for manufactures, without needing to resort (on a net basis) to foreign suppliers; the latter is, of course, not possible because no country can sustain deficits in manufacturing as well as in non-manufacturing trade for any really long period of time. The second reason why successful industrialization is so crucial to the economic progress of a resource-poor economy is because it needs to produce an export surplus of manufactures, in order to finance its deficit in non-manufacturing trade.

Thus, in a country possessing a relatively modest endowment of natural resources, a high per capita output of manufactures is required not only to satisfy the high per capita domestic demand for manufactures, to which successful development gives rise, but also to maintain external balance. In the absence of rapid industrialization, successful development in an economy such as this is bound to be constantly threatened by a dearth of foreign exchange.

During the early and intermediate stages of development of a resource-poor, 'workshop' economy, a rapid growth of manufactured exports is the *sine qua non* for sustaining the momentum of economic advance.[11] The reason for this is that in order for an immature, 'workshop' economy to maintain external balance, it has to find some means of paying for a rapidly growing volume of imported primary products, as well as increased imports of non-government services and capital goods.[12] This is why a rapid growth of manufactured exports is so crucial to the economic success of a country like this, and it is in this sense that the young 'workshop' economy may be thought of as an example of manufactured 'export-led' growth.[13]

The fact that it is so important for a resource-poor, 'workshop', economy to expand its manufacturing export surplus certainly does not mean that it should refrain from importing manufactures. In fact, in the case of most medium-sized 'workshop' economies, there is a powerful case for a considerable measure of industrial specialization. However, if a resource-poor country does import manufactures, then it has little choice but to export manufactures in order to pay for them.

Mature 'workshop' economies continue to rely on a rapid growth of manufactured exports in order to sustain their economic progress. However, in the case of the mature 'workshop' economy, rapidly expanding manufactured exports are needed, not so much to pay for imports of food and raw materials, which may be declining relative to GDP,[14] but in order to finance rapidly growing imports of manufactures and non-government services.

Manufacturing: the engine of growth in the non-manufacturing specialist

Compared to the case of the 'workshop' economy it is, perhaps, more difficult to appreciate why virtually all non-manufacturing specialists (e.g. primary producers and service exporters) also have to industrialize if they are to attain a high level of economic development.

By definition, non-manufacturing specialists are in a position to run a deficit on their manufacturing trade. As a result, they are able to depend on foreign suppliers (on a net basis) to satisfy part of their domestic requirements for manufactures. Nevertheless, the vast majority of non-manufacturing specialists still need to produce a reasonably high proportion of their manufacturing requirements themselves if they are to attain a high level of development. The reason for this is that if they were to depend exclusively on imports to satisfy their manufacturing needs, then most non-manufacturing specialists would find that the rate of growth of their export receipts and, hence, of their capacity to import manufactures would be unsatisfactory in relation to their potential rate of growth of income and, hence, their demand for manufactures. This is partly a consequence of the fact that the domestic demand for manufactures is income-elastic and partly due to adverse factors affecting the growth of many non-manufacturing specialists' export receipts. Thus, as far as the vast majority of non-manufacturing specialists are concerned, a reasonably high per capita output of manufactures is necessary, both to satisfy the high per capita demand for industrial products to which successful development gives rise, as well as to maintain external balance.

There are three main reasons why the non-manufacturing specialist, who remains completely dependent on imported manufactures, is likely to find the rate of growth of its capacity to import far from satisfactory.

First, there is the question of the volume of non-manufacturing resources which a country committed to such a high degree of specialization would need to export in order to be able to develop successfully. Complete dependence on imported manufactures calls not only for a high ratio of net non-manufactured exports to GDP, but for one that, at least during the intermediate stages of development, is actually increasing – given that domestic demand for manufactures appears to grow considerably faster than income at this stage of development. However, the vast majority of non-manufacturing specialists are simply in no position to be able to accomplish this. And the fact that the domestic demand for non-manufactures also increases during the course of development is a further factor tending to constrain the growth of non-manufactured exports relative to the required rate. As a consequence of this basic question of resource endowment, only a handful of non-manufacturing specialists (principally small island economies with outstanding tourist potential) are in a position to be able to meet their domestic requirements for manufactures without engaging in any form of domestic industrialization.

The second reason why the vast majority of non-manufacturing specialists cannot possibly contemplate being completely dependent on imported manufactures is based on 'large' country considerations. Most 'large' primary producers, even if exceptionally well endowed with natural resources (e.g. the US, the USSR and Brazil), would find their rate of economic growth thoroughly unsatisfactory if forced to depend exclusively on imported manufactures. The reason for this is that most 'large' primary producers are likely to be significant exporters, in world terms, of many of the commodities which they produce. This has two possible consequences. The first is that they may find themselves operating on the price-inelastic segments of world demand curves for their particular commodity exports: in this case, any attempt to increase their per capita consumption of manufactures by expanding the volume of their primary product exports gives rise to a deterioration in their external terms of trade.[15] As a result, the purchasing power of a 'large' primary producer's exports in terms of imported manufactures may be relatively fixed. The second possible problem a 'large' primary producer may have to face is that, if world demand for its commodity exports is income-inelastic, as well as being price-inelastic, then it is virtually impossible to take successful countervailing action. This is because any attempt by a 'large' primary producer to counter the low income-elasticity of demand for its commodity exports by increasing its market share will result in a weakening of its export prices and, hence, in a deterioration in its external terms of trade.[16]

Thus, because the demand for its commodity exports is either price-inelastic and/or income-inelastic, a 'large' primary producer which is completely dependent on imported manufactures is likely to find the rate of growth of its capacity to import unsatisfactory in relation to the growth of its domestic demand for manufactures.[17] The same arguments apply in the case of a 'large' country attempting to specialize entirely in exporting services. Thus, in the case of the vast majority of non-manufacturing specialists, some measure of domestic industrialization is vital in order to keep the domestic supply of manufactures expanding at a rate which is consistent with the underlying potential for economic growth.

The third reason why most non-manufacturing specialists are likely to find total dependence on imported manufactures far from satisfactory is that such a high degree of specialization makes a country very vulnerable to external shocks, whether due to fluctuations in demand in consuming countries or supply shifts in other producer countries. As a consequence, the rate of growth of real income may be subject to a great deal of variation. Furthermore, if the price movements of different commodities are highly correlated, as was the case during the international recessions of the 1930s and 1980s, then diversification into non-traditional commodity exports may be no solution to the problem. Thus, there is a strong case for most primary producing countries having a reasonably large industrial base, because of the need to diversify their economic structures as an insurance against external shocks.

For these three reasons, most non-manufacturing specialists need to industrialize if their development efforts are not to be constantly frustrated by foreign exchange problems. And they need to produce a reasonably high per capita output of manufactures if they are to attain a high level of per capita income.

For obvious reasons, these kinds of countries usually base their initial industrialization efforts on import-substitution industrialization (ISI) and, only after they have aquired some measure of industrial expertise, do they turn to exporting manufactures. ISI, by augmenting the domestic supply of manufactures, helps to ensure that there is a satisfactory balance between the income-elastic growth of domestic demand for manufactures and the growth of total supply. ISI in non-manufacturing specialists also helps to ensure that the growth of their manufacturing trade deficit is kept in line with the growth in their capacity to import manufactures, as determined by the growth of their export surplus in primary product trade. Thus, successful ISI, by ensuring that a satisfactory rate of economic development can be attained without prejudicing the maintenance of external balance, enables non-manufacturing specialists to grow at a rate which is much closer to their underlying potential.

Furthermore, what starts out as a programme of 'forced' industrialization designed to safeguard the balance of payments and protect the level of activity often results in the development of a dynamic comparative advantage in a number of lines of manufacturing production. When and if this happens, countries can relax their import–substitution efforts and shift the burden of reconciling a satisfactory rate of economic development with the maintenance of external balance away from an exclusive preoccupation with industrial import-saving and towards an expansion of their manufactured exports.

Nevertheless, by remaining in surplus in non-manufacturing trade, the non-manufacturing specialist who has successfully industrialized can continue to take advantage of the undoubted benefits of international economic specialization.

Conclusions

This chapter had two main aims. The first was to examine the empirical evidence on foreign trade structure for a sample of thirteen OECD countries in the period 1952–82. Our principal conclusion was that these thirteen countries exhibit an enormous degree of diversity, not only as regards the overall structure of their foreign trade but also in so far as some countries have experienced virtual constancy in their trade structure, whilst others have experienced major changes. Given this great diversity of experience, it would be quite wrong to argue that there is a unique route, in terms of foreign trade structure, to the attainment of successful economic development. In particular, it is simply not true to suggest that every country has to become a specialist manufacturing exporter in order to attain a high level of development. Furthermore, of the (relatively few) countries which experienced major changes in trade structure in the post-war period, a significant proportion of such changes were the consequence of developments in non-manufacturing trade of a kind which were relatively autonomous with respect to each country's industrial and economic performance as a whole. Moreover, in countries where these developments in non-manufacturing trade were of a semi-permanent character, they were accompanied by offsetting changes of roughly equal size in trade in manufactures.

The second main aim of this chapter has been to emphasize that, although successful economic development is possible under a great variety of foreign trade structures, virtually all countries, both non-manufacturing specialists and specialist manufacturing exporters alike, have to industrialize (i.e. develop the capacity to produce a high per capita output of manufactures), if they are to attain a high level of development. This is the case in almost all countries, except those possessing truly exceptional advantages in the production and export of non-manufactures. The reason why successful industrialization is the key to attaining a high level of development is that it enables countries to reconcile two important objectives: namely, the need to satisfy the high per capita domestic demand for manufactures, to which successful development gives rise, as well as that of maintaining external balance. Attempting to establish this important proposition was the aim of the second part of this chapter.

4

The commercial account and why it tends to balance

Introduction

The last two chapters were concerned with analysing the relationship between economic development and the structure of foreign trade, focussing, in particular, on the factors affecting the non-manufacturing balance during the course of economic development. Several times during the course of that discussion, we made the point that if a country's non-manufacturing balance deteriorates for reasons which are largely autonomous with respect to its own industrial and economic performance as a whole, then, in order to maintain external balance, there must be a corresponding improvement in the manufacturing balance. Similarly, if the non-manufacturing balance improves, then the manufacturing balance can deteriorate without this necessarily endangering the maintenance of growth and external balance. The aim of this chapter is to put this proposition on a more formal footing.

Of course, if the change in non-manufacturing trade is either small and/or temporary, then it is quite possible that there may be no offsetting movement in the manufacturing balance. However, if the change in non-manufacturing trade is either large and/or sustained, then we can normally expect the manufacturing balance to register an offsetting change of roughly equal size.

This argument will probably be quite readily accepted once a more fundamental proposition has been established. Namely, that in most countries the *commercial* account of the balance of payments (to be defined more precisely below but which basically encompasses all trade in goods and non-government services) has a tendency to balance. A subsidiary proposition is that, even in the case of the relatively few countries whose *commercial* account is either persistently in surplus or persistently in deficit, such surpluses and deficits are quite small relative to GDP. We believe these propositions concerning the *commercial account* will prove to be relatively uncontroversial. Once accepted, they imply that changes in a country's non-manufacturing balance, of a kind which are relatively autonomous with respect to its own industrial and economic performance as a whole, must be matched by offsetting changes of roughly equal size in its manufacturing balance.

The chapter is organized as follows. It begins by defining the concepts we have adopted for organizing balance of payments statistics: the *basic balance*, the *commercial balance* and the *residual balance*. Time-series data on each of these balances are then presented for the thirteen OECD countries in our sample. The chapter continues with a discussion of why the *basic balance* tends to be zero. This is followed by the principal piece of analysis in the chapter: namely, the attempt to establish our propositions concerning the *commercial balance*. We do this by examining the various options available to a country for adjusting to an underlying improvement in non-manufacturing trade. This is followed by a brief discussion of the effect of each of these options on a country's internal economic structure. The chapter ends with a summary of our principal conclusions.

Definitions: the basic balance, the commercial balance and the residual balance

A useful summary of a country's transactions with the rest of the world is provided by the so-called *basic* balance of payments. This balance is calculated by adding together all current and long-term capital transactions with other countries during a given period of time. By definition, any surplus on the basic balance must be matched by a net increase in the total stock of monetary and short-term assets held by the government, institutions and residents of the country concerned (e.g. gold, foreign exchange, trade credit to foreigners, deposits with foreign banks, etc.). Conversely, any deficit on basic balance must be financed by means of a net reduction in the stock of such assets or, which amounts to the same thing, a net increase in the stock of monetary and short-term liabilities.

Table 4.1 presents data for the period 1952 to 1980 on the *basic balance*, as a proportion of GDP, for the thirteen OECD countries in our sample.

The data show that, in all countries and in most periods of time, the *basic balance*, whether in surplus or in deficit, is usually extremely small relative to GDP.[1] For eight of the countries in our sample (Japan, Canada, Australia, Belgium, Sweden, the Netherlands, Norway and Austria), periods in which the *basic balance* was in surplus were generally followed by periods in which it was in deficit (and vice versa). As a result, for these countries, the *basic balance* averages out, over a number of years, to be roughly equal to zero. On the other hand, three of the countries in our sample (the US, the UK and France) were persistently in deficit on basic balance, which meant that they were gradually acquiring monetary and short-term liabilities to foreigners.[2] Even so, for most of the time, their deficits on basic balance averaged no more than about

Table 4.1. *Selected OECD countries: commercial balance, residual balance and basic balance as a % of GDP, 1952–80*

	1952–55	1956–60	1961–65	1966–70	1971–75	1976–80
United States						
Commercial	+1.1	+1.0	+0.9	−0.5	−0.1	−1.3
Residual	−1.0	−1.2	−1.0	−0.6	−0.3	+0.8
Basic	+0.1	−0.2	−0.1	−1.1	−0.4	−0.5
West Germany						
Commercial	+1.6	+2.3	+1.0	+1.7	+1.3	+0.5
Residual	+0.5	−0.1	−0.2	−1.3	+0.5	−0.0
Basic	+2.1	+2.2	+0.8	+0.4	+1.8	+0.5
Japan						
Commercial	−2.9	−1.1	−1.0	+0.5	+0.4	+0.4
Residual	+2.9	+0.9	+0.3	−0.4	−1.0	−0.7
Basic	0.0	−0.2	−0.7	+0.1	−0.6	−0.3
France						
Commercial	−0.1	−0.3	+0.8	−0.1	−0.5	−1.2
Residual	+1.8	+0.1	−1.5	−0.5	−0.5	−0.7
Basic	+1.7	−0.2	−0.7	−0.6	−1.0	−1.9
Italy						
Commercial	−1.1	+0.9	+1.5	+2.7	−0.3	+1.6
Residual	+1.2	+0.7	−0.4	−1.1	+0.7	−0.3
Basic	+0.1	+1.6	+1.1	+1.6	+0.4	+1.3
Canada						
Commercial	−0.8	−2.6	−0.3	+0.8	−0.0	−0.3
Residual	+1.0	+2.0	+0.0	+0.7	−0.3	−0.8
Basic	+0.2	−0.6	−0.3	+1.5	−0.3	−1.1
Australia						
Commercial	−0.5	−0.4	−0.7	−1.4	+0.8	−0.8
Residual	−0.7	+0.4	+0.8	+0.7	−0.1	+0.1
Basic	−1.2	0.0	+0.1	−0.7	+0.7	−0.7
Belgium						
Commercial	+0.2	+2.0	+0.7	+0.8	+1.2	−3.3
Residual	−0.5	+1.0	+0.1	−0.6	−1.0	+1.2
Basic	−0.3	+3.0	+0.8	+0.2	+0.2	−2.1
Sweden						
Commercial	−0.5	−0.7	−0.1	−0.5	+0.8	+0.2
Residual	+0.1	+0.3	+0.3	+0.2	+0.1	−1.6
Basic	−0.4	−0.4	+0.2	−0.3	+0.9	−1.4

Table 4.1. (*cont.*)

	1952–55	1956–60	1961–65	1966–70	1971–75	1976–80
Netherlands						
Commercial	+1.7	−0.2	−0.3	−0.9	+3.1	+1.2
Residual	+0.6	+0.8	+0.2	+0.7	−1.2	−1.8
Basic	+2.3	+0.6	−0.1	−0.2	+1.9	−0.6
Norway						
Commercial	−3.8	−0.8	−1.4	−0.0	−1.4	−2.6
Residual	+1.9	+1.4	+1.8	+0.4	+3.2	+2.9
Basic	−1.9	+0.6	+0.4	+0.4	+1.8	+0.3
Austria						
Commercial	−1.8	−0.7	+1.0	−0.2	−1.0	−3.4
Residual	+2.0	+0.4	+0.7	+0.6	+0.4	+0.2
Basic	+0.2	−0.3	+1.7	+0.4	−0.6	−3.2
UK						
Commercial	−1.9	−0.6	−0.1	+0.2	−1.3	+0.8
Residual	+0.2	−0.3	−0.4	−0.3	+0.2	−1.3
Basic	−1.7	−0.9	−0.5	−0.1	−0.9	−0.5

Source: See Appendix 5

0.5% of GDP. Deficits of this magnitude are so small that these three countries can also be described as having a zero basic balance.[3] Finally, two of the countries in our sample (West Germany and Italy) were persistently in surplus on basic balance, with surpluses averaging about 1% of GDP. As a result, both countries gradually increased their holdings of monetary and short-term assets, and West Germany now possesses the largest gold and foreign exchange reserves of any country in the world.[4] However, with the exception of these two countries, the empirical evidence from the OECD countries in our sample suggests that, in most of them, the basic balance averages out, over a number of years, to be roughly equal to zero.

The various transactions which make up the basic balance can be classified in a number of ways. Table 4.2, containing disaggregated data for the UK for the years 1953, 1963, 1973 and 1983, distinguishes between those items, which make up what we call the *commercial balance*, and the remaining items, which make up the *residual balance*. The *commercial balance* covers all imports and exports of goods and non-government services (including private transfers, such as migrants' remittances to their dependants abroad), whilst the *residual balance* covers all government payments and receipts (including transfers), together with property income from abroad and long-term capital investment.

The meaning of the items separately identified in Table 4.2 is, for the most

Table 4.2. *UK balance of payments: commercial and residual accounts, 1953, 1963, 1973 and 1983 (£m)*

	Commercial account				Residual account				
	(1) Manu-factures[a,b]	(2) Primary products[a,c]	(3) Non-government services[d]	(4) Commercial balance = (1) + (2) + (3)	(5) Government services and grants	(6) Interest, profits and dividends	(7) Long-term investment	(8) Residual balance = (5) + (6) + (7)	(9) Basic balance = (4) + (8)
1953	+1,592	−1,960	+175	−193	−58	+229	−194	−23	−216
1963	+1,976	−2,134	+166	+8	−188	+398	−155	+55	+63
1973	+1,488	−4,201	+929	−1,784	−221	+1,257	−518	+518	−1,266
1983	−2,379	+649	+3,517	+1,787	+174	+1,948	−5,504	−3,382	−1,595

Notes:
[a] Visible trade data on a balance of payments basis
[b] Manufactures = SITC sections 5 to 8
[c] Primary products = SITC sections 0 to 4
[d] Excludes all expenditure in the UK by overseas governments, non-territorial organizations and foreign military forces. These items are included in column (5). See Appendix 6 for further discussion. Column (3) also includes private transfers (migrants' remittances, etc.)
Source: HMSO, *UK Balance of Payments: Pink Book*

part, self-explanatory. However, two points should be borne in mind. First, the distinction between manufactured and non-manufactured goods is somewhat arbitrary. We follow the conventional practice of using the term 'manufactures' to cover those items contained in Sections 5 to 8 of the Standard International Trade Classification; thus, steel, copper and bulk chemicals are classified as manufactures, whereas cheese, whisky and synthetic fibres, which are included in SITC Sections 0–4, are classified as primary products. Second, the term 'government services' includes, on the debit side of the account, expenditure of a military, diplomatic or administrative nature by the British government and its personnel overseas, and on the credit side, expenditure in Britain by foreign governments and their personnel stationed in this country. All other service items are classified as 'non-government services'. Note that our definition of 'government services' is wider than that used in official statistics. For reasons of consistency we assign to the 'government' account certain revenues which are excluded from this account in the Balance of Payments Pink Book.[5] Note that, under the heading 'non-government services', we include the service activities of nationalized industries, universities, polytechnics and the like, in addition to those of the private sector.

As already mentioned, for most of the past thirty years the UK's basic balance has been roughly zero, meaning that total receipts have been roughly equal to total payments. Moreover, as can be seen from Table 4.1, the same has normally been true of the two major components which together make up the basic balance: namely, the commercial and residual balances.[6]

Having briefly examined the commercial and residual balances for the UK, we can now do the same for the other OECD countries in our sample (see Table 4.1). Compared with the UK, most countries experienced much longer periods of being either in surplus or in deficit on commercial account. However, countries which, during the early part of the period 1952–80, were normally in surplus on commercial account (e.g. the US and Belgium) subsequently went into deficit, whilst those which, during the early part of the period, were persistently in deficit (e.g. Japan, Sweden and the Netherlands) were invariably in surplus later on. Of all the countries in our sample, only West Germany was in surplus on commercial account throughout almost the entire period 1952–80, whilst three countries (Canada, Australia and Norway) were normally in deficit. Nevertheless, even in these cases, both surpluses and deficits were quite small relative to GDP.

Thus, the data from our sample of thirteen OECD countries indicate that, when averaged over a number of years, most countries were in balance on commercial account. A small number of countries were persistently in surplus or in deficit, but, even in these cases, both surpluses and deficits were quite small relative to GDP.

Why does the basic balance tend to be zero?

As already noted, a country's *basic balance* is the sum of all current and long-term capital transactions with the rest of the world: it is the sum of the *commercial balance* plus the *residual balance*. Furthermore, the empirical evidence from our sample of thirteen OECD countries indicates that, when averaged over a number of years, the basic balance of most countries is roughly zero. The principal exceptions to this rule were the two reserve currency countries (the US and the UK) and two countries keen not to endanger the momentum of their manufacturing export drives (West Germany and Italy). Are there any systematic forces at work ensuring that, under normal circumstances, a country's basic balance tends to be zero?

Let us begin our answer to this question by examining what happens when a country is persistently in surplus on basic balance, looking, first of all, at the situation under a regime of flexible nominal rates of exchange. Persistent surpluses on basic balance give rise to a steady accumulation of gold and foreign exchange reserves which, under a regime of flexible exchange rates, would be almost bound to trigger a steady appreciation in the nominal rate of exchange and, except in the most unusual circumstances, in the real rate of exchange as well. Appreciation of the real rate of exchange reduces the propensity to export goods and services and/or increases the propensity to import; either way, it gives rise to a deterioration on the commercial account. At the same time, appreciation reduces the cost of acquiring foreign assets and, as a result, causes an increase in long-term capital outflow. Thus, under a regime of flexible nominal rates of exchange, a persistent surplus on basic balance is almost bound to be eliminated as appreciation of the real rate of exchange gives rise to a steady deterioration on both commercial and residual accounts.

By an analogous argument, persistent deficits on basic balance would eventually be eliminated under a regime of flexible nominal rates of exchange via a depreciation of the real rate of exchange. However, because of real wage rigidity, the real rate of exchange may be sticky downwards, and depreciation may be neither a very efficient nor a speedy means of correcting a deficit on basic balance. In addition, a regime of flexible nominal rates of exchange may well be characterized by persistent misalignment of real rates of exchange. Are there any forces ensuring that the basic balance tends to be zero, when real rates of exchange are either sticky or misaligned?

First, there are undoubtedly limits to the extent to which any country can incur persistent deficits on basic balance, the only exceptions to this rule being countries with reserve currency status and those who are significant producers of gold. The reasons for this should be obvious. If a country is persistently in deficit on basic balance then, sooner or later, its reserves of gold and foreign exchange will become exhausted. Of course, when this happens, countries will attempt, as a last resort, to secure short-term bank loans from abroad, and they will also allow commercial arrears (i.e. unpaid bills) to accumulate. However, in time these lines of credit will also become exhausted, leaving the country little choice but to resort to deflation in order to eliminate its deficit on basic balance. Of course, the fact that the IMF occasionally makes an allocation of international reserve assets, such as the SDR, means that in principle countries could be permanently in deficit on basic balance. However, hitherto such allocations have been tiny relative to GDP, and this does not, therefore, constitute an objection of any real significance to the principle that, in a situation of relatively sticky or misaligned real rates of exchange, the vast majority of countries simply cannot afford to be in deficit on basic balance for any lengthy period of time.

On the other hand, if a country is persistently in *surplus*, then, in a situation of relatively sticky or misaligned real rates of exchange, no comparable mechanism exists for forcing it into balance. In such circumstances, there is nothing to stop a country systematically accumulating foreign exchange reserves, and there are certainly a number of examples of steady reserve accumulation (the US in the 1920s, West Germany post-war), which, even if not permanent, have certainly lasted for quite long periods of time.

Even so, in the case of the great majority of countries, there are likely to be powerful pressures on government to correct a persistent surplus on basic balance, simply because the steady accumulation of gold and foreign exchange reserves represents national purchasing power which is failing to be utilized. For example, if there is a steady build-up of reserves in a country where there is a large margin of underutilized resources, then the government is normally likely to come under considerable pressure to use the opportunity to expand the overall level of activity. As output expands, the commercial balance deteriorates and the surplus on basic balance is eroded; as a result, the country's foreign exchange reserves cease to expand and may even contract. On the other hand, if the level of activity cannot be increased, there is bound to be pressure to use the surplus on basic balance to raise domestic absorption by increasing the country's imports. Finally, even if the home population wishes to forgo an increase in absorption, increased foreign aid and/or military expenditure represent further options for disposing of a surplus on basic balance. If none of these options is taken up, a final reason why a country is unlikely to accumulate foreign exchange reserves for any lengthy period of time is that the return to holding the short-term liabilities of other countries (i.e. foreign exchange reserves) is usually lower than that accruing to long-term foreign investment (either direct or portfolio). Thus, foreign investment is likely to be encouraged as an alternative to the continued accumulation of gold and foreign exchange reserves.[7]

Thus, whether we are considering a regime of relatively flexible or one of somewhat sticky or misaligned real rates of exchange, no country can afford to be persistently in deficit on basic balance, and relatively few are likely to be persistently in surplus. Thus, a number of systematic forces exist to ensure that a country's basic balance tends to be zero.

Why the commercial account tends to balance

Introduction

We are now in a position to present the main analytical proposition of this chapter: namely, that the commercial account tends to balance. In order to do this, we shall proceed as follows. We shall assume that the commercial account and the residual account of a particular country are initially both in balance. We shall then assume that an underlying improvement in non-manufacturing trade takes place of a kind which is relatively autonomous with respect to the country's overall industrial and economic performance. This improvement is both large and sustained and takes the form of either an increase in the propensity to export non-manufactures and/or a reduction in the propensity to import. We then proceed to examine the various ways in which an economy can adapt to an improvement in non-manufacturing trade of this kind. This is how we intend to demonstrate why the commercial account tends to balance.

In the light of our earlier analysis of the basic balance, one possible consequence of a sustained improvement in non-manufacturing trade can be ruled out right from the start: namely, that it gives rise to a steady accumulation of gold and foreign exchange reserves. If this possibility can be ignored, then there are two possible outcomes following an improvement in non-manufacturing trade: *either* the commercial account goes into surplus, and this is matched by a deficit of roughly equal size on the residual account, *or*, under the assumption that the commercial account remains in balance, the improvement in non-manufacturing trade is matched by a deterioration in the manufacturing balance.

We shall begin our analysis of why the commercial account tends to balance by examining the case of a country where there is a considerable margin of underutilized resources. We shall then go on to consider a situation in which the level of output is given.

Growth strategies

Suppose there is a large and sustained improvement in non-manufacturing trade in a country in which there is a substantial margin of underutilized resources. In a situation such as this, there will normally be considerable pressure on government to use the opportunity presented by the improvement in non-manufacturing trade to increase the overall level of economic activity. Thus, instead of the improvement in non-manufacturing trade giving rise to a surplus on commercial account, there will usually be pressure to increase the level of activity, so as to eliminate any potential surplus: such pressure is one of the reasons why the commercial account tends to balance. Any attempt to use the opportunity presented by an improvement in non-manufacturing trade to strengthen the domestic economy in some way or another can be described as a 'growth strategy'.

However, before describing two plausible 'growth strategies' and examining their possible effects, it is worthwhile reminding ourselves why it is that an improvement in non-manufacturing trade makes it easier, when there are unutilized resources in an economy, to increase the overall level of activity. The reason lies in the fact that an improvement in non-manufacturing trade not only strengthens the balance of payments but also increases real national income, and, on both counts, makes it easier to expand the overall level of activity. Let us examine each of these points in turn.

Consider a situation in which the economy is operating below a full employment level of activity because of a shortage of foreign exchange (i.e. given the propensity to import, the country's capacity to import is less than that required to sustain full employment). In this case, it is the contribution which the improvement in non-manufacturing trade makes to strengthening the balance of payments that allows the level of activity to rise. This is because any improvement in the country's underlying trading performance serves to relax the foreign exchange constraint on the overall level of activity.[8]

On the other hand, consider a situation in which the existence of unemployed resources is due to the adoption of restrictive monetary and fiscal policies designed, for example, to counter inflationary pressures arising from a persistent wage–price spiral. In this case, it is the contribution which the improvement in non-manufacturing trade makes to increasing real national income that allows the level of activity to rise. This is because the increase in real national income makes it easier to satisfy the various competing claims on national resources and permits the economy to operate at a higher level of activity, without taking off into a hyper-inflationary spiral. Or, to use the conventional but objectionable terminology, the increase in real national income reduces the 'natural' rate of unemployment and thereby allows the economy to operate at a higher level of activity.

Growth strategy I – general reflation

Let us assume in the first instance that the 'growth strategy' simply consists of the adoption of a more expansionary fiscal and monetary stance. Let us further assume that the industrial policy aspect of the 'growth strategy' is limited to using import controls to stem the rise in manufactured imports resulting from economic expansion: thus, import controls are used to try to ensure that the domestic economy receives the maximum possible stimulus from fiscal and monetary expansion, as well as to make sure that the growth exercise is not cut short by balance of payments problems. With the same aim in mind, attempts are also made to curtail the demand for foreign holidays.

What would be the effect of a rise in the overall level of activity on the balance of trade in non-manufactures and manufactures, respectively? The increase in activity would undoubtedly result in an increase in the volume of net primary product imports.[9] However, in the case of the typical OECD country, any such increase would be relatively small. The reasons for this are as follows. The typical OECD country has already completed its 'gastronomic transition' and, thus, any rise in the level of activity would have only a minor impact on either the demand for food or the balance of trade in food. Similarly, since the typical OECD country has by now shed some of its most raw material-intensive branches of industrial production, any increase in activity would have only a limited effect on the demand for imported raw materials. On the other hand, a higher level of activity would undoubtedly result in an increase in the demand for fuel. Thus, if a 'growth strategy' of this kind were adopted, part of the underlying improvement in non-manufacturing trade would undoubtedly be devoted to an increase in the volume of net primary product imports. However, in the case of the typical OECD country, the extent of any such increase would be relatively minor.

In fact, so far as the typical OECD country is concerned, the adoption of 'general reflation' would mean that by far the largest part of the adjustment to the underlying improvement in non-manufacturing trade would take the form of a deterioration in the manufacturing balance. How would this come about? The expansion in economic activity would undoubtedly give rise to an increase in the domestic demand for manufactures. Some of this increase in demand would undoubtedly be satisfied by foreign suppliers and, as a result, there would be an increase in manufactured imports. This would occur even if import controls were successful in restraining the rise in the *propensity* to import manufactures. 'General reflation' would probably also result in some decline in the propensity to export manufactures. Thus, some of the increase in domestic demand for manufactures would be satisfied via a deterioration in the manufacturing balance.

Of course, as long as the increase in domestic demand for manufactures, triggered by 'general reflation', is larger than any resulting deterioration in the manufacturing trade balance, then this particular 'growth strategy' will have a positive impact on both output and employment in domestic manufacturing industry.

Growth strategy II – industrial modernization

An alternative, highly plausible 'growth strategy' would be as follows. Imagine an economy that was characterized by economic collapse and mass unemployment due to the chronically poor competitive performance of its manufacturing sector in both domestic and international markets. A highly desirable 'growth strategy' in this situation would be for the government to devote the entire proceeds accruing from the underlying improvement in non-manufacturing trade to the purchase of advanced types of capital equipment from the leading foreign suppliers. These could then be used to modernize and re-equip the country's manufacturing industry, in order to improve its competitive position in domestic and international markets. Under this 'industrial modernization' strategy, the improvement in non-manufacturing trade would be matched by an equivalent deterioration in the manufacturing balance. However, so long as this programme of industrial equipment spending is additional to the existing level of aggregate demand, then there is no reason why the demand for domestically produced manufactures should in any way be affected, and the same is true of both output and employment in domestic manufacturing industry. Furthermore, since the 'industrial modernization' strategy ought to result in an improvement in the competitive position of domestic manufacturing industry in both domestic and international markets, then domestic manufacturing output should be higher, in the medium to long run, than would otherwise have been the case.

Growth strategies: conclusions

To summarize: one reason why the commercial account tends to balance is that, in a country with a substantial margin of under-utilized resources or one suffering from prolonged economic decline, an underlying improvement in non-manufacturing trade should trigger considerable pressure for the adoption of some kind of 'growth strategy'. In the case of the 'industrial modernization strategy', this improvement is devoted, in its entirety, to increased net imports of manufactures. As a result, the improvement in non-manufacturing trade is matched by an equivalent offsetting deterioration in the manufacturing balance. In the case of 'general reflation' there is a modest increase in net primary product imports, as well as in imports of non-government services; however, in this case as well, much the greater part of the adjustment to the underlying improvement in non-manufacturing trade also takes the form of an offsetting deterioration in the manufacturing balance.

Exchange revaluation: 'consumption strategy'

Suppose an underlying improvement in non-manufacturing trade takes place in a country in which the overall level of domestic economic activity is given, either because the country's resources are fully utilized or because the government sets fiscal and monetary policy so as to keep the level of demand for home-produced output constant. In this situation, an underlying improvement in non-manufacturing trade will, sooner or later, give rise to an appreciation of the real rate of exchange.[10]

Since appreciation causes the price of traded goods to fall in terms of national income, it is responsible for an increase in real national income. In fact, since the level of domestic activity is fixed, appreciation of the real rate of exchange is the only way in which a country in this situation can actually enjoy the benefits of an improvement in non-manufacturing trade. However, because the level of domestic activity is fixed, the whole of this increase in real national income must be spent outside the economy. It is for this reason that we use the term 'consumption strategy' to describe the option of taking the benefit of the improvement in non-manufacturing trade in the form of a revaluation of the real rate of exchange.

The revaluation option is another reason why, in the face of an underlying improvement in non-manufacturing trade, the commercial account tends to balance. Let us, first of all, consider the income effects of revaluation and, subsequently, its price effects.

Let us assume that the pattern of demand remains more or less constant during the course of revaluation. The implication of this is that any increase in real national income is spent in much the same way as total national income. As a result, revaluation leads to an increase in the demand for both traded and non-traded goods. Since total domestic output is fixed, the increase in demand for non-traded goods can only be satisfied by switching resources out of the production of traded goods (principally manufactures). However, since fewer resources are now devoted to producing manufactures, there must be a corresponding deterioration in the manufacturing balance. As for the increase in demand for traded goods, consequent upon the rise in real national income, this will largely be directed towards manufactures, though there will also be an increase in the demand for certain internationally traded services (especially foreign holidays).[11] Of course, given that total domestic output is fixed and that any increase in the demand for non-traded goods must be satisfied domestically, any growth in the demand for manufactures, consequent upon revaluation, must be met via a deterioration in the manufacturing balance. Thus, under the consumption strategy, the manufacturing balance deteriorates on two accounts: first, as a consequence of the switch of resources out of manufacturing production in order to satisfy the increased demand for non-traded goods and, second, because the increased demand for manufactures can only be met out of the trade balance. These then are the income effects of revaluation.

The price effects are simply the means by which the increase in real national income is accommodated. Revaluation reduces the price of traded goods in terms of non-traded goods and thereby encourages resources to be switched out of the production of traded goods and redeployed in the non-traded goods sector.

Thus, following an underlying improvement in non-manufacturing trade, revaluation under the 'consumption' strategy is another mechanism for ensuring that the commercial account is brought back into balance. In this case, much the greater part of the adjustment to the improvement in non-manufacturing trade takes the form of an offsetting deterioration in the manufacturing balance, though the non-government service balance will also experience some deterioration (especially the tourism account). Compared with 'general reflation' (growth strategy I), virtually none of the benefit of the improvement in non-manufacturing trade is devoted to an increase in net primary product imports, which may even fall.

In order to appreciate the importance of assuming that the pattern of demand remains more or less constant during the course of revaluation, let us suppose that a small revaluation is sufficient to trigger a large increase in the demand for foreign holidays. In this case, most of the improvement in non-manufacturing trade would be spent on foreign holidays; any revaluation of the real rate of exchange would be relatively modest, there would be little change in the country's internal economic structure (i.e. in the allocation of resources between the production of traded and non-traded goods) and hardly any deterioration in the manufacturing balance. In the limiting case, in which all of the benefits of the improvement in non-manufacturing trade were spent on foreign holidays,[12] there would be no revaluation, no change in the country's internal economic structure and no deterioration in the manufacturing balance.

Increased foreign aid and/or military expenditure

Of course, the population of the domestic economy may decide to forego the direct economic benefits, which are undoubtedly available as a result of an improvement in non-manufacturing trade. They may decide, instead, to give away these benefits, in the form of either increased aid to less developed countries and/or increased military expenditure abroad. In either case, the underlying improvement in non-manufacturing trade gives rise to a surplus on the commercial account, and this is matched by a deficit on the residual account (which includes foreign aid and military expenditure).

The appearance of a surplus on the commercial account is simply a sign that the country wishes to insulate itself from the domestic economic consequences of the improvement in non-manufacturing trade. By running a surplus, the country avoids the deterioration in its manufacturing balance, which occurs under the two 'growth strategies', as well as under the 'consumption strategy'. It also avoids the changes in internal economic structure which certainly take place under the 'consumption strategy' and may also occur under the 'growth strategies' (see below for a discussion of these effects). However, since the only way in which the population of the domestic economy can themselves enjoy the economic benefits of the improvement in non-manufacturing trade is to submit to the changes in trade and economic structure which it entails, then insulating the economy from such changes ensures that these benefits are foregone.

If the improvement in non-manufacturing trade is thought to be *temporary*, then it is understandable why a country might wish to insulate itself from the ensuing changes in trade and internal economic structure, especially of the type resulting from the adoption of the 'consumption strategy'. In a situation such as this, increased foreign aid and/or military expenditure has obvious attractions. Once the benefits of a temporary improvement in non-manufacturing trade have disappeared, foreign aid and/or military spending can be cut back painlessly – at least as far as the donor country is concerned. By comparison, being forced to reverse the kinds of structural change to which the 'consumption strategy' gives rise can be very painful.

The possibility that the benefits of an improvement in non-manufacturing trade may be devoted to increased foreign aid and/or military expenditure is obviously an exception to the proposition that the commercial account tends to balance. However, it cannot seriously be maintained that the population of any country would be prepared to forgo the domestic economic benefits of a relatively *large* improvement in non-manufacturing trade (i.e. one amounting to several percentage points of GDP), especially if such an improvement were likely to be anything more than temporary.

Furthermore, so far as aid to less developed countries is concerned, the fact that so many OECD countries regularly fail to meet the long-standing UN targets for aid as a proportion of GDP suggests there are powerful constraints to a really significant increase in foreign aid. Moreover, the number of countries that have large military establishments abroad and are in a position to increase them is, in practice, rather limited. Of course, many more countries are in a position to increase their purchases of foreign military equipment. However, in this case as well there are likely to be strong political pressures on government to ensure that not all the benefits of a substantial and fairly sustained improvement in non-manufacturing trade are used to purchase arms. This means that, in general, increased aid to less developed countries and/or higher military expenditure will never constitute more than a minor part of the overall adjustment to a significant and sustained improvement in non-manufacturing trade.

Thus, the conclusions we derived in our discussion of the two 'growth strategies' and the 'consumption strategy' remain intact: much the greater part of the adjustment to an underlying improvement in non-manufacturing trade, especially one which is reasonably large and sustained, is likely to take the form of an offsetting deterioration in the manufacturing balance and this is another reason why the commercial account tends to balance.

Increased foreign investment

Long-term foreign investment, both direct and portfolio, can also be used to insulate the economy from the effects of an improvement in non-manufacturing trade. As in the case of increased foreign aid and military expenditure, the improvement in non-manufacturing trade is reflected in the appearance of a surplus on the commercial account, which is matched by a deficit on the residual account (which includes all transactions related to long-term capital, both capital flows and investment income). However, foreign investment can provide only a temporary respite from the changes in manufacturing trade and in internal economic structure to which a sustained improvement in non-manufacturing trade inevitably gives rise. This is because the foreign assets, created or acquired as a result of net capital outflow, yield an income some of which will sooner or later be repatriated to the domestic economy, where it will be spent on goods and services of one sort or another. When this happens, the country can no longer avoid having to choose between either the 'consumption strategy' or one of the 'growth strategies': the manufacturing balance begins to deteriorate, and the country can no longer postpone any possible consequential changes in its internal economic structure. To see why net foreign investment can only insulate the economy temporarily from the consequences of a large and sustained improvement in non-manufacturing trade requires quite an extensive discussion.[13]

Suppose that the country's net foreign assets are initially zero. The underlying improvement in non-manufacturing trade gives rise, first of all, to a surplus on the commercial account and, as a result, the country is making a transfer of resources to the rest of the world. The residual account, on the other hand, goes into deficit as a result of net capital outflow and, in this way, foreign assets are acquired.

Suppose that the rate of return on foreign investment exceeds the rate of growth of the country's domestic product (quite a plausible assumption). As a result, foreign investment income represents an increasing proportion of GDP. Part of this investment income will be reinvested, and part will be repatriated. However, since the value of the country's net foreign assets is initially quite small, repatriated investment income will also be small relative to GDP. Thus, for a certain period of time, repatriated investment income does not seriously threaten the country's attempt to insulate itself from the domestic economic consequences of the improvement in non-manufacturing trade.

However, if the improvement turns out to be of a reasonably sustained kind then, sooner or later, the stock of foreign assets will grow until it becomes quite large relative to the country's domestic product. There will also be a steady increase in the value of repatriated investment income. This has a number of consequences. First, domestic absorption increases relative to domestic output, and the commercial account surplus gradually declines. At the same time, repatriated investment income rises relative to net capital outflow (including reinvested income), and the deficit on the residual account gradually diminishes. Eventually, repatriated investment income is so large that the residual account goes into surplus and the commercial account starts to record deficits. The country is still acquiring foreign assets, financed out of reinvested profits, but since its commercial account is in deficit it is now a 'rentier' nation, in receipt of a net transfer of resources from the rest of the world.

Thus, a relatively immature capital exporting country can quite quickly find itself in the 'Wealth Trap';[14] namely, in a situation in which it ceases to be a net capital exporter, and becomes a 'rentier' nation – despite the fact that it continues to acquire foreign assets.[15]

Of course, once domestic absorption starts to rise relative to GDP and the commercial account surplus begins to diminish, the country can no longer avoid the deterioration in its manufacturing balance, described earlier when discussing the case of the two 'growth strategies' and the 'consumption strategy'; nor can it avoid any of the ensuing changes in its internal economic structure. Thus, net foreign investment can only insulate a country temporarily from the domestic economic consequences of a sustained improvement in non-manufacturing trade.

Nevertheless, if the improvement is expected to be only temporary, and there is no opportunity for domestic economic expansion and little scope for industrial modernization, there is a persuasive case for devoting the improvement in non-manufacturing trade to the acquisition of foreign assets. The income from these assets can subsequently be used to smooth the process of adjustment, when the temporary improvement in non-manufacturing trade comes to an end. Thus, in a situation such as this, foreign investment can be used to avoid disruptive changes in manufacturing industry.

Why the commercial account tends to balance: conclusions

In our discussion in this chapter we hope to have demonstrated that by far the greater part of the adjustment to an underlying improvement in non-manufacturing trade, of a kind which is both large and sustained, is likely to take the form of an offsetting deterioration in some other area of trade in goods and services, principally in trade manufactures. Foreign investment provides no more than a temporary respite from the changes in manufacturing trade and in internal economic structure which a large and sustained improvement in non-manufacturing trade inevitably entails. Furthermore, it is highly unlikely that any country would forgo direct economic benefits of a really substantial magnitude and give them away in the form of either increased aid and/or military expenditure. Thus, following an improvement in non-manufacturing trade, there exists a variety of forces to ensure that the commercial account tends to balance.

The impact of an improvement in non-manufacturing trade on a country's internal economic structure

In order to round out this discussion, let us briefly discuss the impact on a country's internal economic structure of each of the strategies for adapting to an improvement in non-manufacturing trade just described.

Growth strategy I – general reflation

If 'general reflation', supported by import controls, results in a sufficiently large rise in economic activity, then the ensuing increase in demand for domestically produced manufactures will be greater than any loss of sales due to the deterioration in the manufacturing balance. Thus, 'general reflation' should have a positive impact on the absolute level of manufacturing output and employment, and these effects will be greater the larger is the increase in the overall level of activity. Furthermore, 'general reflation' should also lead to an absolute rise in output and employment in the services.

What happens to manufacturing's share in total employment as a consequence of 'general reflation'? On the basis of our analysis of cyclical recovery, presented in Chapter 1, manufacturing's share ought to rise – at least, initially. However, what happens to manufacturing's share, once the recovery stage is over, depends on the stage of development of each particular country: that is to say, whether it is in the early stages of development, when its labour force is 'industrializing' rapidly; or whether it is in the intermediate or 'transitional' stage, before de-industrialization gets under way; or whether it is in the later stages, when de-industrialization has already started.

Growth strategy II – industrial modernization

This strategy consists of spending the entire proceeds of the improvement in non-manufacturing trade on imports of advanced types of capital equipment, with the aim of improving the international competitive position of the country's manufacturing sector. The impact of such a strategy on output and employment is virtually nil, so far as most sectors of the economy are concerned – apart, that is, from its positive effects on the import and distributive trades. However, if the modernization programme succeeds in improving industrial competitiveness, then the foreign exchange constraint will be relaxed and, sooner or later, the overall level of activity will recover from its depressed state. Furthermore, the economy's longer-run growth performance ought to improve, as a result of which we can expect to see changes in both the level and composition of output and employment. These would be much the same as those described above under 'general reflation', except that a policy of industrial modernization is more likely to produce a really sustained improvement in economic performance.

Consumption strategy – revaluation

Under this strategy, the overall degree of capacity utilization is fixed, and revaluation results in an increase in the share of the non-traded goods sector in both output and employment and a decline in the share of the traded goods sector (principally manufacturing). Thus, revaluation causes manufacturing output and employment to be lower than they would otherwise have been. However, whether manufacturing output and employment actually decline, either absolutely or relatively, depends not only on the size of the improvement in non-manufacturing trade and, hence, on the extent of revaluation, but also on factors such as a country's stage of development and how fast its labour force is growing.

Let us consider just the employment issue. Suppose a country is still at an early stage of development, in which its labour force is growing rapidly, as well as becoming more 'industrialized'. In this situation, revaluation, consequent upon a once-and-for-all improvement in non-manufacturing trade, may do no more than simply slow the pace of expansion of manufacturing employment, both absolute and relative. On the other hand, if the country has reached economic maturity and its labour force is growing slowly, as well as de-industrializing, then revaluation will accentuate the decline, both absolute and relative, in manufacturing employment.

Increased foreign aid, military expenditure and investment

The effect of using the benefits of an improvement in non-manufacturing trade in either or all of these ways is to insulate the economy from the kinds of changes in internal economic structure described above. However, if the improvement in non-manufacturing trade proves to be reasonably sustained, then foreign investment provides no more than a temporary respite from such structural change. The reason is that when foreign investment income begins to be repatriated in large amounts, it is no longer possible to avoid making a choice between the two broad strategies for domestic enjoyment of the benefits of an improvement in non-manufacturing trade described above: either one of the 'growth strategies' or the 'consumption strategy'.

Conclusions and summary

We hope to have demonstrated that both empirical evidence and analytical arguments provide a large degree of support for the proposition that the commercial account tends to balance. On the one hand, the data from our sample of thirteen OECD countries indicate that, when averaged over a number of years, most countries were in balance on commercial account. A small number of countries were persistently in surplus or in deficit, but even in these cases both surpluses and deficits were quite small relative to GDP. On the other hand, a variety of analytical arguments have been deployed to show why the commercial account tends to balance.

The most important consequence of this, as far as the main thrust of the argument in this book is concerned, is that following an improvement in non-manufacturing trade, which is both large and sustained, as well as relatively autonomous with respect to a country's overall industrial and economic performance, much the greater part of the ensuing adjustment will consist of offsetting changes in the manufacturing balance. The main reason for this is that in the typical OECD country, the income-elasticity of demand for primary products, as a whole, is relatively low. Thus, whatever strategy is pursued in response to an improvement in non-manufacturing trade – either the 'consumption strategy' or one of two 'growth strategies' – only a relatively small part of the benefits would be used to increase the country's net imports of primary products. As a result, much the greater part of the adjustment to an improvement in non-manufacturing trade would take the form of an offsetting deterioration in the manufacturing balance, although the precise extent of such a deterioration would depend on which strategy was pursued, as well as on the extent of any simultaneous deterioration in trade in non-government services (especially on the tourism account). This point concerning the manufacturing balance is of the utmost importance for a proper appreciation of the consequence of post-war changes in UK trade in non-manufactures – changes which we shall now describe in some detail.

5

UK trade since the Second World War: an overview

Introduction

For a long time, it has been widely believed that the UK, as an industrial nation, must earn a vast surplus on her trade in manufactures in order to pay for vital imports of food, raw materials and fuel; hence, the post-war slogan 'export or die'. Until fairly recently, this popular perception was correct. During the course of her industrial revolution, the UK became increasingly dependent on imports of food to sustain her growing population, and on imports of raw materials to keep her industries running. Some of these imports were purchased with the income earned from shipping and other services or with income from overseas investment in the form of interest, profits and dividends. However, such 'invisible' income was not in itself sufficient to pay for all of the required imports of food and raw materials and, to make ends meet, the UK was compelled to export manufactured goods. Thus, the UK functioned as an industrial workshop for the rest of the world, exporting manufactured goods to pay for imports of primary products.

The UK's need for a surplus in manufacturing trade reached its high point in the immediate post-war period. There are several reasons for this. First, during the Second World War, the UK had been forced to liquidate many of her overseas assets and, in addition, had acquired massive new debts, with the result that net property income from abroad was drastically reduced compared to the pre-war situation. Second, in the wake of wartime disruption and privation, there was a concerted drive to rebuild the economy and raise living standards. Thus, despite the loss of property income from abroad, the country's appetite for imported food and raw materials was as great as ever. Finally, as a result of world economic recovery and the subsequent Korean War boom, there were world-wide shortages of food and raw materials, and the real cost of net imports to the UK was much greater than during the depressed conditions of the pre-war period.

The combined effect of these various developments was to produce a massive deterioration in the non-manufacturing side of the UK's balance of payments. Taking all non-manufactured items together – primary products, services, property income, transfers and income from overseas investment – the UK's deficit with the rest of the world rose from 5.7% of GDP in 1938 to around 9% in the immediate post-war period (see Table 5.1). And in the freak year 1951, under the impact of the Korean War commodity price boom, the combined deficit on these items reached nearly 16% of GDP. To cover these enormous deficits, the UK required an unprecedented surplus in her manufacturing trade with other countries, and achieving this surplus became one of the main priorities of the Labour government of the day. A vigorous export drive was launched, and human and material resources were channelled into manufacturing industry. As a result, there was a huge rise in manufactured exports, and by 1951 the UK's export surplus in manufactures was equal to 11% of GDP – more than three times its pre-war level.

This post-war drive to increase manufactured exports accounts for much of the increase in manufacturing employment which occurred under the Labour government, and the UK's need to earn a massive surplus on manufacturing trade explains why manufacturing industry assumed such unprecedented importance in the British economy in the immediate post-war years. The experience of these years has left an indelible mark on the conciousness of many Keynesian economists and has often blinded them to developments in the non-manufacturing side of the UK economy. Whilst these economists have correctly stressed the continuing importance of manufacturing production and trade for the country's prosperity, they have frequently ignored or failed to appreciate the huge structural changes which have occurred in her non-manufacturing trade over the past thirty years. The much-publicized discovery and exploitation of North Sea oil is only the latest in a series of changes which have radically transformed the UK's role in the world economy. Some of these changes have been dramatic in their impact. For example, when primary product prices collapsed at the end of the Korean War, Britain's expenditure on imported food, oil and raw materials fell by 4% of GDP. Thus, in the two years between 1951 and 1953, the UK experienced a windfall gain almost as large as the benefit she now derives from North Sea oil.

However, most of the improvements in the UK's non-manufacturing trade have occurred at a slower and less obvious pace, although their cumulative impact has been considerable. *Net imports* of food, drink, tobacco and raw materials have declined, both absolutely and as a proportion of GDP. In 1953, the UK spent 6.1% of her GDP on imported food, drink and tobacco (net of exports), and a further 5.1% on raw materials, making a total of 11.2% in all. By 1980, these figures had fallen to a mere 1.0% and 0.8%, respectively (see Fig. 5.1). This represents a combined saving equivalent to 9.4% of GDP,

Table 5.1. *The UK balance of payments, 1938 and 1946–83. Main items as a percentage of GDP*[a]

	(1) Manufactures[b]	(2) Primary products[c]	(3) Non-government services[c]	(4) Commercial balance = (1) + (2) + (3)	(5) Government services and grants	(6) Interest profits and dividends	(7) Long-term investment[e]	(8) Residual balance = (5) + (6) + (7)	(9) Basic balance = (4) + (8)
1938	+3.5	−9.6	+1.0	−5.1	−0.5	+3.4	n.a.	+2.9	—
1946–50	+8.6	−11.4	+0.2	−2.6	+0.4	+1.8	+0.1	+2.3	−0.3
1951–55	+8.8	−12.4	+0.8	−2.8	−0.4	+1.5	−1.2	−0.1	−2.9
1956–60	+8.0	−9.1	+0.5	−0.6	−0.6	+1.1	−0.8	−0.3	−0.9
1961–65	+6.4	−7.1	+0.6	−0.1	−1.1	+1.2	−0.5	−0.4	−0.5
1966–70	+4.9	−5.7	+1.0	+0.2	−0.9	+1.0	−0.4	−0.3	−0.1
1971–75	+3.5	−6.2	+1.4	−1.3	−0.7	+1.2	−0.3	+0.2	−1.1
1976–80	+3.2	−4.6	+2.2	+0.8	−1.0	+0.4	−0.7	−1.3	−0.5
1981–82	+1.6	−0.4	+1.4	+2.6	−0.6	+0.4	−2.9	−3.1	−0.5
1983	−0.5	+0.3	+1.2	+1.0	−0.6	+0.7	−1.8	−1.7	−0.7

Notes:

[a] GDP at current market prices.

[b] Manufactures = SITC sections 5 to 8, f.o.b.

[c] Primary products = SITC sections 0 to 4, f.o.b.

[d] Excludes all expenditure in the UK by overseas governments, non-territorial organisations and foreign military forces. These items are included in column (5). Their total value varies between 0.2% and 0.3% of GDP. See Appendix 4. Column 3 also includes private transfers (migrants' remittances etc.), whose value is normally around −0.1% of GDP.

[e] For 1946–1951, long-term investment includes the 'errors and omissions' item of the balance of payments.

Total may not add because of rounding errors.

Source: HMSO, *Balance of Payments: Pink Book* and HMSO, *Economic Trends Annual Supplement.*

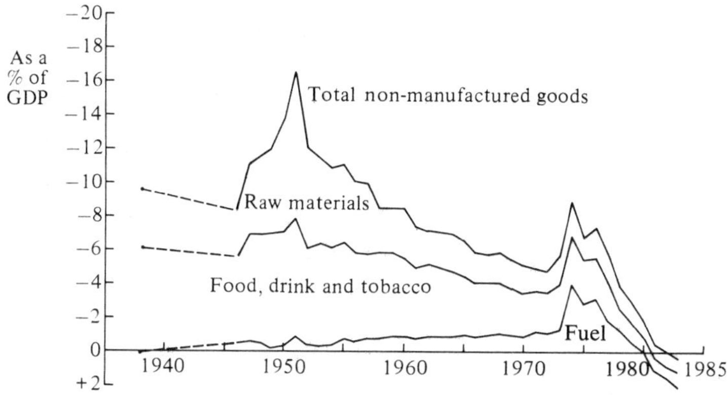

Fig. 5.1 Net imports of non-manufactured goods (as a percentage of GDP)

which is roughly twice the benefit the UK now derives from North Sea oil and gas.[1] Such changes clearly have major implications for the UK's role in the international division of labour and for her internal economic structure, yet they have almost been completely ignored in the debates on British economic development, which are still often cast in terms reminiscent of the late 1940s.[2]

In later chapters we shall discuss these wider implications at some length. However, in the present chapter we shall merely describe what has happened to the UK balance of payments during the past thirty years and examine the evolution of its major components: this will show how extensive have been the changes in the structure of UK trade. In Chapter 6, we shall present a detailed analysis of non-manufacturing's trade, which will help to reveal some of the forces which have been responsible for the transformation of the UK's foreign trade structure.

Overview of the UK's balance of payments since the Second World War

As already mentioned in Chapter 4, the UK's basic balance of payments has been close to zero throughout the past thirty years; thus, total payments and total receipts have been roughly equal. Moreover, as can be seen from Table 5.1, the same has also been true of the two major components which together make up the basic balance: on both the commercial and residual accounts, the balance has been close to zero during this period. On each of these accounts, payments and receipts have been roughly equal, and there has been little of the cross-financing that was such a feature of the pre-war period, when the UK's substantial property income from abroad was used to finance part of the country's huge trade deficit. Since the war, net property income from abroad has normally been positive, but the funds generated have been used elsewhere

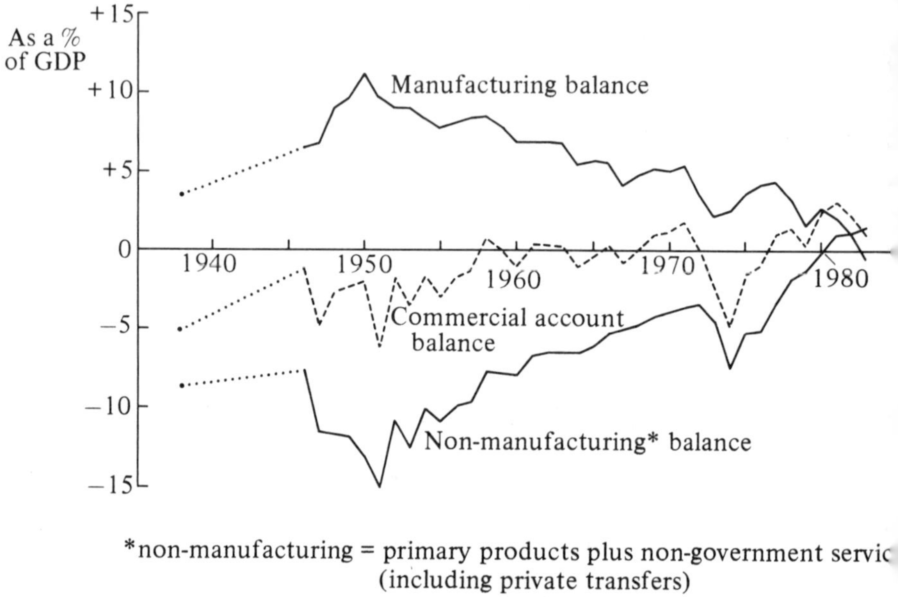

Fig. 5.2 Trade in manufactures and non-manufactures (as a percentage of GDP)

within the residual account itself to finance such items as new investment overseas, government military and diplomatic expenditure abroad and foreign aid. As a result, there has been no surplus of funds available from the residual account to finance deficits on the commercial account. Indeed, apart from a few exceptional years, total exports of goods and non-government services have been virtually the same as total imports of goods and non-government services, so that the commercial account has been self-financing, neither absorbing funds from elsewhere nor generating a surplus for other purposes. Thus, taken as a whole, the UK's commercial account has normally been in balance over the past thirty years.

However, the same is not true of the individual items making up this account. Some of these items have been massively in surplus, whilst others have been massively in deficit. In the immediate post-war period, for example, the UK had a huge surplus on her trade in manufactures. This surplus was used to finance an equally large deficit in non-manufacturing trade, and in this way a rough balance was achieved on the commercial account as a whole. Since that time, the picture has changed almost beyond recognition. The surplus on manufacturing trade has disappeared and so too has the deficit on non-manufacturing trade (see Fig. 5.2). The old picture of the UK as a highly specialized workshop economy, which requires a large surplus in manufacturing trade to finance an equally large deficit in trade in primary products, is now quite out of date. The UK now has a small surplus on her trade in both primary products and non-government services. As a result, UK trade in non-manufactures (goods and services combined) is now self-financing. The UK still exports a large quantity of manufactured goods, of course, but the resulting revenue is no longer used to purchase primary products. It is used, instead, to import an equally large quantity of manufactured goods, and this explains why the UK's previous surplus in manufacturing trade has now disappeared.

The balance of trade in manufactures is often used as an index of industrial strength, and the disappearance of the UK's former surplus in this area is widely interpreted as evidence of the country's industrial decline and loss of international competitiveness. This line of argument is, in our view, mistaken. The UK has undoubtedly suffered a long period of industrial decline and much of her manufacturing industry is now backward compared to that of her main competitors. However, this does not explain why the UK's trade surplus in manufactures has fallen so dramatically. What has happened to the UK manufacturing surplus is not primarily the result of industrial decline, but is mainly a response to *autonomous* improvements in the sphere of non-manufacturing trade. Given the huge autonomous improvements which have occurred in non-manufacturing trade, the UK's manufacturing surplus would have fallen dramatically, no matter how strong or how dynamic the country's industrial base. Before developing this argument at greater length, let us first examine the forces which have shaped the UK's trade in non-manufactured goods and services since the end of the Second World War.

6

UK trade in non-manufactures

Introduction

In this chapter we examine, in considerable detail, post-war developments in each of the main areas of UK trade in non-manufactured goods and services. Trade in these items can be conveniently grouped under five headings:

(1) food, beverages and tobacco;
(2) raw materials;
(3) fuels;
(4) non-government services; and
(5) non-government transfers.

This is the structure we shall adopt for organizing the discussion in the present chapter. The concluding section contains a summary of the main results.

Food, beverages and tobacco

The decline in the UK's deficit in food trade has come about through a combination of almost static consumption of food together with a sustained increase in domestic production (see Fig. 6.1). The latter has largely been the result of increased investment and new techniques of production, since both acreage and employment have declined.

In the fifteen years or so following the Second World War, there was a once-and-for-all increase in total UK food consumption, measured at constant prices. This increase was mainly the result of a shift in the pattern of consumption as 'inferior' foodstuffs, such as bread and potatoes, were replaced by 'superior' and more expensive foodstuffs, such as eggs and meat (Table 6.1). This shift in consumption was itself the result of several factors.[1] As food became more plentiful and rationing was phased out during the 1950s, there was a widespread return to pre-war eating habits, which had been severely disrupted by wartime austerity. Moreover, because of full employment and the newly established welfare state, the 1950s were a period of unprecedented prosperity for previously impoverished sections of the population and, for the first time in their lives,

Table 6.1. *Per capita food consumption in the UK (kg per head per year)*

	Pre-war	1943	1947	1955	1965	1975	1982
Dairy products [a] (excluding butter)	17.4	22.7	22.0	23.9	25.1	26.4	22.9
Meat[b]	53.9	41.1	40.9	53.4	58.6	57.0	54.1
Fish[b]	11.9	8.3	14.5	9.7	9.4	7.9	6.9
Eggs (number)[c]	220	191	191	229	271	246	227
Oils and fats[d]	21.4	17.7	16.3	21.8	22.4	21.8	23.5
Sugars and syrups[e]	43.5	30.3	37.0	48.9	49.2	45.9	46.2
Fresh fruit	35.6	13.0	30.9	30.1	33.4	31.5	35.4
Other fruit[f]	20.6	17.6	20.5	21.2	22.0	22.1	25.7
Pulses and nuts	4.3	2.7	3.6	5.2	5.7	5.4	5.3
Potatoes[g]	86.2	112.9	129.7	106.2	100.9	101.7	105.6
Other vegetables[f]	54.6	57.3	61.6	55.2	60.9	60.5	70.4
Grain products	95.3	112.9	109.6	88.9	77.3	72.1	68.1

Notes: [a] Milk solids, [b] edible weight, [c] shell eggs and egg products, [d] fat content, [e] sugar content, [f] fresh equivalent, [g] potatoes and potato products (raw potato equivalent)
Source: 'The Nation's Food – 40 years of change', L. J. Angel and G. E. Hurdle, *Economic Trends* April 1978

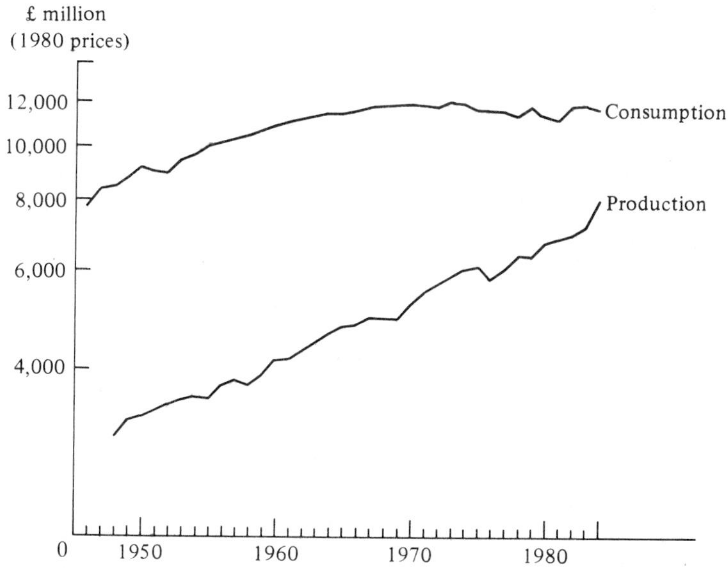

Fig. 6.1 UK food consumption and production since the Second World War

many of them were able to consume high-quality meat and other 'superior' foodstuffs on a regular basis. As a result of these factors, there was a rapid transformation in the average person's diet. However, this transformation was effectively complete by the end of the early 1960s and, since then, both the scale and pattern of food consumption have been remarkably stable. Total food consumption has been rising roughly in line with population at around 0.2% a year, and what changes there have been in the pattern of consumption are fairly minor. For example, domestically produced pork and poultry have replaced Commonwealth mutton and lamb as a source of animal protein, whilst the consumption of cheese has risen substantially and butter has been widely replaced by margarine. This stability in the pattern of food consumption is not due to poverty or slow economic growth but is a result of being a developed economy in which the average dietary standard was already fairly high even before the war. In this respect, the UK's experience has been quite different from that of Italy or Japan, where rapid income growth from a previously low level has been accompanied by a large increase in the consumption of meat and other 'superior' foodstuffs in the post-war period.[2]

The modern rise in UK food production really dates back to 1931, when a century-old policy of free trade was abandoned and, to quote Sidney Pollard (1969), 'British agriculture was turned into a highly protected, organised and subsidised sector of the economy.'[3] However, government policy towards agriculture was rather unsystematic in the 1930s, and it was only when war broke out that a coherent and determined drive to raise food production was undertaken. With modifications, wartime policies were carried over into peacetime and, in one form or another, have continued ever since. Throughout the post-war period, both before and after Britain's entry into the EEC, agriculture has been highly protected, and the government has made strenuous efforts to encourage the adoption of new farming techniques. As in most other European countries, where similar policies have been adopted, the result has been a considerable rise in output. Between 1948 and 1984 agricultural production rose by 160% (see Fig. 6.2). Much of this increase was achieved by the use of artificial fertilizers, weedkillers and pesticides, but some was also due to the use of new varieties of plant and livestock. Over the past fifteen years, for example, milk yields per cow have risen by 24%, whilst it has been estimated that, as a result of new plant varieties alone, wheat production has grown by an extra 2% every year since 1946.[4] In fact, both output and yields have risen dramatically right across the board. The UK now produces over four times as much cereal as in 1938, three-and-a-half times as much butter, five times as much cheese, nearly two-and-a-half times as much meat and twice as many eggs. This massive rise in output has been achieved in spite of a rapid fall in agricultural employment and, despite frequent claims to the contrary, with a relatively small input of

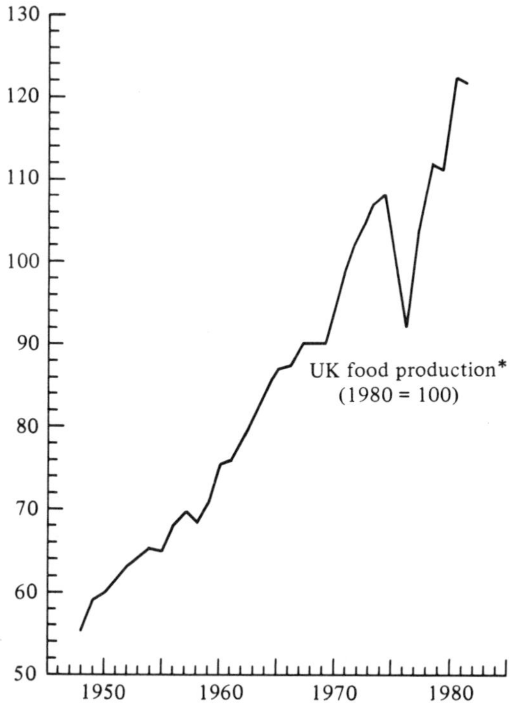

* = Output of Agriculture, Forestry and Fishing at constant factor cost.
Source: Economic Trends, Annual Supplement.

Fig. 6.2 UK food production: volume index (1980 = 100)

energy. Agriculture now employs less than 3% of the national workforce and uses less than 4% of all energy consumed in the economy.[5] This latter figure includes the energy used in making fertilizers and is less than the amount of energy used by just the iron and steel industry alone.[6] There is, of course, a negative side to the spectacular increase in UK food production. The financial cost of agricultural protection and subsidies has been enormous – a cumulative total of more than 63,000 million since 1946, according to one estimate.[7] Some would argue the money could have been better spent in other directions, for example in modernizing the country's manufacturing industry. Quite apart from the financial costs, there are also environmental and even moral aspects to consider. Modern, intensive farming methods involve the widespread destruction of flora and fauna and, in many parts of the country, the result is a monotonous landscape whose recreational value is virtually nil. They also involve considerable mental and physical cruelty to livestock, which are often reared under the most

Table 6.2. *UK percentage self-sufficiency in selected foodstuffs*

	Potatoes	Cereals	Meat	Butter	Cheese	Other milk products	Eggs	Sugar
Pre-war	95	31	47	9	24	31	61[a]	16
1946	99	59	45	8	10	38	80[a]	27
1958	85	46	62	6	41	76	95[a]	23
1966	93	65	69	7	43	82	100	29
1973	93	68	77	23	58	120	97	37
1980	92	88	84	57	70	157	100	47
1981	90	103	86	56	67	141	99	50
1982	87	105	85	63	72	140	100	57
1983	87	103	89	65	71	135	99	52
1984	89[b]	109[b]	90[b]	62[b]	67[b]	159[b]	97[b]	55[b]

Notes: [a] estimate, [b] forecast
Source: HMSO, *Annual Review of Agriculture*, various years

oppressive conditions.[8] Finally, in some cases, the policy of encouraging domestic food production has caused serious harm to former suppliers. For example, the UK, like most other EEC countries, subsidises the production of sugar-beet, and sugar derived from this source has now widely replaced cane sugar previously imported from tropical countries. As a result, the world price of cane sugar has been artificially forced down, and many otherwise viable tropical producers have been impoverished or driven out of business altogether.

The combination of rising production and stationary consumption has made the UK almost self-sufficient in many basic foodstuffs (see Table 6.2). In the four major categories combined – sugar, cereals, milk products and other livestock products – the UK was 83% self-sufficient in 1980.[9] In certain products, such as skimmed milk and cereals, the country has become a net exporter. Of course, the UK will continue to import oranges, bananas and other tropical or Mediterranean foods, but the share of these items in total food consumption is fairly small and is likely to remain so.

The country's shift toward self-sufficiency shows up very clearly in foreign trade. In the immediate post-war period, net food imports rose quite rapidly as a result of changes in the diet; but they stabilized in the late 1950s and then began to fall. Taking 1963 = 100, the volume index of UK net food imports fell from 102 in 1958 to 85 in 1973 and 57 in 1983.[10]

The situation with regard to beverages and tobacco can be summarized as follows. Amongst non-alcoholic beverages, tea has been partially replaced by coffee over the past thirty years; however, apart from this, there is no clear trend in the consumption of such beverages, almost all of which are imported. In the case of alcoholic drinks, the consumption of imported wine has risen

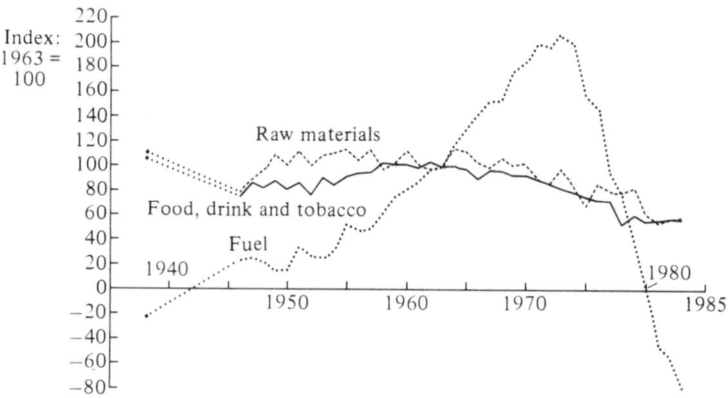

Fig. 6.3 Volume of net imports of primary products (1963 = 100)

a great deal, but this has been more than offset by a big rise in whisky exports. As a result, in value terms, the UK is a net exporter of alcoholic drinks. In the case of tobacco, domestic consumption has fallen and, although the UK still imports as much tobacco as before, an increasing proportion of this is processed and then re-exported in the form of cigarettes. As a result, *net* imports of tobacco have declined.

Taking all these items together – food, beverages and tobacco – the volume of net imports, after reaching a peak early in the 1960s, has fallen steadily ever since (see Fig. 6.3). When compared to GDP, the decline is even more striking. In the 1950s, net imports of food, beverages and tobacco were equivalent to 6.8% of GDP at current market prices (see Table 6.3). By 1960 this figure had fallen to 4.7% and, nowadays, it is around 1.0%.

So far we have been concerned with the volume of net imports. However, there are also prices to consider. As can be seen from Fig. 6.4, imported foodstuffs are now much cheaper in relative terms than they were in the immediate post-war years. To evaluate the importance of this development, we have computed the ratio of net imports of food, beverages and tobacco to GDP, at both current and constant prices. The results, shown in Table 6.4, indicate that, up to the mid-1960s, relative price changes were the main factor responsible for the decline in the ratio of net imports of food, beverages and tobacco to GDP. Since then, however, price movements have been of secondary importance, and the main factor has been the falling of net imports.

To conclude: the ratio of net imports of food, beverages and tobacco to GDP has fallen from 6.8% in 1950 to around 1.0% today. Relative price changes account for about half of this decline, whilst much of the rest is due to a major reduction in the volume of UK net food imports since the early 1960s. As we

Table 6.3. *UK trade in non-manufactured goods and services; net exports as a % of GDP at current market prices, 1938, 1946–83*[a]

	(1) Food	(2) Beverages[b,c]	(3) Tobacco[c]	(4) Basic materials	(5) Fuel	(6) Total (1) to (5)	(7) Non-government services[d]	(8) Grand total = (6) + (7)
1938	−5.5	−0.4	−0.3	−3.5	+0.1	−9.6	1.0	−8.6
1946	−4.4	−0.3	−0.4	−2.9	−0.5	−8.5	+0.8	−7.7
1947	−5.6	−0.5	−0.2	−4.2	−0.6	−11.1	−0.5	−11.6
1948	−5.7	−0.5	−0.2	−4.7	−0.5	−11.6	−0.1	−11.7
1949	−6.0	−0.6	−0.2	−5.1	−0.2	−12.1	+0.2	−11.9
1950	−6.0	−0.5	−0.3	−6.5	−0.3	−13.6	+0.5	−13.1
1951	−6.1	−0.6	−0.3	−8.6	−0.9	−16.5	+0.6	−15.9
1952	−5.2	−0.4	−0.1	−6.0	−0.4	−12.1	+1.3	−10.8
1953	−5.4	−0.4	−0.3	−5.1	−0.3	−11.5	+1.0	−12.5
1954	−4.8	−0.7	−0.3	−4.7	−0.4	−10.9	+0.8	−10.1
1955	−4.8	−0.6	−0.3	−4.6	−0.8	−11.1	+0.3	−10.8
1956	−4.8	−0.3	−0.2	−4.2	−0.6	−10.1	+0.2	−9.9
1957	−4.4	−0.4	−0.2	−4.2	−0.8	−10.0	+0.4	−9.6
1958	−4.5	−0.4	−0.2	−2.6	−0.8	−8.5	+0.9	−7.6
1959	−4.5	−0.3	−0.2	−2.6	−0.9	−8.5	+0.8	−7.7
1960	−4.1	−0.3	−0.3	−2.9	−0.9	−8.5	+0.7	−7.8
1961	−3.6	−0.3	−0.3	−2.4	−0.8	−7.4	+0.8	−6.6
1962	−3.9	−0.2	−0.2	−2.0	−0.9	−7.2	+0.8	−6.4
1963	−3.7	−0.2	−0.2	−2.1	−0.9	−7.1	+0.6	−6.5
1964	−3.5	−0.2	−0.2	−2.2	−0.9	−7.0	+0.5	−6.5
1965	−3.2	−0.1	−0.2	−2.1	−1.0	−6.6	+0.5	−6.1
1966	−3.0	−0.1	−0.1	−1.8	−0.9	−5.9	+0.6	−5.3
1967	−2.9	−0.1	−0.1	−1.7	−1.0	−5.8	+0.8	−5.0

1968	−2.9	+0.1	−0.2	−1.8	−1.1	−5.9	+1.2	−4.7
1969	−2.7	−0.0	−0.1	−1.7	−1.0	−5.5	+1.3	−4.2
1970	−2.5	−0.0	−0.1	−1.7	−0.9	−5.2	+1.3	−3.9
1971	−2.4	+0.1	−0.1	−1.4	−1.2	−5.0	+1.4	−3.6
1972	−2.3	−0.0	−0.1	−1.3	−1.1	−4.8	+1.4	−3.4
1973	−2.5	−0.1	−0.1	−1.7	−1.3	−5.7	+1.3	−4.4
1974	−2.7	−0.1	−0.1	−2.0	−4.0	−8.9	+1.5	−7.4
1975	−2.5	−0.0	−0.1	−1.3	−2.9	−6.8	+1.6	−5.2
1976	−2.2	−0.1	−0.1	−1.8	−3.2	−7.4	+2.3	−5.1
1977	−2.0	−0.2	−0.1	−1.7	−1.9	−5.9	+2.5	−3.4
1978	−1.6	−0.0	−0.1	−1.3	−1.3	−4.3	+2.4	−1.9
1979	−1.6	−0.0	−0.0	−1.2	−0.6	−3.4	+2.1	−1.3
1980	−1.0	+0.0	−0.0	−0.9	−0.1	−2.0	+1.8	−0.2
1981	−1.1	+0.2	+0.0	−0.8	+1.1	−0.6	+1.6	+1.0
1982	−1.2	+0.2	+0.0	−0.7	+1.5	−0.2	+1.3	+1.1
1983	−1.0	+0.0	+0.0	−0.8	+2.1	+0.3	+1.2	+1.5

Notes: [a] Data on exports f.o.b. and imports were taken from HMSO, *Pink Book*, various years
[b] Alcoholic plus non-alcoholic
[c] Data in columns (2) + (3) only from HMSO *Overseas Trade Statistics of the UK*: imports c.i.f. converted to imports f.o.b., using adjustment figure for total imports
[d] Includes private transfers (see notes to Table 5.1)

Table 6.4. *UK net imports of selected items as a % of GDP at current and constant market prices*

	1948–49	1951–52	1954–55	1964–65	1973–74	1978–79	1982–83
	(a) Food, beverages and tobacco						
As % of GDP							
At current prices	6.6	6.4	5.8	3.7	2.8	1.6	1.0
At constant 1964/65 prices	5.0	4.5	4.4	3.7	2.4	1.6	1.5
cf *Volume Index* 1964/65 = 100	86	82	89	100	82	58	58
	(b) Basic materials						
As % of GDP							
At current prices	7.3	4.7	2.2	1.9	1.3	0.9	0.9
At constant 1964/65 prices	3.1	3.0	2.8	2.2	1.4	1.1	0.8
cf *Volume Index* 1964/65 = 100	91	94	99	100	81	72	51

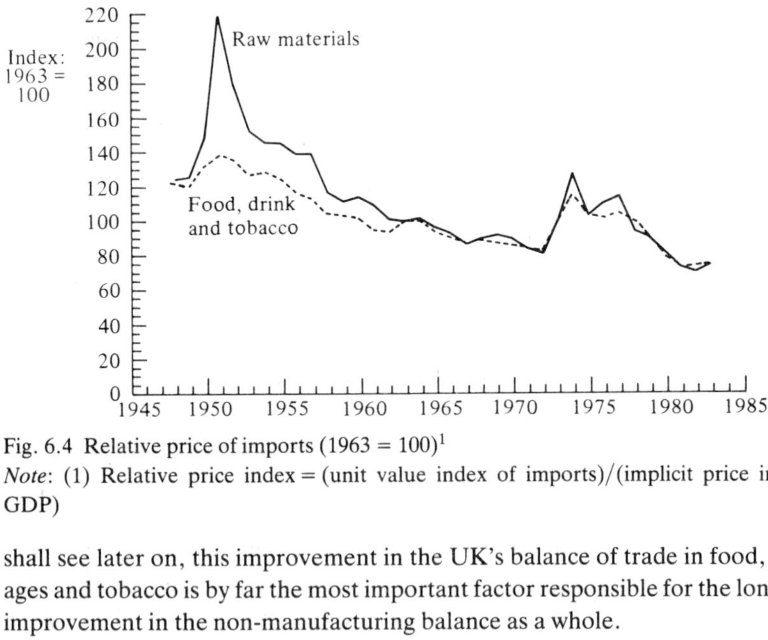

Fig. 6.4 Relative price of imports (1963 = 100)[1]
Note: (1) Relative price index = (unit value index of imports)/(implicit price index of GDP)

shall see later on, this improvement in the UK's balance of trade in food, beverages and tobacco is by far the most important factor responsible for the long-term improvement in the non-manufacturing balance as a whole.

Raw materials

In the course of the nineteenth century, the British economy became heavily dependent on imported raw materials, especially cotton for use in the textile industry and, by the 1870s, net imports of raw materials had reached almost 10% of GDP. However, this period marks something of a watershed and, over

Fig. 6.5 Net imports of basic materials and UK production, 1948–83(1948 = 100)[1]
Note: (1) Indices of production exclude oil and natural gas

the past 100 years, there has been a marked decline in the ratio of net raw material imports to GDP, although this trend has often been concealed, for short periods of time, by large fluctuations in the price of such materials. For example, during the Korean War boom, a sharp rise in prices caused expenditure on imported raw materials to double within two years and, in 1951, the cost of such imports (net of exports) reached almost 9% of GDP. But prices soon fell again and, by 1953, the cost of net raw material imports had fallen back to around 5% of GDP (see Table 6.3). Since then, the share of total UK output spent on raw material imports has continued to fall, apart from a brief interlude in 1973–74, when raw material prices were exceptionally high because of global shortages and speculation (see Fig. 6.4). However, even during this interlude, the cost of net raw material imports never exceeded 2% of GDP, and, in recent years, the figure has been around 1.0%.

To distinguish price and quantity effects, we have compared net material imports with GDP at both current and constant prices (see Table 6.4). The results indicate that, up until the mid-1960s, relative price changes were responsible for most of the decline in the UK's expenditure on net raw material imports. Between the peaks of 1951–52 and 1964–65, expenditure on net raw material imports at current prices fell from 7.3% of GDP to 1.9%. Of this fall, over two-thirds was due to the lower relative price of raw materials and less than a third to the lower volume of raw material imports in relation to real national output. Since the mid-1960s, however, quite the opposite situation has prevailed: price movements have been of secondary importance, and there has been a marked decline in the volume of net raw material imports in the UK, even though GDP has risen somewhat (see Fig. 6.5).

This decline in net raw material imports, both absolutely and relative to GDP, is due to a number of factors. To begin with, there has been a severe industrial depression which has afflicted most sectors of British industry. This depression has greatly reduced both the level of industrial production and the share of industry in total output and, as a result, there has been a dramatic fall in the demand for imported raw materials since 1979. However, even before the recent collapse of British industry, raw material imports were falling, and there were clear signs of a shift towards forms of industrial production which require the use of fewer imported raw materials. Three factors have been mainly responsible for this shift. First, thc structure of industrial production has changed since the 1960s, so that a higher share of production now consists of goods requiring a relatively small input of raw materials. Some of these changes are almost certainly permanent and reflect fundamental shifts in the pattern of demand or in the international division of labour. Others, however, are less fundamental in character and may well be reversed at some time in the future. Secondly, there have been economies in the use of imported raw materials, either because more output has been obtained from a given input of materials or because domestically generated waste has been recycled more effectively. Thirdly, some kinds of imported raw materials have been replaced by domestically produced substitutes. The relative importance of these various factors depends, of course, on the particular material in question, so let us consider briefly the main types of raw material which are imported by the UK.

The first major category consists of the organic materials: cotton, jute, wool, hides, skins and natural rubber. During the 1950s and 1960s, these materials were strongly affected by competition from oil and gas-based synthetics, and demand for them fell, even though the industries which used them were in many cases expanding. For example, the production of pullovers, jumpers and cardigans rose from 75 million in 1955 to 150 million in 1973, yet the number made of wool declined from 61 million to 30 million during this time. A similar transformation occurred in the weaving of yarn, with the share of cotton yarn falling from 71% in 1955 to 47% in 1973. Over the same period, the share of natural rubber in total UK rubber consumption fell from 82% to 36%. In the footwear industry, synthetics were slower to take hold but, even so, by 1973, only 60% of shoes made in the UK had leather uppers. Thus, for all of the materials we are considering, competition from substitutes was the major factor responsible for their reduced use and importation during the 1950s. In recent years, however, the situation has been very different. The higher cost of oil and gas has increased the relative price of most synthetics, thereby reducing the incentive to replace natural materials. At the same time, the decline of natural materials has been slowed down by the widespread use of mixtures such as polyester/cotton in the textile industry and, in the tyre industry, by the combination of natural and synthetic rubber in the production of radial tyres. Indeed, over the past decade, the process of substitution seems to have stopped, and natural materials appear to be holding their own. However, despite this, there has been a further decline in the use and importation of wool, cotton and natural rubber; whilst, in the case of hides and skins, the UK has actually become a net exporter (see Table 6.5). This further decline is entirely the result of falling output in the industries using these materials: the textile, footwear and leather goods industries have all been harmed by imports from low-cost producers abroad; whilst in the case of tyres, tubes and rubber goods, the multinational firms which make them have relocated much of their production overseas.

The next major category of imports consists of forest products. Only the crudest of forest products, such as sawnwood, pit props and woodpulp are classified as basic or raw materials, whilst more sophisticated products, such as newsprint and plywood are classified as manufactures. During the 1950s and well into the 1960s, imports of crude timber and woodpulp rose. Since then, however, the total quantity of such products has fallen, although both the timing and extent of this decline have varied from item to item. For example, there was a massive fall in the demand for imported pit props during the 1960s, caused partly by a contraction of the mining industry and partly by the use of steel supports. On the other hand, imports of sawn softwood continued to rise right up until 1974, when the demand for this kind of timber was drastically reduced by a sharp fall in the scale of housebuilding and other types of construction. Any major recovery in the construction industry would see a big increase in imports of sawn softwood. Hardwood imports have also fallen. Such imports are small by volume, but expensive to purchase, and this has led to their gradual replacement by plastic-faced particle board and other substitutes. This is but one example of a more general trend towards the use of particle board in place of solid timber in construction and furniture. Such board is manufactured from wood and forest residues, and much of it is imported. Thus, part of the decline in UK imports of the cruder, less processed, forms of timber reflects a shift towards the importation of more sophisticated forms, which are then classified as manufactures.

In the case of imported woodpulp, the picture is as follows. This kind of import is used to make paper and board, and it competes with both domestically produced pulpwood and wastepaper. Domestic production of pulpwood has risen over the past thirty years, whilst a greater proportion of paper and board is now produced from wastepaper than was formerly the case. Moreover, during the past decade, the domestic output of paper and board has fallen, as imports capture an increasing share of the domestic market. This combination of falling output in the user industry and greater reliance on home supplies of wastepaper and pulpwood has led to a considerable decline in the volume of imported woodpulp since the mid-1960s.

Table 6.5. *UK net imports of selected basic materials, by volume (1963 = 100)*[a]

	(1) Hides and skins	(2) Cotton	(3) Jute	(4) Wool	(5) Crude rubber	(6) Timber	(7) Wood pulp	(8) Iron-ore and scrap	(9) Non-ferrous ores + scrap	(10) Oil seeds	(11) Synthetic fibres	(12) All basic materials
Weight in total index (%)	3.0	7.6	4.4	13.0	4.5	22.4	15.1	6.9	9.8	11.8	0.9	100
1938	n.a.	188	119	152	78	128	68	43	72	128	−31	110
1946–47	256	123	63	96	95	89	41	53	59	91	−33	84
1954–55	170	134	106	122	157	108	80	100	103	101	−67	112
1964–65	119	97	94	93	121	116	113	137	131	98	−98	114
1973–74	43	63	52	59	64	100	97	155	115	111	−533	91
1978–79	−23	48	32	55	93	75	82	115	99	142	−187	82
1980	−82	36	22	30	89	57	72	44	73	157	−338	62
1981	−93	27	18	36	61	60	65	87	71	104	−106	55
1982	−64	35	19	33	79	77	57	58	70	90	−75	58
1983	−76	29	20	16	58	78	59	71	110	69	−18	59

Note: [a] A minus sign indicates that exports exceed imports. In the case of synthetic fibres, the UK was a net exporter in the base year 1963, and hence for synthetic fibres the index for 1963 = −100

Source: Constructed from HMSO, *UK Overseas Trade Statistics*, various years

The third major category of imported raw materials consists of metalliferous ores and scrap-metal (mainly the former). Until recently, the biggest items in this category were iron-ore and steel scrap, whose combined imports rose strongly up until 1973. Since then, however, imports of iron-ore have fallen away, and the UK has actually become a major net exporter of steel scrap. This turnaround is largely due to the collapse of the British steel industry, whose output has fallen by over 40% since its peak in 1973. Any major recovery in the demand for British steel would see a significant rise in imports of iron-ore and a reduction in exports of steel scrap. In the case of other metallic ores and scrap, the picture is more complex. The total quantity of such imports rose up to the early 1960s, but has declined since then. However, this overall movement conceals important differences between what has happened to various metals. In the case of zinc, the decline in ore imports only began in the early 1970s, when Rio Tinto closed some of its domestic smelting capacity and began to import refined metal rather than ore. In the case of nickel, the fall in imports of ore reflects the reduced demand for nickel in the steel and other industries, where it is used to make alloys. In the case of tin, domestic demand has been falling, largely because of competition from aluminium and other substitutes, and this is reflected in reduced production of tin and reduced imports of the materials from which it is made. Finally, in the case of aluminium, demand for this metal has been growing over the past twenty years, and domestic production rose right up until 1980. As a result, raw material imports by the aluminium industry also increased right up to 1980, mainly in the semi-processed form of alumina rather than crude bauxite.

There are two final categories of raw materials to consider: oilseeds and synthetic fibres. Imported oilseeds are mainly used for conversion into animal feeds, and their use for this purpose has grown steadily during the past thirty years. The case of synthetic fibres is more complex. In this area, the UK has always been a major exporter, and what appears statistically as a rise in net imports (see Table 6.5) is really a fall in net exports. This fall has occurred partly because of the reduced demand for synthetic fibres in Western Europe, and partly because of competition from US fibre producers. Like most European countries, the UK produces synthetic fibres from naptha, an oil-derivative, which has become very expensive since 1973. In the US, however, synthetic fibres are produced from natural gas whose price was until recently controlled. This gave American producers a considerable cost advantage and helps to explain the slump in British exports.

It is clear from the foregoing discussion that the question of raw material imports is complex. However, some of the major trends can be identified. Many of the old staples, such as jute and cotton, have been replaced by synthetic substitutes. Even where this has not been the case, many of the industries which used to import these staple materials, have contracted severely over the past decade in the face of competition from low-cost producers abroad. In the realm of non-ferrous metals and forest products, there has been a shift in the pattern of imports away from crude materials towards more sophisticated semi-manufactures, such as refined metal and chipboard. This process is probably inevitable: it reflects the policies of both the supplying countries and the multinational companies responsible for much of this trade. Finally, there are the effects of the recent crisis and longer-term stagnation of the British economy. Certain industries, such as construction, have stagnated for the past decade, whilst others, such as steel, have contracted severely under the Thatcher government. This has significantly reduced the demand for raw materials such as timber and iron-ore.

To sum up. The absolute decline in net material imports over the past twenty years is partly the result of stagnation and crisis in the British economy. Faster and sustained growth in industrial production would have led to much greater imports of timber, iron-ore and certain other kinds of raw material. On the other hand, faster growth would also have meant an accelerated pace of structural change within the industrial sector and perhaps a faster shift towards forms of production requiring fewer imported raw materials per unit of output. Such changes would have helped to keep down the demand for imported materials. It is impossible, unfortunately, to determine accurately what might have happened to raw material imports as a whole if the British economy had grown faster over the past twenty years. But one thing seems fairly certain. No matter how much faster the economy had grown, the same basic forces would have been at work. Even though *total* raw material imports would have been greater, the amount of imported raw materials required per unit of industrial output would have fallen as much, and perhaps even more, than it actually has done.

Fuel

Before the Second World War, the UK was normally in surplus in trade in fuel. She was a major coal exporter, and revenue from this source normally exceeded expenditure on imported oil. After the war, however, the situation was different, and the UK faced a mounting deficit on her trade in fuels. This new situation was caused by a combination of falling exports of coal and rising imports of oil. At the end of the war, coal exports staged a brief recovery from the effects of wartime disruption, but they never returned to anything like pre-war levels. Moreover, even this limited recovery was soon reversed as a result of competition from oil and cheap foreign coal and, by the 1960s, the UK was no longer a significant net coal exporter. Coal also faced competition in the

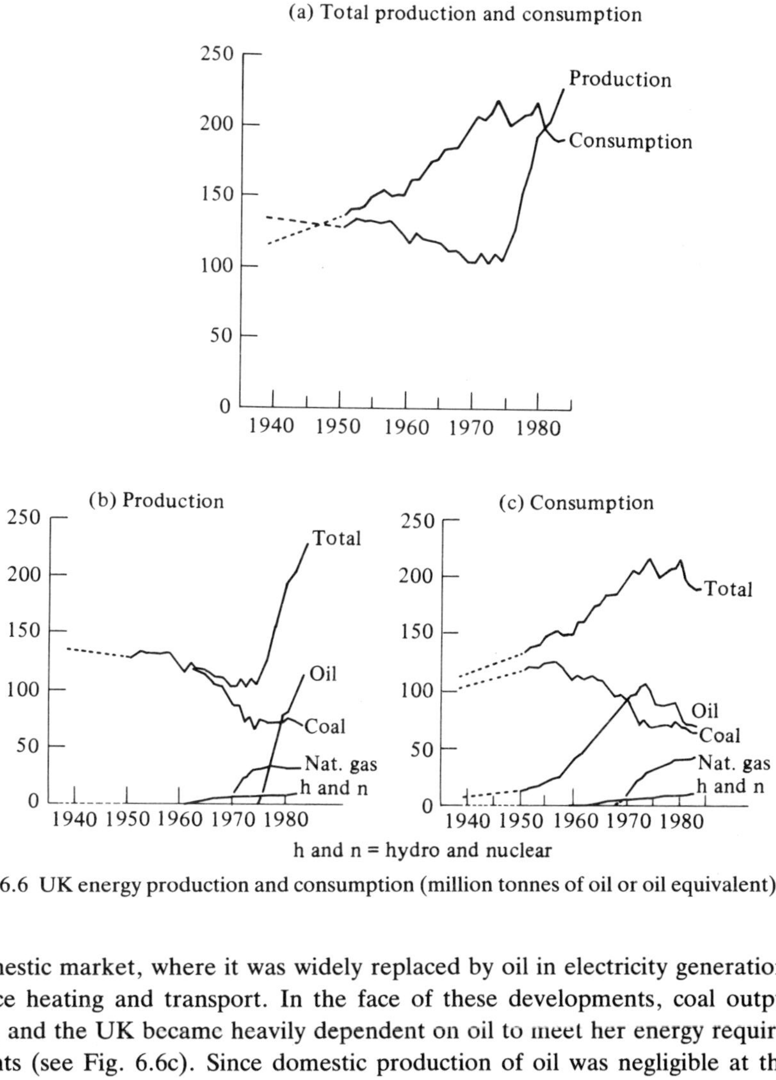

Fig. 6.6 UK energy production and consumption (million tonnes of oil or oil equivalent)

domestic market, where it was widely replaced by oil in electricity generation, space heating and transport. In the face of these developments, coal output fell, and the UK became heavily dependent on oil to meet her energy requirements (see Fig. 6.6c). Since domestic production of oil was negligible at this time, the result was a spectacular growth in oil imports, which rose sevenfold between 1950 and 1973. In the 1960s, the UK also began to import natural gas from Norway, and this further increased the country's fuel deficit. By 1973, roughly half of all the UK's energy requirements were met by imported fuel, and the deficit in fuel trade had reached 1.3% of GDP.

In October 1973, world oil prices quadrupled, following action by the OPEC cartel to restrict output and establish a new price structure. The effect of this on the UK's import bill was immediate; within the space of a year, the fuel deficit had risen from 1.3% of GDP in 1973 to 4.0% in 1974. However, 1974 marks a turning-point and, since then, there has been a sustained improvement in the fuel balance. The deficit has been eliminated, and the UK is now a major net fuel exporter. The country still imports natural gas from Norway, as well as low-grade oil from the Middle East and elsewhere, but the cost of these imports is far outweighed by the revenue from exports of high-grade oil from the North Sea. In 1983, the surplus on UK trade in fuel had reached 6,200 million, which is equivalent to 2.4% of GDP at market prices. Never before in history has the UK had such a large surplus on fuel trade, not even in her heyday as a coal exporter in the early part of this century.[11]

Three main factors have been responsible for this remarkable transformation in the fuel balance. First, there has been a massive increase in UK fuel output since North Sea oil came on stream in 1976. Secondly, the previous growth in energy consumption has been reversed, and total consumption is now well below its 1973 peak. Finally, in the generation of electricity, there has been a shift in the pattern of fuel use away from oil and back to coal: 75% of all the electricity now generated in the UK is derived from coal and most of the rest is nuclear. This shift in demand has provided a new market for British coal and has helped to stabilize coal output after a long period of decline (see Fig. 6.6b).[12]

Let us consider the first two of the above factors in greater detail. The story of North Sea oil is well known and only a brief discussion is needed here.[13] The main facts are as follows. The British sector of the North Sea contains both oil and natural gas reserves. Historically, the discovery and extraction of natural gas preceded that of oil. Gas was first discovered in the British sector in 1965, and production started in 1967. Output built up rapidly to a plateau of around 34 million tonnes of oil equivalent (MTOE) in the mid-1970s, a level at which it has remained ever since (see Fig. 6.6b).[14] This indigenous supply of natural gas is supplemented by imports from the Norwegian sector of the North Sea. At the present time, indigenous natural gas provides about one-fifth of all energy consumed in the UK, and imported gas a further 5%. Thus, natural gas from the North Sea is now a major fuel energy in the British economy.

However, its role is overshadowed by that of oil. Oil was first discovered in the North Sea in 1964, but extraction did not begin in earnest until 1976. Since then production has risen strongly, and the UK is now the world's sixth largest oil producer with a level of production comparable to that of Iran.

Future prospects for oil and gas production are uncertain. They depend on the extent of reserves in place, the future evolution of technology and the amount of exploratory activity in years to come, all of which are uncertain. The range of uncertainty can be gauged from Table 6.6, which contains official estimates

Table 6.6. *Estimated oil and gas reserves in UK continential shelf (as at end 1983)*

	Oil	Natural gas
	MTOE	MTOE
Recoverable reserves originally in place	1977–5847	1189–2378
Cumulative production to end 1983	527	407
Remaining reserves[a]	1405–5275	783–1971
UK production in 1983	115	34
Ratio of remaining reserves to current production	12–46 years	23–58 years

Note: [a] Reserves originally in place minus cumulative production to end 1983
Source: UK Digest of Energy Statistics

for reserves of oil and gas in the UK continental shelf. The amount of recoverable oil still remaining is estimated to lie within the range of 1,405 to 5,275 million tonnes, whilst for natural gas the range is 783 to 1,971 MTOE. For oil, these figures represent between 12 and 46 years' supply at the present rate of extraction, and for gas between 23 and 58 years' supply.

How long these reserves will last in reality depends, of course, on the depletion policy actually pursued. This is of particular relevance in the case of oil. The UK is currently exporting roughly 60% of her North Sea production in the form of crude oil. Although this generates an immediate revenue for the balance of payments, it also implies a faster rate of depletion of oil reserves than would otherwise be the case. With a different export policy the lifespan of these reserves could be increased dramatically. For example, suppose that oil exports were stopped altogether, whilst oil imports continued at the present rate. Then, estimated reserves of North Sea oil would last between 30 and 115 years (given the present level of UK oil consumption). Thus, simply by halting the export of oil from the North Sea reserves, the lifespan of these reserves could be more than doubled. A complete ban on oil exports might be rather an extreme measure, and we mention it here merely to illustrate the role of trade policy in deciding the future of North Sea oil.

So much for energy production. Let us now consider consumption. After rising at an average rate of 2.3% a year over the period 1960–73, total energy consumption has fallen by around a sixth since 1973. The implications of this remarkable turnaround can be seen from the following example. Suppose energy consumption had continued to grow as fast after 1973 as in the preceding period 1960–73. Then, by 1983, the total consumption of energy would have been 278 MTOE, as compared to an actual figure of 192 MTOE in that year. Thus, the actual consumption of energy in 1983 was 86 MTOE below its trend value.

This shortfall is equivalent to three-quarters of the entire output of North Sea oil in 1983.[15] Thus, the reversal of the previous trend in energy consumption is almost as important as North Sea oil in explaining the improvement in Britain's energy balance since 1973.

Two factors explain why there has been such a radical change in the trend of energy consumption since 1973: energy saving and economic stagnation. Table 6.7 shows what has happened to production and the demand for energy in various sectors of the economy between 1960 and 1983. It also gives some information on the demand for energy by households.[16] From the table, we can see there has been a noticeable fall in the amount of energy required per unit of output since 1973; this fall has occurred throughout the economy, but it has been especially pronounced in manufacturing and agriculture. There has also been some reduction in the amount of energy consumed by households, despite the fact that consumers' expenditure in real terms has risen somewhat over the period. From Table 6.7, it is also clear that most of this fall in energy requirements has taken place quite recently – since 1979. Indeed, the fall in energy–output ratios since 1979 has been dramatic, especially in manufacturing industry, and especially in energy-intensive sectors, such as iron and steel or bricks and cement.

There are several factors responsible for the acceleration in the pace of energy saving since 1979. It is partly a delayed response to the huge cumulative rise in world energy prices, which began in 1973. This rise led to intensive efforts to economize on the use of energy, through measures such as better insulation of private and commercial premises, the redesign of products and the adoption of more energy efficient methods of production. However, because of the lags involved, the effect of these measures has only recently become visible in the form of lower energy requirements per unit of output or lower energy consumption by households. In the case of manufacturing industry, there is a further factor to consider. In the period 1979–82, the UK experienced a severe industrial crisis, in which the demand for UK manufactures slumped and manufacturing output fell dramatically. Some firms responded to this slump by modernizing their production methods. However, many firms simply closed down their least profitable plants and scrapped part of their equipment. As a rule, the plant and equipment concerned was relatively old and energy-inefficient, and its elimination has raised the energy efficiency of the manufacturing sector – as conventionally measured. With the disappearance of inefficient capital stock, the amount of energy which is *on average* required per unit of output is less than before. Thus, some of the reduction in energy–output ratios in the UK manufacturing sector since 1979 is a direct result of falling output in the slump of 1979–81. Many firms responded to this slump by scrapping their older, energy-inefficient capital stock and producing a reduced output on the newer, more efficient stock which remained. Such a saving in energy is, of course, entirely negative in char-

Table 6.7. *Economic growth and energy consumption in the UK, 1960–83*

	Annual percentage growth rate				
	(1) 1960–73	(2) 1973–83	(3) 1973–79	(4) 1979–83	(5) Col.(2)–Col.(1)
	Whole economy				
Total energy consumption[a]	2.3	−1.4	−0.1	−3.2	−3.7
GDP	3.0	1.0	1.4	0.4	−2.0
Energy/GDP ratio	−0.7	−2.4	−1.5	−3.6	−1.7
Total energy consumption[a]	2.3	−1.4	−0.1	−3.2	−3.7
Non-oil GDP[b]	2.8	0.3	0.5	−0.1	−2.5
Energy/non-oil GDP ratio	−0.5	−1.7	−0.6	−3.1	−1.2
	Manufacturing[c]				
All manufacturing:					
Energy consumption[d]	1.1	−4.4	−1.8	−8.3	−5.5
Output	3.0	−1.7	−0.7	−3.2	−4.7
Energy/output ratio	−1.9	−2.7	−1.1	−5.1	−0.8
Iron and steel:					
Energy consumption[d]	−0.6	−8.1	−4.4	−13.5	−7.5
Output	0.2	−4.8	−3.6	−6.6	−5.0
Energy/output ratio	−0.8	−3.3	−0.8	−6.9	−2.5
Bricks and cement:					
Energy consumption[d]	0.2	−6.5	−4.6	−9.3	−6.7
Output	4.1	−4.1	−4.0	−4.2	−8.2
Energy/output ratio	−3.9	−2.4	−0.6	−5.1	+1.5
Other manufacturing:					
Energy consumption[d]	2.1	−2.8	−0.4	6.5	−4.9
Output	3.1	−1.5	−0.4	−3.1	−4.6
Energy/output ratio	−1.0	−1.3	0.0	−3.4	−0.3
	Agriculture				
Energy consumption[d]	3.0	−4.6	−3.1	−6.9	−7.6
Output	2.6	2.0	0.5	4.2	−0.6
Energy/output ratio	0.4	−6.6	−3.6	−11.1	−7.0
	Other non-oil GDP				
Energy consumption[d,e]	1.4	−0.3	0.8	−1.8	−1.7
Output	3.0	0.8	1.0	0.6	−2.2
Energy/output ratio	−1.6	−1.1	−0.2	−2.4	−0.5
	Households				
Energy consumption[d,f]	1.8	0.9	1.8	−0.5	−0.9
Total expenditure	2.9	1.2	1.2	1.2	−1.7
Energy/expenditure ratio	−1.1	−0.3	0.6	−1.7	−0.8

Notes: [a] UK gross inland consumption of primary energy including petroleum for non-energy purposes
[b] GDP less extraction of oil and natural gas
[c] Excludes certain minor manufacturing activities which appear under the heading 'other trades' in official statistics
[d] Heat supplied basis
[e] Other transport, public administration, miscellaneous, commercial road transport (i.e. all road transport except cars and motorcycles)
[f] Includes non-commercial road transport (i.e. cars and motorcycles)

acter. It involves no innovation in production methods, and the apparent increase in energy efficiency is purchased at the expense of lower total output.[17] In reality, of course, both negative and positive forms of energy saving have occurred since 1979. Manufacturing output has certainly fallen, and many firms have scrapped their old equipment without replacing it. At the same time, however, many firms have taken positive measures to economize on the use of energy.[18]

Taking the period since 1973 as a whole, the pace of energy saving has been impressive. Moreover, this pace has *apparently* been faster than in the years preceding 1973. Table 6.7 shows what happened to energy consumption during the two periods 1960–73 and 1973–83. In both these periods there was an almost universal fall in energy–output ratios throughout the economy. However, in most sectors this fall was far more rapid in the second period than the first. This in itself suggests that the pace of energy saving has accelerated since 1973. Other evidence which points in the same direction can be gleaned from what has happened to the structure of demand. Since 1973, there have been many energy saving shifts of a permanent kind in the structure of demand. For example, the drive for fuel economy in road transport has led to the use of lighter cars, which contain less steel than the older cars they replace. In other areas, too, there have been economies in the use of steel, which have reduced the demand for this highly energy-intensive metal. Such permanent shifts in the structure of demand are a form of energy saving, which is just as real as any reduction in the energy required to produce a particular good or service. However, the importance of this factor should not be exaggerated. Many of the energy saving shifts in the pattern of demand since 1973 are pathological in character, being the outcome of economic stagnation and industrial decline. They would not have occurred if the UK's economic performance had been stronger over this period. For example, if GDP had grown faster since 1973 the demand for, and output of, manufactured goods would now be much greater than it is. The consumption of energy by the manufacturing sector would also be much greater, both absolutely and as a share of total energy consumption. This difference would be most striking in the case of bricks and cement or iron and steel, both of which are highly energy intensive (see Table 6.8) and both of which have been badly hit by the decline in investment since 1973.

This brings us to the question of economic growth. It is not widely appreciated how much of the improvement in the UK's energy balance since 1973, and especially since 1979, is a result of the country's poor macro-economic performance over this period. After rising at 2.8% per year between 1960 and 1973, non-oil GDP rose by a mere 0.3% between 1973 and 1983. If the pre-1973 growth rate had continued then, by 1983, non-oil GDP would have been 28% higher than it actually was, and GDP as a whole would have been 27% higher. Moreover, in the energy-intensive manufacturing sector, the extra output would

Table 6.8. *UK energy consumption by final user 1960–83 (heat supplied basis)*

	Million therms				
	1960	1966	1973	1979	1983
Manufacturing[a]					
Iron and steel	7092	6849	6575	5025	2924
Bricks and cement	1896	2090	1942	1470	1014
Other industries	10725	11883	14126	13826	10651
Total manufacturing	19713	20822	22643	20321	14589
Non-manufacturing					
Cars and motorcycles[b]	2103	3867	6172	6951	7538
Other road transport	2483	3019	3802	3974	3838
Other transport	4226	2718	2902	3112	2943
Domestic	14425	14407	14917	16501	15494
Public administration	2461	2944	3558	3792	3447
Agriculture	601	643	883	732	555
Miscellaneous	4519	5145	6157	6312	5775
Total non-manufacturing	30818	32743	38391	41374	39590
Grand total	50531	53565	61034	61695	54179

Notes: [a] Excludes certain minor manufacturing activities which are classified in official statistics under the heading 'other trades'
[b] Figures for 1960 and 1983 are estimates
Source: UK Energy Statistics

have been even more than these figures suggest for, as we have mentioned, this sector has suffered disproportionately from the economic stagnation and decline of the past decade. If economic growth had continued at the pre-1973 rate, then UK energy consumption would obviously be much greater than it is now. To determine accurately just how much greater would require a comprehensive analysis which is beyond the scope of the present work. However, rough estimates given in Chapter 7 suggest that that economic stagnation since 1973 has reduced energy consumption by 45–50 MTOE. Since total energy consumption in 1983 was 85 MTOE below the pre-1973 level, this implies that rather more than half the shortfall was caused by the slowdown in economic growth. The remainder was the result of other factors, of which energy saving innovation was probably the most important.

This completes our discussion of the factors which have influenced the UK's balance of trade in fuel since the Second World War. The broad picture can be summarized as follows. Prior to 1973, the main factors were the rise in petrol consumption and the fall in coal production which, between them, led to a growing deficit on the country's fuel account. This deficit increased dramatically following the massive increase in world oil prices in October 1973. Since then, there has been a remarkable turnaround, and the UK is now in surplus in fuel trade. This turnaround is due partly to North Sea oil and partly to a reversal of previous trends in energy consumption. The latter is, in turn, due mainly to the slowdown in economic growth since 1973, although energy conservation and other factors have also played a role. In quantitative terms, North Sea oil contributed 114 MTOE to the domestic supply of energy in 1983, whilst the slowdown in economic growth meant that energy consumption was some 45–50 MTOE less than would otherwise have been the case in 1983. These figures indicate the relative contribution of North Sea oil and economic stagnation to the improvement in the UK's balance of trade in energy over the period 1973–83.

Non-government services[19]

In this section, we consider the various services which appear in the commercial account of the balance of payments. As explained in Chapter 4, this account includes all services except those of a military, diplomatic or administrative nature, which are classified as government services and are placed in a separate account.[20] The adjective 'private' is often used to describe the kind of services which appear in the commercial account. However, this can be misleading. Many of these services are, or were until recently, provided by public corporations, such as British Airways or British Rail, or by public institutions, such as polytechnics or universities, and to describe them as private is a misnomer. For this reason we shall avoid the term 'private' altogether. Instead, we shall use the term 'non-government' to describe all of the services, public and private, which appear in the commercial account.

In the course of British history, the fortunes of her service trade have fluctuated widely. During the nineteenth and the early part of the twentieth centuries, when the UK dominated the world banking and shipping, income from these activities covered most, and sometimes all, of the large deficit on visible trade. However, under the impact of two world wars and a catastrophic slump, the international economy disintegrated and, as it did so, most of the UK's income from services evaporated. Net exports of non-government services, having peaked at around 6% of GDP in the last century, fell to around 1% of GDP by the end of the Second World War. For some years after the war, the service account remained almost in balance, but then suddenly, in the late 1960s, there was a dramatic improvement. Service exports rose strongly, whilst imports stagnated. By 1977, the surplus on non-government services had reached nearly $2\frac{1}{2}$% of GDP – well below the nineteenth-century peak, of course, but still quite a good performance by pre-war standards. However, 1977 marked a high point, and since then there has been a noticeable deterioration on Britain's service

Table 6.9. *UK trade in non-government services[a]; volume indices (1977 = 100)*

	1966	1968	1973	1977	1978	1979	1980	1981	1982	1983
Credits										
Sea transport	69	77	109	100	88	83	78	66	60	53
Civil aviation	40	46	77	100	118	135	146	143	133	136
Travel	33	39	52	100	92	90	79	70	69	74
Financial services[b] (net)	33	62	79	100	106	101	92	104	109	120
Other services	67	75	86	100	107	112	113	112	110	112
Total	54	64	84	100	100	100	96	91	88	89
Debits										
Sea transport	77	90	135	100	95	99	91	84	77	78
Civil aviation	48	56	80	100	115	141	147	151	160	159
Travel	94	74	114	100	123	162	206	220	218	225
Other services	63	67	66	100	90	90	90	87	93	92
Total	72	76	106	100	101	112	116	115	114	115

Notes: [a] Includes public corporation
[b] Includes services rendered by the UK private and public corporations to overseas governments, non-territorial organizations and their personnel
Sources: UK Balance of Payments; Economic Trends

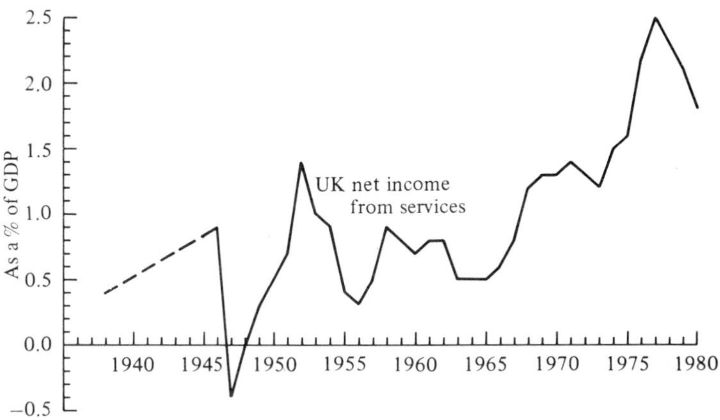

Fig. 6.7 UK net income from services as a percentage of GDP[1]
Source: Table 6.3, column (7)
Note: (1) Excluding Government Services

account. The volume of exports has fallen, whilst that of imports has risen (see Table 6.9), with the result that net income from services has shrunk both in real terms and in relation to GDP (see Fig. 6.7 and Table 6.3.). This deterioration is most striking in the realm of foreign travel and sea transport, where there has been a dramatic reversal of fortunes, but it can also be observed on a smaller scale in certain other service activities.

Table 6.10. *UK trade in non-government services*[a] *(£ million)*

	Average 1953–55	Average 1965–67	Average 1976–78	1981	1982	1983	1984
Credits							
Sea transport	532	799	3272	3784	3267	3054	3235
Civil aviation	39	180	1236	2359	2471	2665	3016
Travel	98	216	2209	2970	3168	3650	4169
Financial services (net)	{	128	1429	2013	2234	2658	2828
Construction work overseas	285	{ 42	757	995	1090	1102	1128
Oil and natural gas[b]			66	173	210	202	194
Other services[c]	}	423	2046	3432	3777	4446	5201
Total	954	788	11015	15726	16217	17777	19771
Debits							
Sea transport	500	803	3221	3944	3890	4067	4386
Civil aviation	39	151	1000	1922	2080	2237	2547
Travel	105	287	1268	3271	3640	4047	4617
Oil and natural gas	{ 188	{ 336	653	598	758	687	756
Other services			1343	2057	2656	3199	3640
Total	832	1577	7485	11792	13024	14237	15946
Balance							
Sea transport	+32	−4	+51	−160	−623	−1013	−1151
Civil aviation	0	+29	+236	+437	+391	+428	+469
Travel	−7	−71	+941	−301	−472	−397	−448
Financial services	{	+128	+1429	+2013	+2234	+2658	+2828
Construction work overseas	+97	+42	+757	+995	+1090	+1102	+1128
Oil and natural gas		{ +87	−587	−425	−548	−485	−562
Other services	}		+703	+1375	+1121	+1247	+1561
Total	+122	+211	+3530	+3934	+3193	+3540	+3825

Notes: [a] Includes public corporations
[b] Services associated with exploration for and production of oil and natural gas
[c] Excludes services rendered by UK private sector to overseas governments, non-territorial organizational and foreign military force
Source: HMSO, *United Kingdom Balance of Payments*

Table 6.10 gives a breakdown of the service account over the past thirty years. During these years, there have been some noticeable changes in the relative importance of the various items in this account and in their net contribution to the balance of payments. For instance, the importance of sea transport has fallen considerably, although it still absorbs nearly a third of all service payments and earns one-sixth of all service revenue. A major factor behind this decline in the importance of shipping has been the reorientation of Britain's trade away from the Commonwealth towards Western Europe (see Chapter 9), where distances are smaller and sea transport plays less of a role.

The main growth areas in the service account have been: civil aviation, travel, construction and finance. Let us consider each of these items in turn. The expansion of civil aviation and travel reflects both the importance of air transport in the modern world and the rise of mass tourism in the form of package tours and the like. Earnings from overseas construction work have benefited from the huge construction boom in the OPEC countries following the rise in oil prices since 1973. At the same time, there has been a recession in the domestic construction industry within the UK itself, and this has forced building contractors and consultants to seek out new opportunities abroad.

The greatly enhanced role of financial services is due to the renewed importance of the City of London as a world financial centre. When the world economy disintegrated during the inter-war period, the City lost many of its former functions. The range of activities shrank, and its role was limited to servicing the Commonwealth and other sterling area countries. Naturally, this reduced the City's earnings of foreign exchange. However, in the 1960s, the City's fortunes improved dramatically. During this period, international trade and finance were liberalized throughout the advanced capitalist world, and there was an explosive growth in international banking and related activities, using the dollar as a common currency. With government help and encouragement, amongst other factors, much of this new business was attracted to London, and the City became the base for British, US and other banks operating in the mushrooming Eurodollar market. There was also a parallel growth in underwriting, brokerage and similar activities, with the result that London became once again an international financial centre of considerable importance.[21]

Another item, which has figured quite prominently in the service account over the past decade, has been the complex of activities associated with the North Sea oil and gas programme. When this programme first began, substantial payments were made by the UK to foreign companies engaged in exploration and development work in the North Sea. However, these payments are now beginning to tail off as the programme reaches maturity, and this item is likely to be less important in the future.

Amongst the various services explicitly identified in Table 6.10, the most consistent net earners have been civil aviation, finance and construction. Most striking, perhaps, if only because it is not widely known, is the case of construction. Taking into account the activities of architects, surveyors, engineers and contractors, total UK revenue from construction work overseas has averaged more than 1,000 million a year during the 1980s. Indeed, the UK construction industry earns more from the export of services than do either the banks or the insurance companies of the City of London, whose contribution in this area is well known.[22]

At one time, in the mid-1970s, tourism was also a big net earner of foreign exchange for the UK, but this is no longer the case. For most of the 1980s the travel account has been in deficit, and the expenditure of UK visitors abroad has normally exceeded that of foreign visitors to the UK. The deterioration in the travel account is partly a result of the tight monetary and fiscal policies pursued by successive British governments in the period 1977–82. Such policies forced up sterling's real rate of exchange and made holidays in the UK very expensive. As a result, the number of foreign visitors coming to this country declined. Meanwhile, there was a spectacular rise in the number of

Table 6.11. *Number of foreign visits and expenditure*

	(1) To UK by overseas visitors	(2) Overseas by UK residents
	000s	000s
1972	7459	10695
1973	8167	11740
1974	8543	10783
1975	9490	11992
1976	10803	11560
1977	12281	11525
1978	12646	13443
1979	12486	15466
1980	12421	17507
1981	11452	19046
1982	11636	20611
1983	12464	20994
1984	13644	22072
1985	14577	21590

Source: British Business (various issues)

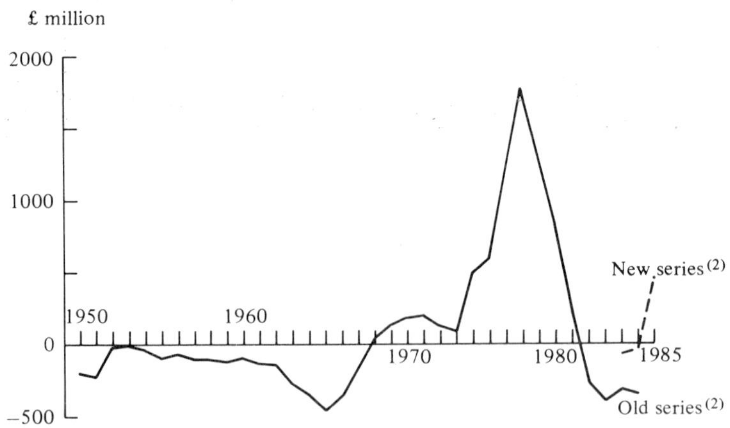

Fig. 6.8 Real value of UK net earnings from travel (at 1980 prices)[1]

Notes: (1) Exports minus imports at current prices deflated by GDP deflator
(2) The old series is consistent with the figures given in table 6.10; the new series is based on revised figures released as this book was going to press

British tourists holidaying abroad (Table 6.11). Following the devaluation of sterling since 1982, the situation has improved somewhat and the number of foreigners, especially Americans, visiting the UK has increased. However, whilst devaluation has certainly attracted more foreigners to the UK, it has not reversed the huge rise in the number of British holiday-makers abroad which took place during the period 1977–82, when the pound was over-valued. During this period, British package tour companies extended their overseas operations, and millions of British people acquired a new taste for holidays abroad. This represents a structural shift in business organization and consumer preferences, which cannot be reversed simply by devaluing the pound. There is clearly a ratchet effect at work in the realm of tourism, and this is a key factor in preventing a major improvement in the travel account. At the time of writing, the travel account is once again in surplus (see Fig. 6.8). However, this may well be an aberration and over the medium term the travel account could easily go back into deficit.[23] Even if this does not occur and the travel account remains in surplus, the amount involved will be quite small and will not compare to the massive surplus achieved in the mid-1970s.

Sea transport

The last major item to consider is shipping. As can be seen from Table 6.10, the sea transport account as a whole remained roughly in balance from the early 1950s right through to 1980. Despite the enormous sums of money involved, total expenditure and total receipts remained roughly in balance during this period, and deficits on some parts of the account were almost exactly offset by surpluses elsewhere. Since 1980, however, this situation has changed rapidly, and there are now clear signs that the sea transport account, as a whole, is moving into permanent and serious deficit.

The stability of the sea transport account prior to 1980 is remarkable and requires some explanation. Broadly speaking, two kinds of shipping are of major importance in this account: (1) the import/export trades, which involve the transport of goods between the UK and other countries, and (2) the cross-trades, which involve the transport of goods between one foreign country and another. The former can, in turn, be subdivided into near and short sea trades, which involve trade between the UK and nearby countries in Europe and the Mediterranean, and deep sea trades, which involve trade between the UK and distant continents. Tables 6.12 and 6.13 give some indication of how British shipping performed in these various trades in the decade prior to 1980. In the near and short sea trades there was a slight improvement, and the share of UK-registered ships rose a little during this period (see Table 6.12). However, this modest improvement was overshadowed by what happened in the value deep sea trades,

Table 6.12. *International seaborne trade of the United Kingdom*

	Share of cargo carried by UK registered vessels (by weight)			
	percent			
	1968	1974	1980	1983
Imports				
Total-all trades	32	29	31	25
Near and short sea trades	27	27	34	25
Deep sea trades	36	30	28	26
Exports				
Total-all trades	45	44	37	24
Near and short sea trades	40	43	40	27
Deep sea trades	59	49	22	11

Source: UK Annual Abstract of Statistics (various issues)

Table 6.13. *The UK sea transport account, 1973–83 (Net earnings £ million)*

	Average 1973–75	Average 1976–78	1979	1980	1981	1982	1983	1984
Freight revenue on UK import/export trade	−443	−535	−912	−931	−1228	−1237	−1374	−1582
Freight revenue on cross-trades[a]	+1278	+1516	+1812	+1776	+1754	+1303	+1205	+1309
Charter revenue	−294	−193	−78	−49	−1	−217	−282	−432
Passenger revenue	+60	+110	+134	+155	+156	+226	+261	+281
Disbursements[b]	−642	−847	−829	−810	−841	−698	−823	−736
Total[c]	−42	+51	+127	+141	−160	−623	−1013	−1151

Notes: [a] Trade between countries other than the UK
[b] Bunkers, port charges, etc.
[c] Totals may not add because of rounding errors
Source: HMSO *UK Balance of Payments* 1984, 1985

where British shipping suffered an enormous loss in market share. In 1968, UK-registered ships carried 59% by weight of all British exports to America, Asia and the other distant continents. By 1980, this share had fallen to 22% (see Table 6.12). On the import side a similar though less spectacular decline occurred. As a result of these losses, there was a large and growing deficit on the import–export section of the sea transport account (see Table 6.13). However, prior to 1980, this deficit was offset by an equally large and growing surplus on cross-trades (see Table 6.13). Having been driven out of the deep sea trades, it appears that British operators responded by expanding their activities in the area of cross-trading, and the revenue they earned was sufficient to keep the sea transport account, as a whole, in balance right up to 1980.

Table 6.14. *Merchant vessels [a] of 500 gross tons and over registered in the UK[b] (Thousand gross tons)*

	1939 3 September	1950	1969	1977	1978	1980	1983
Passenger	3916	2937	1245	654	614	617	602
Cargo liners	9946	10315	5452	2923	2546	1942	1099
Container vessels			194	1624	1827	1600	1543
Tramps			1904	882	743	554	372
Bulk carriers			3265	8181	7174	6428	3911
Tankers	3029	3946	10215	15797	15173	14578	8367
Total	16891	17198	22274	30061	28078	25769[c]	15894

Notes: [a] Steam and motor vessels only, excluding miscellaneous craft
[b] End of year
[c] The discrepancy of 50 thousand gross tons in the total for 1980 was present in the original statistics

Since 1980 the situation just described has changed dramatically for the worse. In the deep sea trades, the long-term decline has continued, and foreign ships now dominate Britain's commerce with distant continents: by 1983, only 11% by weight of all British exports in the deep sea trades were carried in UK-registered ships and only 26% of imports (see Table 6.12). Meanwhile, previous gains in the near and short sea trades have been reversed and after a decade of growth the revenue from cross-trading has fallen away sharply (see Table 6.13).

Thus, the old balancing act – whereby surpluses in one area offset deficits in another – has come to an end, and there is now a general decline affecting every major aspect of UK shipping. The one area where this does not apply is passenger transport, where there has been some improvement (see Table 6.13). But the revenues in question are relatively small and do not affect the overall picture, which is one of decline. This general decline is reflected in a growing deficit on the sea transport account as a whole. By 1984, this deficit had reached 1,151 million (see Table 6.13) – a figure quite without precedent in British history.

The deterioration in the sea transport account since 1980 is not merely a cyclical phenomenon, but is structural in character and will be hard to reverse in the future. To see why, we need only examine what has happened to the UK shipping fleet in recent years (see Table 6.14). Between 1977 and 1983, the total tonnage of ships registered under the UK flag fell by nearly 50% – from 30 million gross tons to 16 million gross tons (see Table 6.14), and the decline is still continuing. This decline affects almost every kind of vessel, including oil tankers, bulk carriers and container ships.[24] Such a decline in the UK fleet has obvious implications for the future. Under ideal conditions, it would be difficult for British operators to regain the ground they have lost in recent years, but, with half their fleet gone, it is almost impossible. Indeed, some British operators have left shipping altogether and have gone into other lines of business so, in their case, the question of regaining lost ground does not even arise. Given what has happened to market shares and to the UK fleet, it is clear that a structural shift has occurred. For the foreseeable future, the UK will continue to have a large deficit on her sea transport account.

Why has all this occurred? Most writers on the subject agree in general terms, but their stress varies (and so too do their remedies). Some, like the Conservative Party's Institute for Policy Studies, stress the high wages and manning levels, which, according to them, have made British ships uncompetitive.[25] Others, like the National Union of Seamen, stress unfair competition from foreign ship operators, who frequently enjoy a degree of protection and state support far greater than that received by UK operators.[26] Other analyses stress the world shipping recession which, they claim, has delivered a body-blow to a UK industry already weakened by the preceding factors. To this list must be added another factor which, although often mentioned, is rarely given the importance it deserves. We are referring, of course, to the strong pound. The sustained appreciation in the value of sterling, which took place between 1976 and 1981, forced up the operating costs of British ship operators, especially labour costs, and put them at a severe disadvantage in competition with their foreign rivals. As a result, markets were lost, profit margins were squeezed, ships were sold off and orders for new ships dried up. Of course, the strong pound does not explain everything, and the other factors listed were also important. Even so, it was a major factor behind both the decline in the UK fleet and the large deficit which has appeared in the sea transport account. Since 1982, the pound has depreciated a fair amount against other currencies. However, the damage has been done, and it will be a long time, if ever, before British shipping recovers and the deficit on sea transport is eliminated.

Determinants of the service balance

This mention of the exchange rate brings us to more general questions concerning the service account. So far, the discussion has focussed on particular items in this account, but little has been said about the systematic factors influencing it. A useful starting-point is to compare the UK's post-war trade performance in manufactures with that in services. For most of the post-war period, services have performed better than manufactures and, despite recent problems, there is still a large surplus on the service account, whilst UK manufacturing trade is now in deficit. This suggests that the UK is comparatively better at producing services than manufactures. Or, to put it another way, the UK has a comparative advantage in producing services. Such a comparative advantage can arise either because a country is particularly good at producing services, or because it is particularly bad at producing other things. In the case of the UK, both propositions are true. The British service sector is often more advanced than that of its foreign rivals or has peculiar advantages, whilst the UK manufacturing industry has been falling behind that of other countries.

Let us consider, first of all, the service sector itself. In the financial sphere, the City of London was uniquely placed during the 1960s and early 1970s to profit from the new opportunities arising in international banking and related activities. The City had long experience of international finance; it had an already established network of overseas operations based largely on the sterling area; it was actively encouraged and supported by successive governments; and it was relatively free from the legal restrictions which hampered its potential rivals in the USA and Continental Europe. In the field of civil aviation, British carriers, both public and private, have led the way in developing non-scheduled services. In construction, as well, British firms have a high reputation and considerable overseas experience, and they were well placed to profit from the post-1973 construction boom in the OPEC countries. Finally, in the realm of tourism and education, the UK has the enormous advantage of being an English-speaking country, where foreign tourists can practise their English and foreign students can learn the world's leading language. The UK is also appealing from a cultural and historical point of view.

The foregoing is an impressive list of intrinsic strengths, which give the UK service sectors an advantage in international competition. There are, however, certain disadvantages to consider. For example, Britain's weather is rather inhospitable, and most British people would prefer to holiday in the Mediterranean and other sunnier climes – if they could afford to. This factor has already harmed the tourist balance and is likely to be of growing importance in the future. In the realm of sea transport, British operators have the disadvantage that their own country's trade is open to all comers, whilst that of their rivals is often protected by law, and restrictions are used to keep out British operators. The same is true in insurance.[27] Thus, British service exporters suffer from a number of disadvantages. But these are outweighed by the advantages described earlier, and there is no doubt that on balance Britain's service sector is intrinsically strong by international standards. This intrinsic strength helps to explain why the UK still enjoys a surplus in international trade in services.

So much for the intrinsic reasons why services have performed comparatively well over the past thirty years. There are also extensive reasons which derive from the poor performance of British manufacturing industry. This poor performance shows up most clearly in the realm of labour productivity. Although rising absolutely, labour productivity in British manufacturing industry has been falling relative to that in other advanced countries over the past thirty years, and output per worker is now well below the level achieved elsewhere (see

Table 6.15. *International comparisons of productivity in 1980*

	GDP per head of population	Output per employee in	
		Whole economy	Manufacturing
Britain	100	100	100
Germany	132–134	134–140	152–163
US	153–186	159–201	276–302
France	134–138	150	180
Belgium	115–132	140	180
Netherlands	102–114	150	230
Italy	84–88	110	150
Japan	113–112	105	200

Source: National Institute Economic Review, August 1982, p. 11

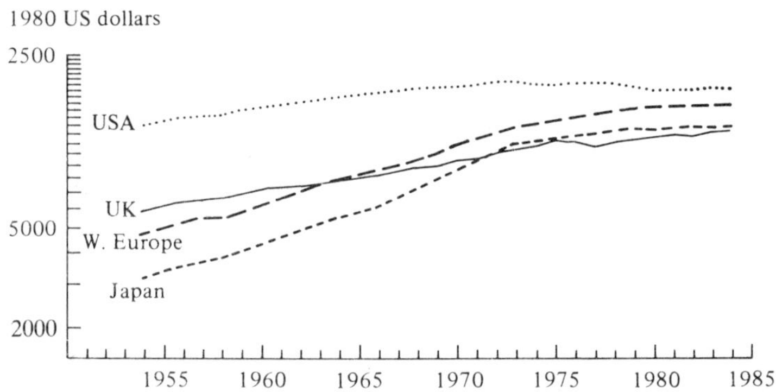

Fig. 6.9 Real cost of labour in selected countries[1]
Note: (1) Employee compensation per year, before tax and including employer's social security contributions measured in 1980 US dollars at purchasing power parity exchange rates. The series for Western Europe is an unweighted geometric mean of the series for France, Germany and Italy.

Table 6.15). As a result of her performance in manufacturing, the UK has become a relatively poor country in which real wages and real incomes, in general, are now lower than in many other Western countries (see Fig. 6.9). This process of relative impoverishment has strengthened the service account in several ways. The relative decline in real wages in the UK has helped the service sector compete with its foreign rivals in North America and Western Europe and given a boost to the country's service exports. Moreover, the slow growth in real incomes has restrained the UK's imports of income-elastic services, such as foreign holidays, whilst exports of these services have been aided by the huge rise in real incomes which has occurred in Western Europe and Japan since the Second World War. Thus, the UK's inferior industrial performance has turned the

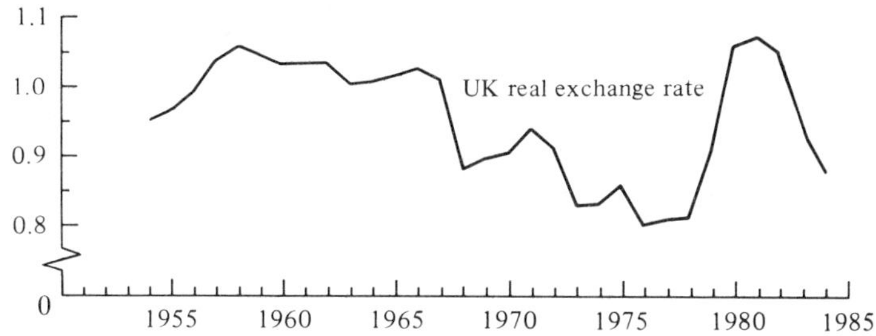

Fig. 6.10 UK real exchange rate[1]

Note: (1) UK real exchange rate $= \frac{\text{Consumer prices in the UK,}}{\text{Consumer prices abroad}}$, where consumer prices in each country are converted to US dollars at current exchange rates. The denominator in the expression is the unweighted geometric mean of the cost of living in the following countries: France, Germany, Italy, Japan and the USA.

country into a relatively poor, low-wage economy and has encouraged her to specialize in the provision of services to foreigners. This helps to explain why there is a surplus on the UK's service account. However, the importance of this factor should not be exaggerated. Poor industrial performance is only part of the story. As we have already mentioned, the UK service sector is strong in its own right and enjoys certain historic advantages over its foreign rivals. Even if British industry had performed better and real incomes had grown rapidly over the past thirty years, these historic advantages would have remained and the service account would probably still be in surplus, although not of course to the same extent.

The shifting pattern of comparative advantage just described is undoubtedly one of the factors explaining the long-term evolution of UK trade in services. However, in the short and medium term other factors have also been important, especially the enormous variations in sterling's real rate of exchange which have occurred in recent years.

In considering how the exchange rate influences trade in services, an allowance must be made for the fact that rates of inflation differ between countries. When such an allowance is made, the result is an index called the 'real rate of exchange'. This index measures the extent to which a different from average rate of inflation in the UK is offset or reinforced by changes in the nominal rate of exchange between sterling and other currencies. Figure 6.10 shows how sterling's real rate of exchange has behaved since 1955. Between 1967 and 1976, there was a sustained decline in the real value of sterling, a development which gave a significant boost to UK service exports. However, this decline was reversed in late 1976, when the then Labour government under pressure from the IMF implemented a severely deflationary policy which was pursued even more rigorously by the Conservative government which replaced it from 1979 onwards. The effect on sterling of this new policy was dramatic. Within a few years the real value of the pound rose by 40% – an appreciation almost without precedent in Britain or any other advanced capitalist country. This huge appreciation is often blamed on North Sea oil, which came on stream at around the same time but, as we argue elsewhere, this was only one of the factors responsible, and the main cause was deflationary policies pursued by governments of the day. With a more expansionary policy, the economy would have grown faster, the demand for imports would have been greater, interest rates would have been lower, and sterling would never have appreciated to anything like the same degree.[28]

The huge rise in the real value of sterling in the years 1977 to 1981 dealt a severe blow to the UK service account. Holidays in this country became extremely expensive in comparison with holidays abroad (see Fig. 6.11) and as a result there was a massive shift in the flow of tourists away from the UK. In most other services relative prices rose by much less, either because of international competition, as in the case of sea freight and finance, or because of international agreements, as in the case of scheduled air fares. However, even in these other services, the appreciation in sterling had a harmful effect on net exports. By increasing the relative costs paid by the UK service sector, this appreciation made exporting unprofitable and led to a diversion of capital into other activities. A clear example of this can be seen in the case of sea transport, where a combination of world recession and an overvalued pound has led British shipowners to sell off much of their fleet or else switch to flags of convenience, which allow them to cut costs by employing cheap Third World labour.

In early 1981, the rise in sterling came to an end and its real value began to fall once again towards a more normal level. This fall has helped service exports, and the service account, as a whole, has been improving. However, because of the damage inflicted during the period of sterling's extreme overvaluation, this improvement is patchy and certain service activities, such as shipping, may never recover.

The above discussion may be summarized as follows. The long-term evolution of the service account has been influenced by two major factors: intrinsic strengths in the provision of internationally traded services, together with a growing weakness in manufacturing industry. Together these factors have given the UK a comparative advantage in services, relative to manufactures, and they explain why there is now a large surplus on the service account as a whole. In addition to these underlying forces, there is also the effect of exchange rate

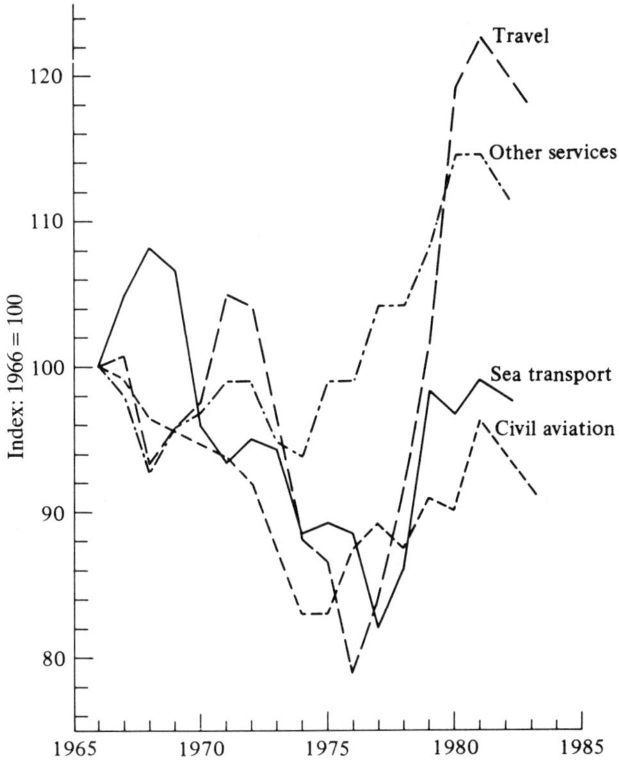

Fig. 6.11 Relative price of UK services (exports/imports) (1966 = 100)

variations to consider. British service exports were severely harmed, in some cases permanently, by the overvaluation of sterling during the late 1970s and early 1980s. During these years, the previous improvement in the service account was reversed, and the surplus on this account reduced. Since 1982, the pound has fallen back again to a more normal level, and the service account has partially recovered. However, in real terms, the surplus on this account is still below the peak achieved in the mid-1970s.

Non-government transfers

The final item in the commercial account of the balance of payments consists of non-government transfers, such as gifts, migrants' remittances and the like. These are of minor significance in the case of the UK, and at no time during the post-war period have such transfers exceeded 0.15% of GDP. This is in marked contrast to the situation in Continental Europe, where non-government

Table 6.16. *Migration to and from the UK (thousands)*

	Population at beginning of period	Immigration	Emigration	Net civilian migration[a]
1951–1961	50290	n.a.	n.a.	−70
1961–1971	52807	n.a.	n.a.	−320
1971–1981	55907	1862	2248	−386[b]

Notes: [a] Minus sign indicates net outflow
[b] The figure for 1971–81 is obtained by adding together the preceding two columns
Source: UK Annual Abstract of Statistics

transfers have occurred on a massive scale and have been a major element in the balance of payments of certain countries. This difference can be explained as follows.

Prior to the economic crisis in 1973, there was a continuous flow of migrant labour from Southern to Northern Europe as the poor and unemployed from Greece, Portugal, Spain and elsewhere sought work in West Germany, the Netherlands and other prosperous countries. Under the Continental 'guestworker' system, such migrant workers are often classified as temporary residents and forced to leave their dependants behind in their country of origin. To maintain these dependants migrant workers have to send much of their wages back home and the result has been a massive transfer of funds from Northern to Southern Europe. Since the crisis the flow of new migrants has slackened but, even so, the scale of transfers is still considerable.

The UK's experience with migrant labour differs from that of other North European countries in two respects. First, the UK has not been a net importer of labour during the post-war period. There has, it is true, been considerable immigration from Ireland and the Black Commonwealth, but this has been more than offset by emigration to the White Commonwealth and elsewhere, with the result that Britain has actually been a small net exporter of labour (Table 6.16). The second difference is concerned not with the scale of migration, but with its character. Although increasingly strict, the UK's immigration laws have usually treated immigrants as permanent residents, and most of them have eventually been allowed to settle here with their families. As a result, immigrants living in the UK have relatively few dependants to support in their country of origin, and the amount of money they send home is, therefore, fairly small. Similar considerations apply to the people who have left the UK over the past thirty years. Most of them have emigrated permanently with their families; they have few dependants to support in this country, and they send relatively little money home.

Thus, in the case of the UK migration has been a rather balanced affair, in which large flows of labour into and out of the country have almost cancelled out. At the same time, most migration has been of a permanent kind and has not, therefore, generated the huge international transfer of funds associated with the Continental guestworker system. These two factors explain why non-government transfers are so much less important in the UK than on the Continent.

Conclusions

In this chapter we have described a number of autonomous factors which influenced UK trade in non-manufactures since 1950. Most of these factors have had a positive impact on the balance of payments, either reducing expenditure on imported non-manufactures or increasing revenue from the export of such items. Amongst the positive factors have been a massive fall in the real cost of imported food and raw materials during the 1950s, greater domestic food production, economies in the use of materials, North Sea oil and the rise of new service activities. There have also been some negative factors at work. The rise in world oil prices in 1973, for example, greatly increased the cost of Britain's fuel imports, although its negative impact on the balance of payments was later reversed when North Sea oil came on stream a few years later. Moreover, such negative factors are the exception and, taken as a whole, the autonomous factors described in this chapter have had a positive impact on the balance of payments. They are responsible for most of the huge improvement in Britain's balance of trade in non-manufactures which has occurred since 1950. However, autonomous factors do not account for all of this improvement. Part of it is merely a by-product of the UK's poor overall economic performance since 1950. The British economy has grown slowly by international standards, and her manufacturing sector has become increasingly backward compared to those of other Western countries. Indeed, since 1973, non-oil GDP has remained virtually constant, and manufacturing output is now below the level achieved in that year. Economic stagnation has helped to strengthen the balance of trade in non-manufactures by holding down the demand for non-manufactured imports of all kinds and, in some cases, encouraging the export of such items.

Thus, the long-term improvement in the UK balance of trade in non-manufactures is partly a result of economic stagnation, caused by the poor performance of her manufacturing industry, and partly a result of autonomous factors whose operation was largely independent of the country's manufacturing performance. Such autonomous factors would still have operated in much the same form even if the UK economy had grown more rapidly and her manufacturing industry had been more dynamic. Several obvious questions arise at this point. How much of the long-term improvement in UK non-manufacturing trade is the result of autonomous factors? And how much is merely a reflection of poor industrial performance and slow economic growth? It is to these questions the next chapter is devoted.

7

UK trade and economic growth: a quantitative assessment

Introduction

The aim of this chapter is to quantify the effect on UK trade of some of the factors described in the previous chapter. The questions it sets out to answer are as follows. How much of the improvement in the UK's balance of trade in non-manufactures in the period since 1950 has been due to poor industrial performance and slow economic growth? And how much has been the result of other autonomous factors that have influenced UK trade in non-manufactures? Of these factors, which have been the most important and how great has been their impact? Such questions, by their very nature, cannot be answered with great accuracy, and the best one can hope for is some general indication of the orders of magnitude involved. To provide such an indication, we consider a number of hypothetical scenarios, which explore the link between economic growth and trade in non-manufactures. These scenarios indicate, under a variety of assumptions, what might have happened to trade in non-manufactures if UK industrial performance had been stronger and the economy had grown more rapidly over the period 1950–83.

After examining the various scenarios, we conclude that poor economic performance is of only minor importance in explaining the massive improvement which has occurred in the UK balance of trade in non-manufactures since 1950. This improvement is mainly the result of autonomous factors, such as greater domestic food production, economies in the use of materials, cheaper food and material imports, new service exports, North Sea oil, etc. Given these autonomous factors, there would still have been a massive improvement in the non-manufacturing balance since 1950, even if industrial performance had been stronger and the economy had grown more rapidly over this period.

The final section of this chapter is concerned with trade in manufactures. In Chapter 5 we described how the UK balance of trade in manufactures has undergone a massive deterioration since 1950. Using the device of hypothetical scenarios, we now consider how much of this deterioration can be ascribed to poor industrial performance and how much to other factors. Our conclusion is that poor industrial performance is certainly one of the factors responsible for what has happened to the manufacturing balance. However, it is not the principal factor. The deterioration in the manufacturing balance is mainly a response to developments elsewhere in the balance of payments; it is mainly a counterpart to the autonomous improvements which have occurred in non-manufacturing trade. In 1950, the UK required a huge surplus in trade in manufactures to finance the huge deficit on her trade in non-manufactures. This huge deficit in non-manufactures has now disappeared, and with it has gone the need for a huge surplus in manufactures. The UK no longer has a huge surplus on her trade in manufactures because she no longer needs one, and poor industrial performance has only a marginal bearing on the matter. This is the main conclusion of the present chapter.

The hypothetical scenarios

To analyse UK trade since 1950 we shall make use of three hypothetical scenarios covering the period 1950–83. All three of these scenarios make exactly the same assumptions about economic growth and the exchange rate. However, they differ in their assumptions concerning foreign trade. The assumptions which they have in common are as follows:

(1) real GDP per capita rises at an annual rate of 3.0% over the period 1950–83. This is considerably faster than the actual growth rate of 2.1% per annum, and as a result by 1983 hypothetical GDP is some 40% above its actual level.

(2) the real rate of exchange follows a smooth trajectory in the years following the discovery and exploitation of North Sea oil, appreciating gradually after 1976 to the level actually observed in 1983. Thus, under the hypothetical scenarios, the UK avoids the massive but temporary overvaluation of her currency which caused the economy so much harm during the period 1979–82.

The above assumptions have opposite implications for the balance of trade in non-manufactures: *ceteris paribus*, faster economic growth implies a more rapid increase in the volume of net imports, whilst a lower exchange rate implies a reduction in this volume. The three hypothetical scenarios differ in their assumptions concerning the magnitude of these effects. At one extreme is the *Worst Case Scenario*, which takes a very pessimistic view. Under this scenario, the negative impact of fast growth on the non-manufacturing balance is very large, whilst the positive impact of a lower exchange rate is very small. At the other extreme is the *Best Case Scenario*, which takes a far more optimistic

Table 7.1. *Impact of faster growth on UK non-manufacturing trade: assumptions*

	Volume of trade (1983 = 100)						
	Food, beverages and tobacco		Basic materials		Non-government services[a]		
	Exports	Imports	Exports	Imports	Exports	Imports	GDP
Actual							
1973	61	101	64	110	94	92	91
1977	77	100	78	93	112	87	92
1979	86	101	90	107	112	97	98
1983	100	100	100	100	100	100	100
Hypothetical scenarios							
1983 best case (B)	105	105	105	145	125	125	140
1983 intermediate (I)	102	110	103	155	120	130	140
1983 worst case (W)	100	115	100	165	115	135	140

	Energy (million tonnes of oil or oil equivalent)									
	Production					Consumption[b]				
	Coal	Oil	Natural gas	Hydro & nuclear	Total	Coal	Oil	Natural gas	Hydro & nuclear	Total
Actual										
1973	78	0	25	7	110	78	109	26	7	220
1977	72	38	35	10	155	72	90	37	10	209
1979	72	78	34	9	193	76	91	42	2	219
1983	70	115	34	12	231	66	70	44	12	192
Hypothetical scenarios										
1983 best case (B)	79	115	34	14	242	85	110	44	14	253
1983 intermediate (I)	79	115	34	14	242	85	118	44	14	261
1983 worst case (W)	79	115	34	14	242	85	126	44	14	269

Notes: [a] Includes private transfers
[b] Gross inland consumption including petroleum for non-energy uses

view on both counts. Between these two extremes lies the more realistic *Intermediate Scenario*.

Table 7.1 lays out the assumptions concerning foreign trade which underlie the various scenarios. Before discussing these assumptions in detail, one general observation is in order. The numbers shown in Table 7.1 are not estimates in a formal econometric sense. They are merely informed guesses reflecting our subjective judgement of the likely magnitudes involved and the plausible range of variation. In choosing these numbers, we have consulted some of the main econometric models of the UK economy. However, for a variety of reasons, these models are of only limited use in the present context, and the information they provide must be supplemented by evidence of a less formal kind.[1] This is particularly the case for trade in services, whose treatment in existing econometric models of the UK economy is extremely sketchy.[2] It also applies to trade in energy, where observed historical relationships may be a poor guide to what might have happened if the British economy had grown at the faster rate which is assumed under the hypothetical scenarios.

Let us now examine Table 7.1. For each scenario and each major category of non-manufactures, the table shows the assumed volume of imports and exports. Information is given in the form of index numbers, taking the actual volume in 1983 as 100. For comparison the actual volume of trade in selected years (1983 = 100) is also given. Running quickly through the individual items shown in Table 7.1, the picture is as follows.

Food, beverages and tobacco

The income-elasticity of demand for imports of this kind, taken as a whole, is low. The hypothetical volume of imported food, beverages and tobacco in 1983 is between 5 and 15% above the actual level, depending on the scenario concerned. On the other hand, the volume of exports is only 0 to 5% higher than the actual figure. This small increase is an allowance for the delayed effect of a lower rate of exchange in the period 1979–82.

Basic materials

If the economy had grown at the faster rate of 3.0% per annum assumed under the hypothetical scenarios, then by 1983 manufacturing output would have been 50–60% above the level actually achieved. As a result, the demand for imported materials would have been much greater. To allow for this, we assume an increase in the volume of imported materials of between 45 and 65%, as compared to the actual level in 1983. Exports of materials are assumed not to alter very much.

Non-government services

Under the hypothetical scenarios, the assumed volume of imported services in 1983 is between 25 and 35% above the actual level for that year. This is a plausible range, given that hypothetical GDP in 1983 is 40% above its actual level; and the exchange rate during the period 1979–82 is well below its actual level. It is also assumed that service exports are between 15 and 25% above than their actual level in 1983. There are two reasons why service exports are higher under the hypothetical scenarios. On the one hand, manufacturing industry performs much better under these scenarios than it did in reality, and the result is a much greater volume of manufactured exports. This in turn generates a demand for complementary service exports in such areas as shipping, banking and insurance. Service exports are also helped by the exchange rate. We have argued in the previous chapter that the UK's service exports were permanently damaged by the large, but temporary, overvaluation of sterling which took place during the period 1979–82. Under the hypothetical scenarios this over-appreciation does not occur and hence service exports avoid the damage which it caused. In view of these considerations, an additional 15 to 25% in the volume of service exports seems plausible.

Fuels

Trade in fuels is discussed in detail in Chapter 12, and here we shall mention only the main points. The hypothetical scenarios assume a modest rise in the output of both nuclear electricity and coal (as compared to the level actually achieved in 1983). There is no change in the output of hydro-electricity, oil or natural gas. Moreover, it assumed that coal imports are limited by handling capacity to 5.9 MTOE [= 10 million tonnes of coal by weight], whilst natural gas imports are limited by available supply to 10 MTOE. On the demand side, an energy coefficient of between 0.8 and 1.0 is assumed. This implies that energy consumption under the hypothetical scenarios is between 32 and 40% above its actual level in 1983.[3]

The non-manufacturing balance

Table 7.2 shows what happens to the UK balance of trade in non-manufactures under the assumptions just described. In this table, the balance of trade in 1983 in each of the items is shown both in absolute terms and as a percentage of GDP. Looking at the figures, the following points stand out. In the actual economy, there was a surplus in non-manufacturing trade in 1983 equal to £4,400 million, or 1.5% of GDP at market prices. However, under the hypothetical scenarios, non-manufacturing trade as a whole is in deficit in 1983. Depending on the scenario concerned, the size of this deficit ranges from £2,100 million to £9,000 million. As a fraction of GDP, the deficit lies in the range of 0.5 to 2.1%. Thus, under the hypothetical scenarios, the balance of trade in non-

Table 7.2. *UK balance of trade in non-manufactures in 1983*

	Food, beverages and tobacco	Basic materials	Non-government services[a]	Fuel	Total[b]
£ million in 1983 prices					
Actual	−3,000	−2,400	+3,500	+6,200	+4,400
Hypothetical:					
Best case (B)	−3,100	−4,100	+4,400	+700	−2,100
Intermediate (I)	−3,600	−4,600	+2,900	−300	−5,600
Worst case (W)	−4,100	−5,000	+1,300	−1,200	−9,000
Percent of GDP at market prices					
Actual	−1.0	−0.8	+1.2	+2.1	+1.5
Hypothetical:					
Best case (B)	−0.7	−1.0	+1.0	+0.2	−0.5
Intermediate (I)	−0.9	−1.1	+0.7	−0.1	−1.3
Worst case (W)	−1.0	−1.2	+0.3	−0.3	−2.1

Notes: [a] Includes private transfers equal to £200 million in 1983
[b] Columns may not add because of rounding error

manufactures is worse than in the actual economy. The difference is most striking in the case of fuels. In the actual economy, the UK had a surplus of £6,200 million on her fuel account in 1983. However, under the Best Case Scenario, there is a surplus on this account of only £700 million whilst under the remaining scenarios this account is in deficit. In the case of non-fuel items, the balance of trade under the hypothetical scenarios is usually worse than in the actual economy, but the difference is less striking than in the case of fuels.

Historical perspective

In the previous chapter we described the massive improvement which the UK has experienced in her balance of trade in non-manufactures since 1950. Under all three hypothetical scenarios, the improvement in this period is smaller, though still very large. This can be seen from Table 7.3. In the actual economy, the non-manufacturing balance improves by 14.6 percentage points between 1950 and 1983 (from −13.1% of GDP in 1950 to +1.5% in 1983). Under the hypothetical scenarios, the size of the improvement in the non-manufacturing balance varies from +12.6% to +11.0% of GDP. Thus, even if the economy had grown at the much faster rate envisaged by these scenarios, there would still have been an enormous improvement in the non-manufacturing balance. Since the

Table 7.3. *UK balance of trade in non-manufactures 1950–83 (% of GDP at market prices)*

	Food, beverages and tobacco	Basic materials	Non-government services[a]	Fuel	Total[b]
Balance of trade					
(1) 1950 actual and hypothetical	−6.8	−6.5	+0.5	−0.3	−13.1
(2) 1983 actual	−1.0	−0.8	+1.2	+2.1	+1.5
(3) 1983 hypothetical B	−0.7	−1.0	+1.0	+0.2	−0.5
(4) 1983 hypothetical I	−0.9	−1.1	+0.7	−0.1	−1.3
(5) 1983 hypothetical W	−1.0	−1.2	+0.3	−0.3	−2.1
Change in balance 1950–83					
(6) actual [(2)–(1)]	+5.8	+5.7	+0.7	+2.4	+14.6
(7) hypothetical B [(3)–(1)]	+6.1	+5.5	+0.5	+0.5	+12.6
(8) hypothetical I [(4)–(1)]	+5.9	+5.4	+0.2	+0.2	+11.8
(9) hypothetical W [(5)–(1)]	+5.8	+5.3	−0.2	0.0	+11.0

Notes: [a] Includes private transfers
[b] Columns may not add because of rounding errors

economy is performing well under the hypothetical scenarios, this improvement cannot be ascribed to poor economic performance. It is clearly a result of autonomous factors such as cheaper imports, increased domestic food production, economies in the use of materials etc.

Looking at Table 7.3, it is obvious that most of the historic improvement is concentrated in just two items: food and materials. The actual deficit on these items combined actually fell from 13.3% of GDP in 1950 to 1.8% in 1983, which represents an improvement of 11.5 points. A small part of the improvement was due to slow growth in the domestic economy, which held in check the demand for imports especially after 1973. But even when allowance is made for this factor, the improvement is still enormous. Under all three hypothetical high-growth scenarios the combined deficit in food and materials improves by more than 11 points between 1950 and 1983. Thus, the huge improvement in the food and materials balance since 1950 is not mainly the result of poor economic performance; it is primarily due to the autonomous factors which have reduced the cost of imported food and materials and reduced Britain's dependence on such imports.

In the case of services, the picture is somewhat different. In the actual economy, there was only a modest improvement in the service balance over the period 1950–83 as a whole (Table 7.3). Moreover, much of this improvement was due to slow economic growth which held back the demand for imported services. When allowance is made for slow growth, there is hardly any improvement at all in the service balance between 1950 and 1983.

The same remarks apply with even greater force in the case of fuel. In the actual economy there was a considerable improvement in the fuel balance between 1950 and 1983 (Table 7.3). However, this improvement was mainly the result of slow economic growth in the domestic economy and only a minor part of it was the result of autonomous factors such as North Sea oil. This is not to say that North Sea oil was not important, because it clearly was. The point is that the huge rise in oil prices in 1973 increased Britain's fuel deficit dramatically, whilst North Sea oil merely served to redress the balance by providing a domestic source of fuel. Taking all the autonomous factors together – the 1973 oil price rise, the 1979 price rise, North Sea oil, nuclear power etc. – their combined effect on the balance of trade in fuel is very small. It is this combined effect which is measured in lines (7) to (9) of Table 7.3.

To sum up: between 1950 and 1983, a huge improvement took place in the UK balance of trade in non-manufactures. Most of this improvement was the result of autonomous development in the realm of food and raw materials. Lower import proces, increased domestic food production, economies in the use of raw materials, the widespread use of synthetic materials and new patterns of consumer demand all helped to reduce expenditure on imported food and materials (net of exports), either absolutely or as a percentage of GDP over the period in question. There was also some improvement in the service balance, although this was negligible compared to what happened to food and materials. Finally, there was a considerable improvement in the fuel balance, which moved from deficit to surplus between 1950 and 1983. However, this latter improvement was almost entirely the result of poor economic performance, which held in check the demand for fuel at a time of rising domestic oil production after 1976. Had the economy grown faster, the UK balance of trade in fuel would have been much the same in 1983 as it was in 1950.

Trade in manufactures

So far, the discussion has been entirely concerned with trade in non-manufactures. However, one of the main themes of this book is that any major deficit on the non-manufacturing side of the balance of payments must, in the long run, be offset by a corresponding surplus on the manufacturing side. Only in this way can an economy remain financially viable. Moreover, any major and permanent change in the non-manufacturing balance must eventually be matched by a roughly equal and opposite change on the manufacturing balance.

Table 7.4. *UK commercial balance 1950–83 (% of GDP at market prices)*

	Non-manufactures	Manufactures	Total commercial balance
Balance of trade			
(1) 1950 actual and hypothetical	−13.1	+11.2	−1.9
(2) 1983 actual	+1.5	−0.5	+1.0
(3) 1983 hypothetical B	−0.5	+0.5	0.0
(4) 1983 hypothetical I	−1.3	+1.3	0.0
(5) 1983 hypothetical W	−2.1	+2.1	0.0
Change in balance 1950–83			
(6) actual [(2)–(1)]	+14.6	−11.7	+2.9
(7) hypothetical B [(3)–(1)]	+12.6	−10.7	+1.9
(8) hypothetical I [(4)–(1)]	+11.8	−9.9	+1.9
(9) hypothetical W [(5)–(1)]	+11.0	−9.1	+1.9

Table 7.4 shows what happens to UK trade under the hypothetical scenarios during the period 1950–83. It also shows what happened in the actual economy during the same period. Let us describe this table briefly.

Line (1) shows the actual situation in 1950. Since the hypothetical scenarios coincide with the actual economy in 1950, line (1) also indicates the situation under the hypothetical scenarios in that year. Line (2) shows the actual situation in 1983, whilst lines (3) to (5) show the situation under each of the hypothetical scenarios also in 1983. Finally, lines (6)–(9) show how the various balances change between 1950 and 1983.

Looking at Table 7.4, several points stand out. In the closing year, 1983, there is a surplus on manufacturing trade under all three of the hypothetical fast-growth scenarios. This surplus is required because under all three scenarios there is a deficit on non-manufacturing trade which must be financed by earnings from the export of manufactures. In absolute terms, this manufacturing surplus is quite large. However, relative to GDP it is quite small. For example, under the Worst Case Scenario, the surplus on manufacturing trade is equal to 2.1% of GDP in 1983, whilst under the Best Case Scenario it is only 0.5% of GDP. Thus, if the UK economy had grown rapidly, as envisaged under the hypothetical scenarios, the country would have required a manufacturing surplus of between 0.5% and 2.1% of GDP to finance the trade deficit in non-manufactured goods and services.

Comparing the situation in 1983 with that in 1950, there is a massive deterioration in the manufacturing balance, both in the actual economy and under all three hypothetical scenarios. In the actual economy the manufacturing balance

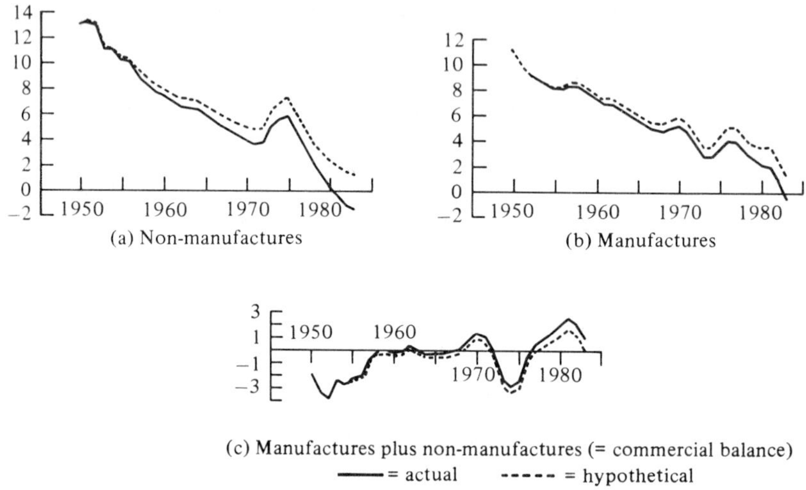

Fig. 7.1 UK balance of trade (% of GDP): actual and hypothetical

declines by 11.7 percentage points (from +11.2 percent of GDP in 1950 to −0.5% of GDP in 1983). Under the hypothetical scenarios, there is a fall of between 9.1 and 10.7 points. Although slightly less than in the actual economy, this is still a massive decline.

So far we have considered only the end points, 1950 and 1983. To provide a more complete picture, Fig. 7.1 shows what might have happened in the intervening years.[4] For convenience, the non-manufacturing balance is drawn with the scale inverted, so that an improvement in this balance appears as a downward movement. Moreover, for clarity, only the Intermediate Scenario is illustrated. The most striking feature of Fig. 7.1 is the degree of similarity between actual, historical experience and what happens under the hypothetical scenario. In each case there is a sharp deterioration in the non-manufacturing balance in 1951 as a result of higher import prices during the Korean War boom. This is then followed in each case by an almost continuous improvement, which lasts right up to 1983. The only major interruption occurs during the mid-70s and is caused by a sudden rise in the price of imported oil and other primary products. Looking now at the manufacturing balance, there is once again a clear similarity between the actual and hypothetical curves. In both cases, there is an almost continuous deterioration from 1951 onwards in the balance of trade in manufactures. The only major interruption occurs in the mid-70s, when an increase in net manufactured exports is required to help finance the greater deficit on non-manufacturing trade caused by inflated import prices.

Thus, the general feature is much the same both in the actual economy and under the hypothetical scenario. In each case there is a massive improvement in the non-manufacturing balance over the period 1950–83 and an almost equally massive deterioration in the manufacturing balance. The extent of change is greater in the actual economy than the hypothetical, fast-growth scenario, but the difference is fairly small and the general picture is much the same in each case. From this observation, it follows immediately that poor economic performance is not the main factor responsible for the transformation which has occurred in the structure of UK trade since 1950. This transformation is mainly the result of the autonomous factors whose effect is indicated by the hypothetical curves in Fig. 7.1.

Conclusions

The principal conclusions to be drawn from the preceding discussion are as follows. If the UK economy had been more successful and grown at the faster rate envisaged under the hypothetical scenarios, the balance of trade in non-manufactures would still have improved dramatically over the period 1950–83. Moreover, this improvement in the non-manufacturing balance would have induced a roughly equal and opposite change in the manufacturing balance. Thus, even if UK industry had been more dynamic and the economy had grown more rapidly, the surplus on manufacturing trade would still have fallen dramatically. The figures given in Table 7.4 suggest that of the 11.7% point deterioration in the manufacturing balance over the period 1950–83, between 9.1 and 10.7% points were a response to autonomous improvements in the non-manufacturing balance. The remainder was the result of poor industrial performance and of the resulting loss of international competitiveness.

8

UK trade structure in an international perspective

Introduction

In Chapter 6, we described the truly dramatic transformation which has occurred in the UK's foreign trade structure since the early 1950s. Thirty years ago, the UK had massive deficits in non-manufacturing trade and required equally massive surpluses in trade in manufactures in order to finance them. However, by the early to mid-1980s, the situation was radically different. The UK was no longer in deficit in non-manufacturing trade, and the overall structure of her foreign trade was much more balanced. Developments in the UK during this period give rise to an obvious question: was the UK's experience exceptional or did other advanced countries register a similar transformation in the structure of their foreign trade. To answer this question is the principal aim of the present chapter.

The discussion is organized as follows. We begin by focussing on developments in non-manufacturing trade as a whole, comparing the UK's experience in the period 1952–82 with that of twelve other OECD countries. This is followed by an analysis of comparative trends in each of the main areas of non-manufacturing trade: food, raw materials, fuel and non-government services and transfers. We then review comparative developments in trade in manufactures. Next, we ask whether there is any evidence to suggest growing convergence in foreign trade structure amongst the OECD countries in our sample. Finally, we discuss whether the massive shift in the structure of UK trade, which occurred in the post-war period, has been a causal factor in the UK's relatively poor economic performance. The chapter ends with a summary of our main conclusions.

Comparative developments in non-manufacturing trade as a whole

In Chapter 3, we briefly examined post-war trends in trade in non-manufactures (primary products plus non-government services and private transfers) for our sample of thirteen OECD countries.[1] Figs. 3.1(a) and 3.2(a) show very clearly how exceptional has been the UK's experience in non-manufacturing trade compared with that of other advanced countries. In the early 1950s, the UK had deficits in non-manufacturing trade to a degree unrivalled by any other country in our sample – either then or since. However, from the early 1950s onwards, apart for a brief period following the quadrupling of oil prices in 1973, the UK's non-manufacturing balance improved almost continuously right up until the early to mid-1980s. Indeed, by the early 1980s, there was actually a small surplus in Britain's non-manufacturing trade. Thus, the period 1952 to 1982 witnessed a truly dramatic transformation in UK trade in non-manufactures. How does Britain's experience in this respect compare with developments in other OECD countries?

Consider, first of all, the three 'workshop' economies (West Germany, Japan and Belgium), all of whom run deficits in non-manufacturing trade. In the 1950s, these deficits were almost as large as those of the UK and, like the UK, all three experienced improvements in their non-manufacturing balance in the period 1952 to 1972 – although on nothing like the same scale as in Britain (see Table 3.1). This improvement was largely the result of favourable trends in trade in food (West Germany and Belgium), as well as in raw materials (all three countries). However, the favourable trend in the non-manufacturing balance of these three 'workshop' economies was reversed in the late 1970s, as a consequence of higher oil prices; as a result, by the early 1980s, their non-manufacturing deficits were actually larger than they had been in the early 1950s (see Table 3.1). Thus, whereas the foreign trade structure of these three 'workshop' economies was very similar to that of the UK in the early 1950s, quite radical differences had emerged by the early 1980s.

Now let us turn to France and the US: both are normally in deficit in non-manufacturing trade, although neither country ever came close to matching the extreme degree of dependence on net imports of non-manufactures exhibited by Britain in the early 1950s. Between the early 1950s and the mid-1970s, both France and the US experienced a steady improvement in their non-manufacturing balance (see Table 3.1), due largely to favourable trends in trade in food and raw materials. However, this well-established improving trend was reversed in the late 1970s, largely as a result of higher oil prices. In consequence, by the early 1980s both France and the US had non-manufacturing deficits which were at least as large as they had been during the early 1950s. Thus, the experience of France and the US in non-manufacturing trade was also radically different from that of the UK.

Similarly, neither Australia nor Canada, who have been continuously in surplus in non-manufacturing trade, experienced much if any change in foreign trade structure in the period 1952–82. The same was true of Holland, which is also usually in surplus in non-manufacturing trade. In Holland's case, gains in trade in raw materials and fuel were more or less equally offset by adverse developments in trade in food and non-government services and transfers. As a result, Holland experienced very little change in its foreign trade structure in the period 1952–82.

Unlike these other countries, Sweden and Italy both experienced major changes in their non-manufacturing balance in the period 1952–82, with both recording steadily increasing deficits (see Table 3.1). This was partly due to factors which were independent of economic performance (falling timber prices in the case of Sweden and higher oil prices in both countries) and partly the consequence of successful economic development which, in the case of Sweden, gave rise to increased tourist spending abroad and, in the case of Italy, to larger deficits in food trade. However, in neither country was the change in non-manufacturing trade as a whole anything like as large as in the case of the UK – and it was, of course, in completely the opposite direction.

Like Sweden and Italy, Norway also experienced major changes in its non-manufacturing balance in the period 1952–82. Starting from a position of surplus, Norway's non-manufacturing balance deteriorated sharply during the 1970s, mainly as a result of a dramatic erosion in earnings from merchant shipping, as well as increased tourist spending abroad. However, at the end of the 1970s, North Sea oil came on stream and, by the early 1980s, Norway's surplus in non-manufacturing trade was even larger than it had been in the early 1950s. Thus, Norway, like the UK, registered a significant improvement in its non-manufacturing balance in the period 1952–82; however, the size of the improvement was considerably smaller. Furthermore, it was very much concentrated in the years right at the end of our period (see Table 3.1).

Austria was the one other country in our sample to register a change in its non-manufacturing balance which was on anything like the same scale and in the same direction as that experienced by the UK. During the 1950s, Austria was in deficit in non-manufacturing trade. However, the period 1952–72 saw a significant improvement in her non-manufacturing balance as a result of growing surpluses in tourism, as well as improvements in food trade. In consequence, Austria moved into surplus in non-manufacturing trade in 1961, and these surpluses increased steadily until 1972. Indeed, the improvement in Austria's non-manufacturing balance in the period 1952–72, amounting to +9.3% of GDP, was somewhat larger than that recorded by the UK (+6.4%). However, this well-established, improving trend was reversed during the late 1970s, largely as a result of higher oil prices. Thus, taking the period 1952–82 as a whole, the change in Austria's non-manufacturing balance, though in the same direction, was only half as great as that recorded by the UK (see Table 3.1).

Conclusions on comparative developments in non-manufacturing trade

This discussion of comparative developments in non-manufacturing trade in the period 1952–82 shows very clearly how exceptional was the UK's experience within the context of our sample of OECD countries. First, the UK experienced a far larger change in her non-manufacturing balance – an improvement of +11.6% of GDP – compared with any other country in our sample. No other country came anywhere close to recording such an enormous change. Second, the UK was the only country to experience a virtually continuous improvement in her non-manufacturing balance throughout the period 1952–82. A number of other countries registered quite significant improvements in the period 1952–72, but, in all cases, these previously favourable trends were reversed by the dramatic rise in oil prices after 1973. Norway and Austria were the only other countries to come anywhere close to matching that UK's experience in non-manufacturing trade – either in terms of the size or the direction of change. Thus, no other country recorded such a large and continuous improvement in their non-manufacturing balance as that which the UK registered in the period 1952–82.

A finer breakdown

Table 8.1 enables us to compare the UK's experience in each of the main areas of non-manufacturing trade (food, raw materials, fuel, and non-government services and transfers) with developments in the twelve other OECD countries in our sample. The periods compared are 1952–5 and 1981–2. The following picture emerges. Of all the countries in our sample, the UK registered the largest improvement in trade in food, as well as in raw materials. The UK also experienced a small improvement in non-government services and private transfers. Finally, as a result of the build-up of North Sea fuel production, the UK avoided the deterioration in fuel trade which affected most of the other large OECD countries in our sample. Thus, although a number of other countries experienced favourable trends in several areas of non-manufacturing trade, the UK's experience was quite exceptional: the UK was the only country to register improvements in all four of the main areas of non-manufacturing trade: moreover, in the case of food and raw materials, she recorded the largest improvements of all. Furthermore, of the thirteen countries in our sample, seven actually registered a deterioration in their non-manufacturing balance, taking the period 1952–82 as a whole. Let us now examine each of the main areas of non-manufacturing trade in somewhat greater detail.

Food, beverages and tobacco

From Table 8.1 we can see that there is a rough inverse correlation between, on the one hand, a country's initial (i.e. in the early 1950s) strength or weakness

Table 8.1. *Trade in non-manufactured goods and services: the UK and other OECD countries compared, 1952–5 and 1981–2 (as % of GDP)*

	Food, beverages and tobacco			Raw materials			Fuel			Non-government services			Non-manufactures overall		
	1952–5	1981–2	Change	1952–5	1981–2	Change	1952–5	1981–2	Change	1952–5	1981–2	Change	1952–5	1981–2	Change
UK	−5.8	−1.0	+4.8	−5.1	−0.8	+4.3	−0.5	+1.3	+1.8	+0.9	+1.5	+0.6	−10.5	+1.1	+11.6
West Germany	−2.9	−1.2	+1.7	−3.3	−1.1	+2.2	+0.5	−4.2	−4.7	−0.5	−2.7	−2.2	−6.2	−9.2	−3.0
Belgium	−3.5	−0.7	+2.8	−4.3	−2.8	+1.5	−0.9	−7.7	−6.8	+0.1	+1.2	+1.1	−8.6	−10.0	−1.4
Japan	−1.9	−1.1	+0.7	−4.1	−1.6	+2.5	−1.0	−5.7	−4.7	−0.9	−1.2	−0.3	−8.0	−9.6	−1.6
Italy	+0.1	−1.3	−1.2	−2.6	−1.8	+0.8	−1.2	−6.5	−5.3	+1.5	+2.2	+0.7	−2.3	−7.4	−5.1
Sweden	−2.0	−1.1	+0.9	+5.8	+1.8	−4.0	−3.3	−4.9	−1.6	+0.1	+0.3	+0.2	+0.6	−3.9	−4.5
Australia	+4.7	+3.4	−1.3	+8.0	+3.2	−4.8	−1.7	+0.2	+1.9	−1.9	−1.5	+0.4	+9.1	+5.3	−3.8
Canada	+2.6	+1.4	−1.2	+2.8	+2.8	+0.0	−1.7	+1.2	+2.9	−1.1	−0.7	+0.4	+2.6	+4.6	+2.0
Netherlands	+5.1	+3.9	−1.1	−4.6	−0.4	+4.2	−1.6	−0.3	+1.3	+3.9	+0.5	−3.4	+2.8	+3.8	+1.0
Norway	−0.1	+0.3	+0.4	+2.6	−0.6	−3.2	−2.7	+12.4	+15.1	+7.3	+1.9	−5.4	+7.0	+14.0	+7.0
France	−1.0	+0.9	+1.9	−1.9	−0.5	+1.4	−1.0	−4.5	−3.5	−0.1	+1.0	+1.1	−4.0	−3.2	+0.8
US	−0.3	+0.4	+0.7	−0.4	+0.4	+0.8	+0.1	−2.1	−2.2	−0.1	−0.1	−0.0	−0.7	−1.4	−0.7
Austria	−3.9	−0.8	+3.1	+1.1	−0.4	−1.5	−2.4	−4.8	−2.4	+0.2	+5.8	+5.6	−4.9	−0.2	+4.7

Source: See Appendix 5

in food trade and, on the other hand, subsequent changes in its food balance. Countries which were in surplus in food trade in 1952–5 subsequently experienced a reduction in their surpluses, and, in the case of Italy, actually went into deficit. On the other hand, countries which were in deficit in food trade in the early 1950s subsequently experienced an improvement in their food balance; either their deficits diminished, or, as in the case of France, the US and Norway, deficits gave way to surpluses.

Thus, amongst the net food-importing countries in our sample, the UK's experience was far from unique. In fact, exactly the same set of factors as those identified in Chapter 6 as being responsible for the improvement in the UK's food balance were also at work in other net food-importing OECD countries: falling food prices (in the 1950s), declining population growth, a relatively low income-elasticity of demand for both quantitative and qualitative improvements in the diet and continuously rising agricultural output.[2] The fact that so many other net food-importing OECD countries experienced improvements in their food balance confirms our view that developments in UK food trade were the result of factors which were largely independent of the UK's relatively poor industrial and economic performance.

However, the reasons why the UK, of all the countries in our sample, registered the largest improvement in food trade are not immediately obvious. One of them is that the rate of growth of agricultural output was higher in the UK than in most other countries in our sample – at least as far as the period 1960–83 is concerned. Secondly, food consumption has been relatively stable in the UK, and so most of the growth in production was used to reduce food imports; in the rest of Western Europe, by contrast, a large part of the growth in production was devoted to increases in consumption.[3] The final reason why the UK experienced the largest improvement in food trade of all the countries in our sample is as follows. During the 1950s, the UK was relatively more dependent on net food imports (relative to GDP) than any other country in our sample. This was partly the consequence of higher levels of consumption, but it was also a reflection of Britain's historical commitment to agricultural free trade. Because of this greater degree of dependence on net food imports, the UK benefited to a relatively greater degree than other countries in our sample from the subsequent fall in food prices. This is the third main reason why the improvement in the UK's food balance was larger than that of any other country in our sample.[4]

Trade in raw materials

As with trade in food, Table 8.1 indicates that there is a rough inverse correlation between a country's initial (i.e. early 1950s) strength or weakness in raw materials trade and subsequent changes in its raw materials balance. Thus, with the exception of Canada, all those countries that had raw materials surpluses in the early 1950s subsequently experienced a deterioration in their raw materials balance: either their surpluses declined or, as in the case of Norway and Austria, surpluses were transformed into deficits. On the other hand, all those countries which had raw materials deficits in the early 1950s subsequently experienced an improvement in their raw materials balance: either their deficits declined or, as in the case of the US, a deficit was turned into a surplus.

Thus, amongst the net raw material-importing OECD countries in our sample, the UK's experience in the period 1952–82 was far from unique. This suggests that the same factors as those identified in Chapter 6 as being responsible for the decline in the UK's dependence on net raw material imports were also at work in other OECD countries – factors such as the fall in raw material prices (in the 1950s), materials-saving technical progress, the development of domestically produced, synthetic substitutes for imported raw materials and changes in industrial structure. The fact that other net raw material-importing OECD countries, whose industrial and economic performance was far superior to that of the UK, also experienced a reduction in their dependence on net raw material imports confirms our view (see Chapter 7) that, even if British industrial performance had been stronger, the UK would still have experienced a significant improvement in its raw materials balance in the period 1952–82.

However, it is far from clear why the UK, of all the OECD countries in our sample, should have experienced the largest improvement in trade in raw materials. One possible explanation is that at the beginning of our period, the UK's industrial structure was somewhat more oriented, compared with other OECD countries, to sectors of production having an above-average input of raw materials per unit of output. This may have been due to Britain's extremely high degree of dependence on net manufactured exports, and the important role played by materials-intensive products (such as cotton textiles) in her export trade. The fact that the UK recorded such a large improvement in her raw materials balance could then be partly attributed to the subsequent decline in Britain's dependence on net manufactured exports. A further contributory factor was that, since Britain was initially more dependent on net raw material imports than any other country in our sample, she benefited to a relatively greater degree from the fall in raw materials' prices which occurred during the 1950s. A final factor explaining why Britain experienced the largest improvement in raw materials trade is that, at the end of our period, namely 1981–2, the demand for raw materials was somewhat more depressed in the UK than in the other OECD countries in our sample because at that stage in the international business cycle, the level of economic activity was relatively more depressed in the UK.

Trade in fuel

Of the thirteen countries in our sample, five experienced an improvement in their fuel balance in the period from 1952–5 to 1981–2. They were: Australia, Canada, the Netherlands, Norway and the UK. Within the context of this group, the size of the improvement in the UK's fuel balance was not particularly large; this is because, in 1981–2, North Sea oil and gas production had yet to reach their peak. However, within the context of the large number of OECD countries who experienced a deterioration in their fuel balance, the UK's experience was exceptional. In particular, the UK was the only one of the large OECD countries not to experience a deterioration in fuel trade. Thus, from a comparative point of view, the main effect of North Sea oil and gas production, prior to 1981–2, was that it enabled the UK to avoid the substantial deterioration in fuel trade experienced by many other OECD countries – especially the larger ones.

Non-government services (including private transfers)

The UK was also far from being the only country to register an improvement in 'non-government services' during the period from 1952–5 to 1981–2. Austria (with an improvement of +5.6% of GDP), France (+1.1%), Belgium (+1.1%), Italy (+0.7%), UK (+0.6%), Australia (+0.4%), Canada (+0.4%) and Sweden (+0.2%) all experienced an improvement on this account (see Table 8.1). Furthermore, amongst this group, the improvement in the UK trade in non-government services was comparatively modest.

One of the reasons why the UK, along with Austria and the two Mediterranean countries, experienced an improvement in trade in 'non-government services' is that they all benefited from increased tourist expenditure being undertaken by inhabitants of the Northern European countries in our sample. The UK and France also enjoyed substantially increased receipts from banking and 'other services', but, unlike France, Britain experienced hardly any increase in migrant workers' remittances.

By contrast, many of the Continental Northern European countries in our sample (West Germany, the Netherlands and Norway), as well as Japan, experienced a deterioration in their 'non-government services' balance (see Table 8.1). Increased tourist expenditure abroad, not matched by anything like an equivalent increase in tourist receipts, was much the most important factor. In addition, Norway suffered a drastic decline in earnings from merchant shipping, whilst West Germany and the Netherlands experienced growing migrant worker remittances.

To conclude, the size of the improvement in UK trade in 'non-government services' was relatively modest by international standards. However, the UK did avoid the substantial deterioration on this account that was registered by a number of other countries in our sample.

Conclusions

The UK's comparative performance in each of the separate areas of non-manufacturing trade can be summarized as follows. In trade in food, as well as in raw materials, the UK registered the largest improvement of all the countries in our sample. On the 'non-government services' account, the UK also recorded an improvement – but on a relatively modest scale compared with the gains made by some of the countries in our sample. Finally, in trade in fuel, the advent of North Sea oil and gas production meant that the UK avoided the big deterioration in fuel trade registered by many other OECD countries – especially the larger ones. Thus, the UK registered favourable developments in each of the four main areas of non-manufacturing trade. Other countries experienced favourable developments in certain areas, but, in most cases, these were offset by adverse developments elsewhere. The UK was the only country to experience an improvement across the whole spectrum of non-manufacturing trade, and this is the reason why Britain, of all the countries in our sample, experienced by far the largest improvement in non-manufacturing trade as a whole in the period 1952–82.

Comparative developments in trade in manufactures

Figs. 3.1(b) and 3.2(b) show extremely clearly how large and sustained was the deterioration in the UK's manufacturing balance in the period 1952–82. In the 1950s, the UK had a stronger manufacturing balance, as a proportion of GDP, than any other country in our sample. However, by 1981–2, Britain's manufacturing surplus had virtually disappeared. This trend deterioration in the UK's manufacturing balance was reversed on just two occasions: first, in 1968–71, following the devaluation of sterling (in November 1967) and the subsequent austerity measures, designed to make depreciation effective; and, second, in 1975–7, following the implementation of a number of policies designed to adjust the British economy to the effects of higher oil prices: incomes policy, currency depreciation and monetary and fiscal restraint. However, except for these two relatively short periods of time, the UK's manufacturing balance experienced a steady deterioration throughout the period 1952–82, the total adverse shift amounting to between −8% and −9% of GDP.

How did the UK's experience in manufacturing trade compare with developments in the other OECD countries in our sample? Consider the three 'workshop' economies (West Germany, Japan and Belgium) which, in the early 1950s, were almost as dependent on net manufactured exports as Britain. By the early 1980s, these three 'workshop' economies had somewhat larger manufacturing surpluses than they had had in the early 1950s. Thus, they experienced virtually no change in their dependence on net manufactured exports taking the period 1952–82 as whole (see Table 3.2). Similarly, the two 'primary producers' (Australia and Canada) experienced relatively little change in their dependence on net imports of manufactures in the period 1952–82. And much the same can also be said of Holland, although her manufacturing balance improved slightly towards the end of the period (see Table 3.2). Thus, the UK's experience in manufacturing trade was radically different from that of all of these countries.

Turning to the US and France, both countries were in surplus in manufacturing trade in virtually every year between 1952 and 1982. However, for much of the period, they both experienced a deterioration in their manufacturing balance although, in the case of France, this adverse trend appears to have been arrested in the late 1970s. Even so, in neither country was the deterioration in manufacturing trade on anything like the same scale (relative to GDP) as that experienced by the UK.

Sweden and Italy, on the other hand, did experience a major change in their manufacturing balance – amounting to about +6% of GDP, taking the period 1952–82 as a whole. However, in neither case was this shift anything like as large as in the case of the UK and it was, of course, in quite the opposite direction. Norway's manufacturing balance also registered an improvement of between +4% and +5% of GDP in the period 1952–82, although, once again, the change was opposite in direction and on nothing like the same scale as that recorded by the UK.

Of all the countries in our sample, only Austria matched the UK in terms of the size and direction of the change in its manufacturing balance in the period 1952–82. In the 1950s, Austria had manufacturing surpluses averaging between +2% and +3% of GDP. However, by the late 1970s, these surpluses had turned into deficits of roughly the same size. However, the scale of the overall shift in Austria's manufacturing balance in the period 1952–82 (amounting to between −4% and −5% of GDP) was nothing like as great as that experienced by the UK (between −8% and −9% of GDP).

What conclusions can be drawn from our analysis of comparative developments in trade in manufactures in the period 1952–82? The main one is that of all the countries in our sample, the UK experienced by far the largest change in manufacturing trade during this period. Furthermore, the UK was one of only two countries – Austria was the other – to experience a significant deterioration in its manufacturing balance.

Evidence of convergence in foreign trade structure

In Chapter 3, we emphasized how enormous was the degree of variation in foreign trade structure amongst the OECD countries in our sample. Is there any evidence of a reduction in the extent of variation and, hence, of convergence in foreign trade structure in the period 1952–82?

Trends in trade in food and raw materials were, by themselves, certainly a source of convergence during this period. Between 1952 and 1982, all net food-importing countries experienced an improvement in their food balance, whilst all net food-exporters experienced a deterioration (see Table 8.1). The same was true of trade in raw materials (see Table 8.1).

However, these developments in food and raw materials trade making for convergence were, for the most part, offset by developments in fuel trade. Many of the countries which experienced an improvement in trade in food and raw materials registered a deterioration in their fuel balance. On the other hand, many of the countries which experienced a deterioration in trade in food and raw materials recorded an improvement in their fuel balance. The main exceptions to this pattern were the UK and the Netherlands, where improvements in fuel trade were superimposed on improvements in trade in food and raw materials, and Italy and Sweden, where the opposite happened. Thus, developments in fuel trade tended to offset the tendencies towards convergence resulting from developments in trade in food and raw materials. Nor were changes in the 'non-government services' account a source of convergence either.

As a result, the variation in foreign trade structure amongst the OECD countries in our sample was just as great in the early 1980s as it had been in the early 1950s. Furthermore, the two extreme patterns of specialization – that of the primary producer, on the one hand, and that of the specialist net manufacturing exporter, on the other – were just as much in evidence as ever.

Does the future hold out the possibility of a greater degree of convergence in foreign trade structure amongst the advanced countries? The short answer is, probably, no. The reasons for this are as follows. First of all, there is not much scope for further convergence in trade in food. This is because there is likely to be growing political resistance in the OECD countries to meeting the cost of increased agricultural surpluses (whether for export or for disposal). In addition, there is likely to be little further convergence in trade in raw materials: in net raw material-importing countries, raw material imports are already very compressed, whilst relatively few possibilities exist for expanding raw material exports.

Thus, so far as the future is concerned, differences in foreign trade structure will come to depend increasingly on the distribution of surpluses and deficits in fuel trade, as well as in trade in non-government services, especially tourism.

These patterns are extremely difficult to predict. However, if the real price of fuel rises in the future, then fuel balances are likely to exhibit a growing degree of variance, depending on the degree of self-sufficiency in each country. Tourist balances are also likely to display increased variance. Thus, in the future, the foreign trade structures of the OECD countries are likely to exhibit as much variation they have in the past.

Changes in trade structure and eonomic performance

The fact that the UK, of all the countries in our sample, experienced by far the largest change in foreign trade structure in the post-war period, as well as the weakest performance in terms of economic growth, suggests that the former might be causally related to the latter. On the other hand, it could also be argued that the fact that the UK's non-manufacturing balance improved almost continuously throughout the entire post-war period should have had a beneficial effect on the country's economic performance. Let us briefly consider which of these two points of view is the more persuasive.

In a typical 'workshop' economy, the ability to reconcile rapid economic growth with the maintenance of external balance depends, as has already been argued in Chapter 3, on being able to produce a large and rapidly expanding manufacturing export surplus. Failure to do so will cause the level and rate of growth of economic activity to be constrained by the availability of foreign exchange and, as a result, economic performance will prove to be unsatisfactory. In such an economy, any improvement in the non-manufacturing balance, as long as it is not the product of economic failure, is bound to result in a reduction of external pressure and, consequently, presents the 'workshop' economy with the opportunity of improving its performance.

To what extent is this argument applicable to the UK? In the 1950s the UK was without a doubt the world's foremost example of a 'workshop' economy, and external pressures on the British economy were accentuated by sterling's role as an international reserve currency undermined, as it constantly was, by the UK's generally weak balance of payments. Thus, a number of attempts to increase the level of aggregate demand with the aim of improving the economy's long-term economic performance foundered amidst currency speculation and a rapid loss of foreign exchange reserves. Thus, both the level of UK national income and also, possibly, its underlying rate of growth were at various times constrained by a weak balance of payments.

Given this situation, what is likely to have been the effect of virtually continuous improvements in non-manufacturing trade – bearing in mind that a large proportion of such improvements were autonomous with respect to the UK's industrial and economic performance as a whole? Given the external pressures on the economy, such improvements ought surely to have had a beneficial effect on performance, because they enabled the UK to reduce its net manufactured exports, both absolutely and as a proportion of GDP. Indeed, had Britain not experienced such a substantial improvement in its non-manufacturing trade then, under the assumption of unchanged industrial performance, the country's post-war balance of payments problems and the ensuing bouts of deflation would have started earlier and been more frequent. As a result, the trend rise in UK unemployment, which got under way in the mid-1960s, would have begun even earlier, and the UK would have probably slipped even further down the international per capita income league table.

Thus, there is a strong case for believing that the very considerable improvements which occurred in UK non-manufacturing trade in the post-war period ought to have had a beneficial effect on the country's economic performance – and, without them, things might well have been very much worse.

On the other hand, it must be remembered that part of the improvement in non-manufacturing trade was obtained as a result of policies which were highly conducive to an expansion of agricultural output. Such policies were not costless and, if an equivalent volume of resources had been devoted to modernizing and reconstructing Britain's industrial base, then the country's overall industrial and economic performance might well have been stronger in the post-war period. Furthermore, we ought not to ignore the possibility that developments in non-manufacturing trade, by making it easier for the UK to adjust to the consequences of poor industrial performance, actually had a detrimental effect on post-war British economic development. The argument is as follows. If developments in UK non-manufacturing trade had been less favourable and economic performance in the fifties and sixties even worse, then it is conceivable that much more radical measures might have been adopted, especially in the field of industrial policy, to modernize the British economy and improve its performance. Such measures might have succeeded in arresting and even reversing Britain's economic decline. Thus, not only did the UK fail to grasp the opportunities for improving her economic performance, presented by favourable developments in non-manufacturing trade, but these self-same developments reduced the pressure to tackle the country's deep-seated problems in a really radical way.

As between these two points of view – namely the suggestion that improvements in non-manufacturing trade should have had a beneficial impact on economic performance, because of their contribution to relaxing the foreign exchange constraint, and the idea that they, in fact, had a detrimental effect, because they made it easier to adjust to the consequence of industrial failure, whilst improvements in food self-sufficiency were purchased at the cost of a lower level of industrial support – we have little choice except to be agnostic.

Can anything be gleaned from the experience of Austria – the only other country in our sample to experience a significant deterioration in trade in manufactures – as to the impact of changes in trade structure on economic performance?

As in the case of the UK, the origins of the improvement in Austrian non-manufacturing trade lay mainly in developments, which were independent of the country's industrial and economic performance as a whole, namely in increasing surpluses in tourism and in an improving food balance. However, unlike the UK, Austria's post-war industrial and economic performance was exceptionally strong. Austria took advantage of the improvements in her non-manufacturing trade to expand the domestic demand for manufactures, thereby strengthening the country's industrial base, despite adverse long-term trends in trade in manufactures. Thus, Austria's experience provides no support whatsoever for the view that changes in trade structure necessarily have a detrimental impact on economic performance, though it has much to say concerning the benefits of a coherent and consistently applied industrial policy.

Summary and conclusions

The main conclusion of this chapter is that changes in the structure of UK foreign trade in the post-war period were exceptional within the context of developments in other OECD countries. In non-manufacturing trade as a whole, the UK experienced by far the most continuous and largest change of any country in our sample – an improvement of +11.6% of GDP between 1952–5 and 1981–2. This was the result of improvements in every area of non-manufacturing trade: of all the countries in our sample, the UK experienced the largest improvements in trade in food and raw materials, and she also registered modest gains in trade in fuel and non-government services. Only Norway came anywhere close to matching the UK's experience in non-manufacturing trade; however, the improvement registered by Norway (amounting to +7.0% of GDP) was not as great as that recorded by the UK; it was also less broadly based and very much concentrated in the years at the end of our period. In trade in manufactures, the UK also registered much the largest change – a deterioration of between −8% and −9% of GDP. Only Austria came anywhere close to matching the size of the deterioration in manufacturing trade experience by the UK – though, in Austria's case, the adverse shift was much more modest (between −4% and −5% of GDP).

This chapter also considered the issue of whether there is any evidence of increased convergence in foreign trade structure amongst our sample of OECD countries during the period 1952–82. We concluded that, despite increased convergence in trade in food and raw materials, offsetting developments in fuel trade ensured that there was as much variance in trade structure at the end of our period as there was at the beginning. Furthermore, since there is likely to be growing dispersion in fuel and tourist balances in the years ahead, we are unlikely to see greater convergence in foreign trade structure amongst the advanced countries in the future.

Finally, this chapter considered whether the major transformation in the UK's foreign trade structure in the post-war period could possibly have been one of the factors contributing to the country's relatively poor economic performance. Our conclusions on this question are somewhat agnostic. We are unable to determine whether, in the absence of such substantial improvements in non-manufacturing trade, UK economic performance would have been worse (because they served to relax the foreign exchange constraint) or better (because they made it easier for the UK to adjust to the consequences of industrial failure and because improvements in food self-sufficiency were purchased at the cost of a lower level of industrial support). However, Austria's experience suggests that improvements in non-manufacturing trade do not necessarily have a detrimental impact on industrial and economic performance.

9

The changing geography of UK trade since the Second World War[1,2]

Introduction

The deficits being incurred by the UK in trade in manufactures with most other industrialized countries are universally regarded as a symptom of economic failure. Meanwhile, the fact that the country continues to earn surpluses in trade in manufactures with primary producing countries is generally interpreted as a sign that British manufacturers, having been chased out of advanced country markets, can only survive by 'trading-down' (i.e. selling technologically unsophisticated products) in Third World markets. The aim of this chapter is to demonstrate that these propositions are entirely false. The fact is the appearance of deficits in trade in manufactures with other industrialized countries is an unavoidable consequence of the increased triangularity of UK trade, resulting from structural change on the non-manufacturing side of the economy, combined with the enhanced purchasing power of OPEC. The consequence of these two developments is that, although the UK has reduced her imports of primary products (including oil) from primary producing countries (including OPEC), she continues to earn surpluses in trade in manufactures with primary producers. Meanwhile, the UK's overall manufacturing surplus with all areas diminished (due largely to autonomous developments in non-manufacturing trade); eventually the point arrived where her overall manufacturing surplus was no longer any larger than the surpluses which she continued to earn with primary producing countries. Thus, unless Britain was to run huge surpluses in merchandize trade (manufactures plus primary products) overall, she had to go into deficit in trade in manufactures with other industrialized countries. This increased triangularity of UK trade – resulting from structural change at home and the enhanced purchasing power of OPEC – has not received the attention it deserves.

This chapter also examines the contribution of changes on the non-manufacturing side of the economy to the major reorientation in the geography of British trade which occurred in the post-war period; namely, its contribution to the huge increase in trade with other industrialized countries (on both the export and the import sides), together with the dramatic reduction in trade with the White Dominions and the non-OPEC LDCs – parts of the world over which Britain, until comparatively recently, exercized considerable political sway.

The organization of the chapter is as follows. It begins by presenting a broad overview of long-term developments in the geography of UK trade since 1913. This is followed by separate, more detailed, discussions of the geography of UK imports and exports for the period since the Second World War; the effects of the dissolution of the Empire on the geography of British trade, as well as of Britain's membership of the EEC, are also analysed. This is followed by a discussion of the causes and consequences of the increased triangularity of UK trade, which developed in the early to mid-1980s. The chapter concludes with a summary of its main points.

Changes in the geographical direction of UK trade since 1913

General overview

In the period since 1913, the geography of British trade has been subject to a number of truly dramatic changes. One of the most striking has been the changing importance of trade with Western Europe. In 1913, Western Europe was the UK's principal trading partner. However, between then and the late 1940s, under the impact of two world wars and the inter-war economic crisis, UK trade with Western Europe underwent a significant decline. Meanwhile, Britain's trade with the White Dominions[3] and with the countries in her formal and informal Empire in the Third World expanded somewhat. However, after the Second World War, Britain rebuilt and expanded her trading links with Western Europe to the point where, by 1983, Western Europe was even more important as a trading partner for Britain than it had been in 1913. Meanwhile, from the early 1950s onwards, trade with the White Dominions and the 'other LDCs'[4] underwent a dramatic decline, both absolutely and as a share of the total. The other major development since the war has been the growth of trade with Japan and OPEC.

In 1913 Western Europe, as a whole, accounted for 37.2% (the present EEC countries:[5] 29.8%) of total UK trade (imports plus exports) (see Table 9.1). On the import side, Western Europe's share was 37.4% (EEC: 29.4%) (see Table 9.3). Imports of manufactures from France and Germany were particularly important at this time, and, between them, these countries may well have supplied as much as one-tenth of all the manufactured goods consumed in the UK prior to the First World War. Moreover, such imports were rising rapidly and

Table 9.1. *UK trade (imports plus exports), by area, 1913–83 (%)*

Area	1913	1929	1938	1948	1951	1958	1961	1965	1967	1970	1973	1974	1977	1979	1982	1983
EEC	29.8	27.7	20.7	15.4	17.7	19.9	21.8	25.0	26.5	28.1	32.8	33.4	37.5	42.4	43.2	44.6
Other W. Europe	7.4	8.0	8.8	10.3	10.8	10.3	11.9	13.9	14.0	11.3	17.6	15.9	16.0	16.5	13.6	14.7
USA	13.7	12.5	10.0	6.7	8.0	9.0	9.4	11.2	12.3	12.3	11.1	10.1	9.7	9.9	12.4	12.6
Japan	1.3	1.1	0.2	0.2	0.4	0.8	1.0	1.3	1.5	1.7	2.5	2.2	2.2	2.3	2.9	3.2
White Dominions	13.8	15.8	23.2	24.5	22.7	21.2	18.1	18.3	16.1	14.6	10.9	9.8	7.4	5.8	5.9	5.2
OPEC	2.3	3.3	3.7	7.1	7.4	10.0	9.0	7.7	7.2	7.5	8.0	12.5	11.5	7.9	9.0	7.2
New industrializing countries	3.4	2.7	2.5	3.5	4.9	2.9	3.1	3.0	3.1	3.5	3.9	3.6	3.5	3.9	4.0	4.0
Centrally Planned Economies	7.7	4.8	6.9	2.7	2.5	3.2	4.5	3.6	4.6	4.1	3.5	3.2	3.2	3.0	2.1	2.1
Other LDCs	20.8	24.1	24.1	29.7	25.6	22.7	21.4	16.2	14.7	17.1	9.7	9.3	9.0	8.4	7.1	6.4
Total	100.1	100.0	100.1	100.1	100.0	100.2	100.2	100.2	100.0	100.2	100.0	100.0	100.0	100.1	100.2	100.0

EEC: West Germany, France, Italy, Netherlands, Eire, Denmark, Belgium and Luxembourg. Greece is not included
White Dominions: Australia, New Zealand, Canada and South Africa
OPEC: Algeria, Libya, Nigeria, Gabon, Saudi Arabia, Kuwait, Bahrain, Qatar, Abu Dhabi, Dubai, Sharjah, etc., Oman, Iraq, Iran, Brunei, Indonesia, Trinidad and Tobago, Venezuela and Ecuador
Newly industrializing countries: Thailand, Singapore, Taiwan, Hong Kong, South Korea, Philippines, Mexico, Brazil
Centrally Planned Economies: Eastern Europe, Soviet Union, China, Vietnam, North Korea and Mongolia
Notes: For 1913 and 1929, imports are c.i.f. For all other years, imports c.i.f. have been converted to imports f.o.b., using conversion factors for total UK visible trade given in IMF *International Financial Statistics: Annual Report* and assuming a conversion factor of 0.9 for 1938. Exports are f.o.b. in all years
Source: HMSO, *Trade & Navigation Accounts of the UK*, and HMSO, *Overseas Trade Statistics of the UK*

fears were expressed, just as they are today, concerning the superior competitive power of Continental industry. Western Europe was also extremely important as an export market for the UK, purchasing 36.9% (EEC: 30.3%) of total exports in 1913 (see Table 9.7). However, coal accounted for a large proportion of British exports to Western Europe at this time and, in trade in manufactures, Britain was in deficit with the 'core' industrial countries of Western Europe (Germany, France, Belgium and Switzerland).

The pattern of Britain's trade with the rest of the world was rather different. Outside of Western Europe (i.e. in trade with the Empire, the White Dominions, the USA and the Baltic countries), Britain engaged in an international division of labour in which she exported manufactures in return for imports of food and raw materials. The emergence of this division of labour, with the UK at its centre, was both cause and consequence of the rapid growth of income and population in the UK, as well as of the country's adoption of agricultural free trade. Following the Repeal of the Corn Laws, much of British agriculture was, in effect, relocated abroad – in the Dominions, in the Colonies and in Argentina (the 'informal' Empire), as well as in the US and the Baltic. The importance of the Empire in this division of labour can be gauged from the fact that in 1913 the White Dominions and the 'other LDCs' accounted for 34.6% of total UK trade (imports plus exports) (see Table 9.1.).

However, 1913 marked a turning-point in the UK's trading relations with Western Europe. Under the impact of two world wars and the inter-war economic crisis, the UK resorted to tariffs and quotas in order to restrict imports of manufactures from other advanced countries, with the aim of helping British industry increase its hold on the domestic market. As a result of these developments, British trade with Continental Europe, particularly with the present member countries of the EEC, gradually declined – the share of the latter in total trade falling from 29.8% in 1913 to just 15.4% in 1948 (see Table 9.1). As a consequence of these developments, Britain's formal and informal Empire in the Third World and the White Dominions came to play a much more central role in her overall trade. During the 1930s, primary producers in these countries were given quotas in Britain's domestic market and, in return, Imperial Preference and other measures ensured that their manufacturing import trade was made virtually the exclusive preserve of British manufacturing exporters (see Astor and Seebohm Rowntree 1939).

This reliance on protection and Empire reached a peak under the post-war Attlee government, whose strategy for economic recovery was based on excluding virtually all imported manufactures from the domestic market and on a vigorous manufactured export drive in order to pay for the cost of importing primary products from the Third World and the White Dominions. By 1948, the latter areas accounted for 66.8% of UK imports and 62.7% of UK exports compared to 38.3% and 42.5% in 1913) (see Tables 9.3 and 9.7). Meanwhile, since the UK was importing virtually nothing except primary products, British industry supplied almost 95% of the UK's domestic market for manufactures.

This situation started to change during the 1950s, albeit slowly. As the UK's economic and political ties with the White Dominions weakened, so Imperial Preference began to be dismantled. Meanwhile, in the UK itself, protection was also relaxed. However, it was not until the end of the 1950s that a really profound shift in the direction of UK trade began to take place. By then, the nations of Western Europe had fully recovered from the aftermath of war, full currency convertibility had been re-established, and the first steps were being taken towards the liberalization of international trade in manufactures. At the same time, the Empire was beginning to disintegrate and, as it did so, the last vestiges of Imperial Preference were swept aside.

Once the direction of British trade began to alter, the change was really dramatic. Trade with Western Europe, especially with the EEC, mushroomed whilst, with the White Dominions and the 'other LDCs', it plummetted. Between 1958 and 1983, the share of UK trade accounted for by Western Europe increased from 30.2% (30.2% of imports and 30.1% of exports) to 59.3% (62.1% of imports and 56.5% of exports). Of this, the EEC's share increased from 19.9% (20.1% of imports and 19.6% of exports) to 44.6% (45.9% of imports and 43.4% of exports).[6] By contrast, the White Dominions and the 'other LDCs', who had been Britain's key trading partners in the immediate post-war period, were of only marginal importance by the early 1980s. Between 1958 and 1983, the share of UK trade accounted for by the White Dominions declined from 21.2% to 5.2%, whilst that of the 'other LDCs' shrank just as dramatically from 22.7% to 6.4% (see Table 9.1).

Meanwhile, the importance of trade with Japan, OPEC and the NICs increased substantially in the period from 1958 to 1983. Even so Japan, despite a rapid advance, still only accounts for a relatively small fraction of total UK trade (3.2% in 1983). OPEC's importance, on the other hand, has varied considerably in the post-war period. It reached a high point in the years 1974–6, as a consequence of both the dramatic rise in the price of oil as well as OPEC's correspondingly enhanced importance as a market for UK manufactured exports. By 1983, however, although OPEC's importance as an outlet for UK exports was greater than ever, its role as a supplier of UK imports had declined dramatically as a result of the growth of North Sea fuel production and the consequent decline in UK oil imports. Finally, trade with the newly industrializing countries (NICSs) has increased steadily since the 1960s.

Let us now turn to a more detailed examination of both the commodity composition and geography of UK imports and exports in the post-war period, starting with UK imports.

UK imports: changes in commodity composition and geographical direction

General

The post-war period has witnessed major changes in the geography of UK imports: there has been a huge increase in imports from other industrialized countries (and, prior to the mid-1970s, OPEC), paralleled by a dramatic decline in imports from the White Dominions and the 'other LDCs'. Changes in the commodity composition of UK imports – in particular, the decline in primary product imports and the increase in imports of manufactures – were a major contributory factor to this change in the geography of UK imports. Let us see how this happened.

Changing commodity composition of UK imports

The post-war period has witnessed an unparalleled expansion of international trade in manufactures, stimulated by worldwide economic growth, increased liberalization of trade in manufactures and growing international integration in consumption and technology. Against this favourable background, UK manufactured exports expanded very rapidly in volume terms (see Table 9.8), albeit nothing like as fast as the manufactured exports of most other advanced countries. More recently, British primary product exports, especially oil, have also increased rapidly (see Table 9.8), though, admittedly, from a rather low base. As a result of this rapid growth in export volume, the UK experienced a considerable expansion in her real capacity to import which was compounded, at least in the period between the early fifties and the early seventies, by a substantial improvement in her external terms of trade.[7]

How did Britain utilize this substantial increase in her real capacity to import? In the period 1950–73 (see Table 9.2) it was partly devoted to purchasing an increased volume of imported primary products (food, raw materials and fuel). As a result, Britain was able to sustain a substantial increase in her real GDP – although GDP rose by less than half the increase in import capacity. Fuel imports increased very rapidly in volume terms (see Table 9.2); however, as a result of the developments in British production and consumption of food and raw materials, described in Chapter 6, the rise in food and raw material imports was much more modest.[8] Thus, despite a large increase in fuel imports, UK primary product imports as a whole did not grow anything like as fast, in volume terms, as the country's real capacity to import. This development, together with a fall in relative primary product prices, resulted in a decline in the share of primary products in total UK imports from 79.8% in 1950–6 to 43.0% in 1970–3 (see Table 9.2).

Table 9.2. *Data on UK imports, 1938 and 1946–83*

	GDP	Total imports	Manu-factures SITC (5–8)	Total primary products SITC (0–4)	Food, beverages and tobacco SITC (0 + 1)	Basic materials SITC (2 + 4)	Fuel SITC (3)
Volume indices (1963 = 100)							
1938	—	—	—	81.5	92.0	95.9	21.1
1946–49	67.5	58.2	34.9	66.0	70.5	81.1	27.1
1950–59	92.6	72.8	51.8	83.6	85.2	97.9	53.3
1960–69	105.6	111.8	125.5	103.9	100.3	103.3	115.9
1970–73	128.1	161.1	245.1	116.5	100.5	106.0	183.1
1974–79	140.4	190.4	368.1	106.5	100.3	100.0	136.8
1980–81	144.8	203.8	457.9	93.4	96.5	91.6	87.5
1982–83	149.6	216.0	520.4	93.6	102.6	92.5	68.3
Imports as a % of GDP		As a % of total imports					
1938	—	100.0	21.3	77.9	46.6	26.1	5.2
1946–49	14.1	100.0	17.2	82.8	40.3	36.8	5.7
1950–59	17.5	100.0	23.0	77.1	37.7	31.7	7.7
1960–69	14.8	100.0	40.8	58.0	30.9	17.9	9.2
1970–73	16.7	100.0	55.4	43.0	21.3	12.3	9.4
1974–79	23.0	100.0	57.3	40.8	15.8	9.4	15.6
1980–81	19.3	100.0	63.9	34.0	12.4	7.2	14.4
1982–83	19.8	100.0	67.1	30.9	12.1	6.4	12.4
Import unit values relative to the deflator for GDP (1963 = 100)							
1938		—	—	—	—	—	—
1948–49		123.9	111.0	127.9	121.2	125.1	157.0
1950–59		134.3	125.5	136.1	122.5	149.6	157.8
1960–69		98.0	102.9	95.0	93.7	98.2	93.5
1970–73		92.3	101.2	87.4	88.4	88.2	82.4
1974–79		118.8	113.0	121.5	102.1	106.2	220.9
1980–81		102.9	91.5	106.6	75.5	76.2	277.3
1982–83		104.4	92.2	110.2	74.0	71.7	315.0

Sources and Notes: The series on import volumes for the period 1947–83 were constructed from data in HMSO, *Annual Abstract of Statistics*. This publication contains base-weighted indices for each of the commodity groups listed in the table. Each of our series is a chained index (reference base 1963 = 100) of six different base-weighted series. Observations for the years 1938 and 1946 were obtained from disaggregated data in HMSO, *Annual Abstract of Statistics*. GDP data from HMSO, *Economic Trends Annual Supplement*: 1985. Data on import values: imports c.i.f. for 1938, and 1946–49 HMSO, *Annual Abstract of Statistics 1954* adjusted to imports f.o.b. using the implicit c.i.f./f.o.b. adjustment coefficient for total imports obtained by comparing data from HMSO, *Annual Abstract of Statistics 1954* and HMSO, *Balance of Payments: Pink Book 1946–57*. Imports f.o.b. for the period 1950–83 available directly from HMSO, *Balance of Payments: Pink Book*. Data on import unit values from HMSO, *Annual Abstract of Statistics*. This publication contains base-weighted unit value indices for each of the commodity groups listed in the table. Each of our series is a chained index (reference base 1963 = 100) of five different base-weighted indices. Data on GDP deflator for the UK from HMSO, *Economic Trends Annual Supplement: 1985*

In the period from 1973 to 1983, the growth in Britain's real capacity to import was used somewhat differently. Although there was an increase in real GDP, UK primary product imports as a whole actually declined in volume terms (see Table 9.2). Imports of food, beverages and tobacco remained virtually stationary, but raw material imports fell by at least 10% and fuel imports declined by considerably more. The main factors responsible for this were the changes in UK production and consumption of primary products, described in Chapter 6, as well as poor economic performance. Despite much higher relative prices for fuel in the period 1973–83 (see Table 9.2), this decline in the volume of UK primary product imports resulted in a further fall in the share of primary products in total UK imports (from 43.0% in 1973 to 29.5% in 1983).

To summarize the argument so far: Britain's real capacity to import grew rapidly in the post-war period, and the increase was large enough to sustain quite a substantial expansion in real GDP. Until 1973, this growth in real import capacity financed an increased volume of imported primary products. However, from 1973 to 1983, primary product imports, as a whole, actually fell. Thus, changes on the non-manufacturing side of the British economy, together with economic failure, resulted in a fall in the share of primary products in total UK imports, and the effect of these developments was compounded, at least in the period from the early fifties to the early seventies, by a decline in relative primary product prices.

Since such a relatively small proportion of the post-war increase in the UK's real capacity to import was devoted to primary products, how was it actually spent?

The first point to note is that it was devoted overwhelmingly to increased imports of goods and services: thus, except for the period 1979–81, the UK was hardly ever in surplus on her commercial account. Part of this enhanced capacity to import was undoubtedly spent on imported services of one sort or another (especially foreign holidays). However, spurred on by the steady liberalization of Britain's manufactured import trade, most of the post-war growth in Britain's real capacity to import was spent on increased imports of manufactures. Thus, UK imports of manufactures increased much faster, in volume terms, than UK merchandize imports as a whole and, between 1946–9 and 1982–3, the share of manufactures in total UK imports increased from 17.2% to 67.1% (see Table 9.2).

It should be noted that the share of primary products in total UK imports would have fallen and that of manufactures would have risen even if British economic performance had been stronger in the post-war period. Of course, Britain could only have achieved faster economic growth if her industry had been more dynamic and productivity growth much faster. This is true whether we consider the period prior to the mid-sixties, when the level of economic activity was, generally speaking, not constrained by the level of demand, or the subsequent period, when it most certainly was. If UK industrial and economic performance had been stronger, then UK primary product imports would undoubtedly have been higher; nevertheless, they would not have been that much higher (see Chapter 7). Thus, even if industrial and economic performance had been stronger, the share of primary products in total UK imports would still have fallen; indeed, the decline might have been even more pronounced than it actually was. The reason for this is that if British industrial performance had been stronger, then manufactured exports would have been higher, as would the country's capacity to import: much the greater part of this enhanced capacity to import would have been spent on imported manufactures which would be higher, not only absolutely but, probably, also as a share of total imports than they are now.

It should also be noted that this argument is perfectly compatible with the view that poor industrial performance has been the principal factor responsible for the generally weak performance of the British economy (particularly the trend rise in unemployment in the period since the mid-1960s). As a result of British industry's failure to respond more adequately to the era of heightened competition in international trade in manufactures, the UK's propensity to import manufactures has increased very rapidly, and much of the potential for economic growth, afforded by the increase in the country's real import capacity, has failed to be utilized. In this situation, successive British governments have resorted to deflation, in order to check the growth in manufactured imports, and Britain has experienced a progressive failure to maintain full employment of both labour and capital.

This proposition is perfectly compatible with arguing that, had British industry's response to the challenge of increased competition been more adequate, then UK imports of manufactures would be higher, not only absolutely but, probably, also as a proportion of total imports, than they are now.

The changing geographical origin of the UK imports

These changes in the commodity composition of UK imports obviously had important implications for the geography of Britain's import trade.

As Britain's imports of food and raw materials declined both as a share of total imports and finally in absolute terms, so areas specializing in exporting food and raw materials diminished in importance as suppliers of imports to the UK. As a result, the proportion of UK imports supplied by the White Dominions fell, between 1948 and 1983, from 25.3% to 5.1%, whilst that accounted for by the 'other LDCs' declined from 32.1% to 5.2% (see Table 9.3).

Meanwhile, the rapid growth of UK oil imports in the period prior to 1973 resulted in OPEC becoming increasingly important as a supplier of UK imports – its share rising from 6.9% in 1948 to 9.4% in 1973 and then increasing even further, in the wake of the first oil price rise, to 16.4% in 1974 (see Table 9.3). However, as a result of the subsequent decline in UK oil imports, OPEC's share fell to just 4.3% in 1983 (see Table 9.3).

Table 9.3. *UK visible imports by area, 1913–83 (%)*

UK imports from:	1913	1929	1938	1948	1951	1958	1965	1973	1974	1979	1980	1982	1983
EEC	29.4	27.1	18.5	13.2	17.9	20.1	23.6	33.0	33.4	43.1	40.3	44.6	45.9
Other W. Europe	8.0	8.2	8.6	8.1	10.1	10.1	12.5	17.0	14.8	16.7	15.8	14.9	16.2
USA	17.8	16.1	12.8	8.8	9.7	9.3	11.7	10.2	9.7	10.2	11.7	11.1	11.0
Japan	0.6	0.7	1.0	0.3	0.4	0.9	1.4	2.8	2.5	3.1	3.3	4.7	5.2
White Dominions	12.7	14.3	23.1	25.3	19.0	20.1	18.6	11.0	8.7	5.5	5.9	5.6	5.1
OPEC	1.6	3.1	3.4	6.9	9.1	12.1	9.7	9.4	16.4	7.0	8.4	6.2	4.3
Newly industrialized countries	2.9	1.6	1.9	2.5	4.1	2.3	2.4	3.9	3.2	4.0	4.7	4.4	4.8
Centrally Planned Economies	6.0	5.3	6.5	2.9	2.9	3.2	4.3	3.7	3.2	3.2	2.8	2.4	2.4
Other LDCs	21.1	23.6	24.2	32.1	26.8	21.7	15.8	9.0	8.2	7.3	7.1	6.0	5.2
Total	100.1	100.0	100.0	100.1	100.0	99.8	100.0	100.0	100.1	100.1	100.0	99.9	100.1

Source: See Table 9.1

Meanwhile, as imports of manufactures increased, both absolutely and as a share of total imports, so areas specializing in exporting manufactures become increasingly important in Britain's import trade. Thus, in the period from 1948 to 1983, Western Europe's share of total UK imports increased from 21.3% to 62.1%,[9] whilst that of Japan rose from 0.3% to 5.2% and that of the NICs increased from 2.5% to 4.8% (see Table 9.3). On the other hand, the importance of the US as a supplier of UK imports hardly changed at all; this was because a large proportion of the increase in UK demand for the manufactured products of US business enterprise was satisfied by overseas subsidiaries of these companies, located either on the Continent or in the UK itself. Thus, as UK imports of manufactures grew, so areas of the world specializing in exporting manufactures (Western Europe, Japan and the NICs) were responsible for an increasing share of total UK imports.

Not only did changes in the commodity composition of UK imports, as between primary products and manufactures, have a major impact on the geographical origin of UK imports, but in addition changes in commodity composition at a more disaggregated level – i.e. changes in the composition of imported primary products, as well as of imported manufactures – also contributed to the changing geography of UK imports. It is to these that we now turn.

Changes in the commodity composition and geographical origin of UK primary product imports

Certain primary product imports increased at a faster rate than others, and the resultant changes in composition had an important effect on the geographical origin of UK primary product imports.

Oil and OPEC

For example, as noted earlier, UK imports of oil grew very rapidly in the period prior to 1973 and this, together with the first oil price rise, was responsible for a huge increase in OPEC's importance as a supplier of UK primary product imports: between 1951 and 1974, OPEC's share rose from 10.2% to 33.3% (see Table 9.4). However, the subsequent sharp decline in UK oil imports resulted in an equally dramatic reduction in OPEC's importance – falling to 10.7% by 1983 (see Table 9.4).

Sugar, tea and sisal: trade with the 'other LDCs'

Post-war changes in the structure of British economy had a particularly adverse effect on UK imports of primary products from the 'other LDCs', their share of the total falling, between 1951 and 1983, from 28.5% to 11.4% (see Table 9.4).

Table 9.4. *UK imports of primary products, by area (%)*

	1938	1951	1961	1973	1974	1980	1983
EEC	15.5	14.2	16.7	25.4	24.7	28.9	33.8
Other W. Europe	8.0	9.5	9.5	11.4	9.0	11.8	19.6
USA	11.1	8.0	7.8	6.5	5.2	7.0	5.9
Japan	0.0	0.2	0.8	0.5	0.3	0.2	0.1
White Dominions	26.7	21.3	20.0	15.7	10.8	10.1	10.2
OPEC	2.8	10.2	16.1	20.3	33.3	20.7	10.7
NICs	2.0	4.8	2.1	3.1	2.3	4.7	3.5
CPEs	6.6	3.2	4.9	3.1	2.8	3.1	4.5
Other LDCs	27.3	28.5	22.2	14.0	11.6	13.5	11.4
Total	100.0	99.9	100.1	100.0	100.0	100.0	99.7
Primary product imports as a share of total imports (%)	77.9	78.0	64.4	40.2	45.2	33.9	29.5

The principal factor responsible for this decline was a drastic fall in UK imports of a number of foodstuffs and raw materials of particular importance to producers in the ‘other LDCs’. For example, between the late fifties and early eighties, whereas UK food imports as a whole declined by just 6.3% in volume terms, imports of sugar declined by one-third (with particularly adverse repercussions on producers in the Caribbean) and imports of beef declined by 28% (with especially negative effects on Argentina).[10] Furthermore, whereas UK raw material imports as a whole were virtually stationary in volume terms, taking the post-war period as a whole, imports of raw cotton, jute and sisal were by 1983 just a fraction of their immediate post-war level.[11]

A further factor tending to depress UK primary product imports from the ‘other LDCs’ was the fact that tea imports decreased from 1968 onwards and, despite a steady growth in imports of coffee, UK beverage imports as a whole experienced a steady decline.

Thus, as a result of post-war changes on the non-manufacturing side of the British economy, primary producers in the ‘other LDCs’, especially in the Indian subcontinent, lost important markets in the UK. These markets are most unlikely ever to be recovered; the well-established decline in UK tea consumption will probably never be reversed whilst, even if UK industrial performance were to improve, Britain will never again be a major import market for natural textile fibres.

Mutton, butter, sugar, wheat and wool: trade with the White Dominions

Post-war changes in the structure of the British economy also had an adverse effect on UK imports of primary products from the White Dominions. Their

Table 9.5. *UK imports, consumption and domestic self-sufficiency in foodstuffs of particular interest to Dominions' producers*

	Imports 1963 = 100	UK consumption (000 tons)	UK production (000 tons)	UK self-sufficiency (%)
Mutton and lamb				
1938	101.0	532	192	36
1953	102.9	488	176	36
1963	100.0	589	253	43
1980	55.0	431	289	67
Butter				
1938	114.9	527	47	9
1953	68.1	318	29	9
1963	100.0	484	34	7
1980	49.5	416	171	41
Sugar				
1938	102.6	2585	414	16
1953	117.9	4036	767	19
1963	100.0	3372	776	23
1980	71.1	2075	1079	52
Wheat				
1938	129.1	7282	1675	23
1953	102.2	6517	2672	41
1963	100.0	7532	3013	40
1980	56.5	9610	8457	88
Cheese				
1938	102.9	187	45	24
1953	108.0	240	91	38
1963	100.0	242	104	43
1980	73.2	338	237	70

Source: HMSO, *Trade and Navigation Accounts of the UK*
HMSO, *Overseas Trade Statistics of the UK*
HMSO, *Annual Reports of Agriculture*

share of the total fell, between 1951 and 1983, from 21.3% to 10.2% (see Table 9.4), and this probably represented a decline in absolute terms, as well.

The principal factor responsible for this development was an unusually large decline in UK imports of foodstuffs and raw materials of particular importance to producers in the White Dominions: mutton and lamb, butter, sugar, wheat and wool. UK imports of these commodities fell by much more, in volume terms, than UK imports of food and raw materials as a whole. Between 1963 and 1980, total UK food imports fell by 12.6%. However, imports of mutton and lamb fell by 45%, butter imports by 51%, sugar imports by 29%, wheat imports by 44% and cheese imports by 27% (see Table 9.5). Similarly, whilst the total volume of UK raw material imports declined by 30.5%, wool imports fell by 60.3%.

These drastic reductions in UK imports of commodities of particular importance to producers in the White Dominions were an inevitable consequence of UK import-substitution in competing areas of temperate agriculture reinforced, in the case of a number of items, by reductions in consumption (see Table 9.5). Such changes in UK patterns of production and consumption have a long-term, structural character, such that, even if there were to be a resumption of sustained economic growth in the UK, it would hardly have any effect whatsoever on imports of these particular commodities. Since there is unlikely to be much, if any, reduction in the agricultural protection in the UK – at least in the immediate future – producers in the White Dominions will almost certainly never recover their former hold on the British market.

The second major factor responsible for the decline in UK imports from the White Dominions has been the growth of food imports from the EEC. As a result of the UK's adherence to the Common Agricultural Policy (CAP), producers in the White Dominions were forced to surrender part of an already shrinking British import market to competitors in Continental Europe. Thus, the share of the White Dominions in UK food imports, after being stationary for about ten years, declined, between 1972 and 1982, from 30.0% to 16.2% whilst, over the same period, the EEC's share rose from 32.7% to 52.0%.[12] However, the EEC's growing importance as a supplier of UK food imports was not just the result of substitution in supply following Britain's membership of the CAP. It was also the consequence of genuine changes in taste and the spread of Continental habits of consumption amongst British consumers – an obvious example being growing British consumption of French cheese.

To conclude: the dramatic decline in UK primary product imports from the White Dominions was partly due to factors favouring EEC suppliers, such as the CAP, and changes in consumer tastes. However, increasing UK self-sufficiency in a number of commodities of special importance to producers in the White Dominions was by far the most important factor responsible for the decline in UK imports from these countries. These developments are unlikely ever to be reversed, and Dominions' producers have almost certainly sustained permanent losses in the British market.

Wine, cheese and the CAP: primary product trade with the EEC

Between 1951 and 1983, UK primary product imports from the EEC increased, both absolutely and as a share of the total (from 14.2% to 33.8%) (see Table 9.4). This increase is usually attributed entirely to the effect of the UK's adherence to the CAP. However, this is only part of the story, and the EEC has been an increasingly important supplier across the whole range of UK primary product imports, food and non-food items alike.[13]

Well before the UK's adherence to the CAP, producers in the present member countries of the EEC were capturing a growing share of the UK's shrinking import market for food. However, membership of the CAP undoubtedly resulted in a quickening of this process, whilst EEC producers also benefited from rising real incomes, as well as changes in taste, as a result of which British patterns of consumption moved closer to those in Continental Europe. An example is the spread of the wine-drinking habit: the only primary product category, in which imports expanded rapidly and continuously throughout the entire post-war period, was 'alcoholic beverages'. Between the early fifties and early seventies, imports of alcoholic beverages increased fivefold, in volume terms,[14] and this was largely the result of the rapid growth of wine consumption in Britain.

The EEC was also responsible for a growing share of UK imports of raw materials and fuel (see note 13) as a result of a considerable growth of two-way trade in products such as synthetic rubber, synthetic fibres and refined petroleum derivatives. Although we treat these products as primary commodities (in accordance with the SITC), international trade in them has been affected by some of the same forces which have been responsible for the rapid growth of two-way trade in manufactures between the UK and the EEC: in particular, the role played by multinational companies in internationalizing the process of production.

The changing origin of UK primary product imports: conclusions

During the past thirty years, dramatic changes have taken place in the geography of UK primary product imports: the rise and decline of OPEC, the growing importance of the EEC and, finally, the dramatic marginalization of the White Dominions and the 'other LDCs'. Substitution of EEC for non-EEC sources of supplies, following the UK's adherence to the CAP, was one of the factors responsible for these changes, but a comparatively minor one. Much more important were the growth and subsequent decline in UK oil consumption, as well as the rapid expansion of North Sea production; long-run trends in UK production and consumption of various foods and beverages, which had particularly adverse effects on producers of these commodities in the White Dominions and the 'other LDCs'; and, finally, structural change in British industry, which resulted in a particularly rapid decline in UK imports of wool, cotton and other textile fibres. Unless there is a drastic reduction in the degree of protection afforded to UK agriculture and a determined attempt to revive those sectors of the British textile industry which are based on natural fibres (cotton, jute, wool and sisal) – developments which must be regarded as extremely unlikely

Table 9.6. *UK imports of manufactures, by area (%)*

	1938	1951	1961	1973	1974	1980	1983
EEC	27.6	30.4	32.9	39.1	41.6	46.6	51.2
Other W. Europe	10.6	12.3	14.7	21.5	20.3	18.0	14.8
USA	18.0	15.6	17.7	13.1	13.9	14.3	13.3
Japan	1.7	1.2	1.1	4.6	4.5	5.0	7.2
White Dominions	13.1	10.9	13.6	7.3	6.7	3.6	2.8
OPEC	5.1	5.2	0.7	0.7	0.5	1.6	1.5
NICs	1.6	1.6	3.7	4.6	4.0	4.7	5.3
CPEs	6.5	2.0	4.3	4.2	3.6	2.6	1.4
Other LDCs	15.8	20.8	11.3	5.0	5.0	3.6	2.5
Total	100.0	100.0	100.0	100.1	100.1	100.0	100.0
Manufactures as a share of total imports	19.5	21.6	34.7	58.1	52.5	64.0	68.0

Source: See Table 9.1

– it is difficult to see how the White Dominions and the 'other LDCs' can ever regain their former commanding position in the UK market for primary products.

The changing origin of UK manufactured imports

In the years immediately after the Second World War, when UK manufactured imports were very tightly controlled and the total volume from all areas was comparatively small, quite a high proportion consisted of simple consumer goods supplied, in the main, by producers in the Indian subcontinent: in 1951, for example, the 'other LDCs' were responsible for supplying 20.8% of total UK manufactured imports (see Table 9.6). However, as controls were relaxed, and the volume of UK manufactured imports began to increase, there was an enormous change in their composition. This increase, in both the volume and the range of UK manufactured imports, could only have been satisfied by producers in Western Europe and Japan.[15] As a result, Western Europe's share of UK manufactured imports increased, in the period from 1951 to 1983, from 42.7% to 66.0%, whilst that of Japan rose from 1.2% to 7.2% (see Table 9.6). The UK also turned, on an increasing scale, to suppliers in the NICs, and their share of UK manufactured imports rose, between 1951 and 1983, from 1.6% to 5.3% (see Table 9.6). As a consequence of these developments, the 'other LDCs' have been marginalized as suppliers of UK manufactured imports, their share having declined, in the period from 1951 to 1983, from 20.8% to 2.5%. Thus, changes in the composition of UK manufactured imports resulting from the vast increase in their volume have been an additional contributory factor to the dramatic reorientation of British import trade away from the White Dominions and 'other LDCs' and towards other advanced countries.

The effect of EEC entry[16]

A noteworthy feature of UK trade throughout the entire post-war period has been the rapid growth of manufactured imports from Western Europe. This was an inevitable consequence of the increased volume and, hence, range of UK manufactured imports, since Western Europen producers were obviously well placed to meet British requirements. This increased degree of integration between the UK and the EEC was already very advanced, even prior to Britain's membership of the Community. Thus in 1973 the EEC already supplied 39.1% of UK manufactured imports – up from 30.4% in 1951 (see Table 9.6). The growth of the EEC as a source of supply was in fact held back, in the period prior to British entry, by UK membership of EFTA, since EFTA, by stimulating an expansion of preferential trade in manufactures amongst its members, resulted in part of Britain's manufactured import requirements being satisfied by producers in 'Other Western Europe' at the expense of suppliers in the EEC.[17]

Britain's membership of the European Community undoubtedly reinforced the process of growing recourse to EEC producers as suppliers of imported manufactures. It did so in two main ways. First, membership of the EEC resulted in some unwinding of UK preferential trade in manufactures with EFTA members and, as a result, there was a significant decline, in the period from 1973 to 1983, in the importance of 'Other Western Europe' as a supplier of UK manufactured imports (see Table 9.6). Secondly, EEC membership resulted in some additional liberalization of UK trade in manufactures in favour of EEC suppliers at the expense of all other areas specializing in exporting manufactures, in particular Japan and the NICs. The beneficial effect of this on EEC suppliers was reinforced by the erection of non-tariff barriers against areas competing with EEC producers: voluntary export restraint agreements (in the case of Japan) and the Multi-Fibre Agreement (in the case of the NICs). Thus, UK entry into the EEC, along with these other measures, had the effect of enhancing the EEC's importance as a supplier of manufactured imports at the expense of other areas, with the result that the EEC's share of UK manufactured imports rose, in the period 1973 to 1983, from 39.1% to 51.2% (see Table 9.6).

In addition, there is little doubt that, since membership of the EEC resulted in some additional liberalization of UK manufactured import trade, it was responsible for exacerbating the already severe competitive pressures on UK producers. Since their response to this challenge was far from satisfactory, membership of the EEC can probably be said to have had a damaging effect on UK economic performance, since it resulted in an additional upward shift in the UK's *propensity* to import manufactures and, in this way, served to exacerbate the trend rise in unemployment of both labour and capital. However, it would be quite wrong to argue that EEC entry has been the only factor responsible for the rapid growth in UK manufactured imports during the past ten years. Some of the main ones have already been outlined earlier in this chapter: the growth in British exports and, hence, in the country's capacity to import; changes in the structure of the British economy, which had an adverse effect on the growth of UK primary product imports; and growing liberalization of trade in manufactures amongst all OECD countries. UK exchange rate policy was an additional, important factor.

Furthermore, although EEC entry probably had an adverse effect on UK economic performance, it should be noted that, had UK industrial and economic performance been stronger, then the volume of UK manufactured imports – from the EEC, as well as from Japan and the NICs – would almost certainly be higher than it is today and the share of these countries in total UK imports would probably be higher as well. The reason for this is that if UK industrial and economic performance had been stronger then UK manufactured exports would be higher, and a considerable proportion of the additional foreign exchange would have been spent on imported manufactures – from Western Europe, Japan and the NICs.

The redirection of UK export trade

The main developments affecting the geography of post-war UK export trade have been twofold: first the growing importance, both absolute and relative, of exports to Western Europe, the US and OPEC and, second, the diminishing importance, both absolute and relative, of exports to the White Dominions and the 'other LDCs'. In the period 1948 to 1983, the share of Western Europe in UK exports increased from 30.6% to 56.5%, that of the US from 4.3% to 14.1% and that of OPEC from 7.3% to 10.1% (see Table 9.7). Meanwhile, the share of the White Dominions declined from 23.7% to 5.3%, whilst that of the 'other LDCs' fell from 27.1% to 7.5% (see Table 9.7). At the same time, there was a moderate increase, both absolute and relative, in UK exports to Japan and a moderate reduction in exports to the NICs and the Centrally Planned Economies (see Table 9.7).

In the period prior to the late 1970s, the commodity composition of UK exports remained virtually constant, with the share of manufactures remaining more or less unchanged at well over 80% (see Table 9.8). Thus, in contrast to UK import trade, changes in commodity composition do not account for any of the changes in the geography of UK exports which took place during this period. It was not until the late 1970s, when fuel exports began to grow, that the commodity composition of UK exports changed in any significant way (see Table

Table 9.7. *UK visible exports by area, 1913–83 (%)*

UK exports to:	1913	1929	1938	1948	1951	1958	1965	1973	1974	1979	1980	1982	1983
EEC	30.3	28.7	23.7	17.9	17.4	19.6	26.4	32.6	33.4	41.8	42.0	41.9	43.4
Other W. Europe	6.6	7.6	9.0	12.7	11.7	10.5	15.3	18.2	17.4	16.4	16.4	12.3	13.1
USA	8.8	7.4	5.4	4.3	5.7	8.7	10.6	12.1	10.7	9.5	9.4	13.6	14.1
Japan	2.2	1.6	0.4	0.0	0.4	0.6	1.1	2.2	1.9	1.4	1.2	1.2	1.3
White Dominions	15.0	17.9	22.9	23.7	27.5	22.2	18.0	10.8	11.3	6.2	5.7	6.1	5.3
OPEC	3.1	3.6	4.0	7.3	5.3	7.9	5.5	6.4	7.3	8.9	10.0	11.6	10.1
Newly industrializing countries	4.0	4.3	3.5	4.6	5.9	3.5	3.6	3.9	4.2	3.7	3.4	3.5	3.3
Centrally Planned Economies	9.6	4.2	7.5	2.4	2.0	3.2	2.9	3.3	3.0	2.8	2.7	1.8	1.9
Other LDCs	20.4	24.8	23.5	27.1	24.1	23.7	16.5	10.6	10.7	9.5	9.2	8.0	7.5
Total	100.0	100.1	99.9	100.0	100.0	99.9	99.9	100.1	99.9	100.2	100.0	100.0	100.0

Source: See Table 9.1

Table 9.8. *Data on UK exports, 1938 and 1946–83*

	GDP	Total exports	Manu-factures SITC (5–8)	Total primary products SITC (0–4)	Food, beverages and tobacco SITC (0 + 1)	Basic materials SITC (2 + 4)	Fuel SITC (3)
Volume indices (1963 = 100)							
1938	—	—	—	98.1	87.1	91.1	124.6
1948–49	67.5	59.9	62.7	53.0	58.1	57.8	38.9
1950–59	92.6	77.6	78.9	71.8	74.4	75.9	62.4
1960–69	105.6	107.6	108.8	101.0	111.1	98.7	87.4
1970–73	128.1	156.4	160.2	142.2	172.7	115.2	126.4
1974–79	140.4	201.9	202.2	201.9	255.4	146.7	183.9
1980–81	144.8	225.4	208.4	285.5	311.3	191.1	360.7
1982–83	149.6	230.9	202.0	318.3	329.6	190.2	458.6
Exports as a % of GDP		As a % of total imports					
1938	—	100.0	69.8	27.7	8.9	10.1	8.7
1946–49	12.4	100.0	82.7	14.5	6.5	5.6	2.5
1950–59	16.1	100.0	80.5	17.7	6.5	5.8	5.4
1960–69	13.9	100.0	83.4	13.6	6.4	4.2	3.1
1970–73	15.6	100.0	84.2	12.7	6.6	3.3	2.7
1974–79	20.2	100.0	80.3	16.5	7.1	3.2	6.4
1980–81	20.3	100.0	71.1	26.0	7.0	2.9	16.3
1982–83	20.1	100.0	66.6	30.5	7.1	2.6	21.0
Export unit values relative to the deflator for GDP (1963 = 100)							
1938		—	—	—	—	—	—
1948–49		115.4	110.7	—	—	—	—
1950–59		115.4	112.4	—	—	—	—
1960–69		98.3	98.8	95.7	95.7	94.8	97.0
1970–73		92.7	93.9	83.7	80.8	84.3	89.9
1974–79		105.5	105.0	113.0	81.1	93.7	214.2
1980–81		96.4	94.3	100.0	67.6	68.2	265.5
1982–83		96.8	94.2	111.6	67.0	64.6	279.0

Sources and Notes: Data on export volumes mainly from HMSO, *Annual Abstract of Statistics*. This publication contains base-weighted export volume indices for total exports, as well as for manufactured exports, for the period 1947 to 1983. It also contains export volume indices for food, beverages and tobacco, basic materials and fuel for the years 1947, 1950–62 and 1966–83. Each of our series is a chained index (reference year 1963 = 100) of several base-weighted series. For the missing years, we constructed indices using disaggregated data in HMSO, *Trade and Navigation Accounts of the UK* and HMSO, *Overseas Trade Statistics of the UK*. Constant price GDP data from HMSO, *Economic Trends Annual Supplement 1985*. Data on export values from HMSO, *Balance of Payments: Pink Book*. Data on export unit values from HMSO, *Annual Abstract of Statistics*. This publication contains base-weighted export unit value indices for total exports, as well as for exports of manufactures, for the period 1948–83. Each of our series is a chained index (reference year 1963 = 100) of six base-weighted indices. HMSO, *Annual Abstract of Statistics* contains export unit value indices for food, beverages and tobacco, basic materials and fuel for the period 1966–83 only. Each of our series is a chained index (reference year 1963 = 100) of three base-weighted indices, extrapolated back to 1960, using series on export unit values for total primary products (also found in HMSO, *Annual Abstract of Statistics*)

9.8). Since UK primary product exports are even more strongly oriented to the markets of the industrialized countries (in Western Europe and the US) than are UK manufactured exports, this shift in commodity composition had the effect of accentuating even further the redirection of UK export trade away from the White Dominions and the 'other LDCs' towards the markets of Western Europe and the US.

Let us now turn to the question of changes in the geography of UK exports considering, first, manufactures and, second, primary products.

Table 9.9. *UK exports of manufactures, by area (%)*

	1938	1951	1961	1973	1974	1980	1983
EEC	17.3	14.9	21.6	30.7	31.6	37.2	37.2
Other W. Europe	8.2	12.2	12.5	18.2	17.3	17.2	12.8
USA	3.0	4.4	6.7	12.3	10.8	9.1	12.6
Japan	0.5	0.3	1.0	2.1	1.9	1.3	1.5
White Dominions	28.4	30.6	20.3	11.7	12.4	6.7	7.0
OPEC	4.7	5.5	7.4	6.6	7.5	11.6	13.1
NICs	4.1	6.2	3.9	4.3	4.7	4.1	4.4
CPEs	7.8	1.0	0.6	3.5	3.2	2.9	2.2
Other LDCs	26.1	24.8	26.0	10.7	10.7	10.0	9.3
Total	100.0	99.9	100.0	100.1	100.1	100.1	100.1
Manufactures as a % of total exports	75.2	81.7	82.6	83.1	81.7	73.6	66.1

Source: See Table 9.1

The changing direction of UK manufactured exports

In the immediate post-war period, exchange controls and tariff protection in Western Europe represented formidable obstacles to British manufacturers wishing to increase their share of Continental European markets. However, in compensation, British producers enjoyed preferential access to a large protected trading area in the Empire and the White Dominions, largely made up of primary producing countries. In the immediate post-war period, these countries enjoyed exceptionally favourable external terms of trade; moreover, their real capacity to import was given an additional boost by the Korean War primary commodity price boom. British manufacturers were obviously well placed to benefit from this tremendous increase in purchasing power, not only on account of Imperial Preference but also because the efforts of competitors in Western Europe and Japan were hampered by the effects of wartime dislocation and post-war reconstruction. These factors explain why the White Dominions and the 'other LDCs' occupied such a prominent position as markets for UK manufactured exports in the immediate post-war period, the White Dominions accounting for 30.6% of the total in 1951 and the 'other LDCs' for 24.8% (see Table 9.9). In effect, there was a surge of British manufactured exports to markets, experiencing an unusual increase in purchasing power, in which British producers faced little effective competition. This extreme geographical concentration of UK manufactured exports was hardly a healthy characteristic, and it was one which did not survive the return to more orderly conditions in international commodity markets and the dismantling of restrictions on international trade in manufactures.

By 1961, the White Dominions absorbed only 20.3% of UK manufactured exports and, by 1983, their share had fallen to just 7.0% (see Table 9.9). This decline in share, which probably represented an absolute reduction as well, was due to a number of factors. During the 1950s, virtually all primary producing countries experienced a substantial deterioration in their external terms of trade and were forced to reduce their net imports of manufactures (relative to GDP). The White Dominions were no exception. In addition, the rate of economic growth in the White Dominions was relatively slow in the post-war period. Meanwhile, following the dismantling of Imperial Preference, British producers lost their privileged position in Dominion markets and, once economic reconstruction in Western Europe and Japan had been successfully completed, they also faced a renewal of stiff competition. Finally, given that UK imports of food and raw materials from the Dominions were on the decline, consumers in these countries could hardly have been expected to remain loyal to British products.

By contrast, the 'other LDCs' became even more important as markets for British manufactured exports in the period from 1951 to 1961 – both absolutely and as a share of the total. This was partly because in many colonial markets Imperial Preference was retained right through the 1950s. However, when the Empire finally disintegrated during the course of the 1960s, British producers lost many of their remaining privileges in Third World markets.[18] British exports to many less developed countries were also adversely affected by the growth of competition from producers in Western Europe and Japan, and by the fact that most developing countries adopted a substantial degree of industrial tariff protection in the post-war period, with the result that in many lines of production British exporters also had to contend with growing competition from local producers.

In reviewing all these developments, it is clear that the post-war redirection of UK manufactured exports away from markets in the White Dominions and the 'other LDCs' was, to a large degree, inevitable. Britain was simply in no position to maintain the privileged position which her exporters had previously enjoyed in these markets – during the 1930s and in the immediate post-war period. First, there were important political factors at work. The US favoured a rapid return to multilateralism, and the UK's international position, both politically and economically, was far too weak to resist US pressures. In addition, as the White Dominions flexed their political muscles, and former colonies gained their independence, British exporters were bound to lose out. Second, to these political factors must also be added the effects of structural change in the British economy. So far as the Dominions were concerned, a major rationale for the Empire as a political entity and as a framework of agreements had been Britain's importance as a market for primary products. As British imports of food and raw materials, from both the White Dominions and the 'other LDCs', went into steady decline, it was clearly impossible to transfer from Empire to Commonwealth the preferential position which British manufacturing exporters had previously enjoyed in these markets. Thus, as a result of both economic and political factors, the White Dominions and the 'other LDCs' came to occupy a more normal position relative to their economic size as markets for British manufactured exports.

Meanwhile, other advanced countries became much more important as outlets for British manufactured exports, both absolutely and as a share of the total. Between 1951 and 1983, Western Europe's share rose from 27.1% (EEC: 14.9%) to 50.0% (EEC: 37.2%) (see Table 9.9).[19] The main factors responsible for this development were the relaxation of exchange controls in the late fifties, the subsequent liberalization of trade in manufactures amongst all OECD countries and the rapid growth of income and purchasing power in the EEC. UK entry into the Community undoubtedly resulted in a further increase in the EEC's importance, both relative and absolute, as a market for UK manufactured exports (see Table 9.9), although some of this growth represented an unwinding of UK exports to 'Other Western Europe', previously stimulated by EFTA trade preferences. The post-war period also saw an increase in the importance of the US and Japan as markets for UK manufactured exports. In the case of the US, this was largely the result of trade liberalization whilst, in the case of Japan, the main factor was rapid income growth. Thus, over time, UK manufacturers directed an increasing proportion of a rapidly growing volume of manufactured exports to markets in Western Europe, the US and Japan and, compared with the situation in the early 1950s, these countries began to assume a much more normal position, relative to their economic size, as markets for British manufactured exports.

Finally, OPEC's importance as a market for British manufactured exports also expanded rapidly in the post-war period – a process which was accentuated by the oil price rices of the 1970s. In fact, OPEC's share of UK manufactured exports increased from 7.5% in 1974 to 13.1% in 1983 (see Table 9.9). Thus, just at the time when the UK was cutting back on its imports of oil from the area, OPEC constituted a rapidly expanding market for UK manufactured exports. These two developments resulted in significant increase in the overall degree of triangularity of UK trade – an issue to which we shall turn in a moment.

The changing direction of UK manufactured exports: conclusions

The geography of British manufactured exports has been subject to truly dramatic changes in the post-war period, the main features of which have been a rapid growth of sales to other advanced countries and OPEC and a decline in the importance of markets in the White Dominions and the 'other LDCs'. The main factors responsible for these developments have been the gradual liberalization of trade in manufactures amongst all OECD countries (including the White Dominions), the growth of industrial protection in many Third World countries and, finally, rapid income growth in Western Europe, Japan and more recently OPEC.

UK primary product exports: commodity composition and geographical destination

Commodity composition

General

Before the Second World War, primary products constituted about 30% of UK exports; however, following the collapse of coal exports in the 1950s, primary products were a relatively minor item, averaging no more than 15% to 20% of total exports (see Table 9.8). Indeed, it was not until the early 1960s that UK primary product exports advanced beyond their pre-war (1938) level in volume terms (see Table 9.8). However, by 1983, primary products were once again responsible for about 30% of total UK exports and, by this time, they were about three times as important, in volume terms, as they had been in 1963. Oil exports obviously played a central role in this revival. However, all the major commodity categories experienced a marked increase during the 1970s. Between 1963 and 1983, UK food exports increased six times, tobacco exports four times and raw material and beverage exports doubled.[20]

Fuel: Fuel played an extremely important part in UK primary product exports both at the beginning and again at the end of the period 1938 to 1983. In 1938, coal and coke accounted for 8.7% of total UK exports; however, coal exports never really recovered after the war and, following a sudden collapse in the mid-1950s, UK fuel exports consisted mainly of small quantities of refined petroleum products. However, in the late 1970s, as a result of exports from the North Sea and higher prices, the share of fuel in total UK exports began to rise, reaching 21.0% in 1983. Thus the UK was once again an important fuel exporter.

Raw materials: For most of the post-war period, raw materials were one of the main items in UK primary product exports. In the immediate post-war period, re-exports of wool and hides were the principal items. However, they gradually declined in importance, and domestically produced materials such as clay, synthetic rubber and fibres, took their place. Finally, during the late 1970s, there was a drastic decline in exports of synthetic rubber and fibres, and scrap metal (iron and copper) took over as the principal item in UK raw material exports.

Table 9.10. *UK exports of primary products, by area (%)*

	1938	1951	1961	1973	1974	1980	1983
EEC	40.2	31.3	18.7	41.9	42.3	56.2	56.7
Other W. Europe	11.2	9.3	13.5	18.2	18.3	14.1	13.9
USA	11.7	12.4	12.7	11.3	10.0	10.2	17.3
Japan	0.3	0.7	1.7	2.8	2.0	0.9	1.0
White Dominions	8.8	10.0	9.2	6.4	6.1	2.9	1.9
OPEC	2.1	3.7	4.3	5.5	6.6	5.2	3.7
NICs	1.9	4.3	2.6	1.9	1.9	1.5	0.8
CPEs	6.9	7.7	21.7	2.6	2.4	2.0	1.1
Other LDCs	16.7	20.5	15.6	9.5	10.5	6.9	3.7
Total	99.8	99.9	100.0	100.1	100.1	99.9	100.1
Primary products as a % of total exports	22.0	16.5	14.3	13.8	14.6	23.5	31.3

Source: See Table 9.1

Food, beverages and tobacco: Following a twenty-year period in which they were virtually stationary, UK exports of food, non-alcoholic beverages (mainly cocoa products) and tobacco experienced a sudden spurt in the 1970s. The expansion in food exports was focussed on cereals, meat and dairy products. Meanwhile, increased consumption of blond tobacco products in Western Europe and OPEC led to a sudden expansion in UK tobacco exports during the 1970s, this being a part of the tobacco market in which UK multinationals are important producers on a world scale.

Alcoholic beverages: Amidst the ups and downs of these other commodities, UK exports of alcoholic beverages (principally whisky) expanded almost continuously in the post-war period. By 1982, UK alcoholic beverage exports were worth at least £1.0b, with whisky exports (£0.86b) being worth more than twice as much as total UK motor vehicles exports (£0.38b).

Geographical destination of UK primary product exports

UK exports of primary products are mainly sold in the markets of other advanced countries – to a much greater degree than in the case of UK exports of manufactures. This particular characteristic has become even more pronounced in recent years as a result of the very rapid growth of oil and food exports to other advanced countries. Thus by 1983 Western Europe absorbed 70.6% of UK primary product exports and the US 17.3% (see Table 9.10). Since the EEC is of such crucial importance as a market for UK primary product exports, it is to this market that we shall devote most of our attention.

Of the six broad primary product categories, the EEC's share is highest in the case of fuel exports:[21] as a result of exports from the North Sea, the UK became an important supplier of fuel to Continental Europe and, by 1983, the EEC absorbed 62.0% of UK fuel exports.

The EEC is also an important market for UK food exports, absorbing 59.5% of the total in 1983. UK food exports are an important, though often neglected, aspect of Britain's adherence to the CAP. Since joining the CAP, trends in food trade between the UK and the EEC have actually been in Britain's favour: the UK's export–import ratio in food trade with the EEC rising, between 1972 and 1983, from 0.22 to 0.43. Indeed, if the UK were not a member of the CAP, British food exports would almost certainly be considerably lower than they are at present. Not only would they face insurmountable barriers in EEC markets, but, if sold on world markets, they would have to be subsidized directly at the British taxpayer's expense.

The EEC absorbed 54.3% of UK raw material exports in 1983. This is the result of a considerable growth of two-way trade between the UK and the EEC, dating largely from before Britain's membership of the Community, in what are essentially manufactured products.

Compared with these other commodities, the markets for British exports of non-alcoholic beverages, tobacco and drink are much more evenly distributed throughout the world; however, in these products, as well, the EEC has also been an increasingly important market.

To conclude: the rapid growth of UK primary product exports, which are mainly directed to markets in the EEC, has been a further factor contributing to the growth of trade between the Community and the UK.

Conclusions on post-war changes in the direction of UK trade: political consequences and the effect of loss of Empire

Summary of post-war changes in the direction of UK trade

Developments on the non-manufacturing side of the economy, described in Chapter 6, were one of the principal factors responsible for the far-reaching changes in the geographical direction of British trade which occurred in the post-war period. One of the most notable features of this process has been the decline, both relative and, in some cases, absolute, in trade with the White Dominions and the Third World – areas over which Britain, until comparatively recently, exercised considerable political sway.

Imports from the White Dominions have been adversely affected by growing UK self-sufficiency in many of the foodstuffs of which the Dominions are specialist producers: butter, sugar, wheat, mutton and lamb. Imports from the Dominions were also adversely affected by developments benefiting EEC suppliers, namely Britain's adherence to the CAP and changes in consumer tastes.

UK imports from the 'other LDCs', especially from the Indian subcontinent, also declined dramatically: on the one hand, UK tea imports declined whilst, on the other, radical changes in the structure of British industry resulted in a reduction in UK imports of cotton, jute and other vegetable fibres to just a fraction of previous levels.

As the UK reduced its imports of primary products from the White Dominions and the 'other LDCs' they, in turn, could hardly have been expected to maintain the preferential position which British manufacturing exporters previously enjoyed in their domestic markets. And they did not. As a result, the exceptionally important position which these areas occupied in Britain's manufactured export trade in the immediate post-war period was gradually whittled down to the point where, today, these parts of the world assume a much more normal role, relative to their economic size, as markets for British manufactured exports.

Meanwhile, Britain's trade with other industrialized countries has mushroomed in the post-war period. The main factors responsible for this have been, on the import side, the rapid growth of UK imports of manufactures and, on the export side, rapid economic growth in Western Europe and Japan and increased liberalization in trade in manufactures throughout the OECD area. In addition, the UK's growing exports of primary products, especially oil, were mainly directed to markets in Western Europe and the US.

The only area of former British political influence with which trade has increased has been OPEC. However, although OPEC is now crucial as a market for UK manufactured exports, its importance in Britain's import trade has been greatly reduced, as a result of greater UK self-sufficiency in oil.

But it is worth mentioning that changes in Britain's internal economic structure had more than just economic effects. Because they gave rise to an irreversible weakening of the economic links which helped, especially during the inter-war years, to bind the British Empire together, these economic changes had important political consequences as well; in particular, structural change in the British economy is one of the reasons why the Commonwealth failed to evolve into a coherent political entity. Let us briefly examine this point.

Throughout the nineteenth century, Britain's growing domestic market for primary products provided a tremendous stimulus to primary producers throughout the entire world, and the strong economic links, generated by this development, obviously enhanced Britain's political domination over the White Dominions, as well as over countries in her formal and informal Empire in the Third World. During the 1930s, the UK became even more dependent on the Empire as an economic system. After abandoning free trade at home, thereby reducing her trading links with Western Europe and the US, the UK retreated into the Empire, creating a preferential trading area for UK manufactured exports in imperial markets, in return for granting imperial producers quotas in Britain's domestic market for primary products. Although Britain attempted to hang on to her Empire after the war, she found it impossible to resist the powerful political pressures, both internal and external, making for dissolution. And all the time changes in Britain's economic structure were eroding the economic foundations of her political domination over these areas. In retrospect, it is easy to appreciate that British political domination of these areas could not survive such major economic changes and to understand why the Empire disintegrated so rapidly.

The weakening of Britain's economic links with these areas also helps to explain why the Commonwealth has failed to evolve into a coherent political entity. The UK's vastly reduced dependence on imported primary products meant that the other members of the Commonwealth, most of whom still remain extremely dependent on exporting primary products, were forced to find alternative markets. Thus the material basis, which could have been used to transform the Commonwealth into a dynamic economic union, has simply disappeared, and this is a major reason why the organization lacks any real political cohesion.

The economic effects of loss of Empire

Can the deterioration in the UK's manufacturing balance be ascribed to the loss of Empire? The answer is emphatically no. To see why, let us make two assumptions: first, that the UK had been able to transfer to the Commonwealth the preferential position which her manufacturing exporters had previously enjoyed in imperial markets: second, that UK imports of primary products from the Commonwealth had declined just as they have done in practice. What would have happened? First of all, both the volume and the price of UK manufactured exports to the Commonwealth would have been higher. As a result, the UK's balance of payments would have been stronger and, as a consequence, the UK *might* have experienced greater prosperity, faster growth and a higher level of economic activity. What would have been the effect on the UK's overall balance of trade with the Commonwealth? If UK manufactured exports to the Commonwealth had grown as fast as those to the rest of the world, whilst UK imports from the Commonwealth had declined, just as they have done, then the UK would have developed a huge surplus in her overall trade with the Commonwealth. How would this surplus have been utilized? Part of it might well have been devoted to increased overseas military expenditure, a higher level of overseas investment, more aid to less developed countries and greater expenditure on foreign holidays. However, the bulk of the UK's surplus on trade with the Commonwealth would have been used to purchase more manufactured imports from Western Europe, the US, Japan and, perhaps, the NICs. The reason for this is that given the changes in Britain's internal economic structure which have taken place, there would have been no reason to spend the surplus earned in trade with the Commonwealth on increased imports of primary products.

Therefore, even if the UK had been able to maintain a preferential position for her manufacturing exporters in Commonwealth markets, there would still have been a substantial deterioration in the UK's manufacturing balance of trade. Of course, UK trade would be considerably more triangular than it is at present: there would be a surplus in trade with the Commonwealth and a deficit in trade with the rest of the world. Indeed, this was exactly the position prior to the First World War, when the UK was in surplus on trade with the White Dominions and the Third World, and she used this surplus to finance a deficit in trade in manufactures with the 'core' industrial countries of Continental Europe.

Thus, although the loss of Empire has affected the geographical direction of UK manufactured exports and has meant that the UK balance of payments has probably been weaker than it might otherwise have been, it does not account for the deterioration in the UK's manufacturing balance: the latter, as we have already argued in Chapter 6, was mainly the consequence of favourable developments in UK non-manufacturing trade, of a kind which were largely autonomous with respect to the UK's industrial and economic performance as a whole.

Deficits in trade in manufactures with other industrialized countries and surpluses with primary producing areas

During the 1970s, the UK slipped into deficit in trade in manufactures with most other industrialized countries, and this development has given rise to a great deal of anxiety. These deficits are frequently held up as the single most obvious index of Britain's industrial decline, whilst Britain's membership of the European Community is usually credited with responsibility for the UK's growing manufacturing deficit with the EEC. Meanwhile, the fact that Britain continues to earn surpluses in trade in manufactures with less developed, primary producing countries is often interpreted as a sign that British industry, having been chased out of advanced country markets, can only survive by 'trading down' (i.e. selling technologically unsophisticated products) in Third World markets.

These propositions are, however, quite erroneous. They ignore the fact that, as a result of developments on the non-manufacturing side of the economy together with the enhanced purchasing power of OPEC, British trade had become much more triangular by the early to mid-1980s. This had a number of importance consequences. Whilst the UK continued to earn surpluses in trade in manufactures with primary producing countries, the deterioration in her overall manufacturing balance of trade with all areas (consequent upon improvements in non-manufacturing trade) reached the point where going into deficit in trade in manufactures with other industrialized countries was the only way of avoiding big surpluses on her merchandise trade as a whole. Thus, the appearance of deficits in trade in manufactures with other industrialized countries was the inevitable consequence of dramatic developments on the non-manufacturing side of the economy, together with the enhanced purchasing power of OPEC.

The causes and consequences of the increasing triangularity of British trade can be looked at in a number of slightly different ways, each of which, we believe, throws some light on the underlying processes at work.

Declining manufacturing balance overall and persistent surpluses with primary producing areas

One way of showing why the emergence of deficits in UK trade in manufactures with other industrialized countries was an inevitable consequence of developments on the non-manufacturing side of the economy, together with the enhanced purchasing power of OPEC, is as follows. Since primary producing countries specialize in exporting primary products and export very few manufactures, when they export to the UK they mainly export primary products. Meanwhile, since the UK mainly exports manufactures, when she exports to primary producing areas her exports consist largely of manufactures. Thus, in her trade with primary producing countries, the UK mainly exports manufactures but imports very few of them in return. As a result, the UK is bound to run surpluses in trade in manufactures with such countries. In 1983, this surplus amounted to +3.1% of Britain's GDP and, although this represented a sizeable reduction compared with the situation in the early 1950s,[22] the UK will probably always be in surplus in her trade in manufactures with primary producing countries. Note also that, as a result of the enhanced purchasing power of OPEC, there was little further decline in the UK's manufacturing export surplus with primary producing areas after 1973 – and there was even a slight increase (see Fig. 9.1).

However, although the UK remained in surplus in trade in manufactures with primary producing countries, her overall manufacturing balance (with all areas) underwent a virtually continuous deterioration. Eventually, the point arrived when the size of the UK's manufacturing surplus with all areas was no larger than the surplus which she continued to earn in trade with primary producing countries (Fig. 9.1); as a consequence, the UK slipped into deficit with manufacturing exporting countries as a group.[23] This happened some time during the course of 1973 (Fig. 9.1) although, with certain manufacturing exporting countries (e.g. West Germany), the UK has almost always been in deficit

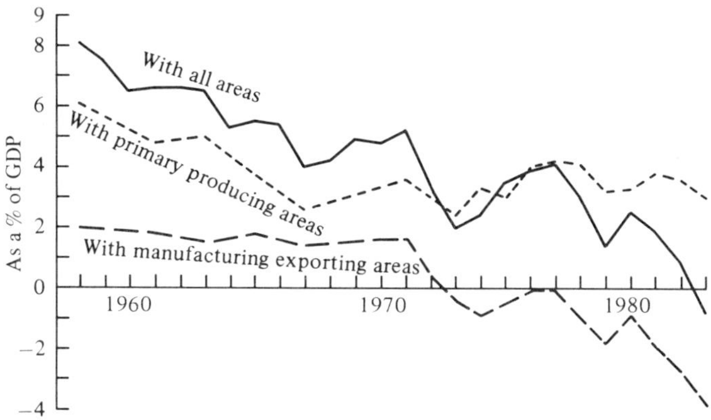

Fig. 9.1 UK manufacturing balance with different areas (as a % of GDP)

in trade in manufactures. Thereafter, as the UK's overall manufacturing balance with all areas continued to deteriorate, her balance with manufacturing exporting countries worsened even further.

Thus, given the deterioration in the UK's overall manufacturing balance, due largely to autonomous improvements in non-manufacturing trade, recent deficits with other industrialized countries must be seen as the inevitable consequence of the fact that the UK remains in surplus in trade in manufactures with primary producing countries. Or, to look at this development in a slightly different way: given that the UK continues to earn surpluses in trade in manufactures with primary producing areas, the appearance of deficits with other industrialized countries has been due to the same set of factors, which have been largely responsible for the improvement in UK trade in non-manufactures: namely, changes in UK consumption and production of non-manufactures and changes in relative primary product prices.

The increased triangularity of UK trade

Another way of looking at these developments is as follows. By the early to mid-1980s, UK trade had become much more triangular: with OPEC, the 'other LDCs' and the US, the UK was normally in surplus in merchandise trade as a whole (manufactures plus primary products) (see Table 9.11). Moreover, in trade in primary products with other industrialized countries, the UK was also normally in surplus (see Table 9.11). With other areas (i.e. the White Dominions, the CPEs and the NICs) Britain was normally in balance, taking trade in primary products plus manufactures together. It follows that unless Britain was to run large surpluses in merchandise trade as a whole, she had to go into deficit in trade in manufactures with other industrialized countries.

Table 9.11. *UK balance of trade in primary products and manufactures (as % of GDP), by area*

	1958			1983		
	Primary products	Manu- factures	Total	Primary products	Manu- factures	Total
All countries	−8.2	+8.0	−0.2	+0.3	−0.7	−0.4
Manufacturing exporters	−2.2	+2.0	−0.2	+1.8	−3.8	−1.9
EEC	−0.8	+0.7	−0.2	+1.5	−2.2	−0.7
Other W. Europe	−0.6	+0.6	+0.0	−0.3	−0.4	−0.7
USA	−0.5	+0.4	−0.1	+0.7	−0.2	+0.5
Japan	−0.1	+0.0	−0.1	+0.0	−0.8	−0.8
NICs	−0.2	+0.3	+0.2	−0.2	−0.2	−0.3
Primary producers	−6.0	+6.0	−0.0	−1.6	+3.1	+1.5
OPEC	−1.6	+1.0	−0.6	−0.4	+1.5	+1.1
White Dominions	−2.2	+2.5	+0.3	−0.5	+0.5	+0.0
Other LDCs	−2.1	+2.4	+0.3	−0.5	+0.9	+0.4
CPEs	−0.2	+0.1	−0.0	−0.2	+0.1	−0.1

Notes: Trade data from HMSO, *Overseas Trade Statistics of the UK*. Imports c.i.f. converted to imports f.o.b., for primary products and manufactures separately, using implicit conversion coefficients obtained from import c.i.f. data in UK, *Annual Abstract* and import f.o.b. data in UK, *Balance of Payments: Pink Book*. Classification of countries by area same as in Table 9.1. GDP at current market prices from *Economic Trends Annual Supplement, 1985*
Source: See Table 9.1

Why was the UK normally in surplus with OPEC, the 'other LDCs' and the US? In the case of OPEC, it was due to the fact that, although North Sea fuel production enabled the UK to reduce her imports of oil from OPEC, the latter continued to be a very important market for UK manufactured exports. As a consequence, the UK's manufacturing surplus with OPEC greatly exceeded her deficit in oil plus other primary products (see Table 9.11). Much the same can be said of UK trade with the 'other LDCs': the decline in UK imports of food, beverages and raw materials reduced the UK's deficit in primary product trade with these countries to the point where it was smaller than the surplus, which the UK continued to earn in trade in manufactures with them (see Table 9.11). Finally, the reason why the UK was in surplus in her overall trade (manufactures plus primary products) with the US was because her surplus in oil trade exceeded her deficit in trade in manufactures.

The fact that in the early to mid-1980s the UK was normally in surplus in her overall merchandise trade (manufactures plus primary products) with OPEC, the 'other LDCs' and the US meant that if she was not to run large surpluses in merchandise trade overall then she had to be in deficit in trade with other parts of the world. However, in trade with the CPEs, the White Dominions and the NICs, the UK was roughly in balance overall, surpluses in trade in manufactures more or less offsetting deficits in trade in primary products (see Table 9.11). Furthermore, as a result of exports of oil and other primary products, the UK was in surplus in trade in primary products with Western Europe and Japan (see Table 9.11). It follows that if the UK was not to run large surpluses in merchandise trade overall, then she had to go into deficit in trade in manufactures with Western Europe and Japan.

This greater degree of triangularity in UK trade, which emerged in the early to mid-1980s, was the inevitable consequence of changes in the non-manufacturing side of the British economy, together with the enhanced purchasing power of OPEC.

Furthermore, had the UK been able to return to full employment at that time, she could still have afforded to run deficits in trade in manufactures with Western Europe and Japan – just as long as the surpluses in her trade with OPEC, the 'other LDCs' and the US, together with any surpluses in trade in primary products with Western Europe and Japan, had exceeded the overall non-manufacturing deficit which would have been incurred at full employment (estimated to be between −2% to −3% of GDP: see Chapter 7).

Differences in the area pattern of UK export and import trade in manufactures

This whole argument – concerning the consequences of changes on the non-manufacturing side of the economy for the increased triangularity of UK trade – can be presented in a somewhat different way, using information on the geography of UK manufactured exports and manufactured imports presented earlier in this chapter. As can be seen from Tables 9.3 and 9.7, the geographical pattern of UK manufactured exports differs from that of UK manufactured imports in quite significant ways. Although the UK exports manufactures to all types of countries (both primary producers and manufacturing specialists), her imports of manufactures come from a rather restricted group of countries – namely, from countries who specialize in exporting manufactures. Thus, primary producing countries (the White Dominions, OPEC, and the 'other LDCs') have always been relatively more important as markets for UK manufactured exports than as suppliers of UK manufactured imports. Meanwhile, specialist manufacturing exporting countries have always been relatively more important as suppliers of UK manufactured imports than as markets for UK manufactured exports. So long as the UK had a sufficiently large surplus in trade in manufactures with all areas, she was in surplus not only with primary producing countries but with manufacturing specialists as well.

However, consider what happened when the UK's overall manufacturing balance deteriorated, and her imports of manufactures increased relative to her exports. The fact that primary producing areas have always been relatively more important as markets for UK manufactured exports than as suppliers of UK manufactured imports meant that the UK continued to be in surplus with such areas. Thus in 1983 this surplus, albeit much diminished since the 1950s, still amounted to +3.1% of GDP. However, as UK imports of manufactures increased relative to her exports, the fact that manufacturing specialists have always been relatively more important as suppliers of UK manufactured imports than as markets for UK manufactured exports meant that the UK began to incur deficits with them.

Thus, when the UK's overall manufacturing surplus was large, she was in surplus not only with primary producing areas but with manufacturing specialists as well. In 1958, for example, the UK's overall manufacturing surplus was +8.0% of GDP, consisting of a surplus with manufacturing exporting areas of +2.0% of GDP and one with primary producers of +6.0% of GDP (see Table 9.11). By 1983, the UK's manufacturing balance with all areas had deteriorated to −0.7% of GDP. Part of the adjustment to this deterioration took the form of a loss of market share in primary producing areas and, hence, a smaller surplus with them. Thus by 1983 the UK's manufacturing surplus with primary producing areas had fallen to +3.1% of GDP (see Table 9.11). The other part of the adjustment consisted of a loss of market share in manufacturing exporting countries, as well as increased imports of manufactures from them. As a consequence by 1983 the UK was in deficit with such areas to the tune of −3.8% of GDP (see Table 9.11).

To what extent has this particular area pattern of surpluses and deficits in trade in manufactures been the inevitable consequence of structural change in the British economy, together with the specific pattern of trade specialization of each group of countries? And to what extent is it the consequence of poor industrial and economic performance – an indicator that British industry, having been chased out of advanced country markets, can only survive by 'trading down' in the Third World?

There is of course no doubt that in many though by no means all areas of manufacturing production, British producers have forfeited the technological leadership they once enjoyed. However, the appearance of deficits in trade in manufactures with manufacturing exporting countries is by no means an index of industrial backwardness. Indeed, given the structural changes which have taken place in the British economy, Britain might well have had even larger deficits with other industrialized countries had her industrial performance been stronger.

The reasons for this are as follows. Imagine a situation in which British industrial technology had, on average, kept abreast of that of rival enterprises in other industrialized countries; as a result, UK economic growth would have been faster, UK real per capita income would now be higher, and the country would be closer to full employment. Under these assumptions, the UK's non-manufacturing balance of trade would certainly have been weaker than it was in 1983, but, as argued in Chapter 7, by no more than between −2% and −3% of GDP. If the UK had aimed to be in balance on her commercial account, then her manufacturing surplus would, therefore, have had to have been between +2% and +3% of GDP – that is to say, a stronger manufacturing balance than in 1983 when there was a deficit of −0.8% of GDP; but not that much stronger. How would this overall manufacturing surplus of between +2% and +3% of GDP have been distributed between primary producing and manufacturing exporting areas?

If British manufacturing industry had been more competitive, then British manufactured exports would be higher. British exporters would have a bigger share of the market in primary producing countries, and the UK's manufacturing surplus with such countries would be larger than it is now – both absolutely and, possibly, also as a proportion of GDP. Of course, British manufactured exports to manufacturing exporting areas would also be higher, but, so long as the UK's surplus with primary producing areas was larger than +2% to +3% of GDP (compared to +3.1% in 1983), the UK could still have afforded to run modest deficits with manufacturing exporting areas – though not, to quite the same extent, as a proportion of GDP, as in 1983. Thus, if UK manufacturing industry had been more competitive and UK manufactured exports higher, then, given the structure of her non-manufacturing trade as it was in the early to mid-1980s, the UK could still have afforded to be in deficit in trade in manufactures with manufacturing exporting areas.

The use of import controls to eliminate Britain's manufacturing deficits with other industrialized countries

In the early 1980s, the use of import controls was widely advocated on the grounds that Britain needed to eliminate her manufacturing deficits with other industrialized countries. It should be clear by now, however, that such a justification for import controls was entirely erroneous, at least as far as the situation in the early to mid-1980s was concerned, because it entirely failed to take account of the increased triangularity of UK trade, resulting from structural change at home and the enhanced purchasing power of OPEC. The fact is that as long as the UK remains in surplus in her overall trade with primary producing areas, as well as in her trade in primary products with other industrialized countries, then any attempt to earn a surplus in trade in manufactures with the latter would result in the UK earning a considerable surplus on her merchandise trade overall.[24]

What would the UK have done with such a surplus? Of course, it could have used it to finance an expansion of overseas military expenditure and/or overseas investment. However, those who advocate the need to improve the UK's manufacturing balance with other industrialized countries usually oppose, as we do, any attempt to breathe new life into the UK's global military and overseas investment role. Alternatively, the UK might have used the consequent surplus on her commercial account to increase her programme of overseas aid; equally, such a surplus might have been eliminated by means of massive imports of manufactures from the NICs. However, whilst there is much to be said in favour of both alternatives, it must be recognized, first, that in the past there have normally been considerable domestic political constraints to a really significant expansion of British overseas aid and, second, to be realistic, there are almost certainly limits to the extent to which the UK can sensibly increase her imports of manufactures from the NICs. Furthermore, those wishing to eliminate the UK's manufacturing deficit with the EEC would almost certainly be in the forefront of any campaign to prevent a substantial increase in manufacured imports from 'super-exploited' low-wage countries.

Thus, unless the UK had been prepared to engage in a major expansion of her overseas aid programme and/or a massive increase in manufactured imports from the NICs, it would have been quite pointless, at a time of peak oil production in the mid-1980s, for the UK to have tried to eliminate her manufacturing deficit with other industrialized countries. The fact is that even if the UK had attempted to return to full employment in the mid-1980s, she could still have afforded to run a small deficit in trade in manufactures with other advanced countries, including the EEC and Japan. Indeed, the point can be put more strongly. It would have been Britain's duty to run such a deficit, since this would have been the most effective way of ensuring that money earned in trade with OPEC and other Third World countries was re-cycled back into the world economy.

Finally, although we are critical of basing the case for import controls – at least in the early to mid-1980s – on the need to eliminate Britain's manufacturing deficits with other industrialized countries we do, nevertheless, believe that import controls have a useful role to play: namely, that of protecting Britain's balance of payments during a period of economic recovery and reconstruction, so as to ensure that recovery is not cut short by a dearth of foreign exchange.

UK and the EEC: the effect of British membership on the UK's manufacturing balance with the EEC

In many appraisals of the effect of Britain's membership of the EEC on the British economy, considerable attention has been focussed on the deterioration in the UK's manufacturing balance with the EEC in the years subsequent to entry. The UK went into deficit in manufacturing trade with the EEC in 1974 and by 1983 this deficit amounted to −2.2% of GDP. Can these adverse trends and the appearance of deficits be ascribed to the effects of EEC entry?[25] The answer to this question is, for the most part, no.

As we have just argued, the deterioration in the UK's manufacturing balance with all areas, consequent upon improvements in non-manufacturing trade, was bound to be accompanied by a deterioration in the UK's manufacturing balance with manufacturing exporting areas, including the EEC. Eventually, the deterioration in Britain's overall manufacturing balance reached the point where, because the country was still in surplus with primary producing areas, she was bound to develop deficits with manufacturing exporting areas, including the EEC. This would have happened even if Britain had remained outside the Community.

However, Britain's membership of the Community did cause her manufacturing balance with the EEC to deteriorate further than it might otherwise have done. This is because it led to a certain degree of substitution of EEC for non-EEC sources of supply in Britain's manufactured import trade. As argued earlier, British membership of the EEC resulted in the termination of UK preferences in favour of manufactured imports from EFTA countries. At the same time, UK manufactured imports from other non-EEC sources were restricted by means of non-tariff barriers, such as voluntary export restrictions (in the case of Japan) and the Multi-Fibre Agreement (in the case of the NICs).

Thus, whilst longer-term structural developments in the UK economy were the main factor responsible for the deterioration in the UK's manufacturing balance with the EEC, entry into the Community undoubtedly accentuated this trend. Furthermore, as argued earlier, EEC entry, by subjecting the UK to an additional degree of trade liberalization and preventing the adoption of measures such as import controls, which might have protected the UK's balance of payments and brought about an improvement in industrial performance, was undoubtedly a factor contributory to steadily rising levels of unemployment of both labour and capital.

Conclusions

One of the aims of this chapter has been to describe the links between changes on the non-manufacturing side of the British economy and the major changes in the geography of British trade which occurred in the post-war period. The other has been to show how developments in trade in non-manufactures, together with the enhanced purchasing power of OPEC, resulted in British trade becoming much more triangular in the early to mid-1980s. An inevitable consequence and concomitant of this increased triangularity was the appearance of deficits in trade in manufactures with other industrialized countries; these deficits were not, therefore, the unambiguous indicator of industrial decline they were widely thought to be.

Developments on the non-manufacturing side of the economy were the main factor responsible for the major changes in the geography of UK imports which occurred in the post-war period. As a result of increased self-sufficiency in primary production, there was only a very modest increase in UK primary product imports as a whole, whilst relative primary product prices also fell. As a result there was a dramatic reduction in the share of primary products in total UK imports. In consequence, manufactures constituted an ever-growing proportion of UK imports, and they were, of course, mainly supplied by areas specializing in exporting manufactures, namely Western Europe, Japan and the NICs. Thus, changes on the non-manufacturing side of the economy were the principal factor responsible for the huge shift in the geography of Britain's import trade which occurred in the post-war period, for the rapid growth of imports from other advanced countries and the NICs and the dramatic decline in imports from the White Dominions and 'other LDCs'.

In accounting for the increase in UK manufactured imports since the war, too much attention has been focussed on the growing liberalization of international trade in manufactures and the consequent reductions in UK import barriers. These factors are not as important as is generally thought. The fact is unless the UK had been prepared to devote virtually all of the post-war growth in her real capacity to import to a combination of increased overseas aid, overseas military expenditure, foreign investment and foreign holidays, then manufactures were bound to constitute a growing proportion of total UK imports. The main effect of increased trade liberalization, given the inadequate response of British producers to the growing competition in international trade in manufactures, was that it was responsible for steadily rising levels of unemployment of both labour and capital.

Meanwhile, there were three main factors responsible for the redirection of UK export trade away from the White Dominions and 'other LDCs' and towards Western Europe, the US, Japan and OPEC. First, increased liberalization of trade in manufactures amongst all OECD countries and the growth of industrial protection in the Third World; as a result of these developments, British manufacturing exporters lost the preferential position they had previously enjoyed in the markets of the White Dominions and many Third World countries. However, these losses were more than compensated for by the growth of new markets in the industrialized countries. The second factor responsible for the redirection of UK export trade was the rapid growth of incomes and, hence, purchasing power in Western Europe, Japan and OPEC. The third and final element was the rapid expansion, from the late seventies onwards, of Britain's primary product exports, especially oil, which were mainly directed to the markets of other advanced countries.

Thus, changes on the non-manufacturing side of the economy, together with developments in the world economy such as trade liberalization and above-average income growth in certain parts of the world (namely, Japan and OPEC), were the principal factors responsible for the major redirection in the geography of Britain's trade which occurred in the post-war period.

Developments on the non-manufacturing side of the economy, together with the enhanced purchasing power of OPEC, also made British trade much more triangular. One aspect of this was the appearance of deficits in trade in manufactures with other industrialized countries. The reasons for the increased triangularity were as follows. Although Britain reduced her imports of primary products from primary producing areas (especially OPEC), she continued to earn surpluses in trade in manufactures with such countries (especially with OPEC); as a result, Britain began to run surpluses on her overall trade (manufactures plus primary products) with primary producing areas. On the other hand, as a result of increased exports of oil and other primary products to the EEC and the US, the UK developed surpluses in trade in primary products with other industrialized countries. Thus, if Britain were not to run substantial surpluses on her merchandise trade overall, she had to go into deficit in trade in manufactures with other advanced countries. Therefore, the appearance of deficits in trade in manufactures with Western Europe, Japan and the NICs was not an accurate index of industrial decline nor the persistence of surpluses with primary producing areas an indicator that British firms were 'trading down' (i.e. selling technologically unsophisticated products) in the Third World – though poor industrial performance and persistent weakness in non-price aspects of international trade in manufactures were, without doubt, characteristic features of Britain's post-war industrial record. The fact is the appearance of deficits in Britain's trade in manufactures with other industrialized countries was an inevitable consequence of the huge changes that have taken place on the non-manufacturing side of the economy, together with the growth of OPEC spending. Even so, Britain's entry into the EEC did contribute to the deterioration in the country's manufacturing balance with the EEC – since membership of the Community resulted in a certain amount of substitution of EEC as against non-EEC sources of supply in Britain's manufacturing import trade. Furthermore, membership of the Community, by causing additional trade liberalization and preventing Britain from implementing measures such as import controls, which might have succeeded in protecting her balance of payments and improving industrial performance, undoubtedly contributed to the country's progressive failure to maintain full employment of labour and capital.

However, as things stood in the early to mid-1980s, if import controls had been adopted as part of a programme for improving Britain's economic performance, they ought not to have been used to re-create the huge surpluses which the country previously enjoyed in trade in manufactures with other advanced countries. Instead, the main purpose of import controls should be to protect the UK's balance of trade during a period of economic recovery and reconstruction in order to ensure that recovery is not imperilled by a shortage of foreign exchange. Of course, the prospective deterioration in Britain's fuel balance, arising from the decline in North Sea production, will not only result in a weakening of Britain's non-manufacturing balance, it will also make British trade much less triangular than it was in the early to mid-1980s. Thus, if there is to be a substantial increase in real GDP in the future, Britain will have to have a much stronger manufacturing balance with other advanced industrial countries than she had in the early to mid-1980s.

10

De-industrialization in the UK: three theses

Introduction

In this chapter we take up some of the themes explored in general terms in Chapter 1. We examine what has happened to manufacturing and other forms of industrial employment in the UK since the Second World War. We show how the UK has experienced an enormous reduction in manufacturing employment over the past thirty years – greater than that in almost any other advanced capitalist country. And we consider various hypotheses which might explain why this has occurred. Three possible explanations are identified, namely, the 'Maturity Thesis', the 'Specialization Thesis' and the 'Failure Thesis'. All three theses, it turns out, have *prima facie* evidence to support them. However, this is only a provisional conclusion and a final judgement must wait until the next chapter.

Britain's post-war employment record in an international context

Fig. 10.1 shows what has happened to employment in the major sectors of the British economy since the war. There has been an almost continuous fall in the number of people employed in agriculture, from around 1.8 million in 1946 to under 1 million in 1983. Over the same period, employment in the service sector rose dramatically, from just under 10 million to over 14 million. In the so-called 'production' industries – manufacturing, mining, construction and public utilities – the picture is more complex. Immediately after the war, under the impetus of post-war reconstruction and the export drive, the number employed in these sectors increased rapidly. Then, in the 1950s, the pace of expansion slackened. Employment continued to rise in manufacturing and construction, though at a slower pace than before, whilst coal mining began to shed labour as pits were closed because of competition from oil. For a time, the new jobs created in manufacturing and construction more than offset those lost in mining, with the result that industrial employment, as a whole, continued rising right through into the 1960s. However, this expansion came to an abrupt halt in 1966 when, following a major sterling crisis, the Labour government

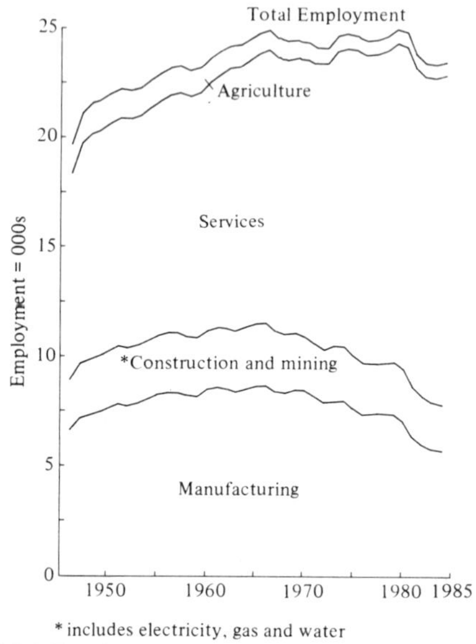

Fig. 10.1 Employment in the UK by sector 1946–83 (millions)

of the day imposed a severe deflationary budget on the economy. Since that time, industrial employment of all kinds – in mining, construction and manufacturing alike – has fallen irregularly at what seems like an accelerating pace. From an all-time peak of 11.5 million in 1966, the total number of industrial workers in employment had fallen to well under 8 million by 1984. Over the same period, manufacturing employment alone has fallen from 8.5 million to well under 5.7 million. About half of this enormous decline took place before the present Thatcher government took office in 1979, whilst the rest has occurred since.

The story is much the same if we look at relative shares rather than absolute numbers, although the timing of events is somewhat different (see Fig. 10.2). After rising strongly immediately after the war, the share of industry in civil employment reached a peak in 1955 of around 48%. In that year, approximately one-third of the entire population between the ages of 15 and 64 were employed as industrial workers, whilst most of the rest were students, housewives and service workers. These figures for industry's share in total employment have rarely been equalled and certainly never surpassed in the whole of British history. Moreover, they are almost without equal in the experience of other capitalist countries. This last point can be verified from Table 10.1, which compares Britain's employment structure in 1955 with that of other highly industrialized economies at an equivalent stage in their development. In the entire history of world

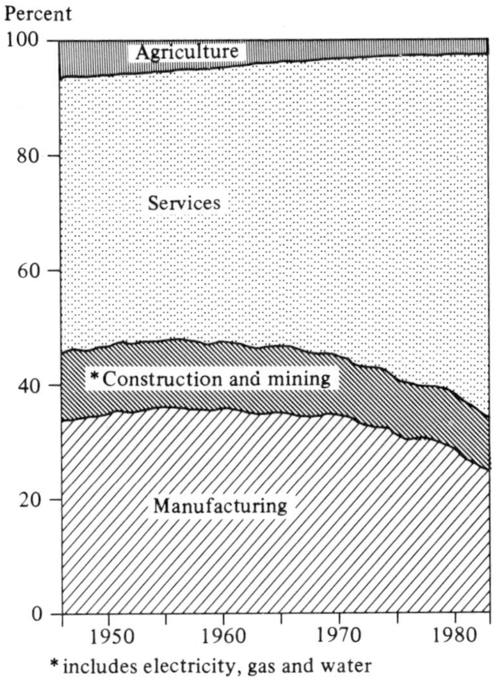

Fig. 10.2 Employment in the UK by sector 1946–83 (percentage shares)

Table 10.1. *Comparative employment structure in the West's most industrialized economies*

	Industrial employment as % of		Manufacturing employment as % of	
	Civil employment	Population aged 15–64	Civil employment	Population aged 15–64
Belgium (1957)	47.0	26.9	36.0	20.6
Germany (1970)	48.5	33.1	37.7	25.8
Luxemburg (1966)	46.9	28.8	35.8	22.0
Switzerland (1963)	47.6	n.a.	38.5	n.a.
UK (1955)	47.9	32.8	36.1	24.7

Source: OECD. The dates in parenthesis refer to the year in which industrial employment reached its all-time peak as a share of civil employment

capitalism, the all-time peak of industrialization (in employment terms) was probably achieved by Germany in 1970 or Switzerland in 1963. In each case, industry accounted for 47–8% of civil employment – which is virtually identical to the figure reached in Britain in 1955. Thus, in employment terms, the British economy in 1955 was one of the most highly industrialized economies the capitalist world has ever seen. Never before, nor since, in any capitalist country at any time has industrial employment been significantly more important than it was in Britain in 1955.

Yet, no sooner had this pre-eminence been achieved, than the process went into reverse. Industrial employment began declining in importance, at first slowly and then with gathering speed. By 1983, the share of industry in total employment had fallen to 34% and that of manufacturing alone to under 25%. To illustrate the scale of the transformation which has occurred since 1955, consider the relationship between industry and the services. In 1955 there were more workers employed in industry than in all of the services combined, both public and private. By 1983 there were almost two service workers for each industrial worker, and the public services alone employed about three-quarters as many people as the whole of the manufacturing industry put together (4.3 million as compared to 5.8 million). Under ideal conditions of prosperity and full employment, such a transformation over such a short period of time would have been disruptive. Under the actual conditions of stagnation and unemployment, it has been traumatic.

Let us now consider the experience of other countries over the past thirty years. We shall concentrate on the manufacturing sector, but our remarks apply with only minor qualifications to the industrial sector as a whole, including mining and construction. Tables 10.2 and 10.3 show what has happened to manufacturing employment in the advanced capitalist countries. Wherever possible the figures go back to 1955 or even before, although in some cases there are gaps caused by a lack of reliable information.

Let us first consider Table 10.2. This shows the rate of growth of manufacturing employment during three distinct periods: 1956–66, 1966–73 and 1973–83. Looking at these growth rates, the following points stand out. In the first period, manufacturing employment increases in every single country shown in the table, often at extremely high rates. In the second period, the pace of expansion slows down, and there are even a few countries in which manufacturing employment starts to fall. Finally, in the third period, 1973–83, there is an almost universal decline in manufacturing employment, with only three minor exceptions: Finland, Iceland and New Zealand. Thus, the first period (1956–66) is one of general expansion in manufacturing employment, the second (1966–73) is one of transition and the third (1973–83) is one of general contraction.

Comparing Britain's performance with that of other countries, we find that between 1956 and 1966 manufacturing employment grew more slowly in Britain than in any other country shown in the table; between 1966 and 1973, it fell by more than in any other country, with the exception of Sweden; and between

Table 10.2. *Manufacturing employment in the advanced capitalist countries*

	Annual percentage change			Cumulative percentage change	
	1956–66	1966–73	1973–83	1956–66	1966–83
Italy	1.0	2.0	−0.9	10.3	5.3
Japan	3.9	2.9	−0.4	47.3	18.3
Finland	n.a.	1.6	0.5	n.a.	17.5
Austria	n.a.	n.a.	−0.6	n.a.	n.a.
Iceland[a, b]	1.5	2.1	2.8	15.6	52.1
France	0.8	0.6	−1.9	8.7	−14.0
Norway	n.a.	n.a.	−0.9	n.a.	n.a.
Denmark[b]	2.2	−1.2	−1.9	24.5	−24.4
Canada	2.4	1.4	−0.4	26.5	6.7
Luxemburg[a]	1.3	0.9	−2.3	14.3	−15.5
Germany	1.2	0.2	−1.9	12.2	−16.2
Sweden[a]	1.0	−1.3	−1.2	10.7	−18.8
Switzerland[a]	1.7	−0.2	−2.0	18.5	−19.9
New Zealand[b]	n.a.	1.9	0.4	n.a.	18.9
Netherlands	1.0	−0.8	−2.4	11.0	−25.7
Australia	n.a.	1.7	−2.7	n.a.	−14.3
Belgium[b]	0.6	−0.3	−3.4	7.1	−30.8
USA	1.3	0.7	−0.4	13.5	0.6
UK	0.4	−1.2	−3.1	+4.1	−33.2

Notes: [a] the initial date is 1957, and the estimate for cumulative change over the period 1955–66 is based on the average annual growth rates for the years 1957–66;
[b] the terminal date is 1981, and the estimate for cumulative change over the period 1966–83 is based on the average annual growth rates for the periods 1966–73 and 1973–81
Source: See notes to Table A7.1 of Appendix 7

1973 and 1983, it fell by more than in any other country, with the exception of Belgium. Taking the period 1955–83 as a whole, or even the subperiod 1966–83, Britain has experienced the greatest percentage decline in manufacturing employment of any Western country.

Table 10.3 shows what has happened to the relative share of manufacturing in total employment. Here the picture is not quite so clear as in the case of absolute numbers. Between 1955 and 1981, the share of manufacturing in civil employment in the UK fell by 9.7 percentage points (from 36.1% to 26.4%). This is certainly a much greater reduction than occurred in most of the countries shown in the table. However, enormous though it is, even greater reductions were recorded in Australia and Belgium, where manufacturing's share fell by 10.2 and 10.6 percentage points respectively. Thus, if we take the share of manufacturing in total employment as our index, the extent of de-industrialization over the last thirty years has been much greater in Britain than in most other advanced capitalist countries, although slightly less than in Australia and Belgium.

Table 10.3. *Share of manufacturing in civil employment, 1950–81*

	Percentage share					Change
	1950	1955	1966	1973	1981	1955–1981
Italy	n.a.	20.0	25.8	28.5	26.1	+6.1
Japan	n.a.	18.4	24.4	27.4	24.8	+6.4
Finland[c]	n.a.	21.3	22.8	25.4	26.1	+4.8
Austria[a]	n.a.	29.8	29.8	29.7	29.7	−0.1
Iceland[b]	21.5	23.7	25.5	25.2	26.3	+3.3
France	n.a.	26.9	28.7	28.3	25.1	−1.8
Norway	22.0	23.1	23.7	23.5	20.2	−2.9
Denmark	n.a.	27.5	29.0	24.7	21.3	−6.2
Canada	24.9	24.1	23.9	22.0	19.4	−4.7
Luxemburg[b]	n.a.	33.2	35.8	33.8	27.4	−5.8
Germany	n.a.	33.8	35.2	36.7	33.6	−0.2
Sweden[b]	n.a.	31.7	31.2	27.5	23.3	−8.4
Switzerland[c]	n.a.	36.1	37.8	35.0	32.0	−4.1
New Zealand[c]	n.a.	23.7	25.4	25.7	24.0	+0.1
Netherlands	29.3	29.3	28.9	25.7	21.1	−8.2
Australia[c]	n.a.	29.6	28.6	25.6	19.4	−10.2
Belgium	35.0	35.3	33.6	31.8	24.7	−10.6
USA	27.9	28.5	27.8	24.8	21.7	−6.8
UK	34.8	36.1	34.8	32.3	26.4	−9.7

Notes: [a] Figure in second column is for 1956; figure in the final column refers to 1956–81
[b] Figure in second column is for 1957; figure in the final column refers to 1957–81
[c] Figure in second column is for 1959; figure in the final column refers to 1959–81
Source: Divers OECD publications and Bairoch (1968)

Three theses

Whether one considers relative shares or absolute numbers the decline in industrial employment in the UK has been spectacular. What accounts for it? Why did this decline begin so much earlier in the UK than in most other countries and why has it been so great? From the general discussion in Chapter 1, we can identify three potential explanations for what has happened.

The Maturity Thesis

The first thesis locates Britain's own historical experience within a more general theory of economic development and structural change. In Chapter 1, we saw how economic development is accompanied by an almost continuous rise in the share of services in total employment, and how the impact of this on industrial employment depends on the stage of development that an economy has reached. In the early and intermediate stages of development, services grow at the expense of agriculture and their share in total employment rises, whilst that of agriculture falls. Meanwhile, the share of industrial employment generally rises. However, at a later stage of development, once an economy has reached 'maturity', the situation is quite different. In such an economy, only a small fraction of the labour force is employed in agriculture and any major increase in the share of services in total employment must be at the expense of industry, whose share must fall. This, in a nutshell, is the Maturity Thesis. It explains why, in a mature economy, the share of industry in total employment falls in the course of time. One cannot lay down general rules which determine exactly when any particular economy will reach the point of maturity, as there are many different factors which can influence the turning-point. However, from the regression analyses of Chapter 1, it seems that the typical capitalist economy reaches maturity when per capita income is in the region of 4,000 US dollars (at 1975 prices). At this stage, agriculture normally accounts for between 5 and 10% of total employment, although the figure may be higher depending on the economy concerned and its pattern of trade speicalization. Before considering how the Maturity Thesis applies to the UK, there are several points which should be noted. The first point concerns employment.

The Maturity Thesis is primarily about employment shares and not absolute numbers. The absolute number of people employed in the industrial sector depends on the behaviour of total employment. Where total employment is growing rapidly, the relative share of industry may fall a considerable amount without there being any reduction at all in the absolute number of people employed in this sector.[1] On the other hand, where total employment is increasing slowly, any major reduction in the relative share of industry will be accompanied by an absolute fall in industrial employment. The second point concerns economic performance. The Maturity Thesis asserts that, at a certain stage in development, the share of industry in total employment will start to fall. In a successful mature economy this fall in industry's share of employment will be accompanied by a rapid growth in output and labour productivity in the industrial sector. The growth in service employment will be enough to provide work for virtually all who require it, including people displaced from the industrial sector through automation and other labour-saving measures. In Chapter 1, we used the term 'positive de-industrialization' to describe the kind of dynamic change in employment structure which occurs in a successful mature economy. In an unsuccessful mature economy, a similar shift in employment structure occurs, but the mechanism is different. In such an economy, industry is in a state of crisis, industrial output is rising very slowly or even falling, and industrial employment may be falling absolutely. Although service employment may be increasing, it is not doing so fast enough to prevent a considerable rise in unemployment. In Chapter 1, we used the term 'negative de-industrialization' to describe this kind of shift in the structure of employment. Thus, in a mature economy, no matter how good or bad is the performance of the industrial sector, the share of industry in total employment will normally fall in the course of time. Depending on what happens to total employment, this fall in the share of industry may or may not be accompanied by an absolute fall in industrial employment. This, at least, is the claim made by the Maturity Thesis and, as we have seen in Chapter 1, there is considerable evidence in its favour.

The Maturity Thesis is of obvious relevance to the UK. In the 1950s, the UK was still one of the richest countries in the world, and her economy was on the verge of maturity. Per capita income in 1955 was $3,305 (at 1975 prices), which is not far short of the turning-point at which the share of industry in total employment starts to fall. Moreover, agriculture accounted for only 5% of total employment, so that any substantial rise in the share of services could only come about at the expense of industry. The situation was very different in most other capitalist countries. Some were still relatively poor and still had enormous reserves of labour in agriculture. These countries were nowhere near mature, and there was still ample room for services to increase their share of employment at the expense of agriculture without reducing the share of industry. Other countries had a higher per capita income than the UK, but even in these countries the share of agriculture in total employment was much greater than in the UK and so, in this respect, their economies were less mature.

The contrast in experience between the UK and other countries can be seen from Table 10.4, which shows what has happened to the structure of employment since 1955. Countries have been divided into three groups, depending on the share of agriculture in total employment in 1955. At one extreme are the 'immature' economies in group A, all of which were still highly agrarian in 1955, having more than 21% of their employed labour force in agriculture. At the other extreme is the UK which stands on its own, being the least agrarian economy in the world in 1955, with just over 5% of its labour force in agriculture. Between these two extremes are the 'transitional' economies of group B, all of which were still moderately agrarian in character in 1955, with agriculture accounting for between 9 and 18% of total employment.

From Table 10.4 and the supporting data given in Appendix 9, we can see how the share of services in total employment has risen dramatically throughout the advanced capitalist world. In the group A (immature) countries, this increase has been matched by an almost equal reduction in the share of agriculture; as a result industry's share has hardly altered. This can be seen from Table 10.5 which summarizes some of the information given in Table 10.4. Between 1955 and 1981, the share of services in total employment rose by 19.2 points in the immature countries of group A (from 36.0% to 55.2%). Over the same period, the share of agriculture fell by 21.1 points (from 31.0% to 9.9%). Meanwhile the share of industry actually rose, though only slightly, from 33.0% in 1955 to 34.9% in 1981. At the other extreme is the UK, where the relative

Table 10.4. *Employment structure and stage of development*

	Percentage share of civil employment				Absolute change in % share		
	1955	1966	1973	1981	1955–73	1973–81	1955–81
				Agriculture			
Group A	31.0	20.6	14.1	9.9	−16.9	−4.2	−21.1
Group B	14.6	9.3	7.0	5.8	−7.6	−1.2	−8.8
UK	5.4	3.6	2.9	2.6	−2.5	−0.3	−2.8
				Manufacturing			
Group A	23.8	26.2	26.6	25.0	+2.8	−1.6	+1.2
Group B	30.5	30.8	28.9	24.7	−1.6	−4.2	−5.8
UK	36.1	34.8	32.3	26.4	−3.8	−5.9	−9.7
				Industry			
Group A	33.0	36.6	37.2	34.9	+4.2	−2.3	+1.9
Group B	40.7	41.2	38.6	33.7	−2.1	−4.9	−7.0
UK	47.9	46.3	42.6	35.7	−5.3	−6.9	−12.2
				Services			
Group A	36.0	42.8	48.7	55.2	+12.7	+6.5	+19.2
Group B	44.7	49.5	54.4	60.5	+9.7	+6.1	+15.8
UK	46.7	50.1	54.5	61.7	+7.8	+7.2	+15.0

Note: The group figures refer to an unweighted average of the countries concerned. Group A contains those advanced capitalist countries in which the share of agriculture in civil employment was at least 21.8% in 1955: Italy, Japan, Finland, Austria, Iceland, France, Norway and Denmark. Group B contains those countries in which the agricultural share was between 9.7 and 18.0% in 1955: Canada, Luxemburg, Germany, Sweden, Switzerland, New Zealand, Netherlands, Australia, Belgium, USA. The UK, with an agricultural share of 5.4% in 1955, is the only advanced capitalist country not in one of these groups
Source: See Table A1 of Appendix 7

expansion of services has been almost entirely at the expense of industry. Between 1955 and 1981, the share of services in total employment rose by 15.0 points in the UK (from 46.7% to 61.7%). There was some decline in agriculture, whose share fell by 2.8 points, but the vast bulk of service expansion was at the expense of industry, whose share fell by 12.2 points. This is hardly surprising. Given the small size of agriculture's share at the begining of the period (5.4%), it was mathematically impossible for this sector to provide the labour required to meet a 15.0% rise in the share of services. As a matter of arithmetic, such a rise in the share of services could only be at the expense of industry, whose *share* was bound to fall.

So, at one extreme are the immature, agrarian economies of group A where, as a rule, services have increased their employment mainly at the expense of agriculture, leaving industry largely unaffected.[2] At the other extreme is the UK, where the share of agriculture was already very small in 1955, and where the relative expansion of service employment has been almost entirely at the expense of industry. Between these two extremes lie the transitional economies

Table 10.5. *Summary of employment changes, 1955–81*

	Absolute change in percentage share		
	Group A (immature)	Group B (transitional)	UK (mature)
Agriculture	−21.1	−8.8	−2.8
Industry	+1.9	−7.0	−12.2
Services	+19.2	+15.8	+15.0
Total	0.0	0.0	0.0
cf. manufacturing	+1.2	−5.8	−9.7

Source: last column of Table 10.4

of group B. These economies were moderately agrarian in 1955, and the increase in the share of services since then has been at the expense of both agriculture and industry, in almost equal proportions (see Table 10.5).[3]

To explore this point a little further, let us go back to Tables 10.2 and 10.3. In these tables, countries are ranked according to the share of agriculture in total employment in 1955. Thus, at the top of the list is Italy, where the share of agriculture was 40.8% in 1955; at the bottom of the list is the UK, where agriculture's share was only 5.4%. Looking at these tables, we find a clear pattern in the behaviour of employment. In the more agrarian economies, towards the top of the list, manufacturing employment has in general grown faster (or fallen less) than in the least agrarian countries towards the bottom of the list. This relationship is illustrated graphically in the scatter diagrams shown in Figs. 10.3 and 10.4. Along the horizontal axis in these diagrams is measured the share of agriculture in total employment in the relevant base year (1955 in Fig. 10.3 and 1966 in Fig. 10.4).[4] Along the vertical axis is measured the change in manufacturing employment since the base year. Looking at these diagrams, we notice immediately a positive association between the variables concerned. This is particularly clear in Fig. 10.3, which shows how manufacturing share has changed since 1955. It is also true of Fig. 10.4, which shows how the absolute numbers employed in manufacturing have changed since 1966. In each case, the least agrarian economies at the beginning of the period have experienced the greatest fall in manufacturing employment, either absolutely or as a share of total employment.

Quite apart from the light they throw on structural change in general, Figs. 10.3 and 10.4 also tell us something about the British economy. As the least agrarian economy, the UK lies well to the left in each diagram, and this in itself helps to explain why the fall in manufacturing employment in the UK, both absolutely and relatively, has been so great. Here, then, we have an explanation for why the decline in industrial employment began so early in the UK and why it has been so great. By the early 1950s, the UK was already approaching economic

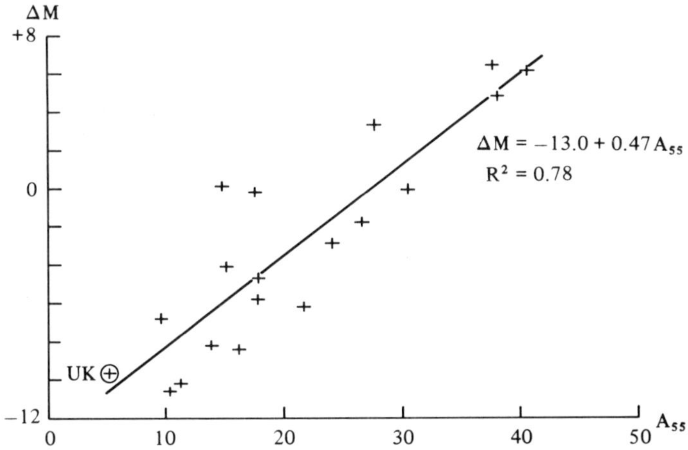

ΔM = Change in percentage share of manufacturing in civil employment, 1955–81.
A_{55} = percentage share of agriculture in civil employment in 1955.

Fig. 10.3 Manufacturing employment and stage of development, 1953–83

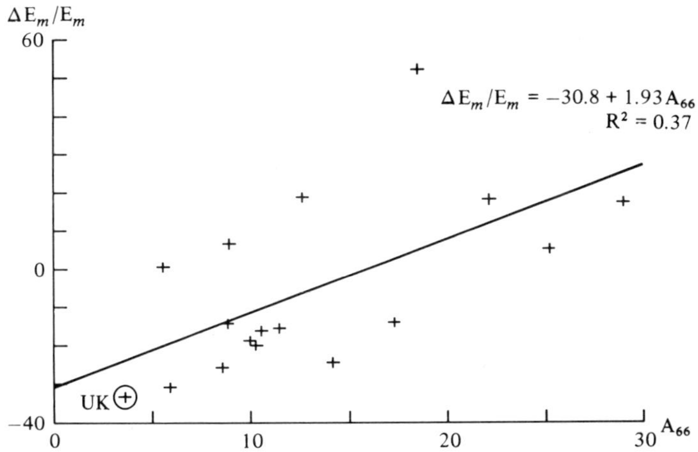

$\Delta E_m/E_m$ = percentage change in manufacturing employment over the period 1966–83.
A_{66} = percentage share of agriculture in civil employment in 1966.

Fig. 10.4 Manufacturing employment and stage of development 1966–83

maturity, and the pattern of employment was bound to shift away from industry towards the services. By contrast, many other currently advanced capitalist countries were nowhere near maturity in the early 1950s: many of them still had a large proportion of their labour force employed in agriculture, and they had simply not yet reached the stage of development at which economic growth involves an absolute or relative decline in industrial employment.

Thus, from the evidence we have examined so far, the Maturity Thesis looks quite convincing as an explanation for what has happened in the UK. It certainly helps to explain why the fall in industrial employment began earlier in the UK and has been more extensive than in most other countries. Further evidence is provided by the fact that many other capitalist countries began to experience a similar decline in industrial employment in the 1960s and 1970s, once their reserves of agricultural labour were depleted and they had reached the stage of maturity at which the service sector increases its share of total employment at the expense of industry.

The Specialization Thesis

A second potential explanation for the decline in manufacturing employment in the UK is concerned with foreign trade, with the huge changes which have occurred in the structure of UK trade over the past thirty years. These changes have been described at length in preceding chapters, so here we outline only their main features. By the time post-war recovery was complete, Britain had once again become a highly specialized 'workshop' economy, importing vast amounts of food and raw materials, as well as oil, in return for manufactured exports. This can be seen from the balance of payments figures. In 1950–2, the surplus on UK manufacturing trade averaged 10.5% of GDP whilst, on non-manufacturing trade, the average deficit was 13.3% of GDP.[5] These are truly remarkable figures, which have never been equalled, before or since, in British history. The reasons for such a remarkable situation are briefly as follows. On the non-manufacturing side, global scarcities in the aftermath of the Second World War had forced up to unprecedented levels the real cost of items which Britain had always imported in bulk, such as food and raw materials. Moreover, Britain's previously massive income from service activities, such as shipping and the City of London, had fallen, whilst receipts from coal exports, which had earlier been enormous, had almost vanished. This combination of inflated import prices and reduced earnings from service and coal exports explains why the deficit in non-manufacturing trade was so large in the early 1950s. To cover this deficit, the UK had no alternative but to export manufactured goods. Her profits from overseas investment had been greatly reduced by the enforced war-time sale of assets in the US and elsewhere, and the scope for overseas borrowing was limited. So, to finance her huge deficit on non-manufacturing trade, the UK required a surplus of almost equal magnitude in her manufacturing trade. This surplus was achieved through a vigorous combination of industrial protection and export promotion.

The early 1950s mark the high point of the UK's role as a 'workshop' economy. Since then, the picture has been transformed beyond recognition. In non-manufacturing trade, the old deficit has disappeared completely, to be replaced by a small surplus averaging 1% of GDP in 1981–3. Meanwhile, in manufacturing trade the opposite has occurred, and the old surplus has been replaced by a small deficit. This transformation is often seen as a symptom of Britain's industrial decline and of the failure of her manufacturing sector to compete successfully in international markets. However, as we have argued in earlier chapters, such an interpretation in unfounded. Certainly, the performance of manufacturing industry has been very poor during the past thirty years, but this is not a major factor explaining why there has been such a dramatic transformation in the structure of UK trade. The cause of this transformation lies mainly in events largely unrelated to the country's industrial performance. Since the early 1950s, there has been a whole stream of autonomous developments whose cumulative impact on Britain's trade structure and pattern of specialization has been enormous. It is these autonomous developments which explain why Britain is no longer a workshop economy, why she no longer has a large deficit on her trade in non-manufactures or a large surplus on her manufacturing trade.

Since the early 1950s, imports of food and raw materials have become much cheaper in real terms; increased domestic food production has reduced the need for food imports; new methods of production and a changing composition of output have reduced the need for imported raw materials; service exports, in such areas as civil aviation, consultancy and finance have risen; finally, the discovery of North Sea oil has turned Britain into a major oil producer. Between them, these developments explain why the UK's balance of trade in non-manufactures has improved so dramatically since the early 1950s. They also explain why the balance of trade in manufactures has deteriorated so dramatically over this period. In the early 1950s, the UK was a 'workshop' economy because she had to be. To finance the huge deficit in non-manufacturing trade, the country required a huge surplus in manufacturing trade. There was simply no other way to remain solvent. Nowadays, however, the situation is quite different. The UK no longer has a huge deficit in non-manufacturing trade and, as a result, she no longer requires a huge surplus in her trade in manufactures. The UK is no longer a massive net exporter of manufactures, because she no longer needs to be, and her poor industrial performance has only a marginal bearing on the matter. The dramatic decline in the UK's manufacturing surplus during the past thirty years is not primarily a symptom of industrial failure but is mainly a response to developments elsewhere in the economy. Autonomous developments in non-manufacturing trade have led to a new pattern of specialization, a new role for the UK in the world economy, of which the loss of her formerly huge manufacturing surplus is but one expression.

Now, for reasons explored in Chapter 1, a country's internal pattern of employment depends on its pattern of specialization, on its role in the international division of labour. *Ceteris paribus*, a 'workshop' economy, such as the UK in the early fifties, with a large trade surplus in manufactures, will have a much larger manufacturing sector than a country with a more balanced trade structure. Moreover, when an economy ceases to be a workshop economy and acquires a less specialized foreign trade structure, its manufacturing sector is likely to contract relatively, if not absolutely.

Here, then, is a potential explanation for what has happened to manufacturing employment in the UK over the past thirty years. In the early 1950s, the UK was a highly specialized manufacturing exporter, perhaps the most extreme example of a workshop economy the world has ever seen. This, in itself, helps to explain why such a large fraction of her labour force was employed in manufacturing industry. Since those days, because of developments in non-manufacturing trade, the British economy has become much less specialized. The country no longer requires such a large surplus in manufacturing trade and, as a result, no longer needs to employ anything like such a large fraction of her labour force in manufacturing. Moreover, no other country has experienced such a massive transformation in its foreign trade structure during the past thirty years. No other country, not even Austria or Norway, has experienced such a vast improvement in its non-manufacturing balance over the period, nor such a deterioration in its manufacturing balance. This may help to explain why the decline in manufacturing employment has been so much greater in the UK than in most other countries.

The Failure Thesis

So far we have considered two explanations for the decline of manufacturing employment in the UK. First, there was the Maturity Thesis, which located this decline within the framework of a general theory of development and structural change. The UK, it argued, was the first country to reach the stage of development known as 'maturity', in which the share of manufacturing in total employment starts to fall. This, in itself, helps to explain why the decline in manufacturing employment began so much earlier in the UK than elsewhere and has been so much greater. A very different explanation was put forward by the Specialization Thesis. According to this thesis, the decline in manufacturing employment is merely an internal consequence of the UK's changing external relations with other countries, in particular of the huge improvements which have occurred in the realm of non-manufacturing trade since the early 1950s. Thus, one thesis argues that a fall in manufacturing employment was inevitable, given the stage of development which the UK had reached by the 1950s, whilst the other argues that improvements in non-manufacturing trade are responsible for this decline.

There is, however, a third possible explanation – the 'Failure Thesis'. As its name suggests, this thesis sees the decline of manufacturing employment as a symptom of economic failure: the growing failure of manufacturing industry to compete internationally or to produce the level of output required for a prosperous and fully employed economy. The Failure Thesis can be summarized in the following set of propositions:

(1) The UK's economic record in the realm of incomes and employment has been poor;
(2) This is largely due to the weak performance of UK manufacturing industry;
(3) If the performance of UK manufacturing industry had been much stronger, UK manufacturing output would have been much greater;
(4) This would have stimulated the non-manufacturing side of the economy and led to the creation of more employment in services and other non-manufacturing activities;
(5) Finally, if UK manufacturing output had been higher, neither the absolute number of people employed in manufacturing, nor this sector's share in total employment, would have fallen anything like as fast as they have done.

Many of these propositions are quite uncontroversial and are universally accepted by economists of all persuasions. Even so, let us examine them briefly.

Consider the question of Britain's economic record. Here the evidence of failure is overwhelming. By international standards, real per capita income has risen slowly in the UK, particularly since 1973. Moreover, growth in GDP since 1973 has been entirely the result of North Sea oil production; indeed, between 1973 and 1983, non-oil GDP actually fell by 2% (Fig. 10.5). The cumulative effect of slow growth on the UK's position in the international hierarchy can be seen from Table 10.6. In 1953, the UK was amongst the half dozen richest countries in the world. By 1983, of all the advanced capitalist countries, she was amongst the poorest. In the realm of employment, the UK's record is equally dismal. In the 1950s, there was almost full employment in the UK, and the bulk of her population had never enjoyed greater economic security. However, by 1984, well over three million people were out of work and, of all the advanced capitalist countries, only Belgium and the Netherlands had a greater fraction of their labour force without employment (see Table 10.7). Not since the 1930s have so many British people faced such a bleak and insecure future.

So much for economic welfare. What about the role of manufacturing industry in all of this? Here again the evidence is overwhelming. By international

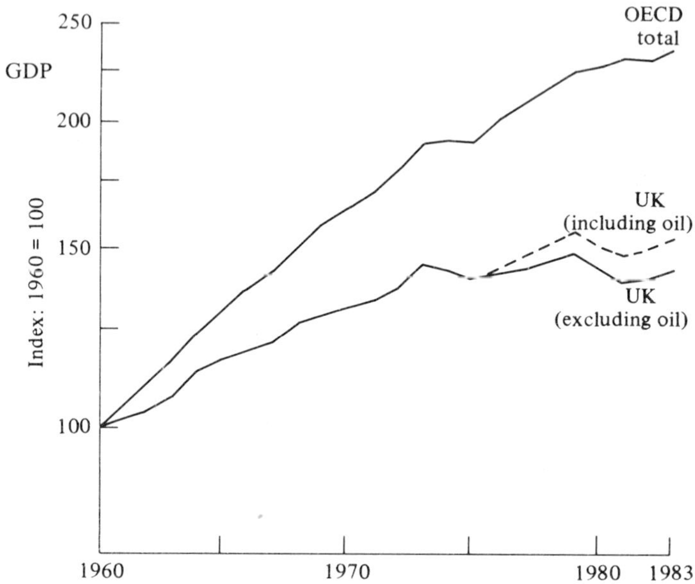

Fig. 10.5 GDP in the UK and OECD, 1960–83

Table 10.6. *GDP per head in selected countries ($US 1975)*[a]

	(1) 1953	(2) 1963	(3) 1973	(4) 1984	Percentage growth per annum 1953–84
Canada	3896	4688	7030	7970	2.3
USA	4946	5503	7371	8511	1.8
Japan	1054	2245	4974	6314	5.9
Australia	3074	3884	5337	6126	2.2
Austria	1735	3031	4785	5752	3.9
Belgium	2499	3384	5253	5959	2.8
France	2432	3476	5437	6362	3.2
Germany	2319	3866	5628	6473	3.4
Italy	1814	2903	4363	4721	3.1
Netherlands	2694	3639	5502	5836	2.5
Norway	3067	4058	5716	7562	3.0
Sweden	3536	4993	6769	7567	2.5
Unweighted average	2756	3806	5680	6596	2.9
UK	3080	3834	5053	5616	2.0

[a] Exchange rates are based on purchasing power parity
Source: OECD, Kravis (1982)

Table 10.7. *Unemployment rates in selected OECD countries*[a] *(percentage of total labour force)*

	1964–73	1974–79	1980	1981	1982	1983	1984
US	4.4	6.6	7.0	7.5	9.5	9.5	7.4
Germany	0.8	3.2	3.0	4.4	6.1	8.0	8.6
France	2.2	4.5	6.3	7.3	8.1	8.3	9.7
Italy	5.5	6.6	7.4	8.3	9.0	9.8	10.2
Canada	4.7	7.2	7.5	7.5	10.9	11.8	11.2
Australia	1.9	5.0	6.0	5.7	7.1	9.9	8.9
Belgium	2.2	3.8	9.0	11.1	12.6	13.9	14.0
Netherlands	1.4	3.8	4.9	7.5	11.4	13.7	14.0
Japan	1.2	1.9	2.0	2.2	2.4	2.6	2.7
Norway	1.7	1.8	1.7	2.0	2.6	3.3	3.0
Sweden	2.0	1.9	2.0	2.5	3.1	3.5	3.1
Austria	1.5	1.6	1.9	2.5	3.5	4.1	4.0
Unweighted average	2.5	4.0	4.9	5.7	7.2	8.2	8.1
UK	3.1	5.0	6.9	11.0	12.3	13.1	13.2

[a] Standardized to accord with the ILO definition of unemployment. Figures given here for the UK differ slightly from those used elsewhere in this book
Source: OECD *Economic Outlook* and *Main Economic Indicators*

standards, the performance of British manufacturing industry has been very poor, especially since the oil crisis of 1973. Prior to 1973, British manufacturing output and productivity rose quite fast compared with the country's previous historical experience. However, in many other countries they rose even faster. As a result, despite moderately fast industrial growth, Britain was overtaken by many of her foreign rivals during this period and, by the time the world crisis broke at the end of 1973, she was no longer a first-rank industrial power. Thus, up to 1973, the decline of British manufacturing was relative rather than absolute. Since then, however, industrial decline has become absolute and manufacturing output is now lower than it was in 1973. Meanwhile, manufacturing output has continued to rise in other countries, albeit irregularly (see Fig. 10.6). Between 1973 and 1982, manufacturing output fell by 18% in the UK, whilst in the six major OECD countries it rose by 15% on average.[6]

In the realm of labour productivity, Britain's performance has also been poor by international standards since 1973. Despite a spectacular shakeout in vehicles, steel and certain other industries in the period since 1979, output per person per hour in British manufacturing rose by only 22% in the decade 1973–83, compared to an average of 34% in the six major OECD countries. Although accurate comparisons in this field are notoriously difficult, available statistics establish beyond doubt that labour productivity in manufacturing industry is

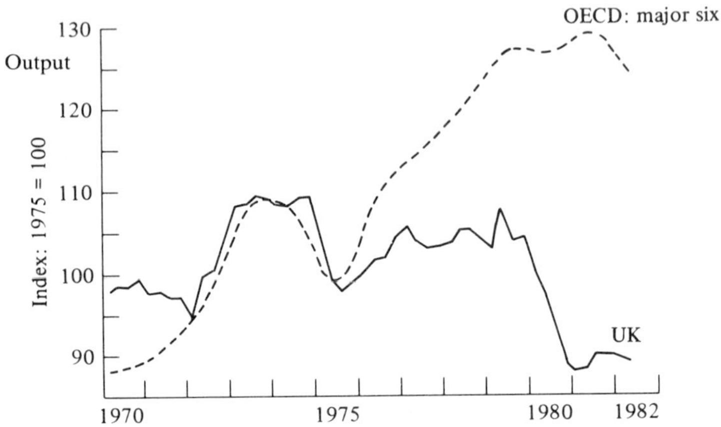

Fig. 10.6 Manufacturing output in the UK and OECD, 1970–82

now much lower in the UK than elsewhere in the advanced capitalist world (see Table 6.15).

The weakness of manufacturing industry is certainly the main reason why the UK has become a relatively poor country and why per capita incomes in the UK are now the lowest in Northern Europe. It also helps to explain why the unemployment rate is so high.

Consider what it would mean if Britain's manufacturing industry were much stronger and more competitive than it is at present, having more equipment, using more advanced methods of production and producing a wider range and higher quality of output. For a start, manufacturing output would obviously be much greater. Part of this additional output would go directly to meet domestic requirements, and part would be exported to pay for imports from foreign countries. Some of these additional imports would be non-manufactures, such as raw materials and services, but there would also be a large increase in manufactured imports. Taking account of additional supplies from both domestic industry and foreign producers, the total amount of manufactured goods available for use in the UK would be much greater than it is at present. Since the production and distribution of manufactured goods involves a wide range of complementary activities, output would be greater in areas such as construction, mining, consulting, transport and retail distribution. Moreover, real incomes would be higher and, consequently, consumers' expenditure of almost every kind would be greater, as would public expenditure on items such as health and education. Thus, with a stronger manufacturing sector, there would be more output in almost every sector of the economy.

What about employment? Would it also be greater? In answering this question, we must distinguish between employment in the economy as a whole and employment in particular industries or sectors. Taking the economy as a whole, total employment would certainly be much higher than it is now, if Britain's manufacturing industry were much stronger and had performed much better over the past thirty years. The weakness of manufacturing industry has been largely responsible for the inflation and balance of payments problems which have plagued the UK for many years. In the face of these problems, successive governments, Tory and Labour alike, have imposed deflationary measures which both reduce employment in the short term and inhibit its longer-term growth. If manufacturing industry had performed better, there would have been less need for such measures. Inflationary pressures would have been weaker, because more output would have been available to meet the rival claims of workers, employers and the state; meanwhile, the balance of payments would have been stronger, because British industry would have been more competitive in home and overseas markets. Thus, governments could have pursued more expansionary policies without jeopardizing their targets for inflation and the balance of payments; as a result, the overall level of employment would have been much higher. How would this increase in total employment have been distributed between one sector of the economy and another? In particular, how would employment in the manufacturing sector itself have been affected, and what would have happened to the share of manufacturing in total employment? To answer these questions by means of a priori argument is not easy, and specific numerical estimates are required if one is to go beyond the most general of observations. In the next chapter we will provide such estimates, but for the present we will limit ourselves to a few general remarks.

As we have just argued, if manufacturing industry had performed much better over the past thirty years, then total employment in the UK would by now be much greater than it is. Given such a large addition to total employment, we can assume that almost every major sector of the economy, including manufacturing itself, would have gained extra jobs: either new jobs would have been created or old jobs saved. As a result, more people would now be employed in construction, in the services and, of course, in manufacturing itself.[7] Thus, employment would be greater than it now is, in both manufacturing and non-manufacturing alike. However, this still leaves open several possibilities. Suppose the stronger performance in manufacturing industry had been accompanied by a large increase in labour productivity; in this case, relatively few additional jobs would have been created in the manufacturing sector itself, despite the large increase in manufacturing output, and most of the additional employment would have been in non-manufacturing, especially services. In this case, the *share* of manufacturing in total employment would have fallen as fast or even faster over the past thirty years than it has done. Conversely, suppose a stronger performance in manufacturing industry had been accompanied by only a modest increase in labour productivity – an unlikely, but logically conceivable combination. In this case, many of the additional jobs would have been in the manufacturing sector itself. As a result, the *share* of manufacturing in total employment would be much greater than it is now and over the past thirty years this share would have fallen much less than it has done. Both these scenarios are logically conceivable and, on a priori grounds alone, there is no way of choosing between them.

All we can say with complete certainty is that if the UK's manufacturing sector had been much stronger, then manufacturing output would have been much higher. It is also likely that more people would now be employed in this sector than at present. However, at this stage, we cannot say how the *share* of manufacturing in total employment would have behaved. We cannot even say whether this share would have fallen more slowly or more rapidly than it has done over the past thirty years. To answer such a question we require something more than a general a priori discussion. We need a specific, quantitative assessment of the various factors involved. In the next chapter we will attempt such an assessment, but for the moment we must leave open the question of how economic performance has affected relative shares.

Conclusions

In this chapter, we have considered three potential explanations for what has happened to manufacturing employment in Britain: the Maturity Thesis, the Specialization Thesis and the Failure Thesis. There is no need to summarize these theses, as their names speak for themselves – and besides they have already been fully described. From the evidence considered in this chapter, there is *prima facie* support for all three theses, and it seems likely that all of them can play some role in explaining what has happened to manufacturing employment during the past thirty years. However, this is only a provisional conclusion, and a more definite answer will have to wait until the next chapter.

11

Towards a better past

Introduction

In this chapter we take up in a more systematic way some of the themes just considered in Chapter 10. Our aim is to quantify the influence of the various factors which have affected manufacturing employment in the UK since the early 1950s, in particular the influence of poor macro-economic performance and the country's changing role in the international division of labour. Our method is that of counterfactual history. We consider various hypothetical scenarios under which the observed, historical behaviour of certain key variables is modified, and we then estimate how such a modification affects other variables in the economy. By its nature, such an exercise is rather speculative in character and may involve considerable guesswork, especially when long periods of time or large variations in the key variables are being considered. Even so, this method can be extremely useful in quantifying the role of individual factors and in providing a rough indication of their relative importance. Indeed, such information is often impossible to obtain except by the counterfactual method. In the present case, for example, there is no other way to assess the relative importance of the major factors which have influenced manufacturing employment in the UK over the past thirty years.

The chapter is organized as follows. It begins with a brief description of several hypothetical scenarios for the period 1946–83. (Further information on this subject is given in Appendix 10.) It then goes on to consider, in detail, what happens to the level and structure of employment under each of these scenarios. By comparing one hypothetical scenario with another – as well as with the actual behaviour of the economy over the period in question – we are able to estimate numerically how far employment in both manufacturing and non-manufacturing has been affected by the UK's poor macro-economic performance and her changing role in the international division of labour.

Our principal conclusions are as follows. If the UK economy had performed much better since 1950 and had remained close to full employment right up to the present, then by 1983 there would have been around 3 million more people in employment than was actually the case. Of these extra jobs, perhaps three to four hundred thousand would have been in the manufacturing sector and some in construction, but the vast majority would have been in the service sector. As a result, the *share* of manufacturing in total employment would have been lower by 1983 than it was in reality. Thus, compared to their peak values in the fifties and sixties, both the level of manufacturing employment and its share would still have fallen dramatically, even if industrial performance had been much stronger. A dramatic fall in manufacturing employment was inevitable for two reasons: (a) because of the massive shift which has taken place in the UK's role in the international division of labour since 1950 and (b) because of the fact that, thirty years ago, the UK economy was already on the brink of 'maturity'. Thus, of the various explanations advanced in the previous chapter to account for falling manufacturing employment, our results in the present chapter strongly support both the 'Specialization Thesis' and the 'Maturity Thesis'. However, they provide ambiguous support for the 'Failure Thesis'. A vast number of manufacturing jobs were lost through factory closures, layoffs and the like. However, virtually as many manufacturing jobs would have been lost through higher productivity, if industry had been dynamic. Thus, the *net* impact of industrial failure on manufacturing employment was rather small. In practice, Britain has been an example of 'negative de-industrialization', due to the weakness of manufacturing, but she would have experienced just as much, if not more de-industrialization of a 'positive' kind, if her manufacturing performance had been stronger. In this sense, most of the loss of manufacturing jobs over the past few decades was unavoidable. These, briefly, are our principal conclusions. Let us now see how they were reached.

Hypothetical scenarios

In this chapter we shall consider two hypothetical scenarios covering the period 1950–83. These will be called Scenario I and Scenario II. Each scenario is defined by specifying the behaviour of four key variables: GDP per capita measured in constant 1975 US dollars (Y), the percentage unemployment rate (U), total employment (E) and net manufactured exports as a percentage of GDP at current market prices (B_m). The behaviour of these variables under the hypothetical scenarios is as follows.

Scenario I

Under this scenario per capita income (Y) starts at its actual level in 1950 and then grows at a uniform rate of 3.0% p.a. right through to 1983. This compares to an actual growth rate over the period 1950–83 of 2.1% p.a. By 1983 GDP per capita under Scenario I is equal to $7,732 (at 1975 prices), which is some 40% higher than the level actually achieved in the UK in that year. With such a per capita income, the UK would have been one of the richest countries in the world, second only to the USA. Note that most of this additional growth occurs after 1973 (see Fig. 11.1a).

Under Scenario I the unemployment rate (U) falls from its actual level of 1.5% in 1950 to 1.0% in 1955. It then remains at this level until 1966, after which time it rises slowly to reach 3.5% in 1983. The general rise in unemployment towards the end of the period under this scenario accords with the experience of successful economies like Austria or Japan. In such economies, unemployment has been creeping upwards over the past decade or more, despite their high rates of growth. We assume the same phenomenon occurs under both hypothetical scenarios (see Fig. 11.1b). Note our assumption that unemployment remains low under Scenario I is merely a working hypothesis. No one can be sure exactly what the impact of faster growth on unemployment would have been in practice. With the faster rate of output growth assumed under Scenario I, we can be sure that total employment would have risen faster than it did in reality, and that unemployment would not have reached the level actually witnessed in the early 1980s. But whether this would have been enough to keep unemployment down to 3.5% is an open question.

The behaviour of total employment under Scenario I is illustrated in Fig. 11.1c. As can be seen from the diagram, total employment rises strongly from 1950 right through to 1983, apart from a brief hiatus in the late 1960s when it drops back for a few years.[1] Comparing the actual and hypothetical curves for total employment, we see that they almost coincide up to 1966. However, from then onwards these curves diverge by an increasing amount. By 1983, total employment under Scenario I is nearly 3 million greater than in the actual economy. This is reflected in a much lower figure for officially registered unemployment: less than 1 million as compared to 3 million in the actual economy. Moreover, there is also much less hidden unemployment in the hypothetical economy, for nearly a million of the extra jobs in this economy are filled by people not officially classified as unemployed: school leavers, housewives, retired persons, and possibly new immigrants from abroad. The formula used to estimate total employment under Scenario I is given in Appendix 10.

In the realm of foreign trade, Scenario I assumes that the ratio of net manufactured exports to GDP (B_m) falls from its actual value of 11.2% in 1950 to 1.3% in 1983. The assumed values for intermediate years are shown in Fig. 11.1(d). These values are baded on the assumption that under normal conditions the surplus on manufacturing trade must be just sufficient to cover the deficit on non-manufacturing trade. In Chapter 7 and Appendix 8, we considered how faster growth would have affected the UK's balance of trade in non-manufactures.

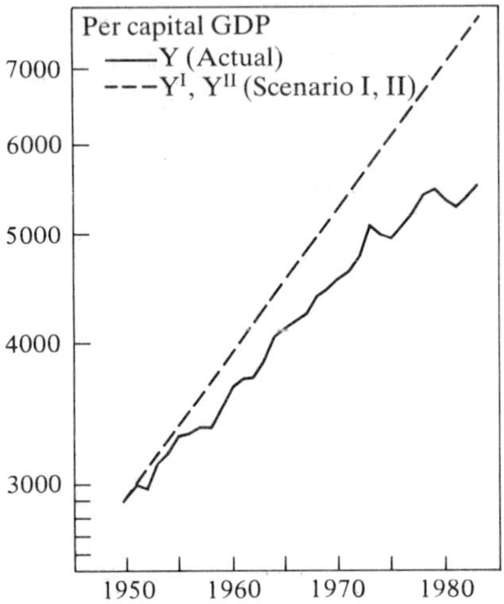

Fig. 11.1a Per capita GDP (Y) (1975 US dollars)

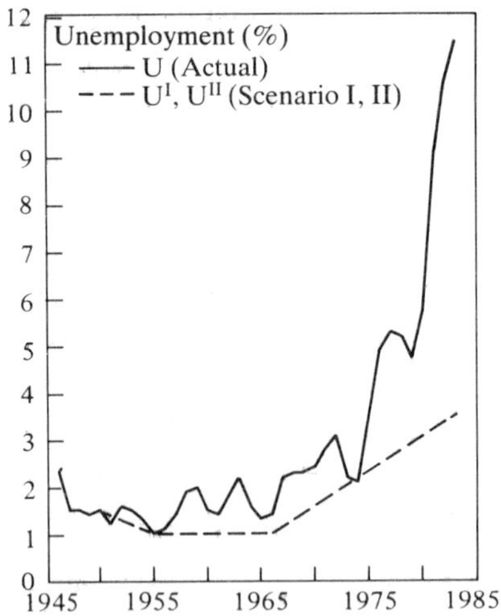

Fig. 11.1b Unemployment (U) (per cent)

Our conclusions were as follows: if the UK economy had grown at the rate assumed under Scenario I during the period 1950–83, then non-manufacturing trade (including services) would have been in deficit to the tune of 1.3% of GDP by 1983 (the 'Intermediate' Scenario in Chapter 7). It is because of the need to cover this deficit that Scenario I assumes a surplus on manufacturing trade equal to 1.3% of GDP in 1983. The manufacturing surplus for earlier years is derived by means of the simple formula described in Appendix 8. With

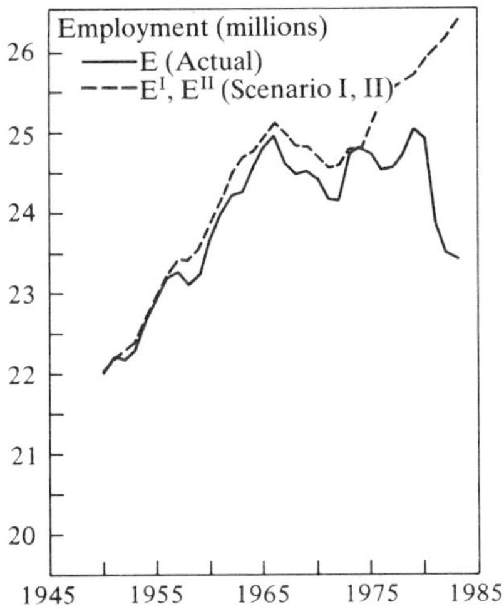

Fig. 11.1c Total employment (E) (millions)

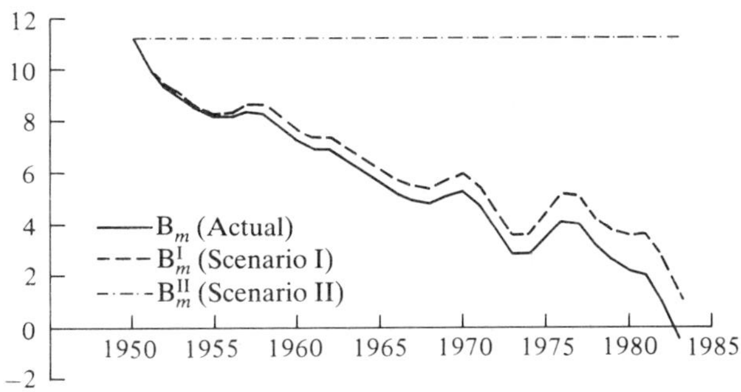

Fig. 11.1d Net manufactured exports (B_m) (% of GDP)

the exception of the abnormal years 1951 and 1973–5, the surplus on manufacturing trade under Scenario I is on average just sufficient to offset the deficit on non-manufacturing trade. Note that the deficit in non-manufacturing trade falls both absolutely and relative to GDP during the course of time under Scenario I. This reflects the influence of the various autonomous factors described in Chapter 6: cheaper food and raw materials; greater domestic food production; economies in the use of raw materials and their replacement by synthetics; the exploitation of North Sea oil and gas; and, finally, the development of new service exports. All of these autonomous factors have been at work in the actual UK economy, and they are assumed to continue operating under Scenario I. This explains why the deficit on non-manufacturing trade gradually falls under this scenario. It also explains why net manufactured exports fall both absolutely and in relation to GDP under this scenario. Such exports are used to finance the deficit on non-manufacturing trade and, as this deficit falls, so too does the required amount of net manufactured exports.

To conclude this description of Scenario I, let us consider briefly the role of the manufacturing sector under this scenario. In a well-known paper, Ajit Singh has given the following definition of what he calls an 'efficient manufacturing sector':

> The evolution of the structure of the U.K. economy over the last century has rendered it a net importer of food and raw materials, which have to be paid for largely by exports of manufactures. . . . given this historical evolution, an efficient manufacturing sector for the U.K. economy may be defined as one which, given the normal levels of other components of the balance of payments, yields sufficient net exports (both currently, but more importantly, potentially) to pay for import requirements at socially acceptable levels of output, employment and the exchange rate.[2]

Under Scenario I, the UK's manufacturing sector is efficient in the sense just described. Since there is rapid economic growth and unemployment is relatively low, we can presume that output and employment are at 'socially acceptable' levels. We can also assume that the exchange rate is at a socially acceptable level, although its behaviour has not been explicitly described here.[3] Finally, net manufactured exports are normally sufficient under Scenario I to finance the deficit in trade in non-manufactures. However, there is one rider to add. Because of autonomous improvements in the realm of non-manufacturing trade, the role of an 'efficient' manufacturing sector gradually changes during in the course of time under Scenario I. In the early 1950s, there is a huge deficit in non-manufacturing trade and in order to achieve external balance British industry must generate a huge export surplus in trade in manufactures. However, at the end of the period in 1983, the situation is radically different. The deficit on non-manufacturing trade has shrunk to around 1.3% of GDP and so, too, has the required surplus on manufacturing trade. Thus, although the manufacturing sector still needs to be competitive internationally, it no longer needs to generate a huge surplus of *net* exports. Whilst gross exports of manufactured goods may be considerable, most of the revenue from such exports will be spent on imports of manufactures, so the volume of net manufactured exports will be quite small. Thus, under Scenario I, the trading role of an efficient manufacturing sector gradually alters during the course of time. Initially, it provides manufactured exports primarily in order to pay for imports of food, raw materials and the like. In the course of time, however, this role becomes less important, and the main function of manufactured exports becomes increasingly that of paying for manufactured imports. This is, of course, just what has occurred in reality during the course of the past thirty years. It is also what happens under Scenario I.

Scenario II

Under this scenario, GDP, the unemployment rate and total employment all behave exactly just as they do under Scenario I. However, net exports behave very differently. Under Scenario I, the ratio of net manufactured exports to GDP (B_m) falls dramatically between 1950 and 1983, as the economy becomes less specialized. Under Scenario II, by contrast, there is no change at all in the pattern of specialization. The UK continues to be a specialist 'workshop' economy throughout the entire period, and the ratio of net manufactured exports to GDP remains constant at 11.2% from 1950 right through to 1983 (see Fig. 11.d).

Scenarios I and II compared

The above scenarios can be summarized as follows. Both scenarios assume that the economy grows much faster over the period 1950–83 than it did in reality; both assume that it remains relatively close to full employment and that total employment rises strongly right through to 1983. However, in their assumptions about foreign trade, the two scenarios differ radically. Under Scenario I, the UK gradually abandons her role as a specialist 'workshop' economy, just as she has done in reality. As a result, her trade surplus in manufactures shrinks dramatically in the course of time. Under Scenario II, by contrast, the UK remains a highly specialized 'workshop' economy throughout the period, exporting a huge surplus of manufactured goods in return for food, raw materials and oil. Thus, the UK's experience under Scenario I is just a more successful version (in terms of growth and employment) of actual history. By contrast, under Scenario II, it is as if the whole range of autonomous improvements in non-manufacturing trade described in Chapter 6 had never occurred. Table 11.1 compares output and employment under the two scenarios with actual experience.

The structure of employment

To determine what happens to the structure of employment under the hypothetical scenarios, we shall use the following equation:

$$M = -1619.8 + 395.81 \log Y - 23.71 (\log Y)^2 - 0.56\,U + 0.70\,B_m + v$$

where M is the percentage share of manufacturing in total employment and v is a residual disturbance term. The functional form is of the same general type as was used in Chapter 1 to anaylse international data on the structure of employment. However, the method of estimation is different in the present case. Previously the coefficient (and the residual) were estimated using annual time-series data for the UK alone. After consulting UK input–output tables and the evidence provided by the regression analyses of Chapter 1, the coefficient on B_m (the ratio of net manufactured exports to GDP) was set equal to 0.70. The remaining coefficients and the residual were thus estimated from UK time-series data using the method of restricted least squares. Full details of the estimation procedure are given in Appendix 10, together with alternative estimates and a discussion of their implications.

Table 11.1. *Summary of UK economic history and hypothetical alternatives*

	Actual						Hypothetical	
	1950	1955	1966	1973	1979	1983	1983I	1983II
Employment and population ('000)								
Manufacturing employment	7657	8270	8678	7977	7378	5791	6164	7989
Non-manufacturing employment	14345	14638	16260	16719	17631	17607	20170	18345
Total employment	22002	22908	24938	24696	25009	23398	26334	26334
Unemployment	327	239	353	557	1235	2986	995	995
Total labour force	22329	23147	25291	25253	26244	26382	27289	27289
Population	50150	50946	54500	55913	55881	56187	56187	56187
Output (1975 US$)								
GDP per head	2915	3305	4173	5097	5475	5506	7732	7732
GDP per civilian worker	6644	7350	9120	11540	12234	13222	16497	16497
Other statistics								
Share of manufacturing in total employment (%)	34.8	36.1	34.8	32.3	29.5	24.7	23.4	30.3
Unemployment (%)	1.5	1.0	1.4	2.2	4.7	11.3	3.5	3.5
Net manufactured exports (% of GDP)	11.0	8.7	5.9	3.0	1.8	−0.5	2.0	11.0

The behaviour of *M* under the hypothetical scenarios is shown in Fig. 11.2, whilst the absolute number of people employed in the major sectors of the economy is shown in Figs. 11.3a–b. Using these diagrams, let us now consider what happens to employment under each of the hypothetical scenarios.

Scenario II [fast growth but no change in trade specialization]

Under this scenario manufacturing employment increases rapidly during the 1950s. However, this expansion comes to an end in the 1960s and, from then onwards, this kind of employment falls almost continuously, both absolutely and as a share of total employment. By 1983, the number of people employed in the manufacturing sector has fallen to 8 million, which as a share of total employment is just over 30%. It is interesting to compare the UK under Scenario II with the situation in other countries. This is done in Table 11.2. By 1983, the UK under Scenario II has an economic structure midway between the two great 'workshop' economies, West Germany and Japan. Like these economies, the UK has a massive trade surplus in manufactures, whilst the share of its workforce employed in manufacturing is lower than in West Germany but greater than in Japan. In terms of per capita income, however, the UK is more prosperous than either of them.

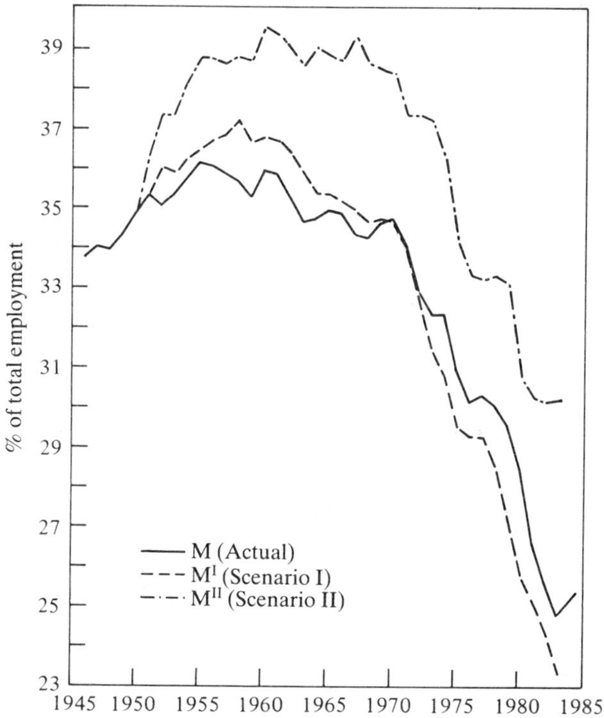

Fig. 11.2 Manufacturing share (M) (% of total employment)

There are several reasons why the share of manufacturing in total employment rises during the 1950s under Scenario II. Of these perhaps the most important is concerned with the agricultural sector. In the 1950s the UK economy is not yet completely 'mature', and there is still room for the manufacturing sector to increase its share of total employment by a fair amount at the expense of agriculture, whose share is falling. (The same is also true under Scenario I and in the actual economy.) However, the potential for this kind of transformation is soon exhausted and, by the 1960s, the economy is fully mature. Once this stage is reached the dominant factor is no longer the shift in employment from agriculture to manufacturing, but rather the shift from manufacturing to the services. The fate of manufacturing in later years under Scenario II is an example of the 'crowding-out' which occurs in all successful economies once they reach maturity. When this stage is reached, service employment begins to crowd out manufacturing employment and, as growth continues, the share of services rises, whilst that of manufacturing falls. What happens under Scenario II is also an example of what we have called elsewhere 'positive de-industrialization'.[4] Under

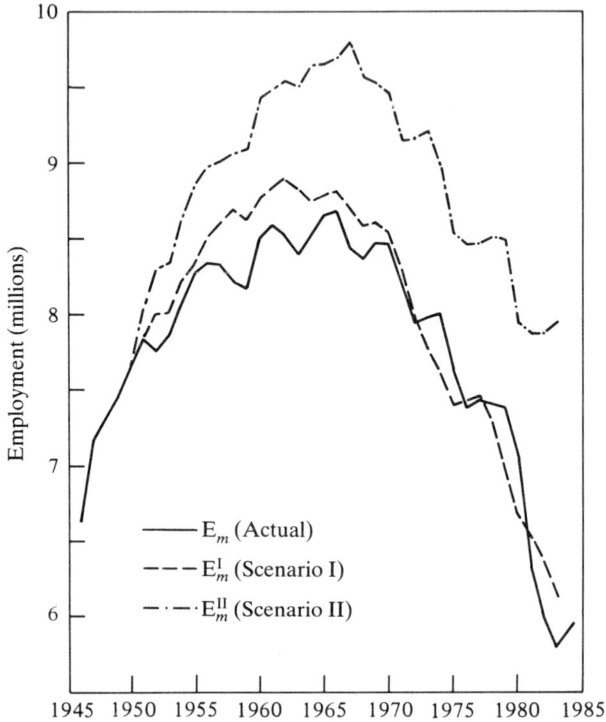

Fig. 11.3a Manufacturing employment (E_m) (millions)

this scenario, manufacturing output rises quite fast in later years, but output per worker rises even faster, with the result that employment in the manufacturing sector falls. However, increased output in the manufacturing sector is able to sustain a high level of output of services and, to provide these services, more workers are taken on by the service sector. Indeed, sufficient new jobs are created in the service sector to keep the economy fairly close to full employment, despite a large increase in the total labour force. This is in stark contrast to experience in the actual economy, which has been beset by 'negative de-industrialization' on a spectacular scale: millions of workers have been shed by an ailing manufacturing industry, and too few new jobs have been created elsewhere in the economy to absorb them, with the result that unemployment has risen dramatically.

Scenario I [fast growth, changing trade specialization]

Let us now consider Scenario I. Under this scenario, the economy grows at the same rate as under Scenario II and, hence, all of the growth-induced shifts

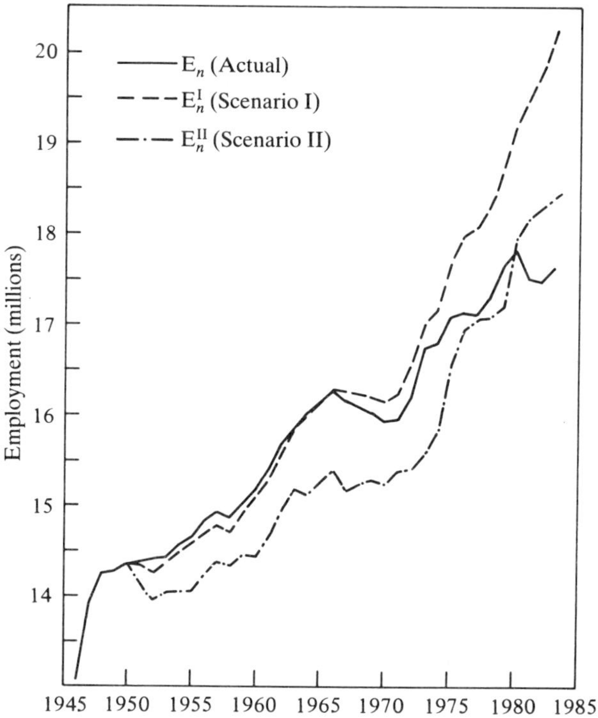

Fig. 11.3b Non-manufacturing employment (E_n) (millions)

in the structure of employment just described also occur under Scenario I. However, superimposed on these are other structural shifts which arise from events in the sphere of foreign trade. Under Scenario II, changes in the UK's pattern of trade specialization were ignored, and the trade surplus in manufactures was assumed to remain constant as a proportion of GDP. Under Scenario I, by contrast, such changes are taken into account and, as a result, the manufacturing trade surplus falls almost continuously. As the surplus falls, there is a transfer of labour from manufacturing to the services, and the result is a growing divergence in the structure of employment between Scenarios I and II. Comparing the two scenarios, we find that, in each case, the share of manufacturing in total employment rises during the 1950s and then undergoes prolonged decline (Fig. 11.2). However, the initial rise is less pronounced under Scenario I and the subsequent decline is much greater. By 1983, the number of people employed in manufacturing is 1.8 million less under Scenario I than Scenario II (see Fig. 11.3a), which is equivalent to 7% of total employment in the economy as a whole (Table 11.1). These figures give some indication of the enormous

Table 11.2. *Some international comparisons in 1983*

	United Kingdom			Other countries					
	Actual	Scenario I	Scenario II	Norway	Canada	USA	Sweden	Japan	Germany
Per capita GDP[a]	5506	7732	7732	7347	7701	8037	7311	6010	6291
Unemployment rate[b]	11.4	3.5	3.5	3.3	11.8	9.5	5.5	2.6	8.0
Net manufactured exports[c]	−0.5	1.3	11.2	−5.7	−2.3	0.9	5.5	11.8	10.1
Share of manufacturing in total employment[b]	24.7	23.4	30.3	19.7	19.8	20.4	22.4	24.8	33.1

Notes: [a] 1975 US dollars
[b] Percent of civilian labour force; all figures are standardized to accord with the ILO definition of unemployment, except for those for the UK which are not standardized
[c] Percent of GDP at market prices; figures for countries other than the UK refer to 1981; for these other countries f.o.b. figures for imports are estimated by multiplying the c.i.f. figures by 0.92
[d] Figures for countries other than the UK refer to 1982

impact which changing trade specialization has had on the UK's internal structure of employment since 1950.

Table 11.2 compares the UK economy in 1983 under Scenario I with the situation in other economies at around the same time. From this table we see that the UK economy under this scenario is rather similar to the Swedish economy. Per capita incomes are somewhat higher in the UK than in Sweden, but the unemployment rate is identical and the share of manufacturing in total employment is much the same. Thus, if the UK had grown as envisaged under Scenario I, her economy would by now be similar to that of Sweden. By international standards a relatively low share of her workforce would be employed in manufacturing (23.4%), although this share would still be greater than in Canada, Norway and the US, where manufacturing now accounts for 20% or less of total employment.

Scenario I and the actual economy compared

Scenario I differs from actual history in one respect only: it assumes that UK industry is more dynamic and that as a result the rate of economic growth is higher, and the economy remains fairly close to full employment right through to 1983. Apart from this difference in macro-economic performance, Scenario I and actual history are identical. (In particular, the same autonomous changes in trade specialization occur in both cases.) Thus, by comparing what happens under Scenario I with what actually happened, we can see how the level and structure of employment were affected by the UK's poor economic performance over the period in question. Perhaps the most striking thing to emerge from this comparision is how small was the net impact of poor industrial performance on manufacturing employment (i.e. over and above any loss which would have occurred if industrial performance had been stronger). Under Scenario I manufacturing employment rises a little faster during the 1950s than in the actual economy, but its subsequent decline is just as dramatic (Fig. 11.3a). By 1983 there are around 6.2 million people employed in manufacturing industry under Scenario I, as compared to an actual figure of 5.8 million – which in each case is over $2\frac{1}{2}$ million below the peak number achieved in the 1960s. Looking at relative shares, the picture is much the same. Under Scenario I, just as in the actual economy, the share of manufacturing in total employment rises up to the mid- or late 1950s and then undergoes a prolonged and massive decline. Indeed, so great is this decline that, by 1983, the share of manufacturing is even lower under Scenario I than in the actual economy: 23.4% as compared to 24.7% (Fig. 11.2). Thus, under Scenario I, the absolute number of people employed in the manufacturing sector in 1983 is somewhat greater than in the actual economy, whilst the share of this sector in total employment is somewhat less. This discrepancy between relative shares and absolute numbers is explained by what happens total employment under Scenario I. Under this scenario, non-manufacturing employment grows extremely fast – mainly in service activities – and by 1983 there are 20.2 million people employed in the non-manufacturing sector as a whole (Fig. 11.3b). In the actual economy the corresponding figure for 1983 is 17.6 million. As result of this massive increase in non-manufacturing employment, the share of manufacturing in total employment is lower under Scenario I than in the actual economy, even though slightly more people are employed in this sector than was actually the case.

As we have just seen, the long-term evolution of manufacturing employment is much the same under Scenario I as in the actual economy. However, the timing of events is rather different. From its peak in the mid-1960s through to 1979, manufacturing employment falls more rapidly under Scenario I, but afterwards the opposite is the case and the fall is greatest in the actual economy (see Fig. 11.3a). The explanation for this difference in timing is as follows. Under Scenario I manufacturing employment declines at a fairly uniform pace during a prolonged period lasting from the mid-1960s right through to 1983. The uniformity and pace of this decline reflect the influence of continuous and rapid structural change. In the actual economy, by contrast, the pace of structural change is slower and fewer manufacturing jobs are lost because of it. This explains why, prior to 1979, manufacturing employment falls more rapidly under Scenario I than in the actual economy. After 1979, however, a new factor enters the situation. In the actual economy, the manufacturing sector is hit by a severe crisis, in which output slumps and there are widespread closures and layoffs. Under Scenario I the economy avoids this slump and output continues to expand without interruption. Of course, even after 1974, manufacturing jobs are still lost under Scenario I as a result of structural change, but the scale of these losses does not compare to the wholescale destruction of manufacturing employment which occurs in the actual economy after 1979 as a result of the industrial crisis. It is this industrial crisis which explains why, after 1979, the fall in manufacturing employment is so much greater in the actual economy than under Scenario I.

Output and productivity under Scenario I: some illustrative figures

The foregoing discussion may be summarized as follows. If Scenario I is any guide, faster economic growth would have had only a minor impact on the long-term decline in manufacturing employment. At most, it would have altered the timing of events and made the pace of this decline more uniform: more manufacturing jobs would have been lost before 1979, and the wholesale collapse of the 1980s would have been avoided. Over the long term, the main impact of faster growth would have been on non-manufacturing employment. With

Table 11.3. *The impact of faster growth: an illustrative example*

	(a) Percentage increase[a]		
	Output per worker	Civil employment	Output
Non-market services	0	20	20
Market services	29	15	49
Other non-manufacturing	15	5	21
Non-manufacturing	18	14.5	35
Manufacturing	46	6.5	55
Total	25	12.5	40.5
	(b) Civil employment (millions)[b]		
	(1) Actual	(2) Scenario I	(3) Difference (2)–(1)
Non-market services	4.3	5.2	+0.9
Market services	10.5	12.1	+1.6
Other non-manufacturing	2.8	2.9	+0.1
Non-manufacturing	17.6	20.2	+2.5
Manufacturing	5.8	6.2	+0.4
Total	23.4	26.3	+2.9

Notes: [a] The hypothetical situation in 1983 (under Scenario I) is compared to the actual situation in 1983
[b] Total may not add because of rounding errors
Source: see Appendix 10

the kind of growth envisaged under Scenario I, there would have been an enormous increase in this type of employment and by 1983 an extra $2\frac{1}{2}$ million people would have been employed in the non-manufacturing sector than was actually the case. The vast majority of these extra jobs would have been in service activities.

To explore further the impact of economic growth on employment, we will now consider a simple numerical example. This example illustrates the kind of output and productivity changes which could account for the behaviour of employment under Scenario I. The main features of this example are displayed in Table 11.3 As can be seen, a finer classification of activities is used here than was used in constructing the original scenarios. As before, manufacturing is taken as one sector, but non-manufacturing is now divided into three subsectors: non-market services (public administration, health, education), market services (transport, distribution, finance, etc.) and other non-manufacturing activities (agriculture, construction, extractive industries, gas, electricity and water). Information on how faster growth affects these sectors is given in a comparative form in the table. For each sector, Table 11.3 compares output, employment and productivity under Scenario I with the corresponding magnitudes in the actual economy. The year chosen for comparison is 1983, so the numbers shown indicate the cumulative impact of faster growth over the entire period 1950–83. In constructing this table the numbers have been chosen so as to be consistent with what we already know about Scenario I. Thus, total output in 1983 is 40% greater than in the actual economy, whilst employment in manufacturing and non-manufacturing is respectively 6½% and 14½% greater. The remaining numbers are consistent with this information. However, these numbers are not, it must be stressed, formal estimates; they are merely informed guesses whose purpose is to indicate the orders of magnitude involved. The example should not, therefore, be taken too literally. Even so, despite this qualification, the example does, in our opinion, provide a reasonably accurate picture of what might have happened to output and productivity if the economy had grown at the pace envisaged under Scenario I. It also lends support to our claim that, over the long term, faster growth would have had only a marginal impact on manufacturing employment.

Looking at Table 11.3, the following points stand out:

(1) There is a huge increase in manufacturing output, which is 55% higher than in the actual economy as a result of faster growth. There is also a 49% increase in the output of market services and some increase in the output of other sectors.

(2) There are considerable intersectoral variations in productivity growth. Output per worker in manufacturing is 46% greater as a result of faster growth, whilst in market services the figure is 29%. Elsewhere in the economy the increase in productivity is considerably less. Indeed, there is no increase at all in non-market services. This last assumption is in line with normal accounting conventions.

(3) Over half of the additional employment resulting from faster growth is in market services, whilst most of the rest is in non-market services, although there is some increase elsewhere in the economy.

Let us consider some of these points in more detail. Take the increase of 55% in manufacturing output. This may seem excessive, given that GDP increases by only 40%, but there are special factors which explain it. In most advanced economies, the long-run income-elasticity of demand for manufactures is around unity (including relative price effects). *Ceteris paribus*, this implies that any given rise in GDP is accompanied by a roughly equal proportionate rise in manufacturing output. In the present case, however, there are a number of reasons why manufacturing output should rise by more than this amount. To start with, the faster growth envisaged under Scenario I provides work and, therefore, additional income for millions of people who would otherwise be unemployed. Since they spend much of this additional income on consumer durables and other manufactured goods, the demand for such goods receives a disproportionate stimulus. Moreover, with a faster rate of growth, the share of investment in GDP is greater, and this too implies a relative increase in the demand for manufactures. Finally, there is foreign trade to consider. In the actual economy Britain had a surplus on her non-manufacturing trade in 1983 and a deficit in her manufacturing trade. However, with the faster growth assumed under Scenario I, this situation is reversed. Net imports of food, raw materials, fuels and services increase, and as a result the non-manufacturing balance goes into deficit.[5] To cover this deficit requires an increase in net manufactured exports and hence an increase in manufacturing output. In view of the special factors just listed, it is clear why faster growth involves such a large increase in manufacturing output.

The second point concerns labour productivity. In Table 11.3, there is a clear correlation between output and labour productivity: activities which experience the greatest increase in output as a result of faster growth also experience the greatest increase in labour productivity. For this reason, the impact of faster growth on employment is more uniformly distributed than the figures on output alone would suggest. Even so, major differences remain, and faster growth has an appreciable effect on the structure of employment. In particular, the increase in manufacturing productivity is so great that the share of this sector in total employment falls despite an above average rise in output.

This concludes our discussion of Scenario I. Before leaving this topic, may we repeat our warning that this example is intended for illustration only. It shows the kind of structural changes which are implied by faster growth and indicates what might have happened had the economy grown at the rate envisaged under Scenario I. The numbers used in the example have been chosen so as to be consistent with estimated values – where these exist – but most of them are not formal estimates and should not be treated as such. They are merely plausible 'guesstimates' designed to indicate the orders of magnitude involved.

The numerical example just considered points to an interesting paradox. The main employment effects of industrial weakness in the UK are to be found not in the manufacturing sector itself, but in other sectors of the economy, especially the services. With a stronger and more dynamic manufacturing industry, there would still have been a precipitous decline in manufacturing employment over the past twenty years or so. However, manufacturing output would have been much greater than it is now and so too would per capita incomes. As a result, there would have been a much greater demand for services (both market and non-market services), and sufficient jobs would have been created in the service sector to absorb the workers displaced from manufacturing. In the present context, the difference between industrial strength and weakness is not measured by the capacity of the manufacturing sector itself to provide employment. Rather, it is measured by the capacity of this sector to generate the material output required to support a prosperous and growing service sector, in which sufficient jobs are available to provide work for all who need it.[6]

Given the stage of development reached by the UK in the early 1950s and the massive changes in trade specialization which have occurred since then, a considerable fall in manufacturing employment was sooner or later inevitable. In actual history, this fall was accompanied by stagnating output and rising unemployment. It was, to use our earlier ternminology, a case of 'negative de-industrialization'. In a more dynamic economy, with a stronger industrial base, much the same fall in manufacturing employment would still have occurred. However, because of higher productivity, this fall in employment would have been accompanied by a rapid growth in manufacturing *output.* This rise in output would in turn have generated sufficient demand for services, and for service employment, to absorb the workers displaced from manufacturing. It would have been a case of 'positive de-industrialization'. In actual history, the decline in manufacturing employment was accompanied by widespread factory closures, rationalizations and layoffs in the face of stagnant or falling demand. In a more dynamic economy, an almost equal fall in manufacturing employment would still have occurred as a result of automation and other measures designed to save labour whilst simultaneously increasing output. Either way, manufacturing jobs would have disappeared, but the implications for real incomes and employment in other sectors of the economy would have been radically different.

The three theses: a quantitative assessment

In the preceding chapter three potential explanations for the decline in UK manufacturing employment were considered. They were as follows: the Maturity Thesis, the Specialization Thesis and the Failure Thesis. Using the hypothetical scenarios developed in the present chapter, we shall now evaluate the explanatory power of these various theses.

Table 11.4 shows what has happened to UK manufacturing employment since 1950, both in absolute terms and as a share of total employment. In this table, changes in manufacturing employment during selected periods are broken down into a number of distinct components. There are three major components, which correspond to the three theses listed above. There is also a catch-all term which measures the effect of miscellaneous factors. The breakdown given in the table is based on the hypothetical scenarios described earlier in the present chapter. Full details of this breakdown are given in Appendix 10, and here we shall merely indicate the main principles involved. The individual components shown in Table 11.4 are defined as follows:

Table 11.4. *Analysis of manufacturing employment since 1950*

	(a) change in relative share of manufacturing in total employment (percentage points)		
	1950–83	1955–83	1966–83
Net failure effect	1.3	1.9	1.4
Maturity effect	−5.5	−7.6	−8.5
Specialization effect	−6.9	−4.8	−3.1
Effect of miscellaneous factors	1.0	−0.8	0.1
Total (= actual change)	−10.1	−11.3	−10.1
	(b) change in manufacturing employment (thousands)		
Net failure effect	−373	−253	−312
Maturity effect	−193	−929	−1830
Specialization effect	−1825	−1344	−859
Effect of miscellaneous factors	525	47	114
Total (= actual change)	−1866	−2479	−2887

(1) *The Net Failure Effect*. This measures the *net* impact of poor economic performance on manufacturing employment. By definition, it is equal to the actual change in manufacturing employment during a given period minus the change which would have occurred during the same period (for whatever reason), if UK industry had performed better and the economy had grown more rapidly. The net failure effect is evaluated by comparing what happens to manufacturing employment in the actual economy and under Scenario I (see Fig. 11.2 and Fig. 11.3a).

(2) *Unavoidable job losses: The Maturity Effect.* This effect indicates the extent to which the fall in manufacturing employment during a given period was inevitable simply because the UK economy was already relatively mature at the beginning of the period concerned. The maturity effect is evaluated by considering what happens to manufacturing employment under Scenario II, after allowing for the effect of miscellaneous factors (see below). Note that much of the fall in manufacturing employment – ascribed here to the maturity effect – was, in practice, the result of layoffs, factory closures and the like. In a proximate sense, therefore, most of the fall in employment under this heading was the result of poor industrial performance. However, these jobs would still have been lost even if UK manufacturing industry had performed better, though the causal mechanism would have been different. With a more dynamic and successful manufacturing industry, the jobs in question would have been eliminated through automation and other

labour-saving measures. Thus, given the stage of development reached by the UK economy, the loss of manufacturing jobs indicated by the maturity effect was inevitable. The only question was, how would this loss come about? In practice, it came about through factory closures and the like. In a more dynamic economy, it would have come about through automation and similar measures.

(3) *The Specialization Effect.* This indicates the extent to which autonomous changes in the structure of UK foreign trade have affected manufacturing employment. (These changes were described in Chapter 6.) The specialization effect is evaluated by comparing what happens to manufacturing employment under Scenarios I and II (See Figs. 11.2 and 11.3a). Note that this effect measures the purely 'structural' impact of foreign trade on manufacturing employment. In evaluating this impact, total output and employment in the economy as a whole are taken as given, and any macro-economic effects resulting from changing trade specialization are ignored. Note also that the 'specialization effect', as measured in Table 11.4, is 'performance adjusted', i.e. the figures embody a correction to eliminate the effect of slow economic growth on the structure of UK trade.

(4) *The Effect of Miscellaneous Factors.* This is a catch-all item which takes into account a variety of factors, such as errors in specification, random disturbances and interaction effects.

After this preamble, let us now examine Table 11.4. As can be seen, three time periods are shown: 1950–83, 1955–83 and 1966–83. The justification for choosing these periods is as follows: 1950 was the year in which the UK economy achieved its largest-ever trade surplus in manufactures (as a percentage of GDP); 1955 was the year in which the share of manufacturing in total employment reached an all-time peak; whilst the absolute number of people employed in the manufacturing sector reached its all-time peak in 1966. Looking at the numbers shown in Table 11.4, perhaps the most striking features is the minor importance of the *net* failure effect. Depending on the time period concerned, this effect accounts for between one-tenth and one-sixth of the absolute fall in manufacturing employment. Moreover, in the case of relative shares, this effect is actually positive and hence accounts for none of the fall in manufacturing's share in total employment.

From the table, it is clear that virtually all of the decline in manufacturing employment, both absolute and relative, is accounted for by two components: the maturity effect and the specialization effect. It is also clear that the relative importance of these two effects depends on the time period concerned. Over the entire period 1950–83, taken as a whole, the specialization effect is the most important: it accounts for most of the absolute fall in manufacturing employment and over half of the fall in this sector's share in total employment. However, if a later starting-point is chosen, the picture is rather different. As the starting-point moves closer to the present, the maturity effect becomes increasingly important, until eventually it supplants the specialization effect as the major component. For example, over the period 1966–83, manufacturing employment fell by 2.9 million. Of this fall, the maturity effect accounts for around 1.8 million and the specialization effect for around 900 thousand.

From the figures shown in Table 11.4, the following points emerge concerning the three theses. The Failure Thesis explains very little of the absolute or relative decline in manufacturing employment. Most of this decline is explained by the other two theses we have considered: the Maturity Thesis, which stresses that Britain was already on the brink of economic maturity in the 1950s, and the Specialization Thesis, which stresses the huge changes that have occurred in the UK's pattern of trade specialization since 1950. Given the stage of development already reached by the British economy in 1950 and the changes in trade specialization which have taken place since then, manufacturing employment was bound to fall dramatically over the coming decades no matter how good or bad the performance of UK manufacturing industry. This is the first and most important point.

Our second point is concerned with the relative importance of the maturity effect and changing trade specialization in explaining what has happened to manufacturing employment. Over the entire period 1950–83, changes in trade specialization have been the major factor. They account for most of the absolute decline in manufacturing employment over the period as a whole, as well as for most of the decline in manufacturing's share in total employment. However, if we take a more recent starting-point, the picture is more complex. In 1950, the UK economy was approaching maturity but had not yet reached it. By the 1960s, the economy was fully mature and, for this reason alone, the share of manufacturing in total employment was bound to fall by a considerable amount in the coming years. Moreover, given the underlying trends in labour supply, this fall in manufacturing's relative share would inevitably be accompanied by a considerable fall in the absolute number of people employed in the manufacturing sector. The extent of this unavoidable fall is indicated by the maturity effect in Table 11.4. According to the figures shown, manufacturing employment was destined to fall by at least 1.8 million between 1966 and 1983, simply because the UK was already a fully mature economy at the beginning of the period in 1966. This fall would have occurred even if there had been no changes in trade specialization during these years and even if UK manufacturing industry had been more dynamic and output had grown more rapidly. Of the 2.9 million manufacturing jobs lost between 1966 and 1983, approximately 60% were bound to go simply because the economy was already mature in 1966, and another 30% were eliminated by changes in the pattern of trade specialization (North Sea oil, greater food self-sufficiency, etc.). The remaining 10% represent the jobs that were lost as a result of poor economic performance and would have been saved if UK manufacturing industry had been more dynamic and the economy had grown more rapidly.

Conclusions

The main conclusions of this chapter are as follows. The post-war decline in manufacturing employment in Britain has been an example of 'negative de-industrialization' (resulting from poor industrial performance), compounded by the effect of changes in trade specialization. However, almost as many manufacturing jobs would have been lost and manufacturing's share would have fallen even further if industrial performance had been more successful. If this had happened, Britain would, instead, have been an example of 'positive de-industrialization'. Thus, a large reduction in manufacturing employment was unavoidable in post-war Britain, since the country was already on the verge of economic maturity in 1950. Manufacturing employment was bound to decline over the coming decades, no matter how good or bad the performance of British industry. Thus, in the last analysis, the number of manufacturing jobs lost as a result of industrial failure was relatively small. The fact is, in a 'mature' economy, the behaviour of manufacturing employment is not always a good indicator of industrial performance. In such an economy, a dynamic manufacturing sector may be shedding labour yet, at the same time, contributing indirectly to the creation of employment elsewhere in the economy as steady increases in industrial production lay the material foundations for a prosperous and expanding service sector.

12

Oil and the UK economy

Introduction

The subject of North Sea oil is complex, and the debate concerning its impact on the UK economy has been confused. There is now an extensive literature on the subject, and some of the previous confusion has dissipated; nevertheless, some of the original disagreements remain. In the present chapter we explore the main issues at stake and consider how North Sea oil has affected the UK economy. As elsewhere in this book, our prevailing concern is with the level of employment and its distribution between various sectors of the economy. Our main conclusion is that the discovery and exploitation of North Sea oil has had some impact on employment; it has been responsible for the loss of perhaps half a million jobs in manufacturing industry and, in the absence of North Sea oil, Britain's manufacturing sector would be somewhat larger, both absolutely and relative to other sectors, than it is now. However, North Sea oil alone is not responsible for the collapse of manufacturing industry which has occurred since oil production first began in 1976, nor for the huge rise in unemployment which has accompanied this collapse. These developments are primarily the result of other factors, such as the world recession, the underlying weakness of British industry and the deflationary policies of the Thatcher government. Given these other factors, the economic collapse was inevitable and would have occurred even in the absence of North Sea oil.

The present chapter is organized as follows. First, there is a description of Britain's trade in fuels since 1950 and an assessment of the role of North Sea oil in this trade. The main conclusion of this discussion is as follows. The North Sea is providing just about enough oil to meet the domestic requirements of a prosperous, fully employed British economy and to keep the fuel account of such an economy roughly in balance. However, because of the present economic depression, the country's demand for fuel is greatly reduced and Britain now has a large surplus on her fuel account. To put it simply: North Sea oil has made Britain self-sufficient in fuel, whilst the depression has made her into a major net exporter of fuels.

The next section is concerned with the link between oil and employment. In considering this question, we distinguish between the structural effects of trade in oil (and other fuels) and the macro-economic effects of such trade. The former are concerned with shifts in the distribution of employment between one sector of the economy and another at a *given* level of employment, whilst the latter are concerned with changes in the level of employment as a whole. This is a distinction we have already made in previous chapters. The discussion of oil and employment is divided into two parts.

One part deals with the recent past and considers the impact of North Sea oil on the British economy. After a brief review of the literature on the subject, we conclude that the macro-economic impact of North Sea oil has been small: without this oil, the evolution of total employment in Britain would have been much the same as it has been, and unemployment would have risen at much the same pace. Meanwhile, structural impact of North Sea oil has been to shift the pattern of employment from tradeables (mainly manufactures) towards non-tradeables (mainly services). The numbers involved in this transfer are fairly large in absolute terms – around half a million – although quite small in relation to the total level of employment of over 23 million.

The second and more interesting part of the discussion takes a longer and wider perspective. It considers the factors which have governed Britain's fuel trade right back to 1950, with the aim of evaluating how far these factors have influenced employment in Britian. Once again, we distinguish between structural and macro-economic effects. On the macro-economic level, we suggest that total employment in Britain has been reduced by some of the factors we identify – partly through their direct influence on the British economy itself and also, indirectly, through their influence on the world economy. Of these, probably the most important was the huge rise in oil prices which took place in 1973. This delivered a shock to the world economy as well as to the UK economy, and its effects are with us to this day. Unfortunately, it is impossible to quantify this effect, although general considerations would suggest it may be very large. The situation is different in the case of structural effects, where we can provide numerical estimates. Using methods already described in the previous chapter, we estimate how far developments in Britain's fuel trade have affected the share of manufacturing in total employment. We also estimate how far this structural component accounts for the fall in absolute numbers in manufacturing employment which has occurred since 1966. Our conclusion is that these developments, taken as a whole, have had only a minor impact on the pattern of employment in post-war Britain. They explain only a small fraction of the shift in employment from manufacturing to non-manufacturing which has occurred over this period and only a small part of the absolute decline in manufacturing employment. Far more important have been developments in other areas of non-manufacturing trade (food, raw materials and services). Between them, these have had a considerable effect on the pattern of employment and the numbers employed in manufacturing.

Britain's trade in fuels

Fig. 12.1 shows what has happened to Britain's balance of trade in fuels since 1950. Looking at this graph, we can distinguish three distinct phases. Prior to 1973, there was a steady shift away from domestically produced coal towards imported oil, and this is reflected in a gradual rise in the ratio of net fuel imports to GDP. Then, in October 1973, there was a huge rise in world oil proces which quadrupled almost overnight (Table 12.1). As a result, the net cost of UK fuel imports leapt from around 1.5% of GDP to over 4%. Finally, from 1974 onwards, there has been a sustained and dramatic improvement in the fuel balance with the result that Britain is now a significant net exporter of fuels. This improvement is due to a number of distinct factors, of which the following are the most important:

(1) Economies in the use of oil in Britain have reduced the amount of oil consumed per unit of final output. Of these economies, the most important has been in electricity generation, where coal (which is domestically produced) has been widely used in place of oil.

(2) Since the 'oil shock' in 1973, Britain's economy has experienced a prolonged recession. As a result, manufacturing output is now below the level achieved in 1973, and the demand for oil and other fuels is greatly reduced (Tables 12.2 and 12.3).

(3) Domestic production of oil has increased steadily since 1976 when supplies from the North Sea first came on stream, and Britain is now a significant world producer of oil.

(4) World oil prices experienced a second major increase in 1978–9, when the dollar price of oil rose by 140% within the space of two years. This occurred just at the time when Britain was about to become a net exporter of oil. Whereas the first major price increase occurred in 1973, when Britain was a net importer of oil (and hence made the fuel deficit greater), the effect of higher oil prices in 1978–9 was to increase the value of Britain's future *surplus* in fuels.

Thus, there are a number of factors behind the sustained improvement in Britain's fuel balance since 1974. Most of these are well known and require no further elaboration. However, there is one factor which is often neglected, and yet it has played a major role in converting Britain into a net fuel exporter.

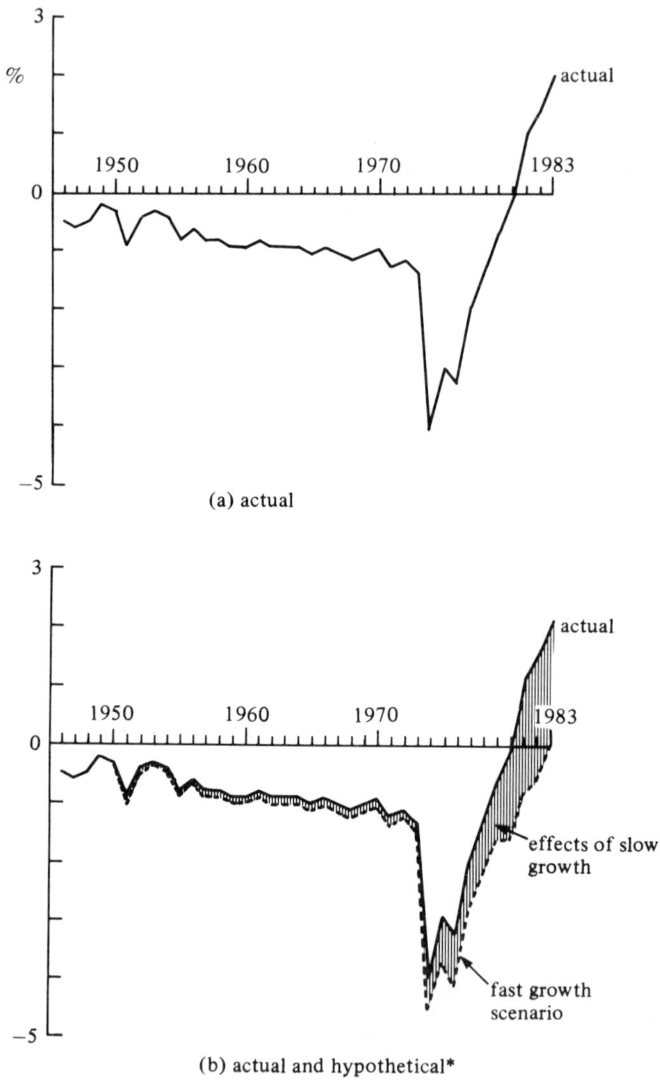

Fig. 12.1 UK balance of trade in fuels, 1950–83 (as % of GDP)
* refers to fast growth scenario 40I (see Appendix 6)

We are referring, of course, to item (2) in the above list: the recession which, with greater or lesser severity, has gripped the UK economy throughout the past decade. If the British economy had grown at a faster pace during this period, the demand for oil would by now be much greater than it is and, to

Table 12.1. *Crude oil prices (OPEC average)*

	US$	Real price of oil[a] (1973 = 100)
1955	1.67	128
1960	1.65	105
1965	1.65	90
1970	1.65	86
1971	1.65	76
1972	1.90	78
1973	2.60	100
1974	9.90	341
1975	10.90	311
1976	11.90	365
1977	12.90	362
1978	13.90	302
1979	19.01	351
1980	31.89	451
1981	35.88	524
1982	34.39	551
1983	30.06	533

[a] $\text{Real price of oil} = \dfrac{\text{price of oil in sterling}}{\text{GDP deflator for the UK}}$

meet this demand, some of the oil now exported would be used domestically, whilst more oil would be imported. As a result, Britain's current surplus in oil would be greatly reduced, and she would no longer be a major fuel exporter.

To illustrate the impact of poor economic performance on UK fuel trade, we have estimated what energy consumption might have been if the economy had grown faster. Full details of these estimates are contained in Appendix 11 and here we shall discuss only the main results. Table 12.4 shows what might have happened under various assumptions to oil consumption if the economy had grown faster. A number of hypothetical scenarios are considered in this table. These scenarios fall into two groups. Those in the group labelled '30' assume that the non-oil economy continues growing after 1973 at the rate actually achieved in the preceding period 1950–73, whilst those in the group labelled '40' assume that GDP per capita grows at a steady 3.0% a year over the entire period 1950–83. By 1983 GDP under the former scenarios is 30% above its actual level whilst, under the latter scenarios, GDP is 40% above its actual level. With each group of scenarios, three variants are distinguished which are denoted by the symbols B, I and W.[1] Looking at Table 12.4 we see that faster growth is accompanied by a massive rise in the demand for oil. Under the most

Table 12.2. *Fuels in the UK economy, 1938–83 (million tonnes oil or oil equivalent)*

	Oil[a]		Natural gas		Coal		Total[b]	
	P	C	P	C	P	C	P	C
1938	0.1	9.2	–	–	133.4	104.7	133.5	113.9
1950	0.2	15.6	–	–	127.0	120.2	127.2	135.8
1955	0.2	24.1	–	–	130.6	127.6	130.8	151.7
1960	0.1	44.1	–	–	114.5	116.8	114.6	160.9
1965	0.1	68.7	–	0.8	110.9	110.3	111.0	179.8
1970	0.2	98.2	9.7	10.6	86.5	92.3	96.4	201.1
1971	0.2	99.2	16.2	17.0	87.9	81.9	104.3	198.1
1972	0.3	106.1	23.3	24.2	71.1	72.0	95.3	202.3
1973	0.4	108.7	25.3	26.1	77.6	78.2	103.3	213.0
1974	0.4	101.9	30.6	31.3	65.0	69.4	96.0	202.6
1975	1.6	90.0	31.8	32.7	75.7	70.8	109.1	193.5
1976	12.1	89.2	33.7	34.7	72.8	71.8	118.6	195.7
1977	38.2	90.0	35.3	36.9	71.9	72.2	145.4	199.1
1978	54.0	91.4	33.9	38.3	72.7	70.5	160.6	200.2
1979	77.9	91.3	34.2	41.8	72.0	76.2	184.1	209.3
1980	80.5	78.3	32.5	41.8	76.5	71.1	189.5	191.2
1981	89.5	72.7	32.4	42.4	75.0	69.6	196.9	184.7
1982	103.2	72.9	33.0	42.2	73.2	65.1	209.5	180.2
1983	114.9	70.5	34.0	44.0	70.1	65.6	219.0	180.1

Notes:
P = Domestic production
C = Gross inland consumption. Prior to 1970, oil consumption is equal to inland deliveries (including refinery fuel) plus losses
[a] Includes oil for non-energy uses, but excludes marine bunkers
[b] Excludes nuclear and hydro-electric
Sources: Annual Abstract of Statistics 1960; Digest of United Kingdom Energy Statistics (various)

conservative scenario, 30B, oil consumption in 1983 is 44% above its actual level. As a result, the surplus of oil production over consumption falls from an actual figure of 44.4 million tonnes to a mere 13.3 million tonnes. Under the most radical scenario, 40W, oil consumption in 1983 is 78% above its actual level, and Britain is a net importer of oil to the tune of 10.7 million tonnes. Thus, in all cases, Britain's oil surplus either falls dramatically as a result of faster growth or disappears altogether.

As a further illustration of the influence of economic growth on UK trade in fuels, Fig. 12.1 shows what happens to the fuel balance under the fast-growth scenario 40I over the period 1950–83. It also shows what happened in reality to the fuel balance over this period. In each case the balance is expressed as a percentage of GDP at current market prices. The effect of slow economic growth on UK fuel trade is indicated in this diagram by the shaded area between

Table 12.3. *UK output and fuel consumption (1973 = 100)*

	Output			Fuel consumption	
	GDP	Non-oil GDP	Manufacturing	Oil	All fuels
1950	54.1	54.1	49.8	14.4	63.8
1955	61.3	61.3	58.5	22.2	71.2
1960	69.3	69.3	67.6	40.6	75.5
1965	80.7	80.7	78.9	63.2	84.4
1970	90.3	90.3	90.5	90.3	94.4
1971	91.6	91.6	89.6	91.3	93.0
1972	94.5	94.5	91.5	97.6	95.0
1973	100.0	100.0	100.0	100.0	100.0
1974	98.5	98.5	98.8	93.7	95.1
1975	96.6	96.6	91.9	82.8	90.8
1976	98.6	97.9	93.7	82.1	91.9
1977	101.4	99.2	95.4	82.8	93.5
1978	104.9	101.7	96.1	84.1	94.0
1979	108.2	103.6	95.8	84.0	98.3
1980	105.0	100.4	87.6	72.0	89.8
1981	103.3	98.1	82.1	66.9	86.7
1982	105.0	99.5	82.3	67.1	84.6
1983	108.4	101.0	84.9	64.9	84.6

Note: Volume indices are computed using 1980 weights

Table 12.4. *Oil in the UK economy 1983[a] (Million tonnes)*

		Production	Consumption	Production–consumption
Actual economy		114.9	70.5	+44.4
Hypothetical scenarios:				
30	B	114.9	101.6	+13.3
30	I	114.9	106.8	+8.1
30	W	114.9	112.0	+2.9
40	B	114.9	110.3	+4.6
40	I	114.9	118.0	−3.1
40	W	114.9	125.6	−10.7

Note: [a] Includes oil for non-energy cases
Source: See Appendix 11

the two curves. Looking at the diagram, the following points stand out. The post-oil shock depression, which has held in check the demand for oil and other fuels, is responsible for about one-third of the improvement in Britain's fuel balance since 1974. The remaining two-thirds is due to a variety of factors, of which North Sea oil is easily the most important. If Britain had grown at the rate envisaged under scenario 40I then, by 1983, there would have been no oil surplus, and the fuel account, as a whole, would have been in deficit.

Thus, it is the economic depression, and not North Sea oil, which has turned Britain into a major net oil exporter and is responsible for the large surplus she now enjoys on her fuel account.

Looking at Fig. 12.1, we see a massive deterioration in the fuel balance in late 1973, followed by a sustained improvement. This is true both in the actual economy and in the hypothetical, high-growth economy. But the *extent* of the post-1973 improvement is rather different in the two cases. In the actual economy, the improvement is so great that, by 1983, Britain's fuel balance is considerably better than it was even before the oil shock in late 1973. However, as we have just explained, part of this improvement was the result of prolonged depression in the non-oil economy and cannot really be ascribed to North Sea oil. This is obvious if we look at what happens under scenario 40I. Under this scenario, the economy continues growing quite fast throughout the period 1973–83. There is some improvement in the fuel balance over this period, but it is quite small. In this hypothetical economy, the post-1973 improvement is considerably smaller than in the actual economy and, by 1983, Britain's fuel balance is only a little better than it was before the 1973 oil shock.

The above argument may be summarized as follows. Viewed in historical terms, the main effect of North Sea oil has been to cancel out the effects of the huge rise in oil prices, which occurred in 1973, thereby restoring Britain's energy situation to a position only a little better than that prevailing prior to 1973. However, in addition to the effects of North Sea oil itself, there are also the effects of economic performance to consider. Since 1973, the British economy has been gripped by a prolonged depression, which has reduced the domestic demand for oil and other fuels, with the result that Britain has become a major *net* exporter of fuel. If the economy had grown at a faster pace, the domestic consumption of fuel would have been much greater and there would have been no surplus available for export. Thus, to put it simply: North Sea oil has made Britain self-sufficient in fuel, whilst the economic depression has made the country into a major net exporter.

Comparision with other areas of non-manufacturing trade

The preceding discussion can be extended to cover other areas of non-manufacturing trade: food, raw materials and services. Table 12.5 shows what happened to the balance of trade in these items between 1950 and 1983. It also shows what would have happened had the economy grown at the faster pace envisaged under scenario 40I.[2] In each case, the balance of trade is expressed as a percentage of GDP at current market prices.

It is clear from Table 12.5 that by far the most important change to occur between 1950 and 1983 was in the realm of food and materials. During this

Table 12.5. *UK balance of trade in non-manufactures, 1950–83*

	Fuel	Food and materials	Non-government services	Total
Balance of trade (as percent of GDP)				
(1) 1950 actual	−0.3	−13.3	+0.5	−13.1
(2) 1983 actual	+2.1	−1.8	+1.2	+1.5
(3) 1983 Scenario 40I[a]	−0.1	−2.0	+0.7	−1.3
Change in balance 1950–83				
(4) actual [(2)–(1)]	+2.4	+11.5	+0.7	+14.6
(5) Scenario 40I [(3)–(1)]	+0.2	+11.3	+0.2	+11.8

Note: [a] Assumes that GDP grows at 3.0% p.a. between 1950 and 1983
Source: Table 7.3

period, the combined deficit on these items fell from 13.3% of GDP in 1950 to 1.8% in 1983 – an improvement of 11.5 percentage points. A small part of this improvement was due to slow growth in the domestic economy, which held in check the demand for imports, especially after 1973. But even when allowance is made for this, the improvement is still enormous: under the high-growth Scenario 40I, the deficit in food and materials is still only 2.0% of GDP in 1983 – a full 11.3% better than in 1950. Thus, the huge improvement in the food and materials balance is mainly structural in character and is not due to poor macro-economic performance. Turning to non-government services, we find a somewhat different picture. There is only a modest improvement in the balance on these items between 1950 and 1983: from a surplus equal to 0.5% of GDP in 1950 to 1.2% in 1983. Moreover, much of the improvement is due to slow growth in the domestic economy, which has held back the demand for imported services. When allowance is made for slow growth, we find there is only a small improvement in the service balance between 1950 and 1983. Finally, there is fuel to consider. The figures given in Table 12.5 confirm what we have said earlier on this subject. From a deficit equal to 0.3% of GDP in 1950, the fuel balance moved to a surplus of 2.1% in 1983 – an improvement of 2.4%. However, most of this improvement is the result of slow growth in the domestic economy, and only a small fraction is the result of structural factors such as North Sea oil. This is not to say that North Sea oil has not been important, because clearly it has been. The point is that the huge price rise in 1973 increased Britain's fuel deficit enormously, and North Sea oil has merely redressed the balance by providing a domestic source of fuel. If we put all the structural factors, both positive and negative, together – the 1973 price rise, North Sea oil, energy conservation, etc. – their combined effect on the fuel balance is quite small. It is this combined effect which is measured in line (5) of Table 12.5.

Thus, comparing 1983 with 1950, the improvement in Britain's trade in fuels is dwarfed by what has happened in the realm of food and raw materials. Moreover, most of this improvement in the fuel balance is the result of slow growth in the non-oil economy, especially over the past decade, during which total output has stagnated. By contrast, the huge improvement in the food and materials balance since 1950 is mainly structural in character, reflecting fundamental changes in Britain's pattern of specialization and her role in the world division of labour.

Oil and employment

We have just described some of the main changes which have occurred in Britain's fuel trade since the Second World War and the factors which account for them. We shall now discuss how these changes have affected the level and pattern of employment. As a convenient starting-point, let us consider North Sea oil, whose impact on the British economy has been the subject of some debate in recent years.

The effects of North Sea oil on employment are of two kinds: structural and macro-economic. The former are concerned with shifts in the pattern of employment between one sector of the economy and another *at a given level of total employment*, whilst the latter are concerned with changes in the level of total employment itself. This is a distinction we have already met in earlier chapters, although our terminology is now slightly different. Here, we use the term 'structural effect' to describe what was previously called the '(pure) specialization effect'. However, apart from this minor difference, our approach is the same as before.[3]

Macro-economic effects

When assessing the impact of North Sea oil on the British economy, it is important to distinguish between what actually happened in reality and what might have happened if the opportunities provided by North Sea oil had been fully exploited. Considering what might have happened, there is no doubt that, properly utilized, North Sea oil could have had a positive impact on both the rate of growth and the level of economic activity, thereby ensuring a higher level of both GDP and total employment. To see the truth of this, one need only consider the condition of the British economy at the time. For many years before North Sea oil came on stream in 1976, Britain had been plagued by inflation and a weak balance of payments. Economic growth had been frequently halted by deflationary government policies designed to curb inflation and defend the pound, and unemployment had been rising since 1966. In this context, North

Sea oil provided new opportunities for expansion which would not otherwise have been available: as a valuable resource, it could be used to meet some of the rival claims on national income, thereby reducing inflationary pressures in the British economy; and as an internationally traded commodity, it strengthened the balance of payments. Thus, North Sea oil both reduced inflationary pressures and strengthened the balance of payments, both of which reduced the need for deflationary policies and made it easier for governments to pursue expansionary policies. Thus, because of its impact on inflation and the balance of payments, North Sea oil provided new opportunities for expansion and, if properly utilized, could have had a positive impact on total employment.

So much for what might have happened. What about the real world? What has been the actual impact of North Sea oil on the British economy, in particular, on total employment? Here there is considerable disagreement amongst those who have written on the subject. Some argue that North Sea oil has been beneficial to the British economy and that without it there would be even fewer jobs and more unemployment than there is today. This is the position taken by Atkinson and others from the National Institute, who estimate that unemployment in Britain is now 700,000 lower than it would be in the absence of oil (Atkinson *et al.*, 1983).[4] At just the opposite extreme are those who argue that North Sea oil has harmed the rest of the economy, causing non-oil output and total employment to fall. Some, like Beenstock and others from the London Business School, regard this as a temporary disturbance, whose effects will wear off quite rapidly as the economy returns to equilibrium (Beenstock *et al.*).[5] However, others take a less complacement view and argue that North Sea oil has done serious damage to the British economy and the effects will be felt for many years to come. This claim has been made most explicitly by Kaldor in his speeches to the House of Lords, but similar views are implicit in several academic papers on the subject.[6] Between these extremes are a variety of authors who see the impact of North Sea oil mainly in structural terms. Whilst conceding that the discovery of oil may have had some impact on total employment, they regard this as minor compared with its much greater effect on the pattern of employment. For example, the numerical calculations given by Forsyth and Kay (1981) imply that manufacturing employment falls by between 8–9% as a result of North Sea oil, but almost as many additional jobs are created in the services and other non-manufacturing activities, with the result that total employment falls by less than 1%. A similar position is taken by a Treasury working paper on the subject, although no explicit estimate is given (Byatt *et al.*, 1982).[7]

Thus, there is a wide variety of views to choose from. We obviously cannot consider them all in detail, so we shall deal only with the main points at issue. Let us begin with a general observation. Disagreements about North Sea oil and its historical impact on the British economy are of two kinds. First, there is disagreement about how the British economy actually works and about the link between North Sea oil and variables such as the exchange rate and the price level. Secondly, there is disagreement about government policy, in particular, about which policies would have been pursued by the government in the absence of North Sea oil. There is also disagreement about how to specify government policy and about what is meant by an 'unchanged' policy or set of policies. Indeed, it is sometimes the case that differences which seem to be economic in nature are really concerned with government policy and its specification. Most participants in the debate on North Sea oil have focussed on the purely economic mechanisms involved, whilst political factors have been mentioned only in passing. This is not very surprising as the authors concerned are virtually all professional economists. However, it does mean that the role of political factors has been underrated, whilst excessive attention has been devoted to purely economic factors which may be of secondary importance in explaining the historical impact of North Sea oil on the British economy.

After this preamble, let us begin by considering the claim of Atkinson *et al.* that North Sea oil has had a large, positive impact on total employment, with the result that far more people are now employed in Britain than would have been the case if this oil had never been discovered. Their argument is on two levels. Using the National Institute econometric model, they first estimate how the economy would have developed in the absence of North Sea oil, assuming unchanged fiscal and monetary policies. Their conclusion is that, in the absence of North Sea oil, there would have been an extra 700 thousand people unemployed by 1982. Having reached this figure on the basis of unchanged policies, they then consider briefly how government policy itself might have been different without oil. They argue that without oil, Britain's economic situation would have been precarious. There would have been a massive current account deficit on the balance of payments and the inflation rate would have been even higher than it was. 'Faced with such a situation', they say, 'it is not at all what the government would have done. Events might well have been taken out of their hands, as they were for example in 1976, by a collapse of confidence in the foreign exchange markets. The likelihood must be that more deflationary policies would have followed, despite an even deeper recession.'[8] Although reluctant to give a precise figure, they suggest that the consequence of such deflationary policies might have been an extra one million unemployed. Thus, taking the higher estimate, the final effect of North Sea oil is to reduce unemployment by 1.7 million, of which 0.7 million is due to the direct effect of oil on the economy with unchanged policies, and the other 1.0 million is because the possession of oil allows the government to pursue less deflationary policies than it would otherwise.

Let us consider first the case of unchanged policies. In reaching their conclusions, the authors make the following assumptions: (1) the impact of oil on the real exchange rate (the 'oil premium') is modest – an appreciation of around 16% by 1982; (2) the impact of this appreciation on foreign trade is small because price elasticities are low, especially in the case of manufactures where the price elasticity of exports is 0.5 and that of imports is 0.3; (3) oil leads to a significant increase in domestic expenditure, partly because it provides additional income, some of which is spent, and partly because it reduces the inflation rate, thereby increasing the value of monetary assets and reducing the propensity to save. So, on the one hand, the discovery of oils leads to a small reduction in non-oil exports (net of imports), but this is more than offset by a relatively large increase in domestic expenditure. As a result, there is an increase in the total demand for non-oil goods and services, so that non-oil GDP rises. This rise in non-oil GDP, in turn, leads to an increase in total employment.

The approach of the National Institute team is open to a number of criticisms. For example, they assume that oil has no effect on the real interest rate, and that its impact on the real exchange rate is therefore quite small. The assumption that North Sea oil has no effect on the real interest rate is what is meant by an 'unchanged monetary policy' in the National Institute approach. They assume that monetary policy is designed so as to keep real short-term interest rates constant at some predetermined level. Thus, if the discovery of North Sea oil leads to an increase in the demand for money, the government ensures that additional money is created on a scale sufficient to meet this demand and prevent any rise in the real interest rate. As we shall see later on, most other economists who have analysed the question of oil use a quite different definition of what constitutes an unchanged policy. They assume that the variable which the government seeks to control is not the real interest rate but the stock of money. A policy is characterized, therefore, by the target stock of money at which it aims. Thus, government monetary policy is said to be 'unchanged' if the target stock of money remains the same. Thus, if North Sea oil creates an additional demand for money, 'an unchanged policy', as defined under this approach, means there is no accommodating increase in the stock of money. As a result, the real interest rate rises and so too does the real exchange rate. Comparing the two approaches, it is clear that what the National Institute means by an unchanged monetary policy in the face of North Sea oil would be described by most other economists as an expansionary shift in policy. Conversely, what these other economists regard as an unchanged policy in the face of North Sea oil would be regarded by the National Institute as a contractionary policy. This difference in terminology has caused a great deal of confusion on the subject of oil and helps to explain why there has been so much disagreement.

However, the main criticism of the National Institute team concerns their trade equations. As we have mentioned, they assume extremely low price elasticities of demand for non-oil exports and imports. If larger elasticities are assumed, the resulting estimates are quite different. For example, Barker and Fairclough (1983) have performed a simulation exercise which is very similar to that of the National Institute team, using a similar model of the economy and making similar assumptions about government policy. However, their approach differs in one important respect: it uses higher and in our view more realistic price elasticities for exports than those assumed by the National Institute. The result is very striking. The effect of oil, according to Barker and Fairclough,[9] is to reduce unemployment by 255 thousand, which is only a third of the National Institute figure of 700 thousand. This result casts serious doubt on the claim that North Sea oil has had a large beneficial impact on the non-oil economy (with unchanged policies). If the other criticisms mentioned above are also taken into account, this claim is even less convincing.

So far the discussion has assumed that monetary and fiscal policies are unaffected by oil. However, as we have seen, the National Institute also considers the possibility that oil has affected government policy. In the absence of oil, they argue, the economic situation would have been much worse. Inflation would have been faster and the balance of payments weaker. Under these conditions, they suggest, the government might have employed even harsher deflationary measures, in which case the result would have been a huge rise in unemployment. Indeed, their own estimates imply that, taking into account the response of government policy, the effect of North Sea oil is to reduce unemployment by 1.7 million. This estimate implies that, in the absence of North Sea oil, there would have been 5.0 million people unemployed in 1984, as compared to an actual figure of 3.3 million.

The above argument cannot be ruled completely out of court, for no one can be absolutely certain how the government would have responded under the conditions envisaged by the National Institute. However, there are strong grounds for rejecting such a pessimistic scenario. The argument takes no account of the political forces which influence government policy and the political constraints under which even the Thatcher government has had to operate. Whilst it is true that unemployment has already reached levels which ten years ago were regarded as intolerable, it is unlikely that it could approach the astronomical levels envisaged by the National Institute without causing a social upheaval and without forcing a major shift in government policy – perhaps not a complete U-turn, but at least a significant reversal. Government decisions are not made in a political vacuum and, if the pressures become too great, they are modified. Old dogmas are abandoned and new pragmatic policies are applied. Such a rule applies as much to the Tories as to anyone else. One sign of this is provided by the evolution of economic policy under the Thatcher government. At one time absolute priority was given to the defeat of inflation, and in government

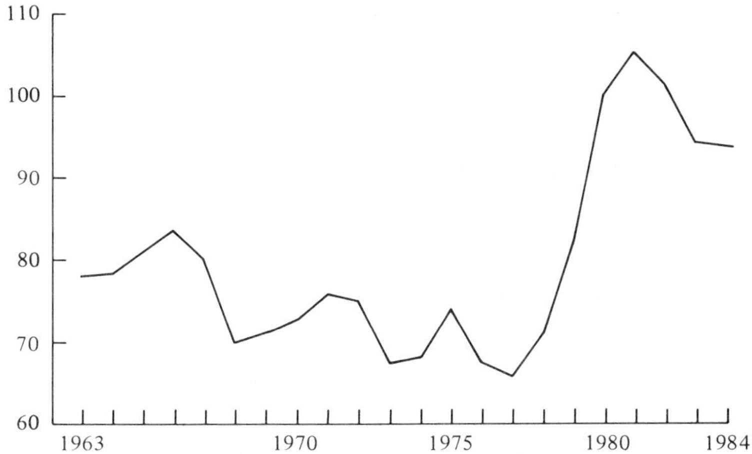

Fig. 12.2 Sterling real exchange rate (1980 = 100)

circles there was talk of zero inflation as a target to be achieved within a few years, no matter what the cost in terms of lost output, destruction of capacity, unemployment and poverty.[10] However, given the electoral risks of mass unemployment and with the example of inner-city riots in Brixton, Toxteth and elsewhere to warn them, wiser councils prevailed in the Thatcher government, and the suicidal nature of the zero-inflation target has been recognized. Even though inflation is still running at 5–6% a year and shows no signs of slowing down, some of the harsher aspects of government policy have been softened, and there is now an evident desire to avoid another major rise in unemployment. One sign of this is the behaviour of the real exchange rate, which has been drifting downwards since 1981 and is now 20% below its earlier peak (see Fig. 12.2). Such a thing would never have been allowed to happen under the old regime and is a sign that something has changed. There has been no U-turn, but the old determination to stamp out inflation at all costs is no longer there. This weakening of resolve is a direct consequence of the political forces acting on the Thatcher government and limiting its freedom of action. Such forces would also have constrained a Thatcher government under the hypothetical scenarios envisaged by the National Institute. Under this scenario there would have been no oil, inflation would have been a little faster and the balance of payments a little weaker. Under these conditions, the government might well have been tempted to impose an even more deflationary policy than it actually did. But it is unlikely that this policy would have been severe enough to drive unemployment up to the levels envisaged by the National Institute. Moreover, had such a policy been imposed, the social conflict and political stresses would have been enormous, and the government would have been forced either to retreat and modify its policies or else be driven from office.[11] Either way, unemployment would not have been allowed to reach the 5 million level envisaged by the National Institute in a Britain without oil.

Our view of the National Institute position can be summarized as follows. We do not accept that, with unchanged policies, there would be an additional 0.7 million unemployed people in Britain in the absence of oil. This figure is much too high and, as we shall see, there are reasons for believing that unemployment is actually higher as a result of North Sea oil (assuming unchanged policies). Nor do we accept that, in the absence of oil, government policies would have been so much harsher that by 1984 unemployment would have risen to 5 million, which is the figure implied by National Institute estimates. Such a rise in unemployment would have been politically unsustainable. Indeed, unemployment has already reached politically dangerous levels and no government, however dogmatic, could have pursued the harsher policies envisaged by the National Institute without committing political suicide. Thus, in our view, North Sea oil has not had a beneficial effect on the non-oil economy; it has not helped to keep unemployment down, nor is total employment greater as a result of North Sea oil than would otherwise have been the case. This still leaves open the other set of questions: has North Sea oil harmed the non-oil economy? Has it helped to increase unemployment? Is total employment less because of it? It is to these questions that we now turn.

There are several theories which seek to explain how the discovery of oil may lead to a reduction in total employment. The most sophisticated of these has been developed by Buiter and Purvis (1980) following the work of Dornbusch (1976) on exchange rate 'overshooting' and by Vines *et al.* (1983). This theory has many subtleties, but the essence of the argument is simple enough. Consider an economy in which monetary policy is used to keep nominal GDP constant. With given prices, this implies that real GDP is also constant, so that any increase in output in one sector of the economy must be matched by an equal reduction elsewhere in the economy. This is of obvious relevance in the case of an oil discovery. With given prices and the given monetary policy, total GDP is fixed. So the addition to GDP represented by oil production must be offset by an equivalent reduction of output in the non-oil economy. Such a transformation in the structure of output will, in general, lead to a fall in total employment, the reason being that output per worker is much greater in the oil sector than elsewhere in the economy. As a result, the additional jobs created in oil production are insufficient to replace those lost in other sectors. Indeed, in the model considered by Buiter and Purvis, no labour at all is used, either directly or indirectly, to produce oil, so a reduction in non-oil GDP must inevitably lead to a fall in total employment. Thus, the essence of the argument is simple. With an unchanged monetary policy and with given prices, high value-added oil production 'crowds-out' low value-added non-oil production, and it is this which explains the fall in total employment. To prevent such crowding out, the government must pursue a more expansionary monetary policy which permits total demand and, hence, real GDP to rise in line with the extra production represented by oil. Indeed, this is just what Buiter and Purvis suggest, as indeed do many of their followers.[12]

The above argument depends heavily on the fact that prices are given. Suppose, however, that in response to the oil-induced recession prices begin to fall. Since nominal GDP is fixed by official monetary policy, the result will be an increase in *real* GDP and the economy will begin to recover. Indeed, according to Buiter and Purvis, this recovery will continue until the original level of employment and output in the non-oil economy are restored. Thus, the effect of an oil discovery on total employment is only temporary and begins to wear off as prices gradually fall.

The above summary of the argument of Buiter and Purvis is, of course, very crude and ignores many of the subtleties and complexities of their analysis. In the fuller version of the story, international capital movements, interest rates, wealth effects and the exchange rate all receive considerable attention. Moreover, the analysis itself is set against the background of continuous inflation and a growing money supply. But, despite these complexities, the essence of their argument is as we have described it. Oil production crowds out non-oil production, because the government is too inflexible and refuses to create the extra money required to support a higher level of total output. Note that this argument applies just as much (or just as little) in a closed economy as an open one, and the question of exchange rates and capital movements is, from an analytical point of view, of secondary importance, despite the attention it receives in the literature on North Sea oil.

The argument of Buiter and Purvis is open to several criticisms, most of which they would almost certainly accept. For example, they assign an importance to monetary policy which seems excessive in the light of experience. It is now widely recognized that the government has found great difficulty in achieving its monetary targets, and that in Britain monetary policy is not a very effective instrument for controlling nominal GDP.[13] Thus, some of the key monetary premises upon which Buiter and Purvis base their argument seem to be false. However, all is not lost, for the analysis may be modified as follows. The essence of the argument is that total GDP is constrained by an external factor, so that an addition to GDP in the form of oil must be matched by an equivalent reduction in GDP elsewhere in the economy. In Buiter and Purvis, this constraint is provided by the money supply, which is fixed exogenously by the government.

But monetary policy is not the only instrument available to the government for controlling nominal GDP. Fiscal policy is an obvious alternative. Suppose the government pursues a fiscal policy whose aim is to achieve a given level of nominal GDP in the economy as a whole. If it is effective, this policy will produce exactly the same results as those ascribed to monetary policy by Buiter and Purvis. With a given fiscal policy and given prices, oil will crowd out non-oil production, and total employment will fall. Moreover, if the recession leads to a reduction in prices, the economy will spontaneously recover just as it does in Buiter and Purvis.

A second objection to the analysis of Buiter and Purvis concerns the nature of economic recovery. After the initial shock, the non-oil economy recovers spontaneously and, as prices fall, output gradually returns to its old level. Thus, the oil shock has no lasting effects. For analytical purposes, this is perhaps a reasonable assumption to make, but it is hardly realistic. In the kind of recession envisaged by Buiter and Purvis, productive capacity is destroyed on a large scale and the rate of investment declines. Thus, unless additional investment is made when recovery occurs – if it occurs at all – there will be less productive capacity than before, and output and employment in the non-oil economy will not return to their old levels. There will be a legacy of unemployment and impoverishment, which can only be eliminated through additional growth over and above that spontaneously arising through the mechanism considered by Buiter and Purvis.[14]

We have dealt at length with the crowding-out effect because, in one guise or another, it appears so frequently in the work of those who believe that the discovery of oil has had a large negative impact on total employment. Indeed, belief in some form of crowding-out effect unifies many diverse economists, ranging from monetarists like Alan Budd and his associates in the London Business School to out-and-out Keynesians like Nicholas Kaldor.[15] However, it is not the only justification for the view that unemployment has been significantly increased by the discovery of North Sea oil. Some writers, for example, point to the 'petrocurrency effect' as the villain. There are a number of different versions of this effect, but the following is the most plausible. Britain has for long been a major financial centre and recipient of surplus funds from the OPEC countries. When world oil prices doubled in 1978–9 many of these countries were slow to spend their additional revenue and acquired a large surplus of funds to invest. Britain was an obvious choice, not just because of her traditional attractiveness as a financial centre and her links with the OPEC countries, but also because, as a major oil producer and potential exporter herself, Britain's currency would almost certainly appreciate in relation to the currencies of oil-importing countries. Thus, according to this argument, Britain attracted a great deal of OPEC funds just because she herself was a major oil producer. Moreover, this inflow of funds drove up the exchange rate far above the level to which it would otherwise have risen and in this way exacerbated an already severe recession.[16]

Another version of the petrocurrency effect is the so-called 'discovery effect'. When the discovery of oil is announced, expectations about the future exchange rate are modified, and capital flows into the country in anticipation of a future appreciation. Unless special measures are taken to counter it, the result or such an inflow is to drive up the exchange rate, even though no oil has yet been produced. This in turn will exert a depressive effect on the domestic economy, causing both output and employment to fall.[17] Interestingly, virtually all writers accept that such a phenomenon might have occurred in the mid-1970s – even the National Institute!

The inflow of funds just described, and the consequent appreciation of sterling, could have been prevented by government action. For example, a tax could have been imposed on sterling deposits, thereby reducing the attractiveness of the currency to foreign investors. A similar result could have been achieved through a more expansionary monetary policy, designed to reduce the interest rate. However, the government rejected these options and, as a consequence, the real exchange rate appreciated dramatically, causing great harm to the non-oil economy. So, just as in the crowding-out theory, we find that the discovery of oil harms the non-oil economy, because an inflexible government refuses to modify its policies and take appropriate action to prevent this happening.

In theoretical terms, the above arguments are formidable. Moreover, they are supported by econometric evidence. For example, the simulations of Bond and Knobl (1982) suggest that North Sea oil has been responsible for a permanent fall of 8% in real income. No figure is given for employment, but the implied loss of jobs is obviously considerable.[18] Another econometric study by Beenstock *et al.*[19] suggests that North Sea oil has had a considerable short-term impact, being responsible for much of the huge appreciation in the real sterling exchange rate which so harmed the British economy in 1979–80. However, in their view, this effect is temporary, lasting only a few years until output and employment in the non-oil economy return spontaneously to their old level. Moreover, the real exchange rate also falls spontaneously but to a level some 14% above its original value. This new exchange rate reflects the permanent impact of oil on the structure of foreign trade. Although we cannot prove it here, the first estimate of Bond and Knobl seems far too high, whilst the claim of Beenstock *et al.* that the negative impact of North Sea oil spontaneously disappears after only a few years is scarcely credible. Note that the latter claim is not supported econometrically, but is *assumed* prior to estimation.

The above argument assumes that government monetary and fiscal policy would have been the same with or without oil. This is, of course, the problem.

To evaluate the historical impact of North Sea oil on the British economy we cannot simply assume that monetary and fiscal policies would have been the same in the absence of oil. On the contrary, there are good reasons for believing just the opposite. Suppose that North Sea oil had never been discovered but the Tory government had pursued the same monetary and fiscal policies. According to the authors we are considering, there would have been less unemployment and, at the same time, faster inflation. Faced with such a combination of faster inflation and lower unemployment, it is fairly obvious how the government would have responded. It would have pursued an even harsher anti-inflationary policy than it has done, thereby creating additional unemployment. Thus, any reduction in unemployment, due to the absence of oil, might well have been offset by the loss of jobs resulting from harsher government policy, in which case the net impact of oil on employment would have been quite small or even non-existent.

Thus, once we allow for the endogenous character of government policy, it is by no means clear that North Sea oil has contributed very much to the spectacular rise in unemployment since 1979. Oil may have influenced the timing of events and the speed at which unemployment has risen, but it has not influenced the final outcome to any great extent. The present level of unemployment is not the result of North Sea oil, but of the government's willingness to pursue its deflationary strategy to the limits of what is politically feasible.

Structural effects of oil production

We have argued that North Sea oil has had no lasting macro-economic impact. It has not significantly affected the level of employment in the economy as a whole. However, as we shall see, it has affected the *pattern* of employment, the distribution of the labour force between one sector of the economy and another. Because of North Sea oil, there are now fewer people employed in the manufacturing sector and more in other sectors of the economy than would have been the case if this oil had never been discovered. Thus, the production of oil has caused a *transfer* of labour from manufacturing to other sectors of the economy. This transfer of labour is what we call the 'structural' effect of oil production. The reasons for the transfer have already been explained in general terms elsewhere in this book, and there is no need to repeat them in detail here. Suffice it to say that North Sea oil has had a profound impact on the structure of Britain's foreign trade, and this, in turn, has influenced the pattern of domestic economic activity. Because of North Sea oil, there has been a permanent (or semi-permanent) appreciation in the real exchange rate of between 10 and 15%, as a result of which net manufactured exports have fallen.[20] This reduction in net manufactured exports is what accounts for the transfer

Table 12.6. *The structural impact of North Sea oil on UK employment, 1976–83 (thousands)*

	Manufacturing	Non-manufacturing	Total
Forsyth and Kay			
Upper	−601	+601	0
Lower	−384	+384	0
Our estimates			
Upper	−600	+600	0
Lower	−480	−480	0

Sources and Methods: See Appendix 12

of labour from manufacturing to non-manufacturing employment (i.e. the 'structural' effect).

Table 12.6 gives some estimates of the structural impact of North Sea oil on employment. Two of these estimates have been derived using the methods developed in the previous chapter, whilst the others are derived from the work of Forsyth and Kay (1980). Details of our procedure are contained in Appendix 12 and the table shows merely the results. In measuring the structural effect, total employment is taken as given, and any loss of jobs in one sector is matched by the creation of jobs in another. As far as manufacturing is concerned, the estimated loss of employment due to North Sea oil ranges from 380 thousand to 600 thousand. Splitting the difference, we arrive at a figure of half a million. This loss is, of course, offset by an equal gain in non-manufacturing employment.

Summary of the effects of North Sea oil on employment

The above discussion of North Sea oil and its effects on employment may be summarized as follows. On a macro-level the theoretical and empirical evidence is inconclusive. Some of the evidence suggests that North Sea oil has had a negative impact on total employment, whilst some of it points in the opposite direction, suggesting that total employment is now higher than it would have been in the absence of oil. One of the major difficulties is evaluating the impact of North Sea oil is in deciding what influence it has had on government policy. Some economists claim that North Sea oil has allowed the government to pursue a more expansionary (a less deflationary) policy than would otherwise have been the case, with the result that total employment is now greater than it would have been in the absence of oil. Others deny this, arguing that the government has responded to North Sea oil in such a way that total employment is now lower than it would have been if this oil had never been discovered. Our own view lies between these two extremes. Whilst North Sea oil may have influenced the timing of events, it has not significantly affected the medium-term evolution of total employment. In our view, government policy has responded to North Sea oil in such a way as to neutralize most of its medium-term effects on employment. As a result, both total employment and unemployment are now much the same as they would have been without oil.

Thus, if induced policy changes are taken into account, North Sea oil has not had a significant effect on total employment.

A wider view

So far, we have taken a rather narrow view and considered North Sea oil in isolation from the other autonomous factors which have influenced Britain's fuel trade since the war. Amongst these other factors are the gradual switch from domestically produced coal to imported oil and natural gas prior to 1973, the huge rise in world oil prices in 1973 and again in 1978–9, and the official decision to revert to the use of coal in electricity generation after 1973. We shall now complement our discussion of North Sea oil by considering the combined effect of *all* these autonomous factors on Britain's fuel trade. This will help us to locate North Sea oil within a wider historical background.

As before, we can distinguish between structural and macro-economic effects. Let us begin with the former. The various autonomous factors we are considering have had diverse effects on the structure of employment. Some have operated against the manufacturing sector, reducing the need for net manufactured exports and encouraging a transfer of labour to other sectors. Of these easily the most important is North Sea oil. Other factors have worked in the opposite direction, increasing the need for net manufactured exports and encouraging a transfer of labour to manufacturing; amongst these are the shift from domestic coal towards imported oil and natural gas in the fifties and sixties and the rise in world prices in 1973. Thus, some of the autonomous factors have encouraged 'de-industrialization', whilst others have had the opposite effect. Taken as a whole, the combined effect of these various factors on the balance of payments and, hence, on the structure of employment (as we define it) has been quite small. We have already considered their impact on the balance of payments earlier in this chapter, and our main conclusions were as follows. There was a gradual deterioration in the fuel balance as a share of GDP prior to 1973; then a sharp deterioration, when world oil prices rose at the end of 1973; and, finally, a sustained improvement over the next decade, due partly to autonomous factors, of which North Sea oil is the most important, and partly to the long depression which has reduced Britain's demand for most kinds of fuel since 1973. Between 1950 and 1983, the fuel balance as a whole improved from a deficit equal to 0.3% of GDP at the beginning to a surplus equal to 2.1% of GDP at the end. However, most of this improvement was due to the slow growth

Table 12.7. *UK manufacturing employment*

(a) *Share in civil employment 1955–83*	
	Percent
1955	36.1
1983	24.7
Change	−11.4
Due to:	
Changing trade specialization	−4.8
(Fuel)	(−0.4)
(Non-fuel items)	(−4.4)
Other factors	−6.6
(b) *Absolute numbers 1966–83*	
	Thousands
1966	8678
1983	5791
Change	−2887
Due to:	
Changing trade specialization	−859
(Fuel)	(−177)
(Non-fuel items)	(−682)
Other factors	−2028

Source: See Appendix 12

of the British economy, especially since 1973 and, when allowance is made for this, we find only a small autonomous improvement in the fuel balance between 1950 and 1983 of around 0.2 percentage points. This is dwarfed by the autonomous improvements which occurred in other areas of non-manufacturing trade (see Table 12.5).

Using methods developed in the preceding chapter, we have estimated the structural impact of these autonomous improvements on manufacturing employment. Details of our procedures are contained in Appendix 12, and Table 12.7 shows only the results. In conformity with previous terminology, the structural impact is shown under the heading 'specialization effect'. Table 12.7 gives estimates for the two periods 1955–83 and 1966–83. These periods have been chosen because 1955 was the year in which the share of manufacturing in total employment was at its historic peak; whilst 1966 is the year in which the absolute number of people employed in manufacturing began to fall. Taking the period 1955–83 first, we find that the share of manufacturing fell from 36.1% of total employment to 24.7% – a decline of 11.4 percentage points. Of this decline, some 4.8 points were a structural shift resulting from autonomous improvements in non-manufacturing trade, of which fuel-related items alone contributed a mere 0.4 points. For the period 1966–83 we find a similar picture. Over this period, manufacturing employment fell by 2,887 thousand. Of this total, some 859 thousand was a structural shift resulting from improvements in non-manufacturing trade as a whole, of which fuel-related items alone contributed a mere 177 thousand. Thus, the structural impact of fuel-related items, taken as a whole, has been very small. Depending on how it is measured, this structural impact accounts for between one-tenth and one-twentieth of the historic decline in manufacturing employment. These figures confirm the argument put forward by the Governor of the Bank of England in his Ashbridge lecture and by economists employed by the Bank.[21] They claim that the main structural impact of North Sea oil has been to cancel out a structural impact in the opposite direction resulting from the 1973 rises in world oil prices. When oil prices rose in 1973, Britain's fuel deficit rose dramatically, and to cover this deficit required an increase in net manufactured exports. *Ceteris paribus*, such an increase in net manufactured exports implies an increase in the output of the manufacturing sector and in the resources devoted to this sector. Conversely, when North Sea oil came on stream in 1976, the opposite was true. Net oil imports were reduced, less manufactured exports were required to pay for them, and less resources were required in the manufacturing sector. Thus, the 1973 price rise induced *re*-industrialization (or at least should have done), whereas North Sea oil induced *de*-industrialization. The Bank's claim is that these two effects largely cancelled each other out, leaving the overall economic structure much the same. This claim is confirmed by our estimates.

So far we have been considering only structural effects, which take the total amount of employment in the economy as a whole as given. What about the macro-economic effects? How far has total employment been affected by the various autonomous factors which have influenced Britain's fuel trade since the Second World War? Here, unfortunately, the picture is extremely confused. There are so many elements involved and the inter-relationships are so complex, that any firm judgement about even the direction of change is difficult to make, and quantitative estimates are impossible. We have already argued that North Sea oil has had no significant effect on total employment, nor on the level of unemployment, because any effect it might have had has been cancelled out by induced modifications in government policy.

In the case of other oil-related factors, however, one cannot be so sure. In particular, there is the spectacular rise in oil prices in 1973 to consider. This almost certainly harmed the British economy, and its effects can be felt to this day. The higher price of oil affected Britain in a number of ways. It contributed to the explosive inflation of 1973–4, it enormously increased the cost of fuel imports and was the main factor behind Britain's large deficit on the balance of payments during the mid-seventies. Internationally, the rise in oil prices helped provoke the world crisis and ensuing stagnation which have seriously harmed

Britain's export performance since 1973. From this list, it is clear that Britain's economy was damaged by the rise in oil prices and, in its absence, both output and employment would have been greater.

Moreover, this is not the end of the story. The economic difficulties of the mid-1970s were tackled by a Labour government whose measures for dealing with them were extremely unpopular, especially the incomes policy which collapsed in the famous Winter of Discontent in 1978–9. The conflict surrounding these policies was a decisive factor in the Labour government's defeat at the polls by a Tory party with Margaret Thatcher as leader. Committed to monetarism and the free market, the incoming government pursued deflationary policies whose result was an economic collapse unprecedented in British history. Whilst it would be presumptuous to blame all this on oil, one can plausibly argue that without the 1973 rise in oil prices, Britain's economy would have been in much better shape in the mid-seventies. With a stronger economy, the Labour government of the time would have pursued more popular policies, thereby preventing a Tory victory in 1979. In this case, a Labour government would have been in power during the early 1980s, pursuing less deflationary policies than those of the Tories. With such a government in power, the economic collapse would have been less dramatic and unemployment would never have risen to its present heights.

This is, of course, a highly speculative line of argument, but it cannot be dismissed out of hand. What is says is that a weak British economy was blown off course by the oil shock of 1973 and has been in grave difficulty ever since. But by its nature, such a claim is impossible to prove conclusively, and we merely state it here to illustrate the difficulties of counterfactual history. The historical development of an economy is not the smooth, reversible process envisaged by most econometricians, but involves many discontinuities and irreversibilities which make it impossible to assess with confidence the influence of a single factor or even combination of factors. This is not so important when we are considering what we have called 'structural effects'. These are concerned merely with the pattern of economic activity at a given level of output or employment, and to analyse them we can use the tools of comparative statics, in which change is assumed to be both continuous and reversible. However, the situation is different in the case of 'Macro-economic effects' which are concerned with the evolution of total employment. Here, dynamics are of central importance, and both discontinuity and irreversibility are the order of the day – if only because of the interplay between economic and political factors.

Take the case of oil. In purely structural terms, as we have seen, the main effect of North Sea oil was to cancel out the effect of the 1973 rise in oil prices. The former effect involved a shift in the pattern of employment away from manufacturing, whilst the latter involved a roughly equal shift of labour into manufacturing. Thus the combined structural effect of these two factors – North Sea oil and the 1973 price rise – was very small and had only a minor impact on manufacturing employment. However, one cannot assert the same thing about their combined macro-economic effect. Even if North Sea oil had only a minor influence on total employment, the 1973 price rise may have been the fatal blow which pushed the British economy off course and set in train a descending and irreversible spiral of political and economic events. If this is so – and it may well be – then the Bank of England is wrong in asserting that the discovery of North sea oil simply cancelled out the effect of the 1973 price rise. On a purely structural level, the Bank is correct: North Sea oil involved a change in the balance of payments and in the structure of employment which were roughly equal and opposite to that arising from the 1973 price rise. On a macro-economic level, however, there is no comparison. The 1973 price rise may have set in train the sequence of events whose impact on total employment in Britain has been enormous. By comparison, the discovery of oil in the North Sea has been of minor importance. It has certainly not reversed the harmful impact on British economic development of the 1973 price rise. Indeed, if anything it may have intensified it, although even this is not very likely.

Conclusions

The main conclusions of this chapter can be summarized as follows. In purely structural terms, North Sea oil has had quite a large impact on the British manufacturing industry, being responsible for the transfer of perhaps half a million workers from manufacturing to other sectors. However, other factors, such as the 1973 rise in oil prices, have operated in the opposite direction. So, taking account of all the various factors which have influenced Britain's fuel trade since 1950, their combined structural effect is quite small and their impact on the pattern of employment is of minor importance. The situation is different in the case of macro-economic effects, which are concerned with the evolution of total employment through time. There are strong reasons for believing that Britain's economic development has been seriously harmed by the factors which have influenced Britain's fuel trade. The 1973 rise in world oil prices certainly harmed the British economy at the time. Moreover, it might well have been the fatal blow which pushed the British economy off course and set in train a process of decline which culminated in the present economic collapse. This is by no means certain, but it is conceivable. Thus, in narrow structural terms, developments in Britain's fuel trade since 1950, taken as a whole, have had only a minor impact on the pattern of employment: shifts in one direction have been largely offset by shifts in another, leaving manufacturing employment much the same as before. However, the macro-economic impact of these developments has been considerable, and total employment is almost certainly much lower than it would have been without the rise in oil prices since 1973. These are our main conclusions.

13

Towards a better future

Introduction

During the 1980s economic debate in the UK has been increasingly dominated by two themes: unemployment and North Sea oil. What can be done about unemployment, which is now officially in the region of 3.5 million, and according to some estimates will remain at or above this level to the end of the century? What will happen as the production of oil and gas from the North Sea declines and the UK again becomes a net importer of energy? These are the themes we take up in the present chapter. Before doing so, however, a few words about our approach will be helpful. Our primary aim is to explore the dimensions of the problem now facing Britain and to indicate the scale of the economic transformation required if the country is to achieve anything like full employment in the foreseeable future. We are not concerned with economic policy *as such*, and we shall not consider in detail how the required transformation might be achieved. Our discussion will, of course, have policy implications and where appropriate we shall point these out. However, our remarks will be of a general nature and there will be no attempt to formulate an explicit programme for economic recovery.

The structure of the chapter is as follows. First, there is a discussion of employment growth, which considers how fast the economy would have to expand in the coming decades to make a real impact on unemployment. Several different scenarios are considered. At one end of the spectrum is the 'Green Scenario', which is based on the principles of the ecology movement and envisages the achievement of full employment with only a minimal rise in GDP. At the other end of the spectrum is the 'Supergrowth Scenario', under which the UK experiences Japanese-style growth and achieves full employment through a gigantic rise in GDP. The next section is concerned with the balance of payments. Our conclusion is as follows. Under the slow-growth Green Scenario, the fuel deficit is relatively small and could be financed from the income generated by service exports. Under the remaining scenarios, however, the rate of economic growth is much higher, far more energy is used and the UK energy deficit is much larger. Under these conditions, service exports would not be sufficient to cover this deficit, and to remain solvent the UK would require a fairly large trade surplus in manufactures.

The section on the balance of payments is followed by an assessment of the role of the manufacturing sector in economic expansion. We argue that rapid growth in GDP requires a massive increase in manufacturing output both to satisfy home demand and for export. However, even under conditions of rapid growth, few additional jobs would be created in the manufacturing sector itself; indeed, employment in this sector would probably fall. Most of the additional jobs required for full employment would be in the service sector, although some would also be in construction.

Employment and economic growth

In mid-1985 the number of people officially recorded as unemployed in the UK was 3.3 million. To reduce this figure significantly would require a large increase in total employment. Just how large would depend on the time-horizon envisaged and the final target figure for unemployment. As an illustration, suppose our target is to reduce officially recorded unemployment to 0.5 million within twenty years (i.e. by the year 2005). How many additional jobs would be required to achieve this target? The answer depends on the number of people seeking work in the UK, and this in turn depends on how the demand for labour affects international migration and participation rates. Official projections for the UK assume a fairly high level of net emigration over the coming decades. This anticipated outflow is, presumably, a response to the lack of employment opportunities within the UK and would be reduced, or even eliminated altogether, under condition of full employment. Under these conditions, fewer people would leave the UK in search of work, whilst migrant workers would be drawn in from abroad, especially from the labour surplus economies of Southern Europe. Official projections also predict an increase in labour-force participation by certain categories of women, especially those with small children. This is expected to occur even under conditions of mass unemployment. With a rapid growth in demand for labour, such as we envisage, female participation rates would increase even faster than is officially predicted. Moreover, premature retirements by both men and women would decline and many older people might be drawn back into the labour market. Making a generous allowance for all these different factors, we estimate that total employment would have to rise by perhaps 5 million over the period 1985–2005.[1] Such an increase in employment would not only bring down officially recorded unemployment dramatically, it would also eliminate much of the hidden unemployment which

Table 13.1. *The road to full employment (millions)*

	Total population	Civilian labour force	Civil employment	Unemployment	Unemployment (%)
Actual					
1950	50.2	22.3	22.0	0.3	1.5
1973	55.9	25.3	24.7	0.6	2.2
1985	56.4	27.2	23.9	3.3	12.1
Hypothetical					
2005	58.5	29.5	29.0	0.5	1.7
2025	60.0	30.4	29.9	0.5	1.6

Note: The series for working population and employment exclude HM Armed Forces. All figures refer to the UK including Northern Ireland

now exists in the UK economy. At first sight, an increase of 5 million in total employment within twenty years might seem overambitious; however, expressed in annual terms, it amounts on average to only 250 thousand jobs a year. This represents an annual growth rate of 1.0% in total employment. Such a growth rate is not unduly high by international standards and is below what has been achieved by a number of capitalist countries in modern times. Perhaps the best-known example is the USA, where employment growth has averaged 1.9% a year since 1960. Moreover, it is predicted that US employment will continue growing at almost this rate into the foreseeable future.[2] Few other capitalist countries can match the US record, but Australia, Canada, New Zealand, Norway and Japan have all had rates of employment growth which exceed our target figure for the UK.[3]

Assuming that officially recorded unemployment falls to 0.5 million by the year 2005, what happens next? Suppose our aim is to keep unemployment at this level over the next twenty years (i.e. up to the year 2025). How many additional jobs would be required to achieve this target? The answer is: not very many. The population of working age should be virtually stable, whilst the rise in participation rates should be slowing down. As a result, the total number of people seeking work would be increasing only very slowly, if at all. Under these conditions an increase in total employment of perhaps 0.2% a year should be sufficient to ensure the achievement of our target. In absolute terms, this would amount to 40–50 thousand additional jobs a year over the period 2005–25. The arithmetic of all this is summarized in Table 13.1.

Thus, to achieve our unemployment targets, total employment must rise at an average rate of around 1.0% a year over the period 1985–2005, and from then onwards by 0.2% a year. At what rate must total output rise so as to ensure this rate of job creation? Unfortunately, there is no simple answer to this question. It all depends on what happens to output per worker. The faster output per worker increases, the faster must total output grow so as to ensure a given rate of job creation. This much is obvious. However, it does not really tell us very much, for output per worker is a subtle variable whose behaviour depends on many different technical and social factors. For example, it depends on the technology in use and on the willingness and competence of the workforce to operate this technology. These in turn are influenced by the prevailing level of real wages. If real wage rates are forced up rapidly, older methods of production and less efficient producers may be driven out of use. This will raise the output per unit of labour performed, and, if hours of work are given, the result will be an increase in output per worker. Thus, output per worker is indirectly a function of real wage rates through their influence on methods of production. It is also influenced by hours of work. With given methods of production, a reduction in working hours will mean that more workers are required to produce a given output than would otherwise be the case. These observations are of obvious relevance in the present context. The behaviour of output per worker is strongly influenced by such variables as real wage rates and hours of work, and hence these variables influence the rate at which total output must grow to achieve the desired rate of employment creation. As a general rule, if hours of work are constant, the faster real wage rates increase, the faster must output rise in order to achieve a given employment target. Conversely, if hourly wage rates are constant, a reduction in hours of work will normally allow this target to be achieved with a smaller rise in total output than would otherwise be the case.[4]

Hypothetical scenarios

To explore the inter-relationship between output and employment we shall now consider some hypothetical scenarios covering the period 1985–2025. These scenarios illustrate how, depending on what happens to labour productivity and hours of work, the same employment targets might be achieved with very different rates of economic growth. The main assumptions underlying the various scenarios are shown in Tables 13.2 and 13.3.

The Green Scenario

As its name suggests, this scenario is based on the ideas of the 'green' ecology movement. It stresses environmental concerns and rejects rapid economic growth as a cure for unemployment. Under this scenario labour-saving technology is introduced only gradually, with the result that labour productivity rises quite slowly. GDP per worker-hour increases at 1.4% a year over the period 1985–

Table 13.2. *Growth rates of output and employment, 1950–2025 (% per year)*

	Population	Employment	GDP	GDP per worker	GDP per head of population
Actual					
1950–73	0.5	0.5	2.7	2.2	2.2
1973–85	0.1	−0.3	1.2	1.5	1.1
Hypothetical					
Green Scenario:					
1985–2005	0.2	1.0	1.0	0.0	0.8
2005–2025	0.1	0.2	0.2	0.0	0.1
Growth Scenario:					
1985–2005	0.2	1.0	3.0	2.0	2.8
2005–2025	0.1	0.2	2.2	2.0	2.1
Supergrowth Scenario:					
1985–2005	0.2	1.0	4.0	3.0	3.8
2005–2025	0.1	0.2	3.2	3.0	3.1

Table 13.3. *Hours and output, 1950–2025 (annual percentage change)*

	GDP per hour	Hours per worker[a]	GDP per worker
Actual			
1950–73	2.8	−0.6[b]	2.2
1973–85	2.5	−1.0[b]	1.5
Hypothetical			
Green Scenario:			
1985–2005	1.4	−1.4	0.0
2005–2025	1.4	−1.4	0.0
Growth Scenario:			
1985–2005	2.7	−0.7	2.0
2005–2025	2.7	−0.7	2.0
Supergrowth Scenario:			
1985–2005	3.7	−0.7	3.0
2005–2025	3.7	−0.7	3.0

Notes: [a] Annual hours, all workers including part-timers
[b] Estimate

2025. However, this is offset by an equal reduction in the number of hours of paid labour performed by the average worker, so that GDP per employed worker remains constant throughout the entire period. Total output rises very slowly and by 2025 GDP is only 26% higher than in 1985 (see Fig. 13.1). With such a small increase in GDP there is obviously little scope for real wage growth.

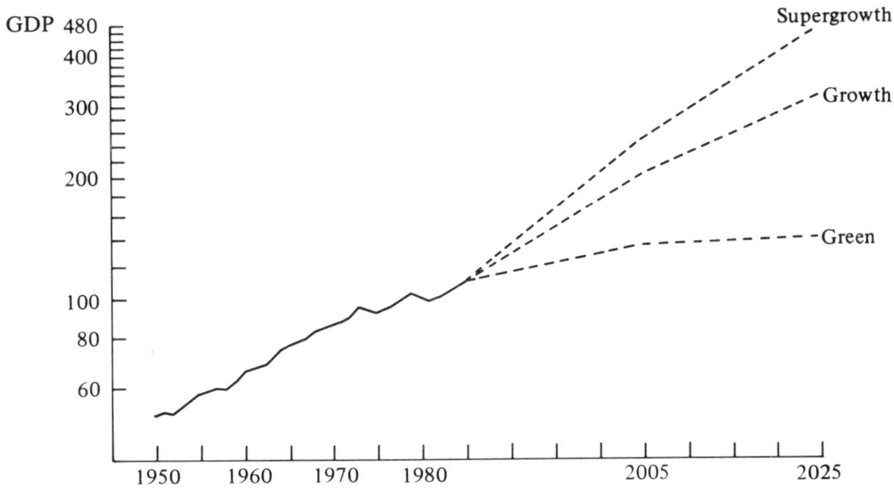

Fig. 13.1 Gross domestic product, 1950–2025 (1980 = 100)

Hourly wage rates certainly rise, but this is matched by a fall in working hours. As a result, by 2025, real take-home pay for the *average* person in employment is not much higher than in 1985. Some people may, of course, gain a great deal through income redistribution, whilst most of the unemployed will enjoy a considerable rise in disposable income simply because they obtain employment. However, although numerically important, such people are still a minority. The fact remains that for most people already in employment there can be little or no increase in real take-home pay under the Green Scenario. However, there is an improvement in the quality of life. Hours of work are much shorter, the environment is more pleasant and the public services, such as transport, health and education, are better. This may be some compensation for the lack of growth in take-home pay.

Under the Green Scenario, working hours decline by 1.5% a year. The cumulative effect of such a fall is dramatic. For the average worker, including part-timers, hours of work decrease from 35 a week in 1985 to just over 19 a week in 2025 (Table 13.4). For full-timers alone, the fall is equally dramatic, from 40 hours a week in 1985 to well under 30 hours in 2025. With such a fall in full-time hours the concept of full-time employment becomes *almost* meaningless, and the distinction between part-time and full-time workers is effectively abolished.[5] Alongside the reduction in weekly hours there is also an increase in the amount of leave for holidays, child care and study (from around 7 weeks a year on average in 1985 to 11 weeks in 2025). Although we shall not explore them here, such a fall in paid working time would have profound social implications.

Table 13.4. *Working time, 1950–2025*[a]

				Hypothetical			
	Actual[c]			Green Scenario		Other Scenarios	
	1950	1973	1985	2005	2025	2005	2025
Weekly hours of work:							
All workers	42	38	35	29	22	32	29
Full-timers	44	42	40	33	—[d]	37	34
Holidays and leave[b]	3	5	7	9	11	9	11

Notes: [a] All full-timers
[b] Weeks per year. Includes leave for child care and study
[c] Most actual figures are estimates
[d] Under the Green Scenario the distinction between full-time and part-time workers becomes virtually meaningless by 2025

It would radically alter the role of paid employment in people's lives, giving them both more leisure time and more time in which to perform useful, but unpaid, labour such as housework. It would also affect the sexual division of labour. At the present time, household tasks such as cleaning and childcare are performed largely by women. With the reduction in hours envisaged under the Green Scenario, this situation would inevitably change – perhaps after a struggle – and much of this unpaid labour would be taken over by men.

The Green Scenario has a number of attractive features, especially the dramatic reduction in working hours. However, it has one obvious drawback. For the majority of people in employment, this scenario involves a virtual freeze in material living standards – as conventionally defined – over at least a 40-year period. Such a prolonged freeze might be viable if implemented universally throughout the advanced countries as a whole. However, for obvious political and economic reasons, it would not be viable if implemented by the UK acting in isolation at a time when most other advanced countries were experiencing fairly rapid growth and rising material consumption. The economic and cultural ties linking the advanced countries to each other are so strong as to preclude such a grossly divergent path in any one of them and, broadly speaking, they must all conform to the same universal norm. Thus, the Green Scenario, as outlined here, is only conceivable as part of a wider international shift towards green policies. The likelihood of such a shift occurring in the near future is remote. Some of the ideas of the Green Movement are certainly being taken up in a piecemeal fashion, but there is no sign of any widespread desire or willingness to abandon economic growth as an objective. Indeed, if anything, economic growth is now more in vogue than it was in the mid-1970s in the wake of the first oil crisis. In practical terms, therefore, the Green Scenario is unlikely to be realized in the extreme form described here. This scenario is included simply as a reference point to indicate how full employment could theoretically be achieved in the UK, and then maintained, with only a minimal rise in total output. Note that when considering the balance of payments implications of this scenario, we shall assume that all advanced countries simultaneously follow the green path of minimal economic growth.

The Growth Scenario

This is the most conventional of our scenarios. It foresees a return to full employment through sustained economic growth at a rate slightly faster than the UK actually achieved during the pre-oil shock years of 1950–73. Output per worker rises at 2.0% a year and by 2025 GDP is 178% above its 1985 level. With such a growth in output there could be a substantial increase in real wages over the period as a whole. Austerity might be required in the initial years to provide the resources required for investment and short-term job creation, but over the long run real wages could certainly rise by a considerable amount. Under this scenario, hours of paid work are reduced from an average of 35 a week in 1985, including part-timers, to 29 in 2025. The hours of full-timers alone decline from 40 a week to 34 a week (Table 13.4). Although less dramatic than under the Green Scenario, this is still a significant reduction in working time. The performance of the UK economy under the Growth Scenario is impressive (see Fig. 13.1). During the 40-year period 1985–2025, GDP grows at an average rate of 2.6% a year, which is just about the rate actually observed during the economic 'recovery' of 1982–5. To maintain such a growth rate over the next forty years would be quite an achievement, though within the bounds of possibility. Given the right government policies and a social consensus around economic goals, an average growth rate of 2.6% a year is certainly feasible for the UK. In this sense, the Growth Scenario is the most credible of all our scenarios.

The Supergrowth Scenario

This scenario accords with the ideas put forward by the Confederation of British Industries in its document *Change to Succeed*.[6] Under this scenario the UK experiences Japanese-style growth, the performance of manufacturing industry is spectacular, and both output and productivity increase rapidly throughout the economy. GDP rises at nearly 4% a year up to 2005 and more than 3% a year thereafter. By the end of the period, in 2025, GDP is four and a half times the 1985 level, whilst output per worker is three and a half times as great. Moreover, hours of work fall significantly, and by 2025 the average full-timer works 34 hours a week as compared to the present 40 hours. The performance of the UK economy under the Supergrowth Scenarios is remarkable, and to achieve this kind of performance would require a virtual revolution in social behaviour. There is no sign at present that such a revolution is in the making, and as a result the UK is not likely to achieve the growth rates envisaged under the Supergrowth Scenario. This scenario is only included as an upper reference point.

The balance of payments

We shall now consider what happens to the balance of payments under the three scenarios just described. Our starting-point will be trade in non-manufactures; later we shall consider the remaining items.

Tables 13.9 and 13.10 show how non-manufacturing trade as a whole behaves under each scenario during the period 1985–2025. The figures shown in the tables, it must be stressed, are not based on formal econometric estimates. Rather, they reflect our subjective evaluation of the disparate evidence which exists regarding the behaviour of non-manufacturing trade and the factors which are likely to influence it over the next forty years. They also reflect our assessment of what kind of policy choices might accompany each scenario. For example, we consider a number of variants of the Green Scenario under all of which the UK demand for energy is reduced and, as a matter of policy, nuclear power is phased out. Under certain variants of the Supergrowth Scenario, by contrast, there is a large growth in energy demand to which the government responds with a fairly rapid build-up of nuclear generating capacity. There is, of course, nothing sacrosanct about these assumptions and the government could, in theory, pursue radically different nuclear policies from those envisaged. For example, the UK could combine slow economic growth, as under the Green Scenario, with a vigorous nuclear energy programme, in which case the country might remain a net fuel exporter for the indefinite future. Alternatively, the UK could pursue a supergrowth strategy without making use of nuclear power, in which case there might be a gigantic fuel deficit. However, although theoretically possible, such combinations are implausible, and it is realistic to assume that the faster the UK economy grows, the greater will be its demand for energy and the greater its eventual reliance on nuclear power. The question of nuclear power is, of course, only one area in which policy choices will influence the future evolution of non-manufacturing trade. The same is also true of agriculture and sea transport, where in each case the question of protectionism will become increasingly important in the coming decades. There is growing pressure to reduce the degree of protection enjoyed by British agriculture under the Common Agriculture Policy (CAP), whilst the opposite is true in the case of sea transport where there is growing pressure to protect the declining UK fleet from foreign competition. How far these pressures will succeed is not yet clear, but in each case the outcome will have implications for the balance of payments.

Because of the long time-horizon, and the numerous economic and political factors involved, there is obviously great uncertainty concerning the future evolution of UK trade in non-manufactures. To handle this uncertainty we shall proceed as follows. For each scenario, three different variants will be considered, labelled A, B and C. Of these, we regard variant B as the most plausible, partly on economic grounds and partly because it reflects most accurately the kind of policy choices which might occur under the scenario concerned. The remaining variants are included so as to indicate the degree of uncertainty involved and the range of potential variation. Thus, variant A takes a uniformly pessimistic view of how non-manufacturing trade might develop and, on every major item, the balance of trade in non-manufactures is worse under variant A than variant B, sometimes by a considerable amount. The opposite is true in the case of variant C, which takes a uniformly optimistic view of non-manufacturing trade.

As elsewhere in this book, trade in non-manufactures will be considered under four main headings: food, beverages and tobacco; basic materials; fuels; and non-governmental services (including transfers). Of these, the most important in the present context is easily fuel. The potential deterioration in the UK fuel balance over the next forty years is enormous. It exceeds any changes which might occur in the remaining items of services, food or materials, and what happens to the non-manufacturing balance as a whole in the coming decades will be largely determined by what happens to UK trade in fuels. In view of this we shall devote a fair amount of space to the question of fuels and energy, whilst the remaining items will be treated in a more cursory fashion.

Fuels[7]

The three main fuels which are traded internationally are coal, oil and natural gas. In addition, there is uranium for use in the generation of nuclear power. However, uranium is not conventionally regarded as a fuel in international trade statistics, but is classified as an intermediate manufactured good. Furthermore, the electricity derived from nuclear power stations is conventionally described as 'primary' electricity and is classified as an indigenous source of primary energy along with domestically produced coal, oil, gas and renewables such as hydro and wind power. In our discussion we shall follow these conventions and ignore uranium imports. The error involved in this procedure is minor, for uranium is a relatively cheap fuel per unit of energy supplied, and the total cost of uranium imports into the UK is comparatively small – and is likely to remain so for the foreseeable future.

Table 13.5. *Description of the scenario variants*

	Variant		
	A	B	C
Energy prices	high	medium	low
UK energy consumption	high	medium	low
UK non-nuclear energy production	low	medium	high
UK nuclear energy production:			
Green Scenario	nil	nil	nil
Other Scenarios	nil	low	medium
UK net energy imports	high	medium	low

The UK balance of trade in fuels depends on a number of factors, of which the following are the most important: primary energy prices, total UK requirements of primary energy and total UK production of primary energy. In addition, there is the composition of energy requirements and energy production to consider, in particular what fuels are used to produce energy and where they come from. In discussing the impact of these factors on the balance of payments, we shall consider three distinct variants of each scenario, whose main features are described in Table 13.5. (Full details are given in Appendix 14.) At one extreme are the A-variants, under which both energy prices and UK energy consumption are relatively high, whilst domestic energy production is relatively low; as a result, there is a large energy deficit and the net cost of fuel imports is considerable. At the other extreme are the C-variants, under which the price of energy and the amount consumed are low, whilst domestic production is high; as a result, both the volume and cost of net fuel imports is relatively small. Between these extremes lie the B-variants which take an intermediate view about prices, consumption and production. One point to note of particular importance concerns nuclear power. Under all variants of the Green Scenario existing nuclear generating capacity is phased out as a matter of policy. Nuclear power is also phased out under the A-variants of the Growth and Supergrowth scenarios. In contrast, under the B and C variants of these growth scenarios, there is an increase in the use of nuclear power.

Let us now consider the main factors in detail. On the question of prices, it is widely agreed that the mid-1980s glut of oil and other fuels is a temporary phenomenon, and that energy prices will recover before the end of the century.[8] In accordance with this view, energy prices are assumed to rise in the long term under all hypothetical scenarios. By 2025 the real price of crude oil, measured in sterling, is between 25 and 90% above its 1983 level, depending on the variant concerned. The price of other fuels rises by a similar amount.[9]

The next factor to consider is energy consumption. For any given rate of

Table 13.6. *Energy and output under the hypothetical scenarios (annual growth rates (%))*[a]

		TPER[b]			TPER/GDP		
	GDP	A	B	C	A	B	C
Hypothetical scenarios for UK 1983–2025							
Green	0.6	−0.4	−0.8	−1.2	−1.0	−1.4	−1.8
Growth	2.6	1.0	0.6	0.2	−1.6	−2.0	−2.4
Supergrowth	3.6	1.4	1.0	0.6	−2.2	−2.6	−3.0
IEA predictions 1983–2000[c]							
UK	1.5		0.8			−0.7	
Japan	3.9		2.4			−1.5	
Denmark	2.9		1.2			−1.7	
W. Germany	2.6		0.1			−2.5	
Sweden	2.1		0.6			−1.5	
O and M estimates for UK 1976–2025[d]							
Low growth	0.6		−1.9 to −2.7			−2.5 to −3.3	
High growth	2.2		−0.8 to −1.3			−3.0 to −3.5	

Notes: [a] Exponential growth rates (i.e. continuously compounding)
[b] TPER = total primary energy requirement
[c] International Energy Association (1985), national tables
[d] Derived from the low energy scenarios contained in Olivier and Miall (1983)

economic growth, future requirements of primary energy depend on the rate of energy conservation. By international standards, the UK's performance in this sphere has been mediocre and is predicted to remain so for the foreseeable future. As explained in Chapter 5, certainly there has been a considerable fall in the amount of energy required per unit of GDP in the UK since 1973. However, much of this is a once-and-for-all effect, resulting from the economic crisis, which has led to the scrapping of old, energy inefficient equipment and to a severe contraction in energy-intensive industries like steel and cement. Despite these improvements, the UK still uses up to twice as much energy per unit of GDP as do energy efficient countries like Denmark, West Germany or Japan.[10] Moreover, as things stand, the disparity is likely to get worse. Energy efficiency is predicted to improve only very slowly in the UK in the coming years, whereas in these other countries impressive gains are expected (see Table 13.6). One reason for this state of affairs is the casual approach of the British government to energy policy in general and its refusal to take the subject of consumption very seriously.[11] However, in constructing the hypothetical scenarios, we take an optimistic view and assume that a vigorous effort is made to save energy, with the result that energy requirements per unit of GDP fall quite rapidly.

Table 13.6 gives an index of how great is the improvement we assume in energy consumption as compared to current predictions for the UK.

The International Energy Agency (IEA) predicts that the energy–GDP ratio in the UK will fall by 0.7% a year on average over the period 1983–2000, whilst under the central B-variants we assume a reduction in this ratio of 1.4 to 2.6% a year, depending on the scenario concerned. This might suggest that our assumptions are rather extreme. However, they do not appear so extreme when compared to current predictions for other countries. For example, the IEA predicts that the energy–GDP ratio for West Germany will fall by 2.5% a year, which is more than we assume under the central B-variant of our Growth Scenario. Further evidence of what might be achieved in the way of energy conservation is provided by the work of low energy enthusiasts such as Olivier and Miall (1983). In a comprehensive and painstaking study of future options, these authors examine what might happen to the demand for energy if the UK were to implement a vigorous programme of energy conservation. With such a programme, they estimate that the energy–GDP ratio would fall by 2.5 to 3.3% a year in the case of low economic growth, and by 3.0 to 3.5% in the case of fast economic growth (see Table 13.6). These estimates imply considerably more energy conservation than we assume under our hypothetical scenarios. For example, in the case of slow economic growth (as under the Green Scenario) we assume a reduction in the energy–GDP ratio of 1.0 to 1.8% a year, depending on the variant concerned, whilst in the case of fast economic growth (as under the Growth Scenario) the reduction is between 1.6 and 2.4% a year. These figures are well below the corresponding estimates provided by Olivier and Miall.

Thus, although ambitious when compared to current predictions for the UK, our assumptions about energy conservation seem modest compared to what low energy enthusiasts claim is feasible. Moreover, they also seem quite reasonable when compared to current predictions for, say, West Germany. In view of this, we shall take the figures shown in Table 13.6 as a realistic indication of what might be achieved with a vigorous programme of energy conservation in the UK. The implications of these figures for energy consumption in the UK are as follows. Taking the period 1983–2025 as a whole, the amount of primary energy required under the Green Scenario falls by 15–40% depending on the variant concerned. This fall occurs because rapid progress in energy conservation is combined with slow economic growth. The Green Scenario, however, is an exception. Under the remaining scenarios, there is a massive rise in GDP, which outweighs any reduction in the energy–GDP ratio. As a result, total energy consumption rises, sometimes by a considerable amount. For example, under the Growth Scenario, the amount of primary energy required rises from 192 MTOE in 1963 to between 210 and 295 MTOE in 2025, depending on the variant concerned.[12] Under the Supergrowth Scenario energy requirements in 2025 are in the range 250 to 350 MTOE. Figure 13.2 shows what happens to energy consumption under the B-variant of each scenario. For comparison the behaviour of energy consumption prior to 1983 is also shown. These diagrams illustrate clearly the impact of economic growth on energy consumption. Generally speaking, the faster an economy grows, the greater is its demand for energy, and with the kind of growth rates envisaged under the Growth and Supergrowth Scenarios a fairly large increase in primary energy consumption would seem likely.

How would the demand for primary energy be satisfied? Supplies of primary energy can be divided into two kinds: nuclear and non-nuclear. As already mentioned, the former is conventionally regarded as a domestic source of energy, whilst the latter can be subdivided into domestically produced and imported energy. Let us begin by considering domestically produced, non-nuclear energy. Under all scenarios and all variants, this kind of primary energy supply declines in the course of time as output of North Sea oil and gas tails off.[13] The falling output of oil and natural gas is partially offset by a small, but rapidly growing, contribution from renewables (wave, solar, wind, etc.) whilst, in some cases, there is also a serious effort to increase domestic coal production. However, these measures are not sufficient to compensate for the loss of oil and natural gas. Hence the fall in non-nuclear energy production as a whole. The significance of these developments depends on the scenario concerned. Under the Green Scenario, declining non-nuclear production of energy is accompanied by a considerable fall in consumption. As a result, even in 2025, the UK is still able to supply the bulk of her energy requirements from her own resources, without recourse to either nuclear power or large-scale imports of energy. However, the Green Scenario is an exception in this respect. Under the remaining scenarios, the fall in non-nuclear production of energy is accompanied by an increase in the demand for energy. As a result, there emerges a large gap between primary energy requirements in the UK and what is produced from the country's own non-nuclear resources. This is the gap which imported energy would have to bridge in the absence of nuclear power.

The actual volume of energy imports depends, of course, on the amount of nuclear power available. Theoretically, with a large enough output of nuclear power, the UK could remain self-sufficient in energy even with the very large energy requirements envisaged under the Supergrowth Scenario. For example, with a nuclear power capacity on the scale forecast for France or Japan in the next century, the UK could dispense with steam-coal almost completely, thereby releasing much of her domestic production of coal for export.[14] Even under the Supergrowth Scenario, such exports might outweigh future imports of oil and gas, in which case the country would continue to have a surplus of energy right through to the end of our period in 2025. However, a massive nuclear

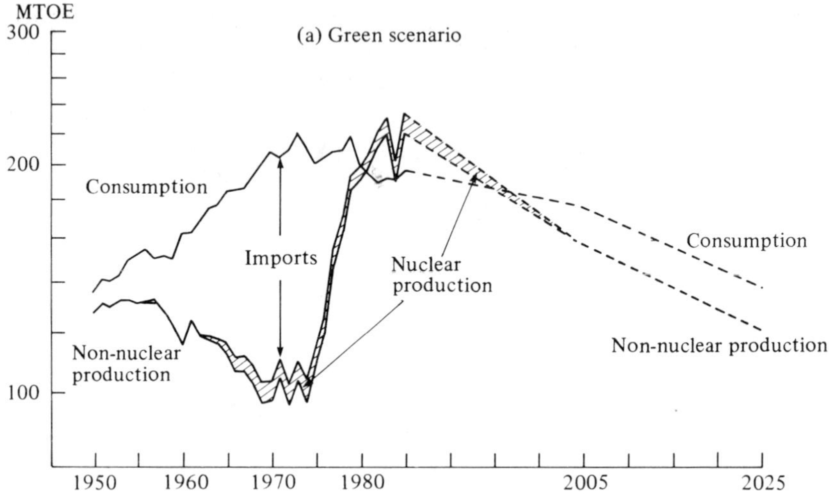

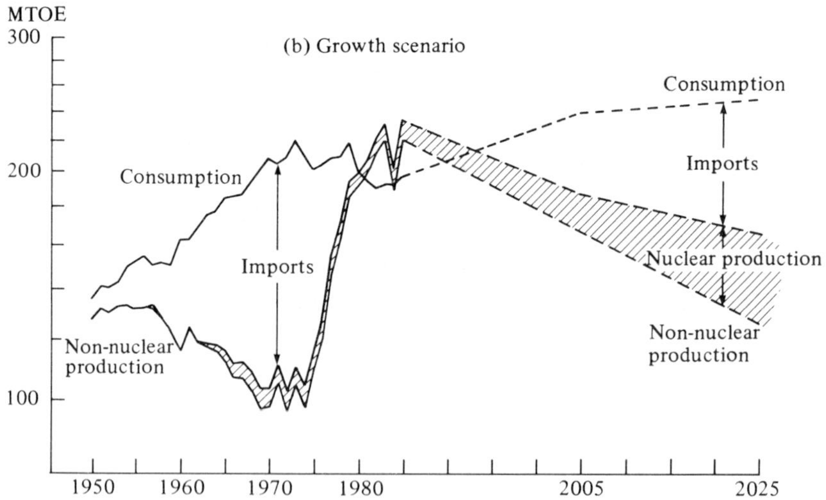

programme on this scale might prove impractical and would certainly meet with enormous political opposition in the UK. For this reason the nuclear programmes envisaged under the nuclear variants (i.e. B and C) of our growth scenarios are much less ambitious than what is planned for France or Japan. Even so, they still involve quite a large increase in nuclear capacity. For example, under

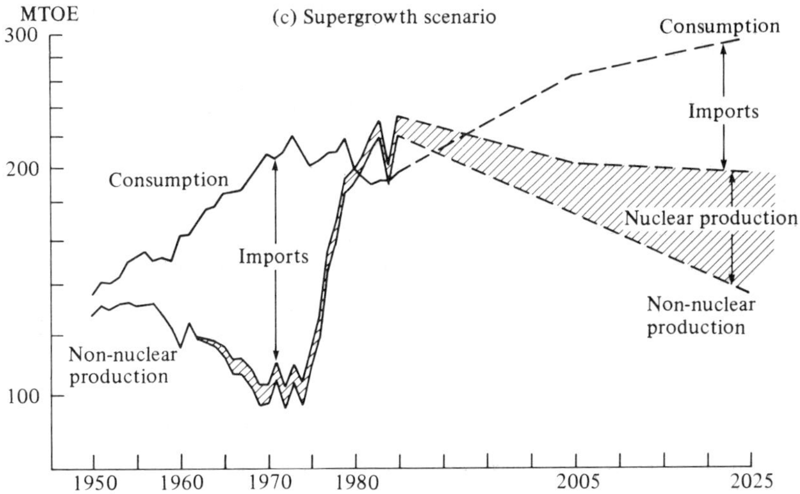

Fig. 13.2 UK energy balance, 1950–2025 (Variant B)
(a) Green Scenario
(b) Growth Scenario
(c) Supergrowth Scenario

the central B-variant of the Growth Scenario, the amount of nuclear electricity rises from 13 MTOE in 1985 to 20 MTOE in 2005 and 40 MTOE in 2025. For the Supergrowth Scenario the corresponding figures are 25 MTOE in 2005 and 60 MTOE in 2025.[15] However, despite this increase in nuclear power, the UK still has a large energy deficit in each case (see Fig. 13.2).

Before leaving the topic of nuclear power, let us make one point clear. We assume that nuclear power plays a major role under the central B-variant of our Growth and Supergrowth Scenarios, and provides about a quarter or all electricity consumed in 2025. This is not because we support nuclear power or are unaware of its dangers, but because we think that economic growth at the rate envisaged under these scenarios might be impractical without it. To obtain fossil fuels on the scale required in the absence of nuclear power might be extremely difficult. Domestic coal production could certainly be stepped up even above the fairly high levels we assume under these scenarios, but the environmental and economic costs might be unacceptable. The UK is a relatively high-cost producer of coal and, although reserves of coal are plentiful, they are often inaccessible or expensive to obtain. Some of the best coal reserves are located in beautiful areas of central England – such as the Vale of Belvoir – whose articulate residents would bitterly oppose and delay any expansion in coal production. At one time, under the ill-fated plan for coal, an eventual coal output of 200 million tonnes (=120 MTOE) was envisaged. However, for environmental and economic reasons, this is now widely seen as over-optimistic and a figure of 140 million tonnes (or less) is sometimes cited as a realistic upper limit.[16] This latter figure is about what we already assume for coal production under the B-variant of the Supergrowth Scenario in 2025. It seems unlikely that domestic coal production could be stepped up sufficiently to replace the nuclear power used under our Growth Scenarios. An alternative would be to import additional coal. However, these scenarios already envisage fairly large imports of coal, and to replace nuclear power by imported coal would require doubling the volume of these imports. Not only might the cost of such imports be prohibitive, but supplies on the required scale might be virtually unobtainable. This would depend, of course, on events in the rest of the world. For example, with a combination of moderate growth in the world economy and widespread use of nuclear power in other countries, world supplies of coal would be plentiful and the UK could import all she required at a relatively low price. Under these conditions, the UK economy could grow rapidly over a long period of time without recourse to nuclear power, using cheap imported coal to generate the electricity required. The same result might be achieved through a quantum leap in the global application of renewable technologies on a scale sufficient to relieve the pressure on fossil fuels and hold down world energy prices. However, this is only one set of possibilities. The alternative prospect is that fossil fuels will become increasingly scarce, in which case sustained and rapid economic growth in the UK may become impractical without recourse to nuclear power. Thus the UK may be faced with a dilemma. If rapid economic growth is the priority, the use of nuclear power on a fairly large scale may be unavoidable. Conversely, if the dangers of nuclear power are too great, there may be no alternative but to accept slow economic growth and make the best of it, as we envisage under the Green Scenario. The UK is not alone in this respect. Other advanced countries are facing a similar dilemma and most have already chosen the nuclear option. Whether they will stick by that choice after the Chernobyl disaster remains to be seen.

Some information about specific fuels has already been given. Further details are contained in Appendix 14. The main points to note are as follows. Under all scenarios imports of natural gas will remain at about their present level through the period we are concerned with. In the case of oil, domestic production remains sufficient to meet most of the UK requirements to around the turn of the century. In the next century, however, the situation is rather different. Under the Green Scenario the UK pursues a conservationist policy designed to reduce oil consumption and conserve existing reserves. As a result the country remains almost self-sufficient in oil right through to 2025. Under the other scenarios, however, oil consumption is much greater, reserves are depleted more rapidly, and net

Table 13.7. *UK primary energy balance (all variants)*

				Green Scenario		Growth Scenario		Supergrowth Scenario	
	1950	1973	1983	2005	2025	2005	2025	2005	2025
Energy self-sufficiency (ratio)[a]									
Variant A				74	65	59	38	55	33
Variant B	94	50	1.20	89	88	78	67	77	66
Variant C				106	117	94	95	92	99
Energy balance (MTOE)[b,c]									
Variant A				−49	−57	−108	−184	−129	−233
Variant B	−8	−110	39	−19	−17	−52	−83	−61	−99
Variant C				10	20	−13	−10	−20	−3
Net fuel exports (£1980 billion)[d,e]									
Variant A				−4.0	−8.1	−8.2	−23.2	−9.8	−28.2
Variant B	−0.3	−2.8	4.9	−1.4	−2.5	−3.6	−10.2	−4.5	−11.9
Variant C				0.8	1.3	−0.7	−2.9	−1.3	−2.9
Net fuel exports as percentage of GDP[d]									
Variant A				−1.4	−2.7	−1.9	−3.4	−1.8	−2.8
Variant B	−0.3	−1.3	2.1	−0.5	−0.8	−0.9	−1.5	−0.8	−1.2
Variant C				0.3	0.4	−0.2	−0.4	−0.2	−0.3

Notes: [a] Self-sufficiency ratio = (production ÷ consumption) × 100
[b] Balance = production − consumption
[c] MTOE = million tonnes of oil or oil equivalent
[d] Net exports = exports (f.o.b.) − imports (f.o.b.)
[e] Current values divided by GDP deflator

imports of oil become progressively larger. Finally there is coal to consider. Here again the picture depends on the variant concerned. Under the optimistic C-variants, UK coal production is more than sufficient for domestic needs, and by 2025 there is a surplus available for export. Under the remaining variants, however, consumption of coal exceeds production, sometimes by a considerable margin, and the gap is covered by imports. To import coal on the scale envisaged would require a large investment in port facilities, and for economic reasons might also require the building of coastal power stations to make use of this coal.

To conclude this discussion let us briefly consider Table 13.7, which compares the UK energy balance under the different scenarios and variants. Under the Growth and Supergrowth Scenarios – despite measures to conserve energy and maintain domestic production – there is still an energy gap which is bridged using imported fuels. As can be seen from the table, the cost of these imports is sometimes very large. For example, under the Growth Scenario (variant B) net fuel imports in 2025 are around £10 billion at 1980 prices, whilst under the Supergrowth Scenario (variant B) the figure is £12 billion. These are equivalent to 1.5 and 5.2% of GDP respectively. Under the Green Scenario the fuel deficit is, of course, much smaller. For example, under variant B of this scenario the value of net fuel imports in 2025 is £2.5 billion at 1980 prices, which is

Table 13.8. *UK balance of trade in non-manufactures (£billion at 1980 prices)*[a]

	Actual		Green Scenario		Growth Scenario		Supergrowth Scenario	
	1973	1983	2005	2025	2005	2025	2005	2025
Variant A								
Fuels			−4.0	−8.1	−8.2	−23.2	−9.8	−28.2
Non-government services[b]			3.0	2.9	2.7	4.7	2.5	1.6
Food, beverages and tobacco			−1.4	−1.7	−1.4	−1.7	−1.4	−1.7
Basic materials			−2.4	−2.5	−3.6	−5.7	−3.8	−7.1
Total			−4.8	−9.4	−10.5	−25.9	−12.5	−35.4
Variant B								
Fuels	−2.8	4.9	−1.4	−2.5	−3.6	−10.2	−4.5	−11.9
Non-government services[b]	2.7	2.8	4.3	6.1	4.4	7.6	3.4	5.2
Food, Beverages and tobacco	−5.8	−2.4	−1.2	−1.2	−1.2	−1.2	−1.2	−1.2
Basic materials	−3.7	−1.9	−2.0	−1.8	−3.0	−4.1	−3.2	−5.1
Total	−9.5	3.5	−0.3	−0.6	−3.4	−7.9	−5.5	−13.0
Variant C								
Fuels			0.8	1.3	−0.7	−2.9	−1.3	−2.9
Non-government services[b]			5.7	10.0	6.2	13.6	5.4	11.9
Food, beverages and tobacco			−1.0	−0.8	−1.0	−0.8	−1.0	−0.8
Basic materials			−1.7	−1.3	−2.5	−2.9	−2.7	−3.6
Total			3.8	9.2	2.0	7.0	0.4	4.6

Notes: [a] Current values divided by GDP deflator
[b] Includes private transfers

equivalent to 0.8% of GDP. As can also be seen from Table 13.7, these figures are subject to a considerable margin of error, and the situation could be either much worse or much better than they suggest.

We have spent so much time on the question of fuel because it is potentially such a crucial item in the non-manufacturing balance of payments. Let us now consider the remaining items in this balance.

Food, beverages and tobacco

As we have seen in Chapter 5, the output of food in the UK has risen strongly since the Second World War, whilst consumption has remained almost stable since the 1960s. If food production were to continue growing as it has in the past, the UK would become a net food exporter by the end of the century and there might be a trade surplus in food, beverages and tobacco as a whole. However, this is unlikely to occur in practice. The sustained growth in UK food production is partly a result of protectionism and government support for agriculture, both under the old deficiency payments system and, more recently, under the EEC Common Agriculture Policy. As the cost of protectionism mounts and its irrationalities become more obvious, public attitudes are beginning to change and it is only a matter of time before reforms are made. In the long

Table 13.9. *UK balance of trade in non-manufactures (% of GDP)*

	Actual		Green Scenario		Growth Scenario		Supergrowth Scenario	
	1973	1983	2005	2025	2005	2025	2005	2025
Variant A								
Fuels			−1.4	−2.7	−1.9	−3.1	−1.8	−2.8
Non-government services[a]			1.0	1.0	0.6	0.6	0.5	0.2
Food, beverages and tobacco			−0.5	−0.6	−0.3	−0.2	−0.3	−0.2
Basic materials			−0.8	−0.8	−0.8	−0.8	−0.7	−0.7
Total			−1.7	−3.1	−2.4	−3.4	−2.4	−3.5
Variant B								
Fuels	−1.3	2.1	−0.5	−0.8	−0.8	−1.3	−0.8	−1.2
Non-government services[a]	1.3	1.2	1.5	2.0	1.0	1.0	0.6	0.5
Food, beverages and tobacco	−2.7	−1.0	−0.4	−0.4	−0.3	−0.2	−0.2	−0.1
Basic materials	−1.7	−0.8	−0.7	−0.6	−0.7	−0.5	−0.6	−0.5
Total[b]	−4.4	1.5	−0.1	0.2	−0.8	−1.0	−1.0	−1.3
Variant C								
Fuels			0.3	0.4	−0.2	−0.4	−0.2	−0.3
Non-government services[a]			2.0	3.3	1.4	1.8	1.0	1.2
Food, beverages and tobacco			−0.3	−0.3	−0.2	−0.1	−0.2	−0.1
Basic materials			−0.6	−0.4	−0.6	−0.4	−0.5	−0.4
Total[b]			1.3	3.0	0.5	0.9	0.1	0.5

Notes: [a] Includes private transfers
[b] Rows may not add because of rounding errors

run, therefore, the degree of protectionism enjoyed by UK agriculture is likely to fall, and the result will be a slower growth in food production. In view of this, we assume the UK continues to have an overall deficit in food, beverages and tobacco over the period 1983–2025 (see Table 13.8).

Basic materials

The net cost of imported materials depends partly on their volume and partly on their price. At present, there is a global surplus of most materials and their prices are depressed. However, this is only a temporary phenomenon and material prices should recover at some time in the future. Under the most plausible B-variant of the scenarios, we make some allowance for higher materials prices but even so the net cost of imported materials continues to fall as a percentage of GDP under most variants (see Table 13.9).

Non-government services (including transfers)

Predicting what might happen to UK trade in services under the hypothetical scenarios is a hazardous business, and to obtain a clear picture of the future is difficult. The difficulties are partly inherent to the subject. Statistics are incomplete and unreliable, and certain internationally traded services, such as banking, are currently experiencing a profound transformation whose long-term consequences for the UK balance of payments are quite uncertain. They are also partly a result of the Cinderella nature of the subject. Few resources have been devoted to the study of UK trade in services, and there exists no comprehensive analysis of the kind which is readily available in the case of energy or manufactures.[17] To undertake such an analysis would be a major task in itself and is certainly well beyond the scope of the present work. All we can do here is provide a general indication of the orders of magnitude involved and make an educated guess as to what might happen to the major items in the service balance under the various hypothetical scenarios. With this observation in mind, let us consider Table 13.10 which shows how UK trade in services is assumed to behave under variant B of each scenario. The other variants will be considered later.

The first item in the table is sea transport. With the decline of the UK shipping fleet there is now a large deficit on this item, which under present government policies is likely to get much worse. However, under the hypothetical scenarios we assume a shift in government policy towards protectionism. Measures are taken to support the UK fleet against foreign competition and, as a result, the deficit in sea transport is held in check. The next item is travel. The underlying trends on this item are unfavourable to the UK. On the one hand, many of the historic tourist spots in the UK are approaching saturation, and the inward flow of tourist is unlikely to increase rapidly under any scenario. On the other hand, the potential for outward tourism for summer and winter holidays is virtually unlimited. The extent to which this potential will be realized depends, of course, on what happens to per capita incomes in the UK. Under the two growth scenarios, per capita incomes increase rapidly, and the result is a massive outflow from the UK and a large and growing deficit on the travel account. Under the Green Scenario, the UK is a much poorer country. Most of its citizens cannot afford frequent holidays abroad, and the deficit on the travel account is therefore relatively small.

The third item is civil aviation. The behaviour of this item is influenced by what happens on the travel account. Most of the payments and receipts which appear under the heading ‘civil aviation’ are associated with travel to and from the UK. *Ceteris paribus*, therefore, an increase in the number of UK residents travelling abroad by air will cause the civil aviation balance to deteriorate, whilst an increase in the number of foreign visitors arriving in the UK by air will have the opposite effect. This inter-relation between the travel and civil aviation accounts is reflected in the figures shown in Table 13.10. Under all scenarios we assume some autonomous increase in aviation earnings from cross-trades (i.e. from the transport of passengers and freight between one foreign country and another). However, under the Growth and Supergrowth Scenarios, this is more than offset by the increased aviation expenditures by UK residents travelling abroad.

At the present time, the two major net earners in the UK services account are 'financial services' and 'other services'. Moreover, the potential for growth in both of these items is considerable, although in each case there is a great deal of uncertainty about the future. In the case of financial services, for example, there are the effects of structural change and de-regulation to consider. In response to competition from abroad and new developments in international finance, the City of London has been forced to implement a series of wide-ranging reforms. Regulations governing both conditions of entry and methods of operation have been relaxed or scrapped altogether, whilst the barriers separating one kind of financial activity from another are being dismantled. The immediate results of these reforms are twofold. By relaxing the restrictions on entry, the reforms are making it easier for foreign firms to operate in the City of London; and by eliminating the barriers between one kind of financial activity and another, they are encouraging the formation of financial conglomerates which combine many different functions previously performed by specialist firms.[18] One of the aims of this so-called 'revolution' is to preserve the City's role as Europe's leading financial centre and to stave off competition from New York, Tokyo and other centres outside of Europe. How far this aim will be achieved is an open question. The City has certain obvious advantages: it is already a well-established financial centre; it is located in the time zone between America and Asia, and can therefore act as a bridge between these two areas; it is also in the same time zone as Western Europe; and the natives speak the global language, English. On the other hand, as telecommunications become more sophisticated, geographical location becomes less important and the reasons for concentrating operations in a particular centre, such as London, become less compelling. On balance, the positive factors are likely to predominate; the City should therefore remain an important financial centre and its earnings of foreign exchange should continue to rise. In Table 13.10 we assume that under the two growth scenarios, net earnings from the export of financial services rise at 2.5% a year in real terms over the period 1983–2025; this is somewhat faster than the rate actually observed over the period 1973–83. Under the Green Scenario, financial exports rise at 1.5% a year.[19]

The item 'other services' is a catch-all for many different activities. Over the decade 1973–83 net earnings from this source increased at around 3% a year in real terms. Under the two growth scenarios shown in Table 13.10 we assume that this rate of increase continues over the entire period 1983–2025, whilst under the Green Scenario the figure is 2% a year.[20] The final item to consider is private transfers. These are normally very small and we assume a deficit of £200 million a year on this item.

Table 13.10. *UK net service exports by category (Variant B)*[a]

	Actual		Green Scenario		Growth Scenario		Supergrowth Scenario	
	1973	1983	2005	2025	2005	2025	2005	2025
£billion at 1980 prices[b]								
Sea transport	−0.3	−0.9	−0.9	−0.9	−0.9	−0.9	−0.9	−0.9
Travel	0.1	−0.3	−0.4	−0.8	−1.2	−2.4	−1.6	−4.0
Civil aviation	0.2	0.3	0.4	0.4	0.0	−0.4	−0.4	−0.8
Financial services	1.7	2.2	3.0	4.1	3.8	6.2	3.8	6.2
Other non-government services	1.2	1.6	2.5	3.7	3.1	5.7	3.1	5.7
Private transfers	−0.2	−0.2	−0.3	−0.4	−0.4	−0.6	−0.6	−1.0
Total	2.7	2.8	4.3	6.1	4.4	7.6	3.4	5.2
Percentage of GDP								
Sea transport	−0.1	−0.4	−0.3	−0.3	−0.2	−0.1	−0.1	−0.1
Travel	0.1	−0.1	−0.1	−0.3	−0.3	−0.4	−0.3	−0.4
Civil aviation	0.0	0.1	0.1	0.1	0.0	−0.1	−0.1	−0.1
Financial services	0.8	0.9	1.0	1.4	0.9	0.9	0.7	0.6
Other non-government services	0.6	0.7	0.9	1.2	0.7	0.8	0.6	0.6
Private transfers	−0.1	−0.1	−0.1	−0.1	−0.1	−0.1	−0.1	−0.1
Total	1.3	1.2	1.5	2.1	1.0	1.1	0.7	0.5

Notes: [a] Net exports = exports − imports. Includes private transfers, but excludes government services (as defined in Appendix 6)
[b] Current values deflated by GDP deflator

Taking the service account as a whole, Table 13.10 indicates a large and growing surplus under all of the scenarios we consider. Under the Green Scenario, real net earnings from services in 2025 are twice their 1983 level and are equivalent to 2.0% of GDP. Under the remaining scenarios the surplus is similar in absolute terms, though considerably smaller as a percentage of GDP. For example, under the Growth Scenario the surplus is 1.1% of GDP, which is much the same as in 1983.

Remember, we are talking here about the plausible B-variant of each scenario. Table 13.9 shows what happens to the service balance under the other variants (see Appendix 14 for details of how these other variants are derived). As can be seen, there are large differences between one variant and another, and the gap between the extreme A and C variants is around 1% of GDP in 2025 under all scenarios.

Non-manufactures as a whole

The overall balance of trade in non-manufactures is shown in Tables 13.10 and 13.11. The main points to note are as follows. There is considerable uncertainty about the behaviour of non-manufacturing trade over the period 1983–2025. Comparing the extreme variants A and C, there is a difference in the overall balance on non-manufactures of between 4 and 6% of GDP in 2025, depending on the scenario concerned (see Fig. 13.3). Under all scenarios, trade in fuels

Table 13.11. *UK balance of payments, 1964–2025 (£billion at 1980 prices)* [a]

	Commercial balance			Balance on other items				
	NM	M	Sub-total	IPD	GE	CM	Sub-total	Grand total
Actual								
1964–68 av.	−9.6	8.8	−0.8	1.8	−1.7	−0.7	−0.8	0
1969–72 av.	−7.5	9.3	1.7	1.8	−1.4	−2.2	1.7	0
1973–76 av.	−11.8	6.7	−5.1	2.8	−1.6	3.9	5.1	0
1977–79 av.	−4.7	6.8	2.1	0.7	−2.4	−0.4	−2.1	0
1980–82 av.	1.4	4.4	5.8	0.6	−1.6	−4.8	−5.8	0
1983–84 av.	2.8	−1.9	0.9	2.0	−1.4	−1.5	−0.9	0
1985 prelim.	4.5	−2.3	2.2	2.4	−2.4[b]	−2.2	−2.2	0
Hypothetical Scenarios (Variant B)								
Green:								
2005	−0.3	0.3	0				0	0
2025	0.6	−0.6	0				0	0
Growth:					Not			
2005	−3.4	3.4	0		individually		0	0
2025	−7.9	7.9	0		specified		0	0
Supergrowth:								
2005	−5.5	5.5	0				0	0
2025	−13.0	13.0	0				0	0

Key: NM = non-manufactures (food, fuels, materials, non-government services and transfers);
M = manufactures;
IPD = interest, profits and dividends;
GE = government expenditure as defined in Appendix 4 (services and transfers);
CM = capital movements (overseas investment and official financing).
Notes: [a] Current values divided by GDP deflator
[b] Estimate

is the major source of uncertainty, which is not surprising as fuels are a large item in total domestic expenditure, and the net cost of imported fuels is extremely sensitive to variations in prices, production and consumption. Despite the uncertainty, several points are clear. The faster the growth rate of the economy, the more unfavourable is the balance of trade in non-manufactures. Faster growth means greater net imports of fuel and basic materials, without any compensating improvement in the remaining items. This is reflected in the behaviour of the non-manufacturing balance as one moves from slow to fast growth scenarios. Under the slow-growth, Green Scenario, there would be a fairly large surplus on services, which would probably be just about sufficient to finance the relatively small deficit in fuels, food and materials. Under the faster growth scenarios, however, the situation would be different. Net imports of fuels and basic materials would be much greater than under the Green Scenario, whilst net earnings from services would be much the same. As a result there would almost certainly be a deficit in non-manufacturing trade as a whole. The size of this deficit is difficult to predict with any accuracy, but the B-variants give some idea of its likely magnitude. They suggest that under the Growth Scenario there would be a deficit on non-manufacturing trade of around £3 billion (at 1980 prices) in 2005 and £18 billion in 2025, which are equivalent to 1.1 and 1.6% of GDP

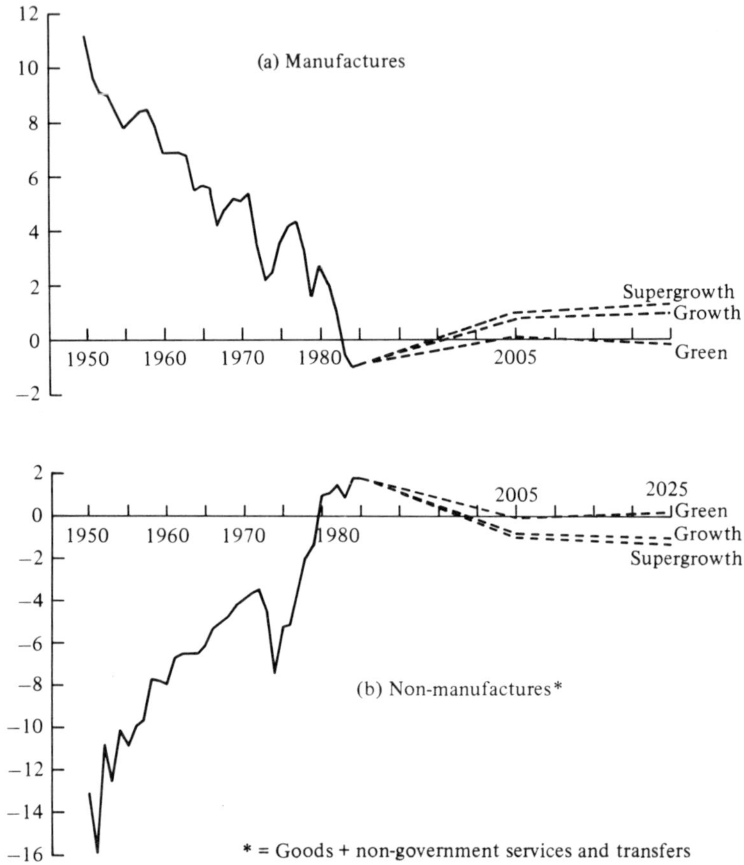

Fig. 13.3 UK balance of trade as a % of GDP (Variant B)
(a) Manufactures
(b) Non-manufactures

respectively. Under the Supergrowth Scenario, the likely deficit on non-manufacturing trade is much greater: £6 billion in 2005 and £13 billion in 2025, which are equivalent to around 1.4 and 1.8% of GDP respectively. Thus, if the B-variants are any guide, the UK would be just about in balance on her non-manufacturing trade under the Green Scenario, but have a large and increasing deficit under the Growth and Supergrowth Scenarios.

As already mentioned, the B-variants are based on plausible assumptions about future trade in non-manufactures. The effect of altering these assumptions can be gauged from Tables 13.9 and 13.10, which show what happens under the pessimistic A-variants and the optimistic C-variants. These other variants, it must be stressed, really are very extreme. Under the A-variants, for example, the UK performs badly in every single area: fuels, food, materials and services. Conversely, under the C-variants the UK performs comparatively well in all of these areas. Such extreme combinations are unlikely to occur in practice and a good performance in certain areas would probably be offset by a bad performance in others. For this reason, the overall balance of trade in non-manufactures is unlikely to be as favourable, or as unfavourable, as the extreme variants suggest, and the B-variants give a more realistic idea of how this overall balance might behave.

Trade in manufactures

It is often said that as North Sea oil runs out the UK will need to build up a surplus on her manufacturing trade so as to finance the resulting deficit. As it stands, this statement is incomplete, for it ignores the question of economic growth. With a slow rate of growth, as under the Green Scenario, net fuel imports would be relatively small, as would net imports of food and materials; earnings from services would probably cover the deficit on these items. A trade surplus on manufactures would not therefore be required. However, the situation would be different if the economy were to grow at a much faster rate, as assumed under the Growth and Supergrowth Scenarios. Under these conditions, import requirements would increase rapidly, and it is most unlikely that service income would be sufficient to finance anything like the entire cost of net imports of fuels, materials and food. As a result, by the turn of the century, there would almost certainly be a large and growing trade deficit in non-manufactures as a whole (i.e. fuels, materials, food, non-government services and transfers). To remain solvent the UK would require a large and growing trade surplus in manufactures. Thus, the need for a manufacturing surplus hinges crucially on the rate of economic growth. With slow economic growth, the UK could probably get by without such a surplus, but with fast economic growth a considerable manufacturing surplus would eventually be required.

To explore this question further, let us begin by examining the so-called commercial balance. This balance, it will be recalled, covers visible trade plus non-government services and transfers; it excludes property income from abroad (interest, profits and dividends), government expenditure overseas (services and transfers), and capital movements (investment and official financing). As we have already seen in Chapter 4, the commercial balance is *on average* fairly close to zero in most advanced capitalist countries, and the often large fluctuations from year to year more or less cancel out in the long run. By the same token, the balance on the remaining items is on average close to zero. Thus, over the long run, net property income from abroad is on average just about sufficient to finance government expenditure abroad and overseas investment. This is not an infallible rule, but it is generally true in advanced economies. It is certainly true in modern Britain, where the commercial balance has been subject to violent fluctuations in recent years, but shows no clearly defined long-term trend. Moreover, the mid-point of these fluctuations has been close to zero.[21]

In the light of the above observations, we shall make the following assumptions about foreign trade under the hypothetical scenarios. For simplicity, we shall ignore fluctuations and assume that the commercial balance is exactly zero in the two benchmark years, 2005 and 2025. This means, of course, that net income from abroad in the form of interest, profits and dividends is *exactly* offset by net government expenditure abroad and net capital movements. It also means that net manufacturing exports must be exactly sufficient to finance any deficit which exists in trade in non-manufactures. Conversely, if non-manufacturing trade is in surplus, any funds thereby generated will be used to finance an equivalent deficit in manufactures.

Table 13.11 shows what these assumptions imply in the case of variant B of the hypothetic scenarios (see also Fig. 13.3). This variant, it will be recalled, is the most plausible of the variants considered in the preceding section. Under the Green Scenario, trade in non-manufactures is just about in balance in the benchmark years 2005 and 2025. This situation arises because falling domestic oil production is partially offset by a combination of greater service earnings and economies in the use of energy. As a result, the UK does not require a surplus in manufactures under this scenario. Under the Growth Scenario, the picture is radically different. There is a large and growing deficit on non-manufactures due mainly to a rapid increase in the net cost of imported fuels. Service income is by no means sufficient to finance these imports, and to cover the gap a large and growing surplus on manufactures is required. The required surplus is around £3 billion in 2005 and £8 billion in 2025. In absolute terms, these are quite large figures, but since output is increasing rapidly under this scenario, they are rather small as a percentage of GDP (0.2 and 1.2% respectively). Finally, there is the Supergrowth Scenario to consider. This is merely a more extreme version of the Growth Scenario. In absolute terms, the deficit on non-manufactures is again quite large, and so too is the required surplus on manufactures: £6 billion in 2005 and £13 billion in 2025. However, because total output is so great, these figures are small as a percentage of GDP (1.0% and 1.3% respectively).

In arriving at the above estimates for the required balance on trade in manufactures, we have assumed that the commercial balance is zero. However, this assumption is not central to the argument, and the general picture would be much the same if this balance was in surplus or deficit to the tune of, say,

£1 or £2 billion. In particular, with fast economic growth, the UK would still require a large and growing surplus on her trade in manufactures. Just how the required surplus might be achieved in practice does not concern us here. Our aim is merely to identify the problem and give some broad indication of the orders of magnitude involved.

The role of manufacturing

We shall now consider what happens to the manufacturing sector under the hypothetical scenarios. This subject has many different facets, but we shall be mainly concerned with output and employment. We shall first estimate how much additional output is required in the manufacturing sector under each scenario, then we shall consider how much additional labour is required to produce this output. For simplicity, we shall examine only the plausible B-variant of each scenario. This is not a serious limitation, for the behaviour of output (and employment) is much the same under all variants.

Output

Under normal conditions, in the absence of either excess demand and supply, manufacturing output is given by the following equation:

Manufacturing output = home sales + exports. Mathematically this equation can be written:

$$Y_m = (D_m - M_m) + X_m$$

where Y_m is manufacturing output, D_m is the total domestic demand for manufactures of all kinds, irrespective of origins, and X_m and M_m are exports and imports of manufactured goods. The above equation can, in turn, be written

$$Y_m = D_m + \bar{X}_m$$

where $\bar{X}_m$ stands for *net* manufactured exports ($= X_m - M_m$). Taking first differences, we get an equation which can be used to estimate what happens to manufacturing output:

$$\Delta Y_m = \Delta D_m + \Delta \bar{X}_m$$

which, in words, can be expressed as follows:

required increase in output of manufactures	=	increase in domestic demand for manufactures (irrespective of origin)	+	increase in net exports of manufactures

To make use of this equation for the UK we shall assume that:

(1) The domestic demand for manufactures (measured at constant prices) rises exactly in step with GDP. Thus, for each 1% rise in GDP, the domestic demand for manufactures increases by 1%. This assumption is in accordance with long-term projections for the UK using the Cambridge Growth Model.[22] It is also in accordance with long-term projections for the US economy.[23]

(2) Net manufactured exports behave as in the preceding section. We are concerned only with the B-variant of each scenario, for which the relevant figures are given in Table 13.11.

Table 13.12 shows what the above assumptions imply for manufacturing output. As might be expected there is very little growth in manufacturing output under the Green Scenario: 1.2% a year over the period 1985–2005 and 0.1% thereafter. Under the remaining scenarios, however, the picture is quite different. For example, under the Growth Scenario manufacturing output must grow at 3.3% a year over the period 1985–2005 and at 2.3% a year in the following period 2005–25. Cumulatively, those growth rates imply an increase in manufacturing output of around 90% during the first period and a further 60% in the second period (see Fig. 13.4). Under the Supergrowth Scenario, the corresponding figures are 140% and 90% respectively. These figures indicate clearly the central importance of manufacturing industry under the two growth scenarios. If fast growth in GDP is the objective, there must of necessity be a very large increase in manufacturing output. Conversely, if growth in GDP is not the objective, the UK can manage with only a modest increase in manufacturing output.

It is interesting to note that under all scenarios, even the Green Scenario, manufacturing output grows faster than GDP. This discrepancy is explained by the need to increase net manufactured exports. Under all scenarios net manufactured exports increase, both absolutely and as a percentage of GDP, and to produce these additional net exports requires an above-average growth of output in the manufacturing sector.

In the opening part of this section, we explained how the required increase in manufacturing output ΔY_m can be divided into two components ΔD_m and $\Delta \bar{X}_m$; the former corresponds to the increase in domestic demand for manufactures which accompanies economic growth, and the latter to the increase in net manufactured exports (which are required mainly to compensate for the loss of North Sea oil and gas revenue).[24] The relative importance of these factors can be gauged by looking at the ratios $\Delta D_m/\Delta Y_m$ and $\Delta \bar{X}_m/\Delta Y_m$. These are shown in Table 13.13 for the two growth scenarios. Under both scenarios, $\Delta \bar{X}_m/\Delta Y_m$ is positive, indicating that part of the additional manufacturing

Table 13.12. *Growth rates by sector, 1950–2025 (% per annum)*[a]

	Manu-facturing	Non-manu-facturing	Whole economy
		Output	
Actual			
1950–73	3.0	2.5	2.7
1973–85	−0.8	2.0	1.2
Hypothetical[b]			
Green Scenario:			
1985–2005	1.2	1.0	1.0
2005–2025	0.1	0.2	0.2
Growth Scenario:			
1985–2005	3.3	2.9	3.0
2005–2025	2.3	2.2	2.2
Supergrowth Scenario:			
1985–2005	4.4	3.9	4.0
2005–2025	3.3	3.1	3.2
		Employment	
Actual			
1950–73	0.2	0.7	0.5
1973–85	−2.9	0.7	−0.3
Hypothetical[b]			
Green Scenario:			
1985–2005	0.7	1.0	1.0
2005–2025	−0.4	0.3	0.2
Growth Scenario:			
1985–2005	0.4	1.1	1.0
2005–2025	−0.6	0.4	0.2
Supergrowth Scenario:			
1985–2005	−0.2	1.3	1.0
2005–2025	−1.3	0.5	0.2
		Output per worker	
Actual			
1950–73	2.9	1.8	2.2
1973–85	2.1	1.3	1.5
Hypothetical[b]			
Green Scenario:			
1985–2005	0.5	−0.1	0.0
2005–2025	0.5	−0.1	0.0
Growth Scenario:			
1985–2005	2.9	1.8	2.0
2005–2025	2.9	1.8	2.0
Supergrowth Scenario:			
1985–2005	4.6	2.6	3.0
2005–2025	4.6	2.6	3.0

Notes: [a] All growth rates are exponential. Columns may not add because of rounding errors
[b] Hypotheticals refer to the B-variant of each scenario

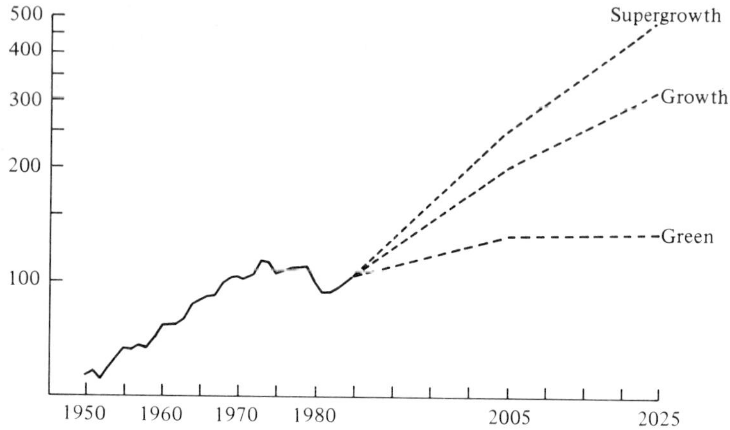

Fig. 13.4 Manufacturing output, 1950–2025 (Variant B) (1980 = 100)

Table 13.13. *Net exports and the structure of demand for manufactures, 1985–2025*

	$\frac{\Delta D_m}{\Delta Y_m}$	$\frac{\Delta \bar{X}_m}{\Delta Y_m}$	Total
Growth Scenario[a]			
1985–2005	0.95	0.05	1.00
2005–2025	0.97	0.03	1.00
Supergrowth Scenario[a]			
1985–2005	0.96	0.04	1.00
2005–2025	0.95	0.05	1.00

Note: [a] Variant B

output must be exported to compensate for the loss of North Sea oil and gas revenue.

However, this part is relatively small and in no case does $\Delta\bar{X}_m/\Delta Y_m$ exceed 5%. At least 15% of the additional manufacturing output is required simply to satisfy the increased domestic demand for manufactured goods resulting from economic growth. This extra demand may be satisfied directly by supplying UK manufactured goods or indirectly by exporting UK manufactures in return for imported manufactures. Either way, there must be a large increase in UK production of manufactures. This would still be true even if North Sea revenues were to continue undiminished at their present rate. The point is that rapid economic growth is accompanied by a greatly increased demand for manufactured goods, and this is the main reason why such a large increase in manufacturing output is required under the growth scenarios.

Employment

Given the behaviour of output just described, the pattern of employment is determined by what happens to labour productivity in each sector. We shall make the following assumptions:

(1) labour productivity in the manufacturing sector rises faster than in the non-manufacturing sector as a whole;
(2) the faster the economy expands the greater is this difference in productivity growth.

These assumptions are in accordance with historical evidence, some of which was reviewed in Chapter 1. They are also in accordance with long-term projections for the UK and other countries.[25] The exact figures assumed for productivity growth under each scenario are given in Table 13.12. These figures show what happens to output per worker in each sector over the period 1985–2025. They are, it must be stressed, purely illustrative. Under the Green Scenario, output per worker now rises quite fast in the manufacturing sector, but this is offset by a rapid fall in hours per worker. As a result, output per worker rises by only 0.5% a year in this sector. In the rest of the economy, taken as a whole, there is a gradual fall in output per worker under the Green Scenario. At first sight, this may seem odd, but the explanation is straightforward. Output per worker-hour rises in the non-manufacturing sector, but hours of work fall even more rapidly; hence a fall in output per worker. Under the Growth and Supergrowth Scenario output per worker rises rapidly throughout the economy, although the increase is much greater in manufacturing than elsewhere. During the period 1985–2025 as a whole, under the Growth Scenario, output per worker rises by 220% in the manufacturing sector and by 105% in the non-manufacturing sector. Under the Supergrowth Scenario, the figures are 530% and 180% respectively.

Table 13.14 shows what our productivity assumptions imply for employment in each sector. This latter differential in productivity growth may appear unrealistic. However, it must be remembered that a considerable part of non-manufacturing employment is located in community and personal services, where measured productivity growth is extremely low. In some cases, this apparently slow growth is genuine; in others it is a statistical artefact created by accounting conventions. Either way, it holds down measured productivity in the non-manufacturing sector *as a whole*, and prevents this sector from exhibiting the kind of spectacular increase in overall productivity which occurs in manufacturing industry under the Supergrowth Scenario. Certain individual subsectors, such as finance or telecommunications, might well experience a spectacular growth rate in labour productivity, but the average growth rate for the non-manufacturing sector as a whole would be dragged down by the performance, as conventionally measured,

Table 13.14. *Employment by sector, 1950–2005 (millions)*

	Manu-facturing	Non-manu-facturing	Total	Share of manu-facturing (%)
Actual				
1950	7.7	14.3	22.0	34.8
1973	8.0	16.7	24.7	32.3
1985	5.7	18.2	23.9	23.7
Hypothetical				
Green Scenario:				
2005	6.5	22.5	29.0	22.5
2025	6.1	23.8	29.9	20.2
Growth Scenario:				
2005	6.1	22.9	29.0	21.1
2025	5.5	24.4	29.9	18.2
Supergrowth Scenario:				
2005	5.4	23.6	29.0	18.7
2025	4.2	25.7	29.9	13.8

of less dynamic sectors like community and personal services. It is for this reason that we assume such a massive differential in productivity growth between manufacturing and non-manufacturing under the Supergrowth Scenario.

Let us begin by considering the Green Scenario. Under this scenario there is a gradual fall in the share of manufacturing in total employment from 23.7% in 1985 to 22.5% in 2005 and 20.2% in 2025. In the first period, up to 2005, the gradual fall in the share of manufacturing is accompanied by a fairly rapid growth in total employment. As a result, there is an increase in the absolute number of people employed in the manufacturing sector. However, the situation is different after 2005. Total employment is almost stationary from then onwards, and the falling share of manufacturing leads to an absolute decline in the number of people employed in this sector, thereby reversing much of the increase in the preceding period. Over the period 1985–2025, as a whole, less than 0.5 million extra manufacturing jobs are created under the Green Scenario. On the other hand, an additional 5.5 million jobs are created elsewhere in the country, mainly in service activities. This shift in employment structure is the result of differential productivity growth. As we have seen, output per worker in the manufacturing sector grows by 0.5% a year, whilst in the non-manufacturing sector it falls by 0.1% a year. This differential may not appear very large, but its cumulative impact is considerable. It accounts for the entire shift in employment structure which occurs under the Green Scenario, and explains why the bulk of additional jobs created under this scenario are located in service activities. As we shall see, the same is also true under the remaining scenarios.

Under the remaining scenarios, there is a rapid increase in manufacturing output over the period 2005. However, this is accompanied by a massive increase in labour productivity, so employment in the manufacturing sector does not alter very much in this period. After 2005, output growth slows down, but productivity continues to increase at a very high rate in the manufacturing sector. As a result, employment in this sector starts to fall, and by 2025 fewer people are employed in manufacturing than was originally the case in 1985. The situation is quite different in the non-manufacturing sector, where labour productivity rises more slowly than output and the result is a large increase in employment. By 2025 some 24–26 million people are employed in this sector as compared to 18 million in 1985. Thus, under the Growth and Supergrowth Scenarios, the manufacturing sector plays a crucial role as a provider of material goods, producing the rapidly growing output required for both home consumption and export. However, over the long run, this sector does not directly provide any additional jobs. It is the non-manufacturing activities, mainly services, but also construction, which provide the extra jobs required to achieve our employment target.

One further point should be noted concerning employment. Under all scenarios – Green, Growth and Supergrowth – the share of manufacturing in total employment falls throughout the entire period 1985–2025. This represents a continuation of trends already well established in the UK economy period to 1985 (see Fig. 13.5c). However, the pace of decline is slower than it has been in recent years. Moreover, total employment is growing, which also helps to slow down the fall in manufacturing employment. Depending on the Scenario concerned, by 2025 the number of people working in the manufacturing sector is between 4.2 and 6.1 million in 2025, as compared to 5.7 million in 1985. Thus, although manufacturing provides few, if any, additional jobs, it remains a significant source of employment throughout the entire period. These figures are, of course, purely hypothetical and are based on the assumption that total employment grows at the rate we assume (0.6% p.a. over the period 1985–2005). Even so, they should help to counter some of the more fanciful notions concerning the future of manufacturing employment and its alleged demise as Britain enters the so-called 'post-industrial' society. Although the share of the manufacturing sector in total employment is falling, this sector will continue to remain a major, though perhaps declining, source of employment for the foreseeable future. This will be true almost no matter what happens to the UK economy.

Economic structure

To round off the discussion let us examine what happens to the structure of the economy under the hypothetical scenarios. We shall consider only the central

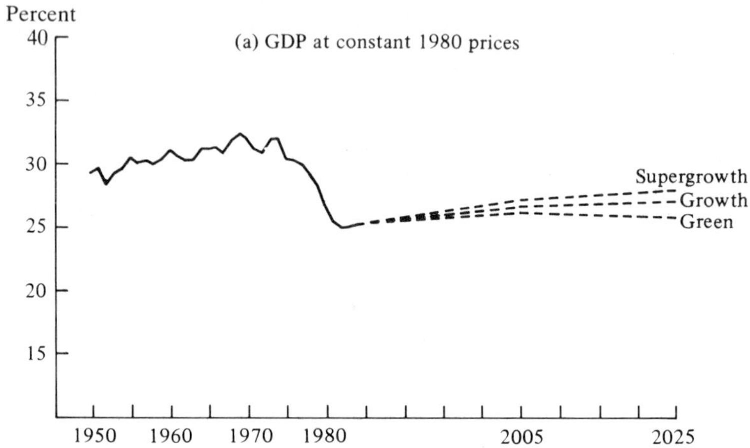

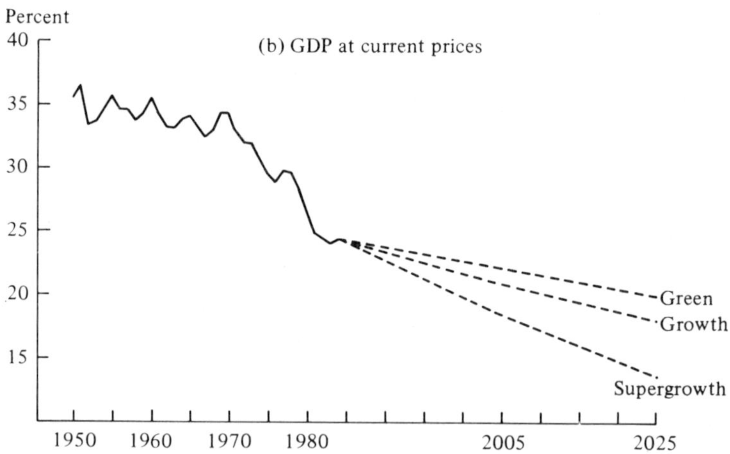

B-variant of each scenario. As indicators of economic structure we shall use the following measures:

(1) the share of manufacturing in GDP measured at constant 1980 prices;
(2) the share of manufacturing in GDP measured at current prices;
(3) the share of manufacturing in total employment.

The behaviour of these shares under the various scenarios is shown in Fig. 13.5a–c. The diagrams also give information for the historical period 1950–85.

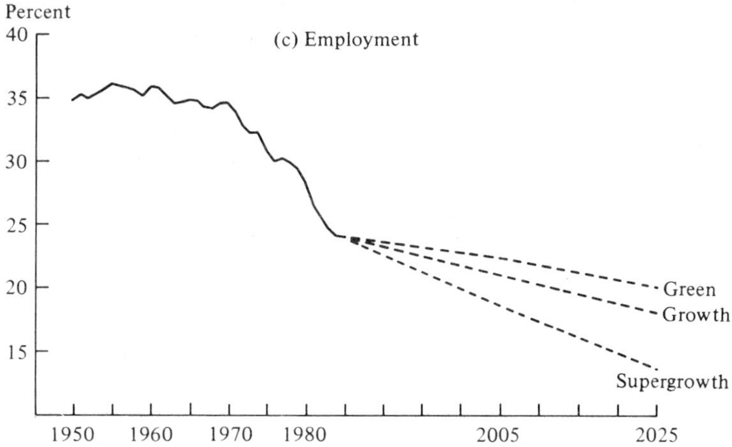

Fig. 13.5 Share of manufacturing, 1950–2025 (Variant B)
(a) GDP at constant 1980 prices
(b) GDP at current prices
(c) Employment

Looking at these diagrams, we see a clear difference in behaviour between the constant price share and the other two shares. Measured at constant prices, the share of manufacturing in GDP remains remarkably constant over the period 1950–2025. It declines somewhat in the subperiod 1974–85, but then partially recovers after 1985. By 2025 this share is almost back again to its original level in 1950. Over the long term, therefore, the general picture is one of stability in the structure of real output.

Looking at the other measures of economic structure the picture is quite different. In the case of both employment and current price output, the share of manufacturing declines almost continuously from 1950 right through to 2025. From a peak of around 36% in the early 1950s, the share of manufacturing in GDP at current prices falls to between 14 and 20% by 2025, depending on the scenario concerned. A similar fall occurs in the share of this sector in total employment. The explanation for the decline is, of course, the same in both cases: differential productivity growth. Over the entire period 1950–2025, labour productivity rises faster in manufacturing than non-manufacturing, sometimes by a considerable margin. This reduces the relative labour requirements of the manufacturing sector, causing the share of this sector in total employment to fall. Moreover, the relatively fast growth of productivity in the manufacturing sector leads to a virtually continuous fall in the relative price of manufactures, thereby forcing down the share of this sector in GDP measured at current prices. Thus, in each case – employment and current price output – the falling share of manufacturing is merely a reflection of differential productivity growth, of the especially fast growth of productivity in the manufacturing sector as compared to the rest of the economy.

When discussing structural change it is a common practice to look only at employment or current price output shares, whilst ignoring constant price shares. In the present context this would be serious mistake. It would give the impression that manufacturing industry is of declining importance under the hypothetical scenario, and create the illusion that a rapid growth in GDP could be achieved without a commensurate rise in manufacturing output. Nothing could be further from the truth. Under all scenarios, the manufacturing sector remains of central importance as a supplier both of goods to the home market and exports to foreign markets. Under all scenarios, manufacturing output rises as least as fast as GDP, and often faster. Indeed, without a huge expansion in the output of manufactured goods, it is quite inconceivable that GDP could increase at the rates envisaged under the two growth scenarios. There is an interesting paradox here. The more dynamic is the manufacturing sector, the faster does the output of this sector increase. Yet, because of differential productivity growth, the more rapid is the fall in manufacturing's share of employment and current price output. It is because of this inverse relationship that employment and current price shares give such a misleading picture of the role of manufacturing industry. Looking at Fig. 13.5b–c, it would seem that manufacturing industry is of least importance under the Supergrowth Scenario and of most importance under the Green Scenario, whereas the truth is just the opposite.

Concluding remarks

In the present chapter we have considered how the UK could return to something like full employment in the coming decades. Amongst the questions discussed were: how many extra jobs would be required to achieve full employment? How much economic growth would be needed to generate these extra jobs? What would be the balance of payments implications of a return to full employment? And what would be the role of the manufacturing sector in all of this? Our main conclusions are as follows.

To reach something like full employment by the year 2005 would require the creation of perhaps 5 million extra jobs over the period 1985–2005. Having achieved this objective, to maintain full employment in the future a further 1 million extra jobs might be required over the period 2005–2025. These estimates include a generous allowance for increased labour force participation and international migration. The amount and kind of economic growth needed to achieve these employment targets would depend on what happened to material living standards. If the material consumption of those already in employment could be frozen indefinitely, these targets could be achieved with only a modest rise in both manufacturing output and GDP as a whole. Under the Green Scenario, for example, virtually full employment could be achieved by the year 2005 with a GDP growth of only 1% per annum combined with a slightly faster growth in manufacturing output. Under this scenario, labour-saving technology would be introduced only gradually and would be used primarily to reduce working time rather than to increase real incomes. There would be some economic growth, but the additional output would be used mainly to help those who are currently poor and/or out of work. For the majority of people already in employment, there would be little or no increase in real take-home pay, and the benefits of this scenario come mainly in the form of reduced working time and improved public services.

From a theoretical point of view, the Green Scenario is perfectly feasible and has much to recommend it. It is certainly preferable to what has been happening in recent years. During the 1980s, slow economic growth in the UK has been accompanied by increasing inequality not just between social classes, but within the working class itself. Millions of people, mainly employed in the private sector, have enjoyed rising material living standards during this period, whilst millions of others have suffered increasing poverty and social deprivation because of unemployment, reduced welfare benefits and deteriorating public services. As a result, the costs of slow economic growth have been borne almost entirely by an unfortunate minority, whilst the majority have been largely insulated from its effects. Under the Green Scenario, this injustice would be remedied. Both income and work would be shared out more widely, and the costs of slow economic growth would be distributed in a more egalitarian fashion. Quite apart from this obvious virtue, the Green Scenario has other attractions. It challenges the conventional wisdom of economists that the only route to human happiness is through the indefinite increase of material wealth. On any rational calculation, the UK already has sufficient material wealth to enable all of its citizens to live in reasonable comfort. However, this wealth is either maldistributed or is of a socially irrational kind, e.g. private cars instead of public transport. Although not rejecting growth entirely, the Green Scenario is just as concerned to remedy these defects as to increase the amount of wealth available. Many economists would consider this to be a defect of the Green Scenario. We consider it to be a virtue.

Another advantage of this scenario is its economy in the use of energy. Under the fast growth scenarios, rapid growth in GDP leads to an increased energy consumption despite attempts to conserve energy. To meet this increasing need for energy, the UK must either resort to nuclear power, with all of its dangers, or else must use an increasing amount of potentially scarce fossil fuels. Under the Green Scenario, however, total energy requirements fall quite rapidly, nuclear power is phased out and UK consumption of fossil fuels declines. From the point of view of environmental safety, the Green Scenario is clearly superior to the faster growth scenario. Moreover, by reducing UK consumption of fossil fuels, it leaves more of these fuels available for developing countries whose requirements must inevitably increase as they industrialize in the coming decades.

Having said this, however, we must admit that, given present attitudes and aspirations, the Green Scenario is politically impractical. Although many people already in employment might be willing to accept a few years of material austerity as the price of full employment and social justice, few would be willing to accept an indefinite freeze in their material consumption. Sooner or later they would expect material consumption to increase, and to provide for such an increase – whilst at the same time creating new jobs – would require a much faster rate of economic growth than is envisaged under the Green Scenario.

Just how fast is difficult to say, but something like the rate envisaged under our Growth Scenario might be required. Under this scenario, it will be recalled, GDP rises at 3% a year during the period 1985–2005, and by just over 2% a year thereafter. With this kind of economic growth, the achievement of full employment could be combined with a large rise in material consumption for the average person already in employment. In the short run, some degree of real income restraint would be needed to release the resources required for investment, emergency job creation and to remedy the anomalies and injustices which have arisen during the Thatcher era. However, over the long run, there could be a substantial rise in material consumption for the average person. To achieve the rate of GDP growth envisaged under the Growth Scenario would require a massive increase in the output of manufactured goods. The reason for this is as follows. With such a rapid growth in GDP, there would be a massive increase in the demand for manufactured goods both for personal consumption and for use in production. In theory, these manufactured goods could be imported from other countries and their purchase financed through the export of services. The UK would then become like the Canary Islands or Bermuda, which produces virtually no manufactured goods of their own, but export services in return for imported manufactures. In reality, of course, such a path would be quite impractical for the UK. Whilst it may be feasible for a small holiday or tax-haven economy to live almost entirely on services, this is quite impossible for a large economy like the UK. The potential for service exports on the required scale does not exist. It is true that net service exports from the UK are likely to increase in the coming decades. However, as we have seen, even under a fairly optimistic assumption, the additional revenue from this source will be more than offset by the loss of revenue caused by falling oil and gas production in the North Sea. When the loss of oil and gas revenue is taken into account, there would be no service revenue left over to finance additional net imports of foreign manufactures. (On the contrary, net imports of manufactures will have to be reduced, either by exporting more or importing less.) Thus, any increase in the UK demand for manufactures in the future must be accompanied by an even greater rise in the domestic production of manufactures. Some of these manufactures may be used to supply the UK market directly, others may be expected to pay for manufactured imports. Either way, domestic production of manufactures must increase even faster than domestic demand. Given this fact, it is clear why GDP growth at the rate envisaged under the Growth Scenario would require such a large increase in manufacturing production. Only in this way would the massive increase in demand for manufactures which occurs under this scenario be satisfied, whilst at the same time preserving balance of payments equilibrium. Some of the increased production of manufactures would be used to supply domestic consumers, some would be used to pay for imported manufactures, and some would be used, along with increased service exports, to make up for the loss of North Sea oil and gas.

To achieve such a massive increase in manufacturing output would not be easy. During the Thatcher era a great deal of production capacity has been scrapped and there has been relatively little investment in new plant and equipment. As a result, manufacturing industry is now operating fairly close to full capacity and there is limited potential for a rapid Keynesian style of reflation. Any major increase in manufacturing output would require an ambitious programme of capacity creating investment, which in turn would require the diversion of scarce resources from other potential uses, such as private or public consumption, or investment in housing, hospitals and the like. The organizational and political obstacles to such a transfer of resources are formidable, though not insuperable. For the transfer to be feasible, there would have to be both a widespread understanding of the need for a large-scale investment programme and a willingness to accept the sacrifices involved in such a programme. There would also have to be some kind of planning mechanism – or at least an 'industrial policy' – to identify what kind of investment was required and to ensure that this investment actually took place. At the present time, these conditions are not satisfied. Whilst there is some popular awareness of the need for a large-scale investment programme there is, as yet, little awareness of the real cost of such a programme and the immediate benefits which must be foregone in order to make it possible. Moreover, on the organizational side, there exists nothing which remotely resembles a coherent planning mechanism for identifying investment requirements and implementing a large-scale investment programme in the UK. Indeed, there is considerable opposition in business circles to the very idea of coherent planning and to set up such a mechanism business opposition would have to be either placated or overcome.

These are some of the internal obstacles to rapid and sustained economic growth. There are also external obstacles. The UK now operates in a far more hostile world environment than was the case twenty or thirty years ago. Its economy is now far more integrated with the world economy than it used to be, the country faces formidable competition from overseas and it no longer has even a vestigial empire to fall back on. All of these conditions make the achievement of rapid economic growth more difficult than it used to be. To achieve rapid economic growth under present conditions, the UK requires a dynamic and modern manufacturing industry, producing the right goods, of the right quality and the right price, to compete with powerful foreign rivals in both home and overseas market. It is not simply a matter of investing in new capacity and producing additional goods. These goods must also be sold. Import controls are sometimes advocated as a way of dealing with this challenge. Such controls, it is said, would reduce the extent of foreign competition in the home market and make it easier for domestic producers to expand; they would also influence the sourcing policies of multinationals and persuade these firms to rely more on local production, instead of imports, to serve the UK market. All of this is true and there is certainly a case for the use of import controls as part of a strategy for rapid economic growth. However, the potential benefit of such controls should not be exaggerated. The scope for using them is limited by the dangers of retaliation, especially from Western Europe, and they do nothing to ease the problems of competition in foreign markets. Even with import controls, the international environment would still impose severe constraints on the UK, and to achieve rapid growth the country would still require a dynamic and competitive manufacturing industry.

The foregoing argument can be summarized as follows. If material consumption of those already in employment could be frozen indefinitely, full employment could be achieved with no improvement at all in Britain's relative economic performance. Only a modest rise in GDP and manufacturing output would be required. However, if the achievement of full employment is to be combined with an eventual increase in material consumption – as most people desire – a definite improvement in Britain's long-term economic performance is required. They key to such an improvement lies in manufacturing industry. Services can make a useful contribution, but rapid and sustained economic growth is impossible without a massive increase in manufacturing output. This in turn requires a large-scale programme of capacity – creating investment within the framework of a coherent industrial policy, whose aim is to create a dynamic and competitive manufacturing sector. If rapid and sustained economic growth is the aim, the expansion and modernization of the manufacturing sector must take priority over other desirable, but less fundamental, objectives.

Appendix 1

Fig. A1.1 Percentage shares of employment by sector in various countries 1846–1982

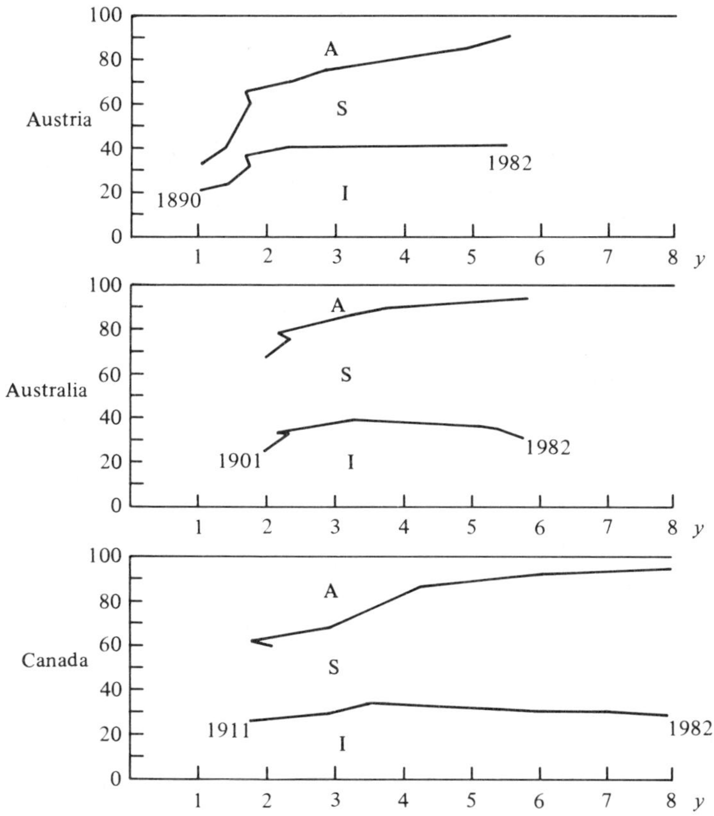

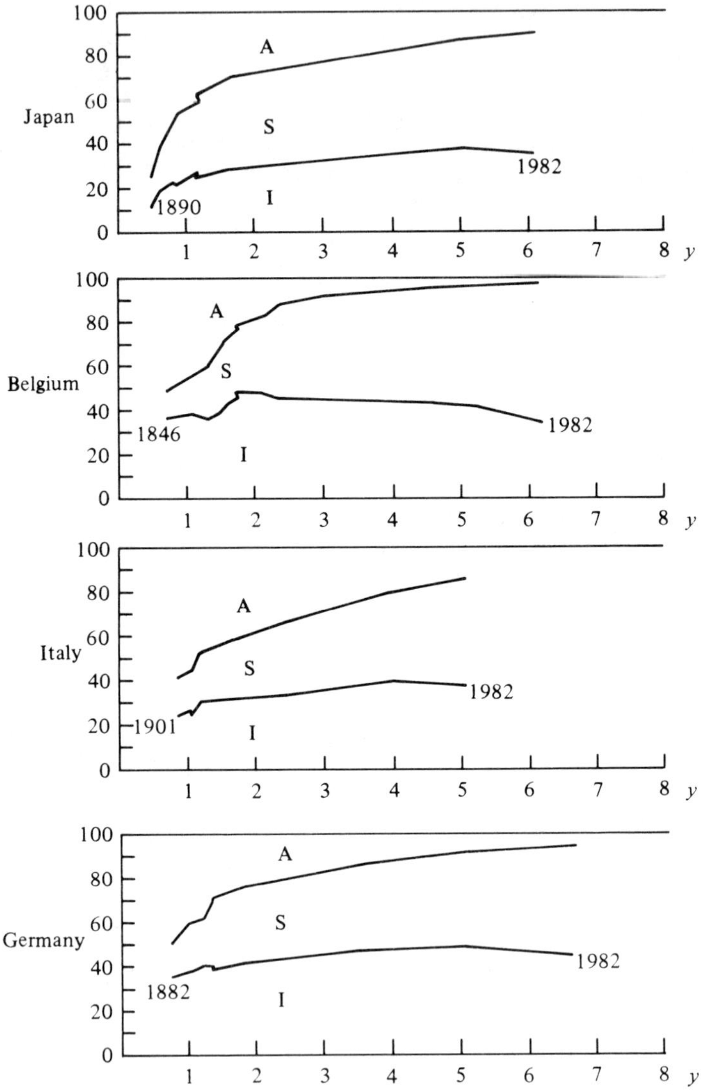
Japan
A
S
I
1890
1982
Belgium
A
S
I
1846
1982
Italy
A
S
I
1901
1982
Germany
A
S
I
1882
1982
100
80
60
40
20
0
1
2
3
4
5
6
7
8
y

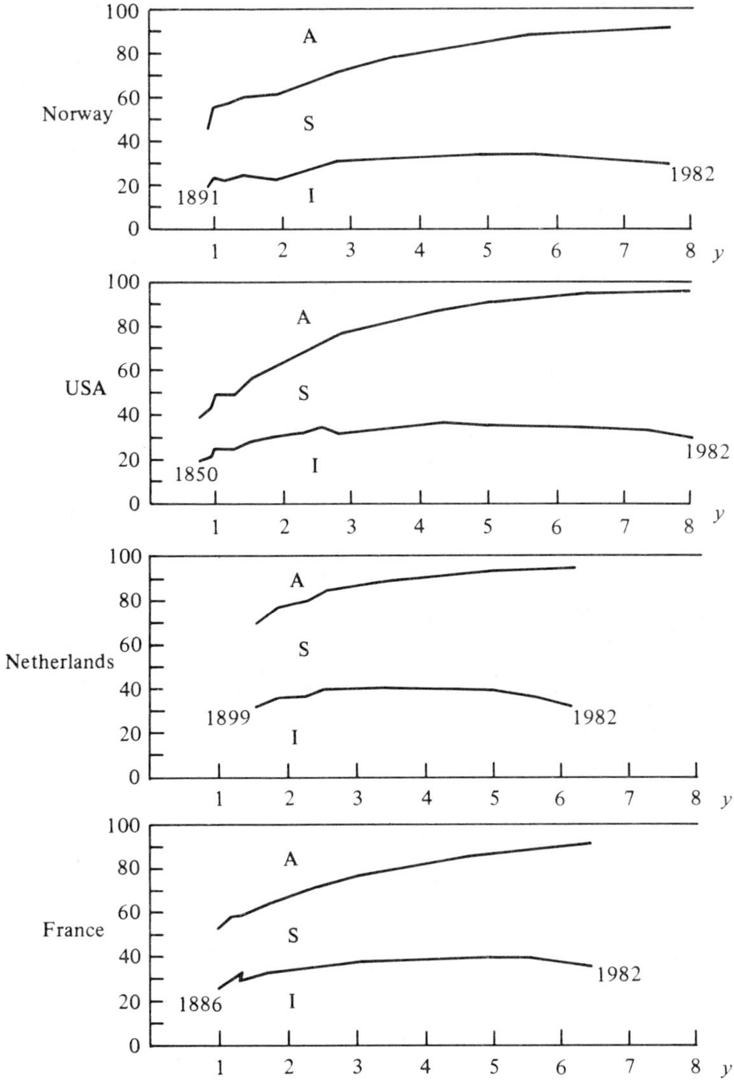
Norway
100
80
60
40
20
0
A
S
I
1891
1982
1 2 3 4 5 6 7 8 y
USA
1850
1982
Netherlands
1899
1982
France
1886
1982

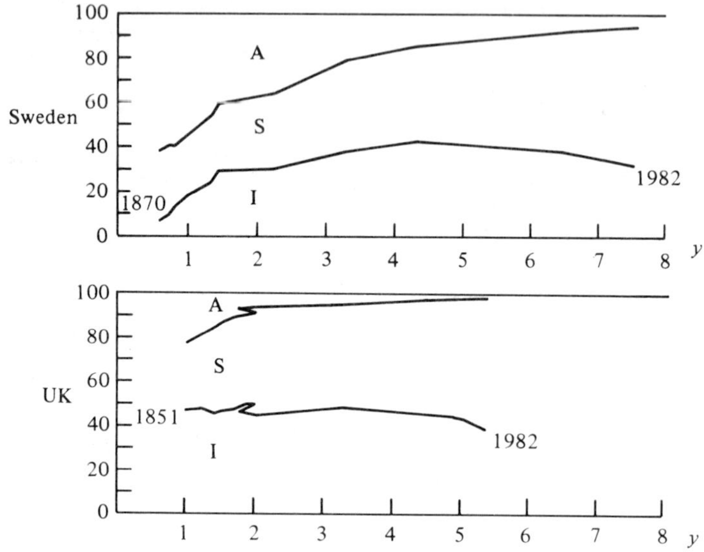

Notes:

A = Share of employment in agriculture, forestry and fishing.

I = Share of employment in industry (mining, manufacturing, construction, public utilities).

S = Share of employment in services (i.e. all other activities).

Y = Per capita income in thousands of 1975 US dollars evaluated at purchasing power parity exchange rates.

Appendix 2

The simple mathematics of structural change

This appendix presents a simple mathematical model which embodies the main features of structural change in all but the most stagnant of economies.[1] It is based on the following propositions which, although not universally true, capture the essence of economic development:

(1) The demand for food is income-inelastic (Engel's Law);
(2) the real demand for services rises roughly in line with real national income;
(3) labour productivity rises more slowly in the service sector than elsewhere in the economy. Moreover, this lag in performance is greatest in the most dynamic economies.

The model shows how these propositions are sufficient to explain both the rising importance of industrial employment during the early phase of economic development and the eventual transition to a 'service' economy in which industrial employment is of declining importance. The model also reveals why in dynamic 'late-comers', such as Japan, industrial employment never achieves the same importance as it has done in their less dynamic forerunners, such as Belgium or the UK. This is explained by the highly uneven character of development in 'late-comers', where productivity rises much faster in manufacturing industry than in the services.

The model

Let us make the following assumptions. The economy is closed and total output in real terms is given by:

$$Z = Z_a + Z_i + Z_s \qquad (1)$$

where Z_a, Z_i and Z_s stand for output in agriculture, industry and the service sector respectively. Assume that food consumption per head of population remains constant through time. Since the economy is closed this implies that

$$Z_a = dN \tag{2}$$

where N is total population and d is a constant. Assume that the proportion for the population in employment remains constant through time. Then,

$$L = fN \tag{3}$$

where L is total employment and f is a constant. From (2) and (3) it follows that:

$$Z_a = bL \tag{4}$$

where $b = d/f$.

Suppose the real output of services is a constant fraction c of total output. Then

$$Z_s = cZ \tag{5}$$

From the above equations, it follows immediately that

$$Z_i = (1 - c)Z - bL \tag{6}$$

Labour productivity

Except in very poor or stagnant economies, the growth of labour productivity is normally uneven, rising more slowly in services than in agriculture or industry. For convenience, we assume that labour productivity grows at the same rate in agriculture as in industry. Although not strictly necessary, this assumption greatly simplifies the analysis without significantly altering the conclusions. Assume also that productivity growth rates remain constant through time, and that units of measurement are chosen so that output per worker is the same in each sector of the economy at time zero. With these assumptions we can write:

$$\begin{aligned} y_s &= y^0 e^{\alpha t} \\ y_i &= y^0 e^{\lambda \alpha t} \\ y_a &= y^0 e^{\lambda \alpha t} \end{aligned} \tag{7}$$

where y_s, y_i and y_a stand for output per worker in the services, industry and agriculture respectively, and $\lambda > 1$, $y^0 > 0$ and $\alpha > 0$ are constants. Note that the parameter λ can be interpreted as an index of uneven development, whose main function is to indicate how much faster productivity grows in industry than in the services. In the present model, λ also indicates something about productivity growth in agriculture, but this is really an accident which derives from our simplifying assumptions. In what follows, this parameter should be interpreted mainly as an index of uneven development between industry and the services.

By definition, output per worker in each sector is equal to:

$$y_s = \frac{Z_s}{L_s}$$

$$y_i = \frac{Z_i}{L_i}$$

$$y_a = \frac{Z_a}{L_a} \tag{8}$$

where the Ls denote employment in the sector concerned. Total employment is given by

$$L = L_s + L_i + L_a \tag{9}$$

which from (8) can be written:

$$L = \frac{Z_s}{y_s} + \frac{Z_i}{y_i} + \frac{Z_a}{y_a}$$

From (7) it follows that

$$L = \frac{1}{y^0}(Z_s e^{-\alpha t} + Z_i e^{-\lambda \alpha t} + Z_a e^{-\lambda \alpha t}) \tag{10}$$

Using (4), (5) and (6), we find that

$$L = \frac{1}{y^0}\{cZe^{-\alpha t} + [(1-c)Z - bL]e^{-\lambda \alpha t} + bLe^{-\lambda \alpha t}\}$$

which, after rearrangement, can be written

$$y = \frac{y^0}{c} e^{\alpha t} \frac{1}{1 + (1 - c/c)e^{-(\lambda - 1)\alpha t}} \tag{11}$$

where $y = Y/L$ is the average productivity of labour in the economy as a whole. The equation implies that

$$y = \frac{y_s}{c} \cdot \frac{1}{1 + (1 - c/c)e^{-(\lambda - 1)\alpha t}} \tag{12}$$

Since $\alpha > 0$ and $\lambda > 1$, it is clear that as t tends to infinity:

$$\frac{y}{y_s} -> \frac{1}{c} \tag{13}$$

Employment shares

Denote the share of the labour force employed in each sector as follows:

$$P_s = \frac{L_s}{L}$$

$$P_i = \frac{L_i}{L}$$

$$P_a = \frac{L_a}{L} \tag{14}$$

We can find the share of agriculture in employment as follows:

$$\begin{aligned} P_a &= \frac{L_a}{L} \\ &= \frac{L_a}{Z_a} \cdot \frac{Z_a}{L} \\ &= \frac{1}{y_a} \cdot \frac{bL}{L} \\ &= \frac{b}{y^0} \cdot e^{-\lambda \alpha t} \end{aligned}$$

which can be expressed as

$$P_a = P_a^0 e^{-\lambda \alpha t} \tag{15}$$

where $P_a^0 = (b/y^0)$. Note that P_a^0 is the share of agricultural employment in time zero.

The share of service employment is given by:

$$P_s = \frac{L_s}{L}$$

$$= \frac{Z_Z}{Z} \cdot \frac{Z}{L} \cdot \frac{L_s}{Z_s}$$

$$= c \cdot y \cdot \frac{1}{y_s}$$

which from (12) implies that

$$P_s = \frac{1}{1 + (1 - c/c)e^{-(\lambda - 1)\alpha t}} \tag{16}$$

From this equation it is clear that the share of service employment at time zero given by:

$$P_s^0 = c \tag{17}$$

Equation (16) can be written as follows:

$$P_s = \frac{1}{1 + (1 - P_s^0/P_s^0)e^{-(\lambda - 1)\alpha t}} \tag{18}$$

Finally, the share of industrial employment is given by:

$$P_i = 1 - P_a - P_s \tag{19}$$

and hence:

$$P_i = 1 - P_a^0 e^{-\lambda \alpha t} - \frac{1}{1 + (1 - P_s^0/P_s^0)e^{-(\lambda - 1)\alpha t}} \tag{20}$$

It is clear from equation (15), (18) and (19) that, as t tends to infinity,

$$P_a \to 0$$

$$P_i \to 0$$

$$P_s \to 1$$

In the case of agriculture and the services, convergence to the final limit is uniform: the share of agriculture in total employment falls steady to zero, whilst that of services rises steadily to 1. However, the case of industry requires further analysis.

The share of industrial employment

Differentiating equation (19); we obtain:

$$\frac{dP_i}{dt} = -\frac{dP_a}{dt} - \frac{dP_s}{dt}$$

which, using equations (15) and (17), we can write:

$$\frac{dP_i}{dt} = \lambda\alpha P_a - (\lambda - 1)\alpha(1 - P_s)P_s$$

$$= \lambda\alpha P_a - (\lambda - 1)\alpha(P_a + P_i)P_s$$

$$= (\lambda - 1)\alpha P_a\left[\frac{\lambda}{\lambda - 1} - P_s\left(1 + \frac{P_i}{P_a}\right)\right] \tag{21}$$

The sign of this derivative depends on the ratio P_i/P_a. In an underdeveloped economy, where the agricultural sector is large and the industrial sector small, this ratio will be small and the above derivative will be positive. In such an economy, therefore, the share of industry in total employment at first rises in the course of development. As development proceeds, however, this begins to stabilize and then at a certain point starts to fall back again.[2]

The relation between the three sectors in the course of development is shown in Fig. A2.1.

It is clear from the diagram, and also from equation (21), that the share of industrial employment is subject to opposing forces. On the one hand, the share of agriculture in total employment is always falling; the share of services, by contrast, is always rising. The balance between the two forces alters in the course on development, and this explains why the share of industrial employment at first rises and then later falls. When development first begins, much of the country's labour force still works on the land, and the exodus of labour from this sector outweighs any expansion in the services, with the result that industry increases its share of total employment. As development proceeds, however, the balance changes. Agriculture declines as a source of labour, whilst the service sector continues to respond and absorb additional labour. Eventually, there comes a point where the shift into services outweighs the shift out of agriculture. At this point, the share of industry starts to fall.

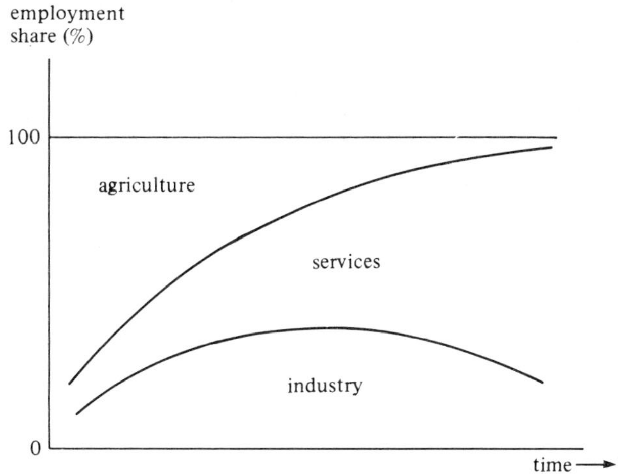

Fig. A2.1 The changing structure of employment

An alternative approach

The evolution of the employment structure in the course of development can be described in a somewhat different fashion as follows. Let us begin by expressing P_i as a function of P_s. From equation (18) it can be shown that

$$e^{-(\lambda-1)\alpha t} = \frac{1-P_s}{P_s} \cdot \frac{P_s^0}{1-P_s^0}$$

Substituting in equation (15), we find that

$$P_a = P_a^0 \left(\frac{1-P_s}{P_s} \cdot \frac{P_s^0}{1-P_s^0} \right)^{\lambda/\lambda-1} \tag{23}$$

Since $P_i = 1 - P_s - P_a$, it follows immediately that

$$P_i = 1 - P_s - P_a^0 \left(\frac{1-P_s}{P_s} \cdot \frac{P_s^0}{1-P_s^0} \right)^{\lambda/\lambda-1} \tag{24}$$

This is the required function.

Differentiating (23) and rearranging, we find that

$$\frac{dP_i}{dP_s} = -1 + \frac{\lambda P_a^0}{(\lambda - 1)P_s(1 - P_s)}\left(\frac{1 - P_s}{P_s} \cdot \frac{P_s^0}{1 - P_s^0}\right)^{\lambda/\lambda - 1} \tag{25}$$

Since $\lambda > 1$, it is easy to show that:

$$\frac{dP_i}{dP_s} \to -1 \text{ as } P_s - 1$$

Let us now consider what happens at the other end of the time scale, when development is just beginning. From equation (25) we find that at $t = 0$:

$$\left(\frac{dP_i}{dP_s}\right)_0 = -1 + \frac{\lambda P_a^0}{(\lambda - 1)P_s^0(1 - P_s^0)} \tag{26}$$

Provided P_a^0 is sufficiently large, as it will be in an underdeveloped economy, this expression is positive. Thus, for an economy which starts with a large agricultural sector, the share of workers employed in industry rises in the initial stage of development, along with that of services. However, in the final stage of development, the opposite is the case, and the share of industry falls whilst that of the services continues to rise. This can be seen from Fig. A2.2 which plots

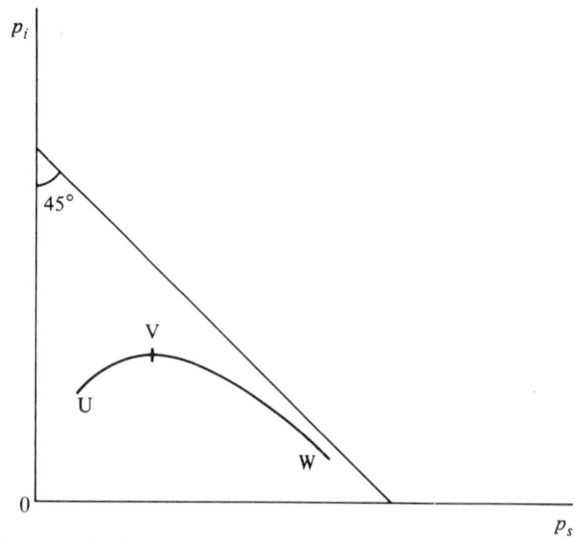

Fig. A2.2 The path of development

P_i as a function of P_s. Starting at the point U, the economy experiences a rapid fall in agrarian employment. This is indicated in the diagram by a movement towards the downward sloping 45° line. Part of the initial shift out of agriculture is taken up by industry and part by the services. This is the phase of 'industrialization'. After a time, this phase comes to an end and the share of industry stops rising. Then comes the final phase of 'de-industrialization' in which the share of industrial employment declines steadily and the service sector becomes the main employer of labour. The economy moves down into the right-hand corner towards the point W in Fig. A2.2.

The share of industry in employment traces out a curve which can be parametized as follows:

$$P_i = 1 - P_a^0 e^{-\lambda\sigma} - \frac{1}{1+(1-P_s^0/P_s^0)e^{-(\lambda-1)\sigma}}$$

$$y = \frac{y^0}{P_s^0} \cdot \frac{e^{\sigma}}{1+(1-P_s^0/P_s^0)e^{-(\lambda-1)\sigma}} \tag{27}$$

where $\sigma = \alpha t$. The shape of this curve is shown in Fig. A2.3.

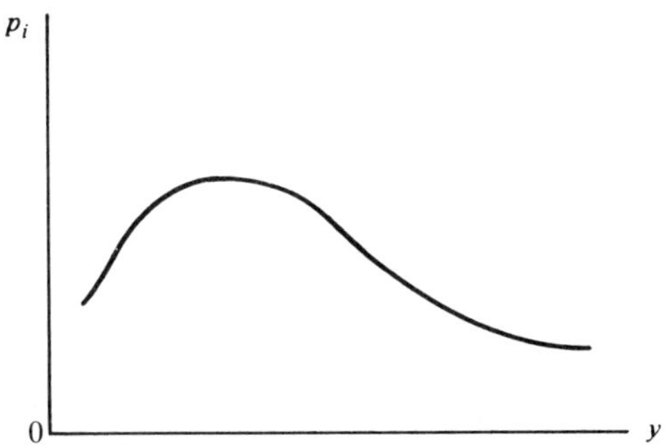

Fig. A2.3 Real income and industrial employment

The effects of uneven development

Between them, equations (24) and (27) determine completely the behaviour of the employment structure in the course of development. As real income rises, the economy follows the trajectory shown in Figs. A2.2 and A2.3. It is clear from the equations that the shape and position of this trajectory depends on the value of λ, but is quite independent of the parameter α. Whilst α affects the speed at which the economy moves along its trajectory, this parameter has no effect at all on the shape of the trajectory itself.

Figs. A2.4(a) and (b), which are derived from equations (24) and (27), illustrate how variations in the parameter λ influence the path of development. Other things being equal, the greater is the value of λ, the more uneven is the growth of productivity and the flatter is the trajectory followed by an economy in the course of its development. At any given level of real income, an economy with a high value of λ will have greater than average labour productivity in industry and less than average productivity in the services. As a result, such an economy will have relatively few workers employed in industry and more employed in the services.

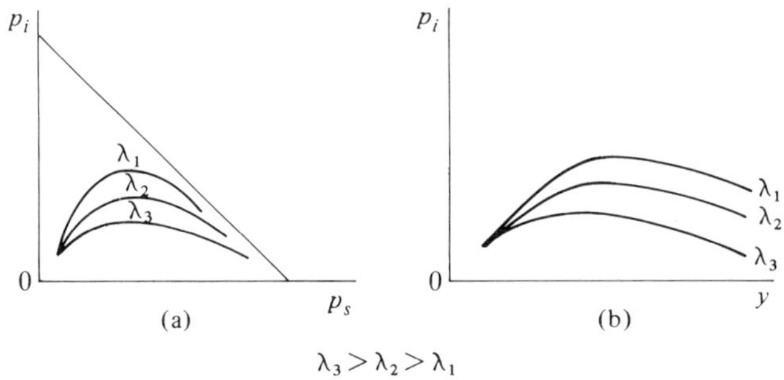

Fig. A2.4 Effects of uneven productivity development

The above conclusions throw some light on the question of 'late-comers' to the development processes as, for example, Japan. When industrialization begins, such countries are normally backward in every sector of the economy as compared to their more advanced forerunners, and in the course of development they experience a rapid increase in labour productivity in all sectors. However, these increases are typically much greater in industry (and sometimes agriculture) than in the services, for the following reasons. First, when industrialization begins, the late-comer is typically more backward in industry (and agriculture) than in the services, and the scope for 'catching-up' is therefore less in the services than elsewhere in the economy. Secondly, dramatic increases in productivity are easier to achieve in industry (and, more questionably, agriculture) than in the services, where social institutions and practices are often more resistant to change. Finally, in a rapidly growing economy, industry may benefit from 'dynamic economies of scale' which are not so readily available to services and other sectors of the economy.[3] So, for all of these reasons, productivity goes not only faster but also more unevenly in the late-comers than it did previously in the established leaders during the course of their own development. In the present model, this implies that for a late-comer the value of both α and λ are greater than for its less dynamic forerunners. Figs. A2.5(a) and (b) compare the trajectories followed by two economies during a given period of time, one a mature industrial economy which is growing relatively slowly, and the other a dynamic late-comer. At the beginning of the period, the late-comer has a much lower real income and is back where the more advanced economy was many years before. By the end of the period, however, the situation has changed radically and the level of real income is now the same in both countries. Looking at individual sectors, we find that by the end of the period the late-comer has actually overtaken the old leader in industry where its labour productivity is now higher. By contrast, in the services its productivity is still some way behind that of the leader. Because of these productivity differences,

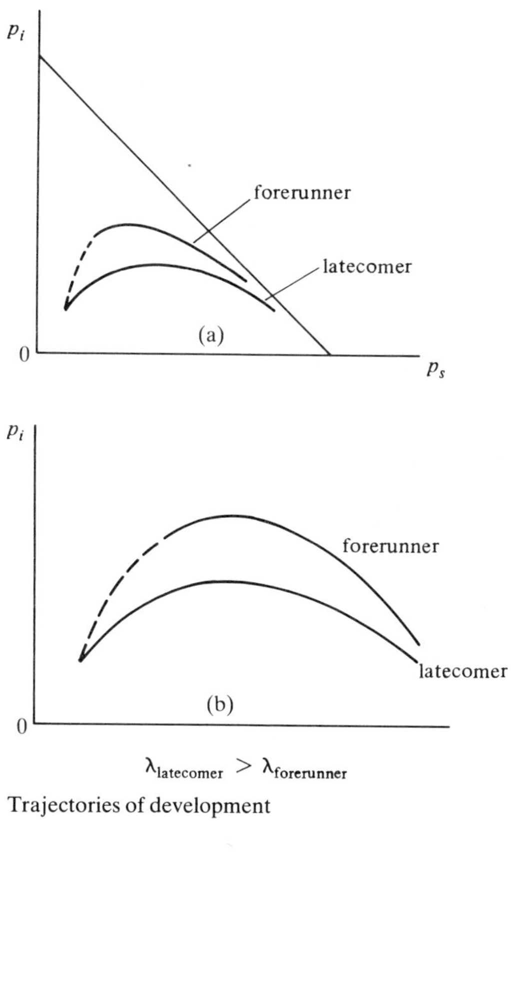

Fig. A2.5 Trajectories of development

the pattern of employment in the two countries is different, even though they now enjoy the same level of real income. In the late-comer, relatively few people are employed in industry, because productivity is comparatively high in this sector. On the other hand, more are employed in the services where productivity is comparatively low. Looking at the trajectory followed by the late-comer in the course of development, it is clear that industrial employment never achieves the same importance as it did in the old industrial country, and the subsequent de-industrialization is therefore less dramatic. Indeed, one of the striking features of development in the late-comer is the rapid growth of service employment, almost from the very beginning, and hence the relatively minor importance of industrial employment. This is due to the extremely uneven pattern of productivity growth, in which the service sector fails to match the spectacular increases in output per worker achieved in industry and, sometimes, in agriculture.

The long run

In the above model, virtually the entire labour force is eventually employed in the service sector, whilst employment in agriculture and industry shrinks to almost nothing. In the case of agriculture, this is a fairly realistic conclusion: in many advanced countries the share of agriculture in total employment has already fallen to around 3 or 4%. In the case of industry, however, there are certain factors which may prevent such an extreme development. To start with, there are some industrial branches, such as construction, where productivity growth is relatively slow, certainly no faster than in the services. As a result, employment in these branches is likely to remain fairly important. Moreover, slow productivity in the service sector will make services even more expensive compared to manufactured goods. This will lead to increasing pressure for modernization in the service sector to cut costs and, simultaneously, will cause the pattern of demand to shift away from services towards manufacture. Taking all these factors into account, it is unlikely that the present shift from industry to services will continue indefinitely in advanced countries. Eventually the share of industrial employment will stabilize. Indeed, if the pressure for modernization in the service sector is great enough, or if the relative demand for services declines considerably, there could even be a shift in the pattern of employment away from the services and back to industry. So far, however, there is no sign of such a reversal occurring.

Appendix 3

Empirical evidence on output and expenditure data at constant and current prices

This appendix contains a brief examination of some of the empirical evidence in support of the assertions made in our discussion of constant and current price data on the question of expenditure. Some of the most convincing evidence is provided by the work of I. B. Kravis and associates for the UN International Comparisons Project.[1] In a comprehensive and extremely detailed study, these authors compared expenditure patterns in a sample of 34 countries in the year 1975. The sample was carefully chosen so as to span virtually the entire spectrum of per capita incomes, ranging from one of the world's poorest countries (Malawi) to one of the richest (the USA). In comparing such a broad range of countries, the intention of the authors was to learn how expenditure patterns vary in the course of the development. Cross-section studies of this kind, it must be said, have their limitations and are not always a reliable guide to what may happen within a single country during the course of time. Even so, the results are striking and are also confirmed by evidence from more limited time-series analysis.[2] So far as it is relevant, the UN study confirms everything said in the text about expenditure patterns and their evolution in the course of development, about the divergence between constant and current price shares, and about the factors responsible for this divergence (i.e. productivity and price differentials). We shall not consider the results of the UN study in detail, but confine ourselves to the question of services.

Table A3.1 presents some of the UN evidence on services. In this table countries are divided into six income groups, I–VI in order of ascending per capita income. For each of these groups, line 3 of the table shows the percentage share of services in total expenditure measured at 'current' (i.e. local) prices. As we move up the income scale, this share rises considerably – from an average of 22.2% in the poor countries of Group I to 43.9% in Group VI. These results appear to support the common view that services are relatively more important in rich countries than poor. However, as the authors point out, this conclusion is open to an obvious objection. Relative prices differ markedly from one country to another, and the apparent difference in expenditure patterns revealed in line

Table A3.1. *Expenditure patterns and relative prices in 34 countries in 1975*

	Income group					
	I	II	III	IV	V	VI
1. No. of countries in group	8	6	6	4	9	1
2. Real GDP per capita (US = 100)	9.0	23.1	37.3	52.4	76.0	100.0
Percentage share of services in total expenditure[a]						
3. At current (i.e. local) prices	22.2	28.4	27.4	25.6	36.9	43.9
4. At constant (i.e. common) prices	33.8	31.7	31.8	30.3	31.2	32.3
Relative prices						
5. Services/goods (US = 100)	36.2	51.7	49.6	49.3	79.5	100.0

Notes: The entries in lines 2 to 5 are unweighted averages of the values for countries in the group. Note that Group VI consists of the USA alone
Line 3: based on expenditure valued at local prices in the country concerned
Line 4: based on expenditure revalued at hypothetical 'international prices'. For a description of the method used see Kravis *et al.* (1982). Ch. 3
[a] Total expenditure includes government expenditure and capital formation
Source: Kravis *et al.* (1983), Table 2

3 could simply be an illusion caused by relative price differences. The potential scale of the distortion can be gauged from the fact that the relative price of services (as compared to goods) is almost three times as great in Group VI as in Group I countries. To eliminate the distortion caused by the use of current (i.e. local) prices, the authors construct a hypothetical set of 'constant' prices.[3] Unlike current prices, which vary from country to country, these constant prices are the same for all countries. The fact is used by the authors to compare real expenditure patterns in the various countries. To this end they recalculate the share of services in total expenditure using constant, instead of current, prices.[4] As can be seen from line 4, the result of this modification is dramatic. Measured in current (i.e. local) prices the share of services in total expenditure is much higher in rich countries than poor. Measured in constant prices, however, the share is virtually the same at all levels of per capita income. In real terms, the ratio of service expenditure to goods expenditure is the same in rich countries as in poor. Thus, the apparent difference in demand patterns, which is indicated by current price shares, is entirely due to relative price differences. The relative price of services (as compared to goods) is much higher in rich countries than poor, and it is for this reason alone that in rich countries services absorb a

greater portion of total expenditure, measured at current (i.e. local) prices. The UN authors also explain why services are relatively so expensive in rich countries. The answer is to be found in productivity differentials. Rich countries have a higher level of labour productivity in all sectors of the economy than do poor countries. However, the difference is much greater for goods than services. In the service sector, output per worker may be 3 to 4 times greater in rich countries than poor, whilst in the goods-producing sectors of the economy the ratio may be 10 to 1 or even more. Thus, as we move from poor to rich countries, *relative* productivity increases in the goods-producing sectors of the economy and falls in the service sector. This has obvious implications for relative prices. As relative productivity falls in the service sector, in the move from poor to rich countries, services become relatively more costly to produce (as compared to goods), and their relative price therefore increases. The opposite is the case for goods, whose relative price falls. Here, then, is the reason why relative prices differ and why in the rich countries services absorb such a large fraction of total expenditure, measured at current prices. Both phenomena are the result of lagging productivity in the service sector. In real terms, the split in expenditure between goods and services is the same in rich countries as poor. However, in the rich countries, labour productivity is *relatively* low in services (as compared to the goods-producing sectors). As a result, the relative price of services is much higher than in poor countries, and for this reason they must absorb a much larger fraction of total expenditure, measured at current prices. This, in a nutshell, is the main conclusion of the UN study.

Let us now consider some evidence of a rather different kind. Table A3.2 shows what happened to output and employment in a sample of 6 major OECD countries over the period 1962–81.[5] The corresponding information on productivity and prices is shown in Table A3.3. Again the evidence confirms the main points of our argument. During the period in question labour productivity rose considerably faster in the goods-producing sectors of the economy than in the service sector. As a result, there was a major shift in relative prices. By 1981 the relative price of services (as compared to GDP as a whole) was 13.2% higher than in 1962, whilst the relative prices of food and manufactures were, respectively, 16.0 and 24.5% below their 1962 level. At constant prices, the share of services in GDP remained almost constant, rising by only 1.6 points between 1962 and 1981 (from 53.7% to 55.3%). However, because of lagging productivity in the service sector, the share of services in total employment rose dramatically by 12.6 points (from 44.6% to 57.2%); lagging productivity also caused the relative price of services to rise, and the result was an 8.0 point increase in the share of services in GDP, measured at current prices (from 48.2% to 56.2%). Thus, in real terms, there was only a very small shift from goods to services in the structure of output during the period 1962–81. However,

Table A3.2. *The sectoral composition of output and employment in six major OECD countries, 1962–81*[a]

	1962	1973	1981	Change 1962–81
	(a) Share of GDP at constant prices (%)			
Agriculture	7.8	4.9	4.2	−3.6
Industry	38.5	42.4	40.5	+2.0
Services	53.7	52.7	55.3	1.6
Total	100.0	100.0	100.0	0.0
(manufacturing)	(26.0)	(30.6)	(30.3)	(+4.3)
	(b) Share of GDP at current prices (%)			
Agriculture	8.4	5.6	3.8	−4.6
Industry	43.4	42.1	40.0	−3.4
Services	48.2	52.3	56.2	+8.0
Total	100.0	100.0	100.0	0.0
(manufacturing)	(31.6)	(30.6)	(27.8)	(−3.8)
	(c) Share of employment (%)			
Agriculture	18.5	10.2	7.8	−10.7
Industry	36.9	37.9	35.0	−1.9
Services	44.6	51.9	57.2	+12.6
Total	100.0	100.0	100.0	100.0
(manufacturing)	(27.5)	(28.0)	(25.1)	(−2.4)

Note: [a] The six major OECD countries are Canada (1971), USA (1975), Japan (1975), France (1970), W. Germany (1976), Italy (1970). For each country, the date in parentheses refers to the base year used for the constant price calculations underlying section (a) of this table. All figures in this table are unweighted averages.

because of lagging productivity in the services, there was a large increase in the share of services both in employment and in GDP at current prices. These results confirm our earlier propositions about the services and their evolution in the course of development.

Table A3.3. *Intersectoral ratios in 6 countries: percentage change 1962–81*

	Relative labour productivity	Relative price
Agriculture/GDP	+27.7	−16.0
Industry/GDP	+10.9	−12.4
Services/GDP	−19.7	+13.2
(Manufacturing/GDP)	(+27.7)	(−24.5)

Source: Table 1.3

Within the goods-producing sectors of the economy, there was actually a small increase in the share of industry in GDP at constant prices over the period 1961-82. However, this was accompanied by a rapid increase in industrial productivity and, as a result, the share of industry in total employment fell over the period in question. Moreover, fast productivity growth led to a fall in the relative price of industrial products, thereby causing a decline in the share of industry in GDP measured at current prices. Thus, measured in real terms, there was a slight shift towards the industrial sector in the structure of output over the period 1962–81. However, this was more than offset by the effects of rapid productivity growth. Hence the reduction in industry's share of both GDP at current prices and employment. These findings also confirm our arguments about relative shares and their evolution in the course of development.

So far we have been talking about the period 1962–81 as a whole. Table A3.2 also shows what happened in each period 1962–73 and 1973–81. Comparing these subperiods, there does seem to have been some change in behaviour after 1973. During the subperiod 1973–81 there was a definite shift from industry to services in the structure of output. For example, the share of industry in GDP at constant prices declined by 1.9 points (from 42.4% to 40.5%), whilst that of services rose by 2.6 points. However, most of this shift was probably cyclical in origin. Since 1973, investment has been at a low ebb and in consequence the demand for industrial products has been unusually depressed. When investment eventually recovers, the share of industry in real GDP should return to a more normal level.[6]

To sum up: cross-section and time-series evidence both support our general argument. If cyclical variations are ignored, there is no sign of a large and permanent shift in the real structure of demand and production away from goods towards services. Nor does the evidence support the idea of a significant decline in the relative importance of industrial products in advanced economies. In real terms, the share of industrial products in both output and expenditure remains approximately constant in advanced economies, fluctuating with the economic cycle, but normally exhibiting no marked trend upwards or downwards over the longer term.[7] The apparent shift in demand from industry to services which is supposed to occur in advanced economies is mainly an illusion created by systematic shifts in relative prices. These relative price shifts are, in turn, a reflection of differential productivity growth.

Appendix 4

Net exports and the structure of employment

In this section, we make use of the UK Input–Output Tables for 1975 to estimate the effect of net manufactured exports on the pattern of employment. Our main assumptions are as follows: (1) there are constant returns to scale, (2) a change in net manufactured exports has no effect on total employment, (3) the composition of domestic demand is given exogenously, so that all components of domestic demand rise or fall together in response to shifts in foreign trade. These are all standard assumptions. In addition, we also require some assumptions about what happens to non-manufacturing trade when net-manufactured exports increase. We shall consider three distinct cases:

Case A Net exports of non-manufactures remain unchanged.

Case B There is a reduction in the net export of private services exactly equal to the rise in net manufactured exports.

Case C There is a reduction in the net exports of agricultural products (i.e. a rise in net imports) exactly equal to the rise in net manufactured exports.

Table A4.1 shows what happens in each case to the structure of employment when net manufactured exports increase. Information is given in the form of

Table A4.1. *Employment coefficients for UK trade in manufactures*

	A	B	C
Agriculture	−0.01	+0.01	−0.77
Manufacturing	+0.62	+0.78	+0.71
Other industrial (mainly construction)	−0.09	−0.01	+0.00
Market services	−0.24	−0.72	+0.05
Non-market services	−0.28	−0.06	+0.00
Total	0.00	0.00	0.00

Source: UK Input–Output Tables for 1975

'employment coefficients'. These coefficients show what happens to the share of each sector in total employment when there is a change in the ratio of net manufactured exports to GDP. For example, consider what happens to private services under case A. Suppose the ratio of net manufactured exports to GDP rises by 1 percentage point (e.g. 5.0% to 6.0%). Then, according to Table A4.1, the share of market services in total employment will fall by 0.24 percentage points (e.g. from 27.0% to 26.76%). The figures given in this table were derived using a 19 sector version of the UK Input–Output Tables for 1975 (as supplied by the UK government to the EEC Commission).

In case A, a 1% rise in the ratio of net manufactures exports to GDP causes the share of manufacturing in total employment to rise by 0.62 percentage points. This is matched by a large fall in employment in the market and non-market services, together with some fall in employment in construction. In case B, the shift in employment is mainly from the market services to manufacturing, whilst the share of most other sectors is hardly affected. Finally, in case C, the shift is mainly from agriculture to manufacturing. This last conclusion is suspect because the assumption of constant returns to scale is extremely unrealistic in the case of agriculture.

Appendix 5

International comparison of trade structure: sources and methods

For sources of UK data on visible and invisible trade, as well as on GDP at current market prices, see Chapter 6. Data sources for the other countries in our sample are as follows.

GDP data

Data on GDP at current purchaser's values for 1952–82 were taken from OECD, *National Accounts*. For the period 1962–82, data from this source are in US billion dollars (at current prices and exchange rates). However, for the years 1952–61, data are in national currencies. The latter were converted to US dollars using annual average par/market rate of exchange (rf) from IMF, *International Financial Statistics*. Where GDP estimates were based on the former System of National Accounts, the earlier series were linked into estimates for more recent years (based on the new System of National Accounts), using a common year in both series.

Data on visible trade

For the years 1952–7 and 1981–2, data on imports and exports for all countries were taken from UN, *Yearbook of International Trade Statistics*. This source was also used to obtain data for the period 1958–80 for the following countries: USA, Australia, Canada, Sweden, Austria, Japan and Norway. For the period 1958–80, trade data for France, West Germany, Italy, Belgium and the Netherlands were obtained from Eurostat, *Monthly External Trade Bulletin*.

The main categories of the Standard International Trade Classification were aggregated as follows:

SITC	Our headings
0 + 1	Food, beverages and tobacco
2 + 4	Raw materials
3	Fuel
5 + 6 + 7 + 8	Manufactures

For the US, Canada and Australia, import data were available on an f.o.b. basis. For all other countries, import data were only available on a c.i.f. basis. In order to obtain estimates of imports f.o.b., the c.i.f./f.o.b. conversion factors in IMF, *International Financial Statistics*, were used.

Where trade data were in national currencies, conversion to US dollars was made using rates of exchange given in IMF, *International Financial Statistics.* Where data were in ECUs (European Currency Units), the ECU: dollar rates of exchange found in Eurostat, *Monthly External Trade Bulletin* were used for conversion into US dollars.

Data on trade in non-government services and transfers

Data on net payments and receipts in respect of non-government services (transportation, insurance, tourism and other services) and private transfers (including workers' remittances) were obtained from the following sources:

(i) *For the years 1952–9*: OECD, *Balance of Payments Statistics, 1950–61*; the data in this publication are in US dollars. It does not contain estimates for either Japan or Australia, for whom data were obtained from IMF, *Yearbook of Balance of Payments Statistics*.

(ii) *For the years 1960–8:* OECD, *Balance of Payments, 1960–77* except for Japan, for which data were obtained from IMF, *Yearbook of Balance of Payments Statistics*.

(iii) *For the years 1969–77:* For Austria, Australia, Canada, Sweden and Norway; OECD; *Balance of Payments, 1960–77*. For France, Germany, Belgium the Netherlands and the United States: Eurostat, *Balance of Payments: Global Data, 1969–80* and for Japan, IMF, *Yearbook of Balance of Payments Statistics*.

(iv) *For the years 1978–80:* IMF, *Yearbook of Balance of Payments Statistics* (for Austria, Australia, Canada, Sweden, Norway and Japan); Eurostat, *Balance of Payments: Global Data, 1969–80* (for France, Germany, Belgium and the Netherlands and the United States).

(v) *For the years 1980–2:* IMF, *Yearbook of Balance of Payments Statistics*.

Appendix 6

The treatment of government services in the UK balance of payments

The treatment of government services in the balance of payments raises certain conceptual problems and our approach differs from that used in official statistics. The official *Balance of Payments Pink Book* contains a heading, 'General Government', which covers transactions of a military, diplomatic and administrative nature between the British government and the rest of the world. This account records, on the debit side, expenditures overseas by the British government and its personnel stationed abroad, including purchases from the private sector in foreign countries. On the credit side, it includes revenue received by the British government from foreign governments and international organizations. However, it does not include the revenue received by the UK private sector from foreign governments and their personnel stationed in Britain. Such revenue is attributed to the private sector and appears in a separate account labelled 'other services'.

There is clearly an asymmetry here between the treatment of credits and debits. On the credit side, the choice of whether or not to include a particular service transaction under government services depends on who *supplied* the service. If the government supplied it, the transaction is recorded in the government account. If not, the transaction is entered in the non-government account. However, so far as debits are concerned, quite a different criterion is used. What matters in this case is who *paid* for the service in question. If it was the government, the transaction is recorded in the government account. If not, it is entered in the non-government account. Thus, on the credit side, transactions are classified as between government and non-government according to who *supplied* the service in question whilst, on the debit side, what matters is who *paid* for the service. Although logical in its own terms, such a procedure can be very misleading. It means that a particular overseas expenditure made by the British government is included in the government account, whereas an identical expenditure in Britain made by a foreign government is excluded.

For example, suppose Britain opens diplomatic relations with a newly independent state. Each country will have to set up an embassy and acquire the appropriate staff and buildings. For convenience, assume that the cost of doing so is the same in each country and that all the goods and services required are supplied by the local private sector. In this case, each government will spend exactly the same amount in the other's territory, so that the net transfer of funds will be zero. Thus, the diplomatic activities in question will have no direct impact on Britain's overall balance of payments, because expenditure in one direction will be exactly offset by expenditure in the opposite direction. However, this is not the impression we get if we look only at the general government account in the Pink Book. In this account, Britain's expenditure on her embassy overseas will be recorded as a debit against the British government. However, the offsetting revenue resulting from the establishment of a foreign embassy in Britain will not appear in the general government account at all. It will appear in a quite different account and be recorded as a credit for the private sector. Thus, the general government account will record a net debit when diplomatic relations are established with a new state, whilst the private sector account will record a net credit. Therefore, the general government account, taken in isolation, gives a misleading impression of how diplomatic activities affect the balance of payments. To get an accurate picture, we must include the receipts normally attributed to the private sector in official statistics. The same argument applies, of course, to the military and administrative activities of the government. Here, again, there are offsetting revenues which do not appear in the general government account, but which should be included to get an accurate picture of what is happening.

To deal with the problem just described we have modified the official general government account by including the offsetting revenues which are normally excluded from this account. The result is a symmetrical account in which government expenditures, whether made by the British government or by foreign governments, are treated in exactly the same fashion. The debit side includes a variety of expenditures overseas of a military, diplomatic and administrative nature by the British government and its personnel, whilst on the credit side we include the equivalent items of expenditure in Britain by foreign governments, international organizations and their personnel. (See Table A6.1 for a complete list of what is included in the modified government account.)

The effect of this modification is striking. At present, roughly two-thirds of all receipts of a military, diplomatic and administrative nature are excluded from the general government account, as conventionally defined. As a result, Britain appears to have a large deficit on what are called 'government services'. For 1983, for example, the general government account records service credits equal to £420 million and debits equal to £1302 million, giving an apparent deficit on government services equal to £832 million. However, these figures ignore £590 million spent in the UK by foreign governments and non-territorial

Table A6.1. *List of items classified as government services*

1. *Military items*

Credits

US Forces' expenditure

These are goods and services supplied by the UK government to the United States Forces stationed in the United Kingdom.

Other military receipts by UK government

This item includes receipts for:
(i) certain goods supplied to the US government ('offshore sales');
(ii) contributions from overseas governments towards common defence projects;
(iii) contributions from other NATO countries towards the cost to the UK of using military facilities in Malta until 1978;
(iv) goods held abroad and then handed over to overseas countries by the UK Forces;
(v) services provided in the UK and elsewhere to overseas residents by the services department, for example, military training schemes. Where no charge is made such entries are offset under military grants.

* Non-government receipts from US military forces

Comprise the personal expenditure of these forces and the purchase of goods and services by military establishments located in the UK from the private sector. The figures are derived from information provided by US military authorities.

Debits

Military expenditure

This item includes expenditure on:
(i) the services of locally engaged staff of UK military bases abroad;
(ii) contributions towards common defence projects;
(iii) goods and services provided to UK Forces by local residents;
(iv) food, equipment, fuel and services purchased locally;
(v) the use by the UK of military facilities in Malta up to 1978.

The items are recorded partly on a net basis, that is after deducting receipts arising locally and receipts arising both from the most recent Anglo-German offset agreement and from the Hong Kong defence costs agreement.

2. *Non-military items*

Credits

European Community institutions

These are services rendered by the UK government acting as an agency for the collection of contributions to the European Community budget, and rendered at the site of the Community's Joint European Torus project in Oxfordshire.

Other receipts

These are for goods and services which the government provides to overseas residents under its economic aid programmes and

Debits

Administrative, diplomatic, etc. expenditure

Goods and services provided by local residents to UK embassies, High Commission offices, consulates, the British Council and the Commonwealth War Graves Commission account for most of this heading. Also included are the services of locally engaged staff, and goods and services provided by local residents to UK diplomatic and other non-military personnel stationed overseas.

Table A6.1. (*contd.*)

which are then offset under economic grants, plus miscellaneous goods and services supplied by the UK government to overseas countries.
* Overseas governments' and non-territorial organizations' expenditure
Comprises the cost of operating and maintaining Commonwealth High Commission offices, foreign embassies and consulates in the UK, including the personal expenditure of diplomatic staff, and similar expenditure by the UK offices of non-territorial organizations. The estimates are based on information supplied by the statistical offices of certain other countries and on numbers of diplomats stationed in the UK.

Note: With the exception of the items marked by an asterisk, all the above items appear under the heading 'General Government' in the official Balance of Payments Pink Book. Those marked with an asterisk are recorded in the non-government account in the Pink Book under the heading 'Other Services'.

organizations, and £416 million spent by US military forces in this country. When these additional items are included in the government account, as they should be in our view, the apparent deficit of £832 million becomes a small surplus of £174 million. Indeed, under our definition, the balance of trade in government services has been in surplus throughout the 1980s, and the deficit in preceding years was much smaller than is suggested by official statistics (see Table A6.2).

The above discussion has obvious implications for the treatment of non-government services. Suppose we transfer to the government account the revenues which are at present located in the non-government account. The net earnings from non-government services will be reduced by an equal amount. To illustrate the orders of magnitude involved, we have computed Britain's net earnings from non-government services according to both the official definition and our own. The results are shown for a number of years in Table A6.3. As can be seen from the table, the difference between the two series is sometimes quite large, being over £1000 million in 1983. However, their general behaviour is quite similar. Under both definitions, non-government services are in surplus in all the years shown in Table A6.3. Moreover, the two series move roughly in unison, rising and falling together: they both indicate a massive improvement in the balance on non-government services, which started in the mid-1960s but has been partially reversed in more recent years. Thus, to get a general picture of the trend in non-government services, it makes no difference which of the two series is used.

Table A6.2. *Government services: a modification (£ million)*

	Average 1953–55	Average 1965–67	Average 1976–78	1981	1982	1983
Credits (official definition)	51	42	237	407	406	470
Additional items:						
Overseas governments' and non-territorial organizations' expenditure	54[a]	47	292	529	575	590
Non-governmental receipts from US military forces		32	111	266	296	416
Total credits	105	121	640	1202	1277	1476
Debits (official definition)	166	319	931	965	1238	1302
Balance	−61	−198	−291	+237	+39	+174

Note: [a] estimate = 0.3% GDP
Source: CSO Pink Book

Table A6.3. *UK balance of trade in government and non-government services (£ million)*

	Average 1953–55	Average 1965–67	Average 1976–78	1981	1982	1983
			Official definition			
Government services	−115	−277	−694	−558	−832	−832
Non-government services	+176	+290	+3933	+5016	+4538	+4734
All services	+61	+13	+3239	+4458	+3706	+3902
			Our definition			
Government services	−61	−198	−291	+237	+39	+174
Non-government services	+122	+211	+3530	+4221	+3667	+3728
All services	+61	+13	+3239	+4458	+3706	+3902

Appendix 7

Overseas investment and the balance of payments

In this appendix we consider a simple model which illustrates how overseas investment influences the balance of payments in the long run. All accounting is done in 'real' terms. Let

$Y =$ net national output of goods and services
$K =$ net capital stock

Assume that

$$K = kY \tag{1}$$

and

$$\frac{\dot{K}}{K} = \frac{\dot{Y}}{Y} = g \tag{2}$$

where k and g are constant. Let

$A =$ net holding of assets overseas

$\pi =$ average rate of return on net assets overseas

Then net national income is equal to $Y + \pi A$. Suppose that a constant function $s > 0$ of this income is saved. Then total net wealth, at home and abroad, increases at the following rate:

$$K + A = s(Y + \pi A) \tag{3}$$

After rearrangement, this can be written:

$$A = s\pi A + (s - gk)Y \tag{4}$$

From (2), it follows that

$$Y = e^{gt}Y_0 \tag{5}$$

for some Y_0. Hence, we can write (5) as follows:

$$\dot{A} = s\pi A + (s - gk)e^{gt}Y_0 \tag{6}$$

If π is constant, the solution to this equation is given by:

$$A = Re^{s\pi t} + \frac{s - gk}{g - s\pi} \cdot Y_0 \cdot e^{gt} \tag{7}$$

where R is an arbitrary constant. Dividing by $K = kY_0e^{gt}$, it follows that:

$$\frac{A}{K} = \frac{R}{kY_0} \cdot e^{(s\pi - g)t} + \frac{s - gk}{k(g - s\pi)} \tag{8}$$

From now on we shall assume that $g > s\pi$. This condition ensures that the above solution converges. Hence as t goes to infinity:

$$Lim \frac{A}{K} = \frac{s - gk}{k(g - s\pi)} \tag{9}$$

Thus, the ratio of net assets abroad to domestic wealth will stabilize in the long run. Note that if $(s/k) > g$, the right-hand side in the above equation is positive, so in the long run the country will be a net creditor. The converse is true if $g > (s/k)$.

From equation (8) we may also get an expression for net income from abroad.

$$\frac{\pi A}{Y} = \pi \cdot \frac{K}{Y} \cdot \frac{A}{Y}$$

$$= \frac{\pi R}{Y_0} e^{(s\pi - g)t} + \frac{\pi(s - gk)}{g - s\pi} \tag{10}$$

Since $g > s\pi$ it follows that

$$Lim \frac{\pi A}{Y} = \frac{\pi(s - gk)}{g - s\pi} \tag{11}$$

An important relationship in the present model is that between national income $Y + \pi A$ and national output Y. From (10) it is clear that:

$$\frac{Y + \pi A}{Y} = 1 + \frac{\pi(s - gk)}{g - s\pi} + \frac{\pi R}{Y_0} e^{(s\pi - g)t} \tag{12}$$

and hence

$$Lim \left(\frac{Y + \pi A}{Y}\right) = 1 + \frac{\pi(s - gk)}{g - s\pi} \tag{13}$$

assuming, of course, that $s\pi < g$. The above expression is greater than unity for $(s/k) > g$ and less than unity for $(s/g)g$.

Let us now consider the balance of payments. Assume that there are no inter-country transfers and let X stand for net exports of goods and services. Since there are no transfers, the balance on current account is equal to $X + \pi A$ and hence:

$$\dot{A} = X + \pi A \tag{14}$$

Thus,

$$X = \dot{A} - \pi A \tag{15}$$

which from (7) can be written:

$$X = -\pi(1-s)Re^{s\pi t} + \frac{(s-gk)(g-\pi)}{g-s\pi} \cdot Y_0 e^{gt} \tag{16}$$

Dividing by $Y = Y_0 e^{gt}$ we get:

$$\frac{X}{Y} = \frac{\pi(1-s)R}{Y_0} \cdot e^{-(g-s\pi)t} + \frac{(s-gk)(g-\pi)}{g-s\pi} \tag{17}$$

By assumption $g > s\pi$. Thus as t goes to infinity:

$$Lim \frac{X}{Y} = \frac{(s-gk)(g-\pi)}{g-s\pi} \tag{18}$$

The mechanism which governs the volume of net exports in the present model is an interesting one, so let us consider it in more detail. National output can be divided into three components as follows:

$$Y = C + X + \dot{K} \tag{19}$$

where C is consumption. Since $\dot{K} = gkY$, this can be written

$$Y = C + X + gkY \tag{20}$$

and hence

$$\frac{X}{Y} = (1-gk) - \frac{X}{Y} \tag{21}$$

Since $1 - gk$ is given, any change in X/Y must be accompanied by an equal and opposite change in C/Y. To see how this change in consumption comes about, we may write C as follows:

$$C = (1-s)(Y + \pi A) \tag{22}$$

where πA is, of course, net income from abroad. Hence

$$\frac{C}{Y} = (1-s)\frac{Y+\pi A}{Y}$$

$$= (1-s)\left(1+\frac{\pi A}{Y}\right) \tag{23}$$

Since s is given, the above equation tells us that variations in C/Y are caused by variations in the ratio of national income to national output $(Y+\pi A)/Y$. The latter are in turn caused by variations in net income from abroad, πA.

The equations listed above establish a definite sequence of causality, which is summarized in Fig. A7.1. This diagram displays the feedback mechanism which regulates net exports. For $g > s\pi$ this mechanism ensures that X/Y converges to the limit given in equation (18).

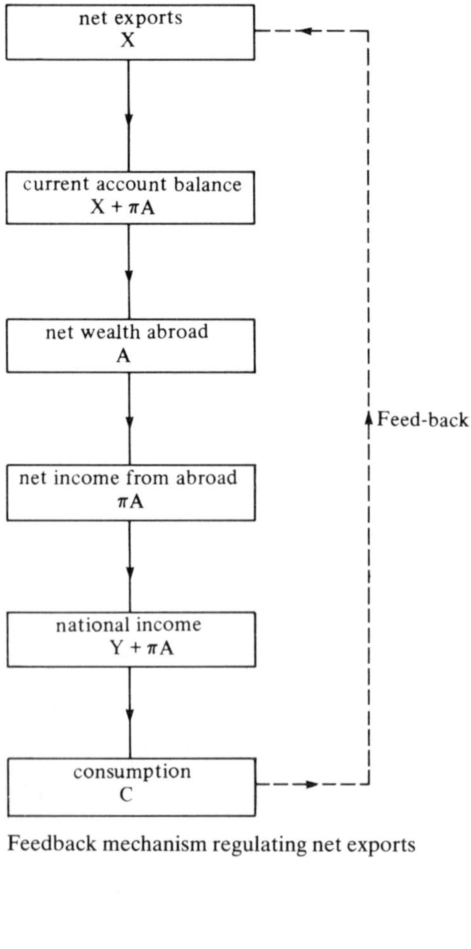

Fig. A7.1 Feedback mechanism regulating net exports

Two types of economy

In the present model there are two main types of economy which we shall call: 'intrinsic capital exporters' and 'intrinsic capital importers'. This classification depends on the relation between savings and investment behaviour, as given by the following conditions,

$$\left.\begin{aligned}&\text{intrinsic capital exporter: } (s/k) > g\\&\text{intrinsic capital importer: } g > (s/k)\end{aligned}\right\} \tag{24}$$

Using previous definitions, these conditions can be written:

$$\left.\begin{aligned}&\text{intrinsic capital exporter: } sY < \dot{K}\\&\text{intrinsic capital importer: } \dot{K} > sY\end{aligned}\right\} \tag{25}$$

The reason for choosing the above names is as follows. Suppose that net income from abroad is zero. Then total savings is equal to sY. If $\dot{K} > sY$, these savings will be less than domestic investment, and to make up the difference the country will have to borrow. Thus, it will import capital. Conversely, if $\dot{K} < sY$, the country will have a surplus of savings over investment which it will use to acquire assets overseas. Thus, it will export capital. The adjective 'intrinsic' is used in the present context because we are ignoring income from abroad. We are considering only income of internal origin and the savings such income would generate given the existing propensity to save.

Some paradoxical results

The above classification of countries into intrinsic capital importers and exporters gives rise to some paradoxical results. Consider an economy whose net income from abroad is zero at time $t = 0$. It can easily be shown that for such an economy:

$$\frac{X_0}{Y_0} = s - gk \tag{26}$$

From equation (17) it follows after manipulation that

$$\frac{X}{Y} = \frac{X_0}{Y_0}\left[\frac{g - \pi}{g - s\pi} + \frac{\pi(1 - s)e^{-(g - s\pi)t}}{g - s\pi}\right] \tag{27}$$

The above solution is convergent since $g > s\pi$. Thus, as t goes to infinity:

$$Lim\frac{X}{Y} = \frac{g - \pi}{g - s\pi} \cdot \frac{X_0}{Y_0} \tag{28}$$

Suppose $\pi > g$. Since $g > s\pi$, it is clear from equation (28) that $Lim(X/Y)$ and X_0/Y_0 are of opposite sign. Suppose the country is an intrinsic capital exporter. Then $(X_0/Y_0) > 0$ and the country initially has a trade surplus. In the course of time, however X/Y will become negative and the trade balance will go into deficit. Conversely, suppose the country is an intrinsic capital importer. Then $(X_0/Y_0) < 0$ and the country initially has a trade deficit. In time, however, X/Y will become positive and the trade balance will go into surplus. In the long run, therefore, an intrinsic capital exporter will have a trade deficit, whilst an intrinsic capital exporter will have a trade surplus. This paradox, it must be stressed, occurs only when $\pi > g$.

Note that we are talking here about foreign trade and not about the current account as a whole. The current account differs from the trade account because it includes property income in addition to imports and exports. When such income is taken into account there is no paradox. Even in the long run the current account of an intrinsic capital exporter remains in surplus. Such a country will eventually have deficit on trade, but this will be more than offset by the income it receives from investments overseas. Conversely, the current account of an intrinsic capital importer remains in deficit even in the long run. The country will eventually have a surplus on trade but this will be more than offset by the service payments on its foreign debt. The situation is summarized in Table A7.1. Note that Table A7.1 assumes that $\pi > g > s\pi$; it also assumes that net income from abroad is initially zero.

Table A7.1. *Evolution of the balance of payments*

	Initial situation		Long run	
	net exports	current account	net exports	current account
Intrinsic capital exporter	+	+	−	+
Intrinsic capital importer	−	−	+	−

The debt trap

The above paradox is familiar in development economies where it has been analysed under the heading 'debt trap'. Consider a country whose domestic savings is just equal to domestic investment. Suppose the rate of economic growth now increases but the country does not increase its propensity to save. The result will be a gap between savings and investment, which will have to be covered by foreign borrowing. The country will become what we have called an 'intrinsic capital importer'. In the course of time, the foreign debt will mount and so too will the cost of servicing it. As this happens, the amount of genuinely new resources obtained from abroad will fall and increasingly the main purpose of borrowing will be to service existing debt. Indeed, suppose the new growth rate g is less than $s\pi$. Then, as we have seen above, the point will eventually come where service payments on existing debt exceed new borrowing. At this point the balance of trade will go into surplus. However, because of the burden of debt service, the current account as a whole will remain in deficit and the foreign debt will continue to rise, though at a slower pace. In the long run, the economy will converge to a situation in which the debt is increasing in line with national output, and a constant fraction of this output is exported to help service the foreign debt. Thus, at first, the country receives a genuine transfer of resources from the rest of the world. At the end the opposite is the case.

The wealth trap

Let us now examine the case of an intrinsic capital exporter. For simplicity we shall assume that net property income from abroad is initially zero. Under these conditions the country will start off with positive net exports, and both the trade account and the current account will be in surplus. Consider what happens when the country begins to invest this surplus abroad. At first the amount of net wealth overseas will mushroom. However, as this wealth mushrooms, so too will the income it generates. This in turn will cause consumption to rise both absolutely and in relation to national output. As a result, net exports will fall and the amount of genuinely new capital provided from the home country will decline (i.e. X/Y will fall). As a result, overseas investment will be financed increasingly from reinvested or recycled profits from abroad and the amount of genuinely new capital will decline. Eventually, the time will come where profits from abroad outrun overseas investment and the country will have a deficit on its trade account. At this point the country will have become a rentier nation living on its past. In accounting terms it will still be investing overseas, but in real terms the opposite will be the case. It will be a net importer of goods and services, and will therefore provide no genuinely new capital to the rest of the world. Any overseas investment undertaken will be directly or indirectly financed out of the income received from existing investment abroad. This is established by equation (18) which shows how net exports, X, became negative for sufficiently large t.[1] In Chapter 4 we use the term 'wealth trap' to describe the *automatic* process by which a country which is intrinsically a capital exporter may become a rentier nation. The mechanisms at work are analogous to those giving rise to the debt trap. Note that in each case the main condition for the trap to operate is that $\pi > g$. It is this condition which accounts for the paradoxical results.

A numerical example

To illustrate the above argument, let us consider the following example. Suppose $g = 3\%$, $s = 12\%$, $k = 3$ and assume the economy begins with zero net income from abroad. These assumptions imply that $(X_0/Y_0) = s - gk = 3\%$. Table A7.2 shows what happens to X/Y for values of π between 0 and 6%. For $\pi > g$, we see that as expected X/Y becomes negative. When π is very much greater than g, this happens very quickly. Indeed, if $\pi = 6\%$ it takes only 25 years for X/Y to become negative. What this table also shows is that, for π fairly close to g, the value of X/Y falls and then remains fairly close to zero for an extremely long time. For example, if $\pi = 4\%$, X/Y falls to 1.0% within 25 years and remains in the range ±1.0% for the next hundred years. If $\pi = 5\%$, X/Y falls to less than 1.0% within 20 years and remains in the range ±1.0% for another 37 years.

Table A7.2. *The evolution of X/Y for different values of π*

t (years)	0	1%	2%	3%	4%	5%	6%
0	3.0	3.0	3.0	3.0	3.0	3.0	3.0
5	3.0	2.9	2.8	2.6	2.5	2.4	2.3
10	3.0	2.8	2.5	2.3	2.1	1.8	1.6
15	3.0	2.7	2.4	2.0	1.7	1.3	1.0
20	3.0	2.6	2.2	1.8	1.3	0.9	0.5
25	3.0	2.5	2.0	1.6	1.0	0.5	−0.0
30	3.0	2.5	1.9	1.4	0.8	0.2	−0.4
35	3.0	2.4	1.8	1.2	0.5	−0.1	−0.8
40	3.0	2.4	1.7	1.0	0.3	−0.4	−1.2
45	3.0	2.3	1.6	0.9	0.2	−0.6	−1.5
50	3.0	2.3	1.6	0.8	−0.0	−0.8	−1.7
∞	3.0	2.1	1.1	0.0	−1.2	−2.5	−3.9

Note: X/Y is measured in % in this table.

Appendix 8

Trade and economic growth: the intermediate scenario

In this appendix we describe how the hypothetical curves in Fig. 7.1a–c of Chapter 7 were derived. The following definitions refer to the period 1950–83. For the actual economy in year t let:

y_t = per capita GDP in 1975 US dollars,

B_{mt} = net manufactured exports as a percent of GDP at current prices,

B_{nt} = net exports of non-manufactures as a percent of GDP current market prices,

$$B_t = B_{mt} + B^{\mathrm{I}}_{nt}$$

Let Y^{I}_t, B^{I}_{mt}, B^{I}_{nt}, B^{I}_t be the corresponding variables under the hypothetical 'Intermediate Scenario'. These variables take the following values:

$$y^{\mathrm{I}}_t = y_{1950}e^{.03(t-1950)}$$

$$B^{\mathrm{I}}_{mt} = B_{mt} + \frac{y^{\mathrm{I}}_t - y_t}{y_t} \cdot \frac{y_{1983}}{y^{\mathrm{I}}_{1983} - y_{1983}}(1.3 - B_{m1983})$$

$$B^{\mathrm{I}}_{nt} = B_n + \frac{y^{\mathrm{I}}_t - y_t}{y_t} \cdot \frac{y_{1983}}{y^{\mathrm{I}}_{1983} - y_{1983}}(-1.3 - B_{n1983}) \qquad (1)$$

$$B^{\mathrm{I}}_t = B^{\mathrm{I}}_{mt} + B^{\mathrm{I}}_{nt}$$

Using the above formulae, it can be verified that for t = 1950 the following is true:

$$y^{\mathrm{I}}_{1950} = y_{1950}$$

$$B^{\mathrm{I}}_{m1950} = B_{m1950}$$

$$B^{\mathrm{I}}_{n1950} = B_{n1950} \qquad (2)$$

$$B^{\mathrm{I}}_{1950} = B_{1950}$$

Moreover,

$$B^{\mathrm{I}}_{m1983} = 1.3$$

$$B^{\mathrm{I}}_{n1983} = -1.3$$

$$B^{\mathrm{I}}_{1983} = 0$$

Note that, under the formulae given in equation (1), a hypothetical trade balance differs from its actual value by an amount which depends on the difference between hypothetical and actual GDP.

Appendix 9

Comparative data on employment shares

The following table shows the pattern of employment in the advanced capitalist countries over the period 1950–81.

Table A9.1. *Percentage shares in civilian employment 1950–81*

	(a) Agriculture 1950	1955	1966	1973	1979	1981
Italy	—	40.8	25.2	18.3	14.9	13.4
Japan	45.2	37.9	22.2	13.4	11.2	10.0
Finland[d]	—	38.3	29.0	17.1	11.8	11.1
Austria[a,b]	39.7	30.6	21.4	16.2	9.2	8.8
Iceland[c]	37.7	27.8	18.6	15.7	12.1	11.7
France	—	26.7	17.3	11.4	8.9	8.6
Norway	28.2	24.2	16.7	11.4	8.6	8.5
Denmark	—	21.8	14.2	9.5	7.2	7.3
Canada	23.2	18.0	9.0	6.6	5.7	5.5
Luxembourg[c]	—	17.9	11.5	7.9	5.9	5.6
Germany	23.8	17.8	10.6	7.5	5.8	5.5
Sweden[c]	20.4	16.3	10.0	7.1	5.8	5.6
Switzerland[d]	—	15.3	10.3	7.7	7.4	7.0
New Zealand[c]	—	15.0	12.7	11.2	11.1	11.2
Netherlands	16.0	14.0	8.6	6.8	5.3	5.0
Australia[d]	—	11.3	8.9	7.4	6.5	6.5
Belgium	12.2	10.4	5.9	3.8	3.2	3.0
USA	12.1	9.7	5.6	4.2	3.6	3.5
UK	6.1	5.4	3.6	2.9	2.6	2.6

Table A9.1 (*contd*)

	(b) Industry 1950	1955	1966	1973	1979	1981
Italy	—	29.2	36.9	39.2	37.7	37.5
Japan	23.2	24.8	32.7	37.2	34.9	35.3
Finland[d]	—	31.7	33.8	35.7	34.4	34.8
Austria[a,b]	36.3	40.0	40.1	40.6	40.1	39.5
Denmark[c]	32.1	34.3	38.2	37.6	38.0	37.4
France	—	36.2	39.9	39.7	36.3	35.3
Norway	31.2	33.0	33.7	33.9	30.1	29.8
Denmark	—	34.9	37.2	33.8	32.5	29.3
Canada	33.9	34.0	33.6	30.6	28.9	28.3
Luxembourg	—	43.4	46.9	44.3	38.8	38.1
Germany	41.7	45.5	48.2	47.5	44.4	43.5
Sweden[c]	38.4	41.9	41.6	36.8	32.5	31.3
Switzerland[d]	—	44.8	46.9	44.1	39.3	39.3
New Zealand[d]	—	35.3	36.4	36.1	33.6	32.6
Netherlands	39.5	40.1	40.5	36.5	32.5	30.2
Australia[d]	—	37.9	37.0	35.5	31.3	30.6
Belgium	45.6	46.1	44.8	41.5	35.5	33.4
USA	36.7	37.6	36.3	33.2	31.3	30.1
UK	46.6	47.9	46.3	42.6	38.8	35.7

	(c) Manufacturing 1950	1955	1966	1973	1979	1981
Italy	—	20.0	25.8	28.5	26.7	26.1
Japan	—	18.4	24.4	27.4	24.3	24.8
Finland[d]	—	21.3	22.8	25.4	25.8	26.1
Austria[b]	—	29.8	29.8	29.7	29.5	29.7
Iceland[c]	21.5	23.7	25.5	25.2	26.9	26.3
France	—	26.9	28.7	28.3	26.1	25.1
Norway	22.0	23.1	23.7	23.5	20.5	20.2
Denmark	—	27.5	29.0	24.7	23.3	21.3
Canada	24.9	24.1	23.9	22.0	20.0	19.4
Luxembourg[c]	—	33.2	35.8	33.8	28.3	27.4
Germany	—	33.8	35.2	36.7	34.5	33.6
Sweden[c]	—	31.7	31.2	27.5	24.5	23.3
Switzerland[d]	—	36.1	37.8	35.0	32.3	32.0
New Zealand[d]	—	23.7	25.4	25.7	24.2	24.0
Netherlands	29.3	29.3	28.9	25.7	22.3	21.1
Australia[d]	—	29.6	28.6	25.6	20.2	19.4
Belgium	35.0	35.3	33.6	31.8	25.9	24.7
USA	27.9	28.5	27.8	24.8	22.7	21.7
UK	34.8	36.1	34.8	32.3	29.5	26.4

Table A9.1 (*contd*)

	(d) Services 1950	1955	1966	1973	1979	1981
Italy	—	30.0	37.9	42.5	47.4	49.1
Japan	31.4	37.3	45.1	49.4	53.9	54.7
Finland[d]	—	30.1	37.2	47.2	53.8	54.1
Austria[a,b]	29.0	29.4	38.5	43.2	50.6	51.7
Iceland[c]	30.2	37.9	43.3	46.7	49.9	50.9
France	—	37.1	42.8	48.9	54.7	56.2
Norway	40.6	42.8	49.6	54.7	61.3	61.7
Denmark	—	43.3	48.6	56.7	60.3	63.3
Canada	42.9	48.0	57.4	62.8	65.4	66.2
Luxembourg[c]	—	38.7	41.6	47.8	55.3	56.3
Germany	34.5	36.7	41.2	45.0	49.8	51.0
Sweden[c]	41.2	41.8	48.4	56.1	61.7	63.1
Switzerland[d]	—	39.9	42.8	48.1	53.2	53.6
New Zealand[d]	—	49.7	50.9	52.8	55.4	56.1
Netherlands	44.5	45.9	50.9	56.7	62.2	64.8
Australia[d]	—	50.8	54.1	57.1	62.2	62.8
Belgium	42.2	43.5	49.3	54.7	61.3	63.6
USA	51.2	52.7	58.1	62.6	65.2	66.4
UK	47.3	46.7	50.1	54.5	58.6	61.7

Notes: [a] Initial year is 1951
[b] Figure in second column refers to 1956
[c] Figure in second column refers to 1957
[d] Figure in second column refers to 1959
Definitions: Agriculture = agriculture, forestry and fishing
Industry = mining and quarrying, manufacturing, construction, gas, electricity and water
Services = all other civil activities
Sources: OECD Labour Statistics (various) and Bairoch (1968). The statistics used in these publications have been used to construct consistent series

Appendix 10

The hypothetical scenarios

This appendix explains how the hypothetical Scenarios I and II which are used in Chapter 11 are derived. Throughout this appendix we use the following notation. For the actual economy in year *t* let:

Y_t = per capita GDP measured in 1975 US dollars

U_t = the percentage unemployment rate as officially recorded

B_{mt} = net manufactured exports as a percentage of GDP at current market prices

E_{mt} = the number of people employed in manufacturing

E_{nt} = the number of people employed in non-manufacturing (excluding the armed services)

E_t = civil employment

M_t = the percentage share of manufacturing in total employment.

With the definitions the following identities hold:

$$E_t = E_{mt} + E_{nt}$$

$$M_t = \frac{E_{mt}}{E_t} \times 100 \qquad (1)$$

Let Y_t^i, U_t^i, B_{mt}^i, E_{mt}^i, E_{nt}^i, E_t^i and M_t^i denote the corresponding values of the above variable under Scenario *i* (*i* = I, II). Then

$$E_t^i = E_{mt}^i + E_{nt}^i$$

$$M_t^i = \frac{E_{mt}^i}{E_t^i} \times 100 \qquad (2)$$

The hypothetical scenarios cover the period 1950–83. To describe them we make use of the following auxiliary variables.

Per capita GDP

$$Y_t^h = y_{1950}e^{.03(t-1950)} \qquad 1950 \leqslant t \leqslant 1983 \tag{3}$$

Thus, starting from the actual value of y in 1950, y^h grows at a steady 3% a year.

Unemployment

$$\begin{aligned} U_t^h &= 1.5 - 0.1(t-1950) && 1950 \leqslant t \leqslant 1955 \\ &= 1.0 && 1955 \leqslant t \leqslant 1966 \\ &= 1.0 + 0.147(t-1966) && 1966 \leqslant t \leqslant 1983 \end{aligned} \tag{4}$$

Thus, U_t^h falls steadily from 1.5% in 1950 to 1.0% in 1955, after which it remains constant at 1.0% up to 1966, and then rises gradually to 3.5% in 1983. Note that $U_t^h = U_t$ in 1950.

Manufactured exports

For $1950 \leqslant t \leqslant 1983$:

$$B_{mt}^h = B_{mt} + \frac{Y_t^h - Y_t}{Y_t} \cdot \frac{Y_{1983}}{Y_{1983}^h - Y_{1983}}(1.3 - B_{m1983}) \tag{5}$$

This is the same formula which is used for the 'Intermediate Scenario' in Chapter 7 (see Appendix 8). From equation (5) it is clear that B_{mt}^h is a modified version of B_{mt}. This modification indicates the effect of superior economic performance on net manufactured exports. If GDP per capita had grown at the hypothetical rate of 3.0% a year from 1950 onwards, there would have been an additional demand for non-manufactured imports (over and above their actual level in any given year). To pay for these additional imports would have required additional net exports of non-manufactures, the amount of which is indicated by equation (5). Note that changes in B_{mt} after 1950 can be broken down as follows:

$$B_{mt} - B_{m1950} = (B_{mt} - B_{mt}^h) + (B_{mt}^h - B_{m1950}) \tag{6}$$

The first term in parenthesis measures the cumulative impact of poor industrial performance on net manufactures, whilst the second term indicates the effect of other, autonomous factors (see Chapter 7).

Total employment

$$E_t^h = \frac{[0.7 + (U_t/1 - U_t)]}{[0.7 + (U_t^h/1 - U_t^h)]} \cdot E_t \quad (7)$$

This formula is derived on the assumption that unemployment is imperfectly captured by official statistics. It assumes that out of every 10 additional jobs created under a hypothetical scenario (as compared to the actual economy in the same year), 7 are taken by people officially registered as unemployed, while the remaining 3 are taken by people who are not recorded as unemployed (school leavers, housewives, etc.). This assumption is in accordance with the rule of thumb used by the Cambridge Economic Policy Group.

The hypothetical scenarios

The hypothetical scenarios start from the actual situation in 1950 and then gradually diverge from it in the following years. The values taken by the key variables under each scenario are shown in Table A10.1.

Table A10.1. *Key variables*

	Scenario I	Scenario II
Y_t^i:	Y_t^h	Y_t^h
B_{mt}^i:	B_{mt}^h	B_{m1950}
U_t^i:	U_t^h	U_t^h
E_t^i:	E_t^h	E_i^h

From this table we see that Scenarios I and II differ only with regard to the variable B_m. Under Scenario I this variable alters in response to the autonomous factors described in Chapter 6, whilst under Scenario II it remains constant.

Estimating employment

The actual percentage of manufacturing in total employment in year t is given by:

$$M_t = 1619.8 + 395.81\, y_t - 23.71\, y_t^2 - 0.56\, U_t + 0.70\, B_{mt} + v_t \quad (8)$$

where $y_t = \log Y_t$ and v_t is a residual error item. The method used to estimate the coefficients in this equation is described elsewhere. For simplicity we shall write the above equation as follows:

$$M_t = f(y_t) - 0.56\, U_t + 0.70\, B_{mt} + v_t \quad (9)$$

The share of manufacturing in total employment under Scenario i is derived as follows:

$$M_t^i = f(y_t^i) - 0.56\, U_t^i + 0.70\, B_{mt}^i + v_t \tag{10}$$

for $i = \text{I, II}$.

Given the behaviour of the relevant variables, it follows that:

$$M_t^{\text{I}} = f(y_t^h) - 0.56\, U_t^h + 0.70\, B_{mt}^h + v_t$$

$$M_t^{\text{II}} = f(y_t^h) - 0.56\, U_t^h + 0.70\, B_{m1950} + v_t \tag{11}$$

where $y_t^h = \log y_t^h$, and y_t^h, U_t^h and B_{mt}^h are the auxiliary variables described above.

From these hypothetical shares the absolute number of people employed in manufacturing can be derived as follows:

$$E_{mt}^i = \frac{M_t^i}{100} \cdot E_t^h \tag{12}$$

for $i = \text{I, II}$. In the formula E_t^h standards for total employment, which is the same under all the hypothetical scenarios. The number of people in employment in the non-manufacturing sector can be derived from the equation:

$$E_{nt}^i = E_t^h - E_{mt}^i \tag{13}$$

The derivation of Table 11.4

To derive the formulae used for Table 11.4 we proceed as follows. Let the operator Δ denote the change in a variable between the years t_0 and t_1. Thus, in the actual economy, the change in manufacturing employment between t_0 and t_1 is given by:

$$\Delta M = M_{t1} - M_{t0} \tag{14}$$

in relative terms, and by:

$$\Delta E_m = E_{mt1} - E_{mt0} \tag{15}$$

in absolute terms. To break down these changes into components shown in Table 11.4, let us define the following auxiliary variables:

$$R_t = -0.56\, U_t^h + 0.70\, B_{m1950} + v_t$$

$$E_{rt} = \frac{R_t}{100} \cdot E_t^h \tag{16}$$

It is easily verified, from equations (11) and (12), that:

$$M_t^{\mathrm{II}} - R_t = f(y_t^h)$$

$$E_{mt}^{\mathrm{II}} - E_{rt} = \frac{f(y_t^h)}{100} \cdot E_t^h \tag{17}$$

Table 11.4 is based on the following identities.

$$\Delta M = \Delta(M - M^{\mathrm{I}}) + \Delta(M^{\mathrm{I}} - M^{\mathrm{II}}) + \Delta(M^{\mathrm{II}} - R) + \Delta R$$

$$\Delta E_M = \Delta(E_M - E_M^{\mathrm{I}}) + \Delta(E_M^{\mathrm{I}} - E_M^{\mathrm{II}}) + \Delta(E_M^{\mathrm{II}} - E_r) + \Delta E_r \tag{18}$$

In each of the above identities there are four terms on the right-hand side. Reading from left to right, these terms are: the *Net Failure Effect*, the *Specialization Effect*, the *Maturity Effect* and the *Effect of Miscellaneous Factors*. These definitions are summarized in Table A10.2.

Table A10.2. *Definition of the terms used in Table 11.4*

Component of change	Change in relative share of manufacturing in total employment	Change in absolute number employed in manufacturing
Net Failure Effect	$\Delta(M - M^{\mathrm{I}})$	$\Delta(E_m - E_m^{\mathrm{I}})$
Specialization Effect	$\Delta(M^{\mathrm{I}} - M^{\mathrm{II}})$	$\Delta(E_m^{\mathrm{I}} - E_m^{\mathrm{II}})$
Maturity Effect	$\Delta(M^{\mathrm{II}} - R)$	$\Delta(E_m^{\mathrm{II}} - E_r)$
Effect of Miscellaneous Factors	ΔR	ΔE_r
Total (=actual change)	ΔM	ΔE_m

The Maturity Effect

Using equation (18), it can be shown that in the case of relative shares the Maturity Effect is given by:

$$\text{Maturity Effect} = \Delta f(y^h) \tag{19}$$

In the case of absolute numbers, it is given by

$$\text{Maturity Effect} = \Delta\left(\frac{f(y^h)}{100} \cdot E^h\right) \tag{20}$$

From these formulae, in conjunction with equations (1) and (9), the following proposition can be easily established.

> *Proposition* The Maturity Effect indicates how manufacturing employment would have behaved if the following conditions had been satisfied:

(1) per capita income had grown at the hypothetical rate of 3% p.a. from 1950 onwards (and hence $y_t = y_t^h$)
(2) net exports had been zero (in $B_{mt} = 0$);
(3) there had been no unemployment (i.e. $U_t = 0$);
(4) there had been no random disturbances (i.e. $v_t = 0$);
(4) total employment had grown at the hypothetical rate from 1950 onwards (and hence $E_t = E_t^h$).

The Maturity Effect is negative for most of the period covered by our analysis. This means that even if all of the other conditions just listed had been satisfied, manufacturing employment would still have fallen simply because the economy was already relatively mature at the beginning of the period in 1950. In actual fact, of course, these conditions were not satisfied. The economy was not successful and grew rather slowly; net exports of manufactures were not zero and changed considerably over the period; unemployment rose dramatically; there were random disturbances; and total employment rose at less than the hypothetical rate. As a result, the fall in manufacturing employment was greater than is indicated by the Maturity Effect. From the Maturity Effect we can infer how much of the fall in manufacturing employment was inevitable simply because the economy was already relatively mature at the start of the period, whilst from the remaining components given in Table A10.2 (19) we can infer how much of this fall was the result of other factors.

Estimation procedures

In Chapter 1 we showed how the share of manufacturing in total employment could be explained using a function of the following form:

$$M_t = a + by_t + cy_t^2 + dU_t + eB_{mt} \tag{21}$$

where $y = \log y$. We then estimated the coefficient in the equation using data drawn from a number of countries and a number of different years. In constructing the hypothetical scenarios, the same basic equation was used, but the estimation procedure was different. As a first step, the coefficients in equation (21) were estimated using ordinary least squares applied to annual UK time-series data for the period 1950–83. This revealed strong evidence of autocorrelation, so equation (21) was replaced by the following equation, which incorporates a lagged dependent variable:

$$M_t = fM_{t-1} + a + by_t + cy_t^2 + dv_t + eB_{mt} \tag{22}$$

The coefficients were again estimated using ordinary least squares. This reduced the extent of autocorrelation but did not eliminate the fundamental objection

Table A10.3. *Estimates of the equation* $M = a + b \log y + c(\log y)^2 + dU + eB_m + fM_{-1}$

	No. of observa-tions	Constant	log *y*	$(\log y)^2$	U	B_m	M_{-1}	R^2	DW	Turning point
Unrestricted										
A	34	−1402.1	350.43	−21.35	−0.67	0.14		.983	0.844	3666
		(6.96)	(7.23)	(7.31)	(12.06)	(1.30)				
B	34	−683.13	171.50	−10.47	−0.41	0.09	0.47	.987	1.29	3605
		(2.26)	(2.30)	(2.32)	(3.99)	(0.91)	(2.94)			
Restricted										
C	34	−1619.8	395.81	−23.71	−0.56	−0.70*		.966	1.16	4217
		(5.95)	(6.01)	(5.95)	(1.86)					
D	34	−979.17	239.69	14.37	−0.40	0.45*	0.36	.980	1.31	4189
		(2.77)	(2.75)	(2.71)	(3.20)		(1.92)			

Note: The restriction on equation C is $e = 0.7$; in equation D the coefficient e is restricted so that $e/(1-f) = 0.7$
Absolute t-values are shown in parenthesis
The turning-point is measured in 1975 US dollars and is equal to $exp(-b/2c)$

to the results, namely the extremely small coefficient of B_m. In the case of equation (21), the estimated value of e was 0.14, whilst in the case of equation (22) the long-run coefficient $e/(1-f)$ was equal to 0.17 (see Table A10.3). These estimates are quite implausible. They imply that huge changes in the volume of net manufactured exports have virtually no impact on the domestic structure of output and employment. Moreover, they conflict with the evidence provided by the UK input–output tables. For example, the UK input–output table for 1975 implies that, *ceteris paribus*, a rise in net manufactured exports equal to 1% of GDP will cause the share of manufacturing in total employment to rise by between 0.62 and 0.78 percentage points, depending on what happens to non-manufacturing trade (see Appendix 4). This conclusion is confirmed by the regression analyses of Chapter 1, which on almost every occasion puts the coefficient of B_m in the region of 0.7 (see Table 1.6). Admittedly, these latter estimates were derived from international cross-section data, but this is not a fundamental objection in the present context. In view of the conflicting evidence from other sources, equations (21) and (22) were re-estimated with a restriction placed on the coefficient of B_m. Where there was no lagged dependent variable, the restriction $e = 0.7$ was imposed; where there was such a variable, the restriction $e/(1-f) = 0.7$ was imposed. The results are shown in Table A10.3.

When the coefficient of B_m is restricted in the fashion just described, the lagged dependent variable plays only a minor role. There is slightly less evidence of autocorrelation when the lagged variable is included, but otherwise there is not much to choose between the two equations. In particular, both equations yield similar predictions for manufacturing employment under the hypothetical scenarios (see, for example, Table A10.4). In view of this similarity, we have chosen the simpler version without a lagged dependent variable (i.e. equation C in Table A10.3). It is interesting to note that all four of the estimated equations suggest that faster economic growth would have had only a marginal impact on manufacturing employment. This can be seen from Table A10.4 by comparing the actual figures for 1983 with those under Scenario I.

Table A10.4. *Manufacturing employment in 1983*

	Thousands	Percent of total employment
Actual	5791	24.75
Scenario I		
Equation A	5762	21.88
Equation B	6068	23.04
Equation C	6160	23.42
Equation D	6123	23.25

Appendix 11

Alternative energy scenarios for 1983

In this appendix we describe a number of alternative energy scenarios for 1983. The purpose is to indicate how faster growth in the years prior to 1983 might have influenced Britain's consumption of energy and trade in fuels. A complete description of the assumptions underlying these scenarios is given in Table A11.1. As can be seen from this table, the scenarios can be classified into two groups designated by the numbers 27 and 40. Scenarios in the former group assume that non-oil GDP grows as fast between 1973 and 1983 as it did between 1950 and 1973. As a result, GDP in 1983 is 27% greater under these scenarios than the level actually achieved. Scenarios prefaced by the number 40 assume that per capita GDP (including oil) oil rises at 3.0% a year between 1950 and 1983. As a result, GDP in 1983 is 40% greater under these scenarios than the level actually achieved. Under all scenarios, it is assumed that 10% of the additional energy required is provided by natural gas and the rest by coal and oil. Within each group there are four scenarios denoted by the following combination of letters:

LL = low energy, low oil consumption
LH = low energy, high oil consumption
HL = high energy, low oil consumption
HH = high energy, high oil consumption

On the production side, each scenario assumes that the domestic output of coal, oil, natural gas and primary electricity (nuclear, hydro, etc.) in 1983 is equal to the amount actually produced in that year. Any change in domestic consumption is met by increasing imports or reducing exports of the fuel concerned. In calculating the balance of trade in fuels, these additional net imports are evaluated at their actual 1983 prices.

The energy balance

Table A11.2 shows what happens to energy consumption under the various scenarios. Under every scenario, total consumption of energy in 1983 exceeds

Table A11.1. *Assumptions underlying the various scenarios*

	27LL	27LH	27HL	27HH	40LL	40LH	40HL	40HH
Energy production				no change in quantity or type				
Increase in GDP[a]	27	27	27	27	40	40	40	40
Increase in energy consumption (%)	24.3	24.3	29.7	29.7	36.0	36.0	44.0	44.0
Energy coefficient[b,c]	0.9	0.9	1.1	1.1	0.9	0.9	1.1	1.1
Share of additional energy provided by (%):								
Coal	50	30	50	30	50	30	50	30
Oil[c]	40	60	40	60	40	60	40	60
Natural gas	10	10	10	10	10	10	10	10
Primary electricity (nuclear, hydro, etc.)	0	0	0	0	0	0	0	0
Price of additional net imports (£ per t.o.e.)[d]								
Coal[e]	68	68	68	68	68	68	68	68
Oil	124	124	124	124	124	124	124	124
Natural gas[f]	110	110	110	110	110	110	110	110

Notes: [a] Hypothetical GDP in 1983 compared to actual GDP in 1983
[b] Energy coefficient = % rise in energy consumption ÷ % rise in GDP
[c] Includes petroleum for non-energy uses
[d] Import prices are f.o.b.
[e] Price shown is equivalent to £40 per tonne
[f] Price shown is equivalent to £0.26 per therm

the amount actually produced in 1983. As a result, Britain becomes a net importer of energy. However, under scenarios 27A–D there is still a financial surplus on the fuel account as a whole (see Table A11.3). This is explained by the fact that Britain continues to export oil, which is expensive, whilst importing coal and natural gas which are relatively cheap. Under scenarios 40A–C, Britain is still a net exporter of oil, but the resulting revenue is not sufficient to pay for net imports of coal and natural gas. Hence the fuel account as a whole is a deficit. Finally, under scenario 40D, domestic consumption of oil exceeds production, and Britain is a net importer of all three major fuels: coal, oil and natural gas. As a result, there is a large deficit on her fuel account. Expressed as a percentage of GDP at market prices, the balance on the fuel account varies from +0.5 to +0.1 under scenario 27 and from −0.1 to −0.6 under scenario 40.

It is interesting to compare the demand for coal under the various scenarios with the output target laid down by the 1974 Plan for Coal. According to this plan the output of coal was supposed to reach 135 million tonnes by 1985, which in energy terms is equivalent to 79.4 million tonnes of oil. Under scenario 27LH, such an output would be just about sufficient to meet the demand for coal without net imports. Under all other scenarios, consumption of coal would exceed the Plan for Coal target, in most cases by a considerable amount.

Table A11.2. *UK production of energy in 1983 under various scenarios (million tonnes of oil or oil equivalent)*[a]

Type	Production		Gross inland consumption							
	All cases	Actual	27 LL	27 LH	27 HL	27 HH	40 LL	40 LH	40 HL	40 HH
Coal[a]	70.1	65.6	88.9	79.6	94.2	82.7	100.2	86.4	107.9	91.0
Oil	114.9	70.5	89.2	98.5	93.3	104.8	98.2	112.0	104.3	121.2
Natural gas	34.0	44.0	48.7	48.7	49.7	49.7	50.9	50.9	52.4	52.4
Primary electricity	12.0	12.0	12.0	12.0	12.0	12.0	12.0	12.0	12.0	12.0
Total	231.0	192.1	238.8	238.8	249.2	249.2	261.3	261.3	276.6	276.6
		Production–consumption								
Coal[a]		4.5	−18.8	−9.5	−24.1	−12.6	−30.1	−16.3	−37.8	−20.9
Oil[b]		44.4	25.7	16.4	21.6	10.1	16.7	2.9	10.6	−6.3
Natural gas		−10.0	−14.7	−14.7	−15.7	−15.7	−16.9	−16.9	−18.4	−18.4
Primary electricity		0.0	0.0	0.0	0.0	0.0	0.0	0.0	0.0	0.0
Total		38.9	−7.8	−7.8	−18.2	−18.2	−30.3	−30.3	−45.6	−45.6

Notes: [a] The conversion factors used to derive this table are as follows:
1 million tonnes of oil = 1.7 million tonnes of coal
= 425 million therms
= 3,800 Gwk of electricity produced

[b] Consumption includes petroleum for non-energy uses

Table A11.3. *UK net fuel exports in 1983 under various scenarios*[a]

	Actual	27 LL	27 LH	27 HL	27 HH	40 LL	40 LH	40 HL	40 HH
Million tonnes of oil or oil equivalent[b]	+36.9	−7.8	−7.8	−18.2	−18.2	−30.3	−30.3	−45.6	−45.6
£ million at 1983 prices[c]	+6240	+1905	+1385	+927	+283	−221	−994	−1666	−2613
% of GDP	+2.1	+0.5	+0.4	+0.2	+0.1	−0.1	−0.2	−0.4	−0.6

Notes: [a] Net exports = exports–imports

[b] Note that in the actual economy production exceeds consumption by 38.9 m.t.o.e. (see Table A11.2). The difference between this figure and the figure for net exports given here is due mainly to stock-building. Under the hypothetical scenarios, stocks are ignored and net exports are assumed to equal production minus consumption.

[c] Exports and imports are both valued f.o.b.

Appendix 12

North Sea oil

Derivation of Table 12.6

According to the figures given in Forsyth and Kay (1980), North Sea oil leads to a reduction of between 5.7% and 8.9% in manufacturing output and a corresponding rise in the output of other non-oil sectors. Assuming that labour productivity in manufacturing is unaffected, this implies a reduction of between 5.7% and 8.9% in manufacturing employment. In the base year considered by the authors (1976), the total number of people employed in manufacturing was 7372 thousand. So the loss of jobs in this sector is between 420 thousand and 656 thousand. According to Forsyth and Kay this loss is partially, although not completely, offset by the creation of new jobs elsewhere in the economy. They argue that, because value-added per worker is lower than average in manufacturing, a given transfer of value-added from manufacturing to other sectors of the economy will raise average productivity and so reduce total employment. And from this observation, they go on to estimate that for each 250 thousand jobs lost in manufacturing only 180 thousand are created in other sectors, giving a net loss of 70 thousand. From their own estimates about the impact of North Sea oil on manufacturing, it follows that total employment falls by between 118 thousand and 184 thousand, which in percentage terms is between 0.5% and 0.8%.

Using the above information, we may express the results of Forsyth and Kay in a different fashion. The impact of North Sea oil on employment can be regarded as a combination of two effects: (1) a uniform proportional reduction in employment across all sectors of the economy (macro-economic effect), plus (2) a simple transfer of workers from manufacturing to non-manufacturing (structural effect).[1] In the case of Forsyth and Kay, the macro-economic effect involves a uniform reduction of employment in each sector of between 0.5% and 0.8%; whilst the structural effect involves, respectively, the transfer of between 5.2% and 8.1% of the manufacturing workforce to other employment. The absolute number of workers involved in these changes is shown in Table A12.1. Of particular interest is the structural effect which involves the transfer of between 380 thousand and 600 thousand workers from manufacturing to non-manufacturing.

Table A12.1. *Impact of North Sea oil on employment (Forsyth and Kay) (thousands)*

	Manufacturing	Non-manufacturing	Total
Lower estimate			
Macro-economic	−36	−82	−118
Structural	−384	+384	−0
Total	−420	+302	−118
Upper estimate			
Macro-economic	−55	−129	−184
Structural	−601	+601	0
Total	−656	+472	0

Our own estimates of the impact of North Sea oil are derived as follows. The value of North Sea oil production in 1983 was equal to 5.6% of GDP at market prices. Suppose this is the amount by which the non-oil balance of trade deteriorates as a result of North Sea oil. Suppose also that two-thirds of this deterioration is in manufacturing trade and the rest in services and other non-manufactures. Then the manufacturing balance (as a percentage of GDP) deteriorates by 3.7 percentage points ($=\frac{2}{3}\times 5.6$). According to the assumptions used throughout the present work, this implies a reduction of 2.6 percentage points in the share of manufacturing in total employment ($=0.70\times 3.7$). Since total employment in 1983 was 23,298 thousand, the result is a fall of just over 600 thousand in manufacturing employment. This measures the purely structural impact of North Sea oil and is based on the assumption that total employment is unaffected.

The above procedure is open to one obvious objection. It ignores many of the costs (and also benefits) associated with North Sea oil, such as imported goods and services, capital inflows and interest, profits and dividends. To get a truer picture of the impact of North Sea oil on the balance of payments, these various items should be included in the calculations. This reduces the estimated impact of North Sea oil by around a fifth and the resulting estimate of lost manufacturing jobs is 480 thousand.

Derivation of Table 12.7

In deriving Table 12.7 we make use of the estimates shown in Table 11.4. These estimates suggest that over the period 1966–83 changing trade specialization caused the loss of 859 thousand jobs in manufacturing, and other factors the loss of a further 2028 thousand jobs in this sector. Similar calculations for the period 1955–83 indicate that changing trade specialization caused the share of manufacturing in total employment to fall by 4.8 percentage points over the period, whilst other factors caused this share to fall by a further 6.6 points.

The next step is to break down these global figures for the effects of trade specialization so as to differentiate between fuel and non-fuel items. Our method is, in essence, quite simple. After correcting for cyclical distortions, we examine what happens to the balance of trade in non-manufactures over the period concerned, and we calculate how much of the improvement in this balance is due to each particular item. We then assume that the employment effect of each item is proportional to its impact on the balance of payments. This provides us with the required estimates. As an example, take the period 1955–83. 'Performance adjusted', the trade balance in non-manufactures (as a percentage of GDP) improved by 9.70 percentage points over the period, of which 0.82 points were contributed by fuel and the remaining 8.88 points by non-fuel items (see Table A12.2). Thus, fuel alone accounted for a fraction 0.82/9.70 of the total improvement. Now according to the estimate given above for the effects of trade specialization, all non-manufacturing items together accounted for a reduction of 4.8% in the share of manufacturing in total employment over the period 1955–83. Our method for breaking down this global figure implies that fuel items alone accounted for a reduction in the share of manufacturing equal to $4.8 \times 0.82/9.70 = 0.4$ percentage points, whilst non-fuel items accounted for the remaining 4.6 points. A similar calculation for the period 1966–83 shows that of the 859 thousand manufacturing jobs lost as a result of changing trade specialization, $859 \times 0.99/4.80 = 177$ thousand were associated with developments in the realm of fuel, and the remainder with other non-manufacturing items.

Table A12.2. *Balance of trade in non-manufacturing (performance adjusted)*[a] *% of GDP at market prices*

	Fuel	Other non-manufactures	Total
(1) 1955	−0.88	−10.12	−11.0
(2) 1966	−1.05	−5.05	−6.10
(3) 1983	+0.06	−1.24	−1.30
Change			
(4) 1955–83	+0.82	+8.88	+9.70
(5) 1966–83	+0.99	+3.81	+4.80

Note: [a] Performance-adjusted figures are derived by estimating the balance of trade under Scenario 40I (see Chapter 7).

The above procedure is obviously very crude. In the case of fuel, it ignores many of the various manufacturing and other costs involved in the exploitation of North Sea oil, and for this reason it almost certainly overstates the negative impact of fuel trade on manufacturing employment.

Appendix 13

Holland and the Dutch disease: a case of severe hypochondria

> The improvement in the energy balance was matched by a corresponding deterioration in the balance of manufactured trade. And this meant that . . . the Netherlands . . . suddenly faced stagnation of industry, mass unemployment and what is now called the Dutch disease. (Kaldor, 1981)

The term 'Dutch disease' has entered our vocabulary because Holland's successful development of its indigenous natural gas resources is widely assumed to have had a negative effect on Dutch manufacturing output and employment, as well as on the Dutch economy as a whole. The main symptoms of the Dutch disease are reckoned to have been as follows:[1]

(a) a deterioration in Holland's balance of trade in manufactures, resulting from the improvement in her balance of trade in fuel;
(b) stagnant industrial production; and
(c) mass unemployment.

The aim of this brief discussion is to see whether this correctly describes the impact of natural gas on the Dutch economy. We conclude that these stylized facts are so wide of the mark, as far as Holland is concerned, that the 'Dutch disease' should be treated more as a case of severe hypochondria.

Before examining the statistical data on the Dutch economy, let us briefly review the possible economic effects of a 'minerals boom'. This involves summarizing some of the results of the discussion in Chapter 4.

The economic effects of a minerals boom[2]

A 'minerals boom' results in an increase in net output of the 'mining' sector and, thereby, constitutes an addition to real national income. If this additional real income is used to increase domestic expenditure, either on consumption and/or investment goods, then there is almost bound to be some ensuing change in the country's internal economic structure. Of course, structural change can be and often is extremely painful – especially to those sectors of the community who are directly affected by it – but structural change can only be avoided if the real income benefits of the 'minerals boom' are actually given away – either in the form of increased foreign aid and/or higher military expenditure abroad. Increased foreign investment can also be used to avoid internal structural change, but it provides only a temporary respite; nevertheless, where the 'minerals boom' constitutes only a temporary windfall, foreign investment is a useful means of smoothing internal structural change.

'Minerals' are fully traded, and the 'minerals boom' results in an improvement in the balance of trade in 'minerals', because it leads to either an increase in exports and/or a decline in imports. As a consequence of this improvement in one area of trade, some other part of the country's balance of payments must undergo a corresponding deterioration. There are basically three possibilities: either (a) a deterioration in the manufacturing balance and/or (b) a deterioration in the non-manufacturing balance (i.e. in food, raw materials or non-government services) and/or (c) a deterioration in the residual account (increased capital outflow and/or increased government aid or military spending abroad).

If the benefits of the 'minerals boom' are used to increase domestic expenditure, then either (a) and/or (b) must take place. It is often assumed, usually for ease of exposition, that manufactures are the only traded goods in existence. However, there is no reason why the manufacturing balance should bear all the burden of adjusting to an improvement in 'minerals' trade: the balance of trade in food or raw materials, or the 'non-government' service balance are equally plausible candidates for adjustment. This point is often ignored.

Let us assume, nevertheless, that the manufacturing balance does bear the entire burden of adjusting to the improvement in fuel trade. How does this adjustment take place? And what are the implications of different forms of adjustment for the level of employment in the manufacturing sector, as well as in the economy as a whole?

Consider first an *investment* strategy, in which the benefits of the 'minerals boom' are used to modernize the domestic capital stock, so as to improve the country's underlying industrial and economic performance; meanwhile, in all other respects, macro-economic policy remains unchanged. Since the proceeds of the 'minerals boom' are spent on imports, there is no reason for the exchange rate to be any different from what it would have been in the absence of the 'minerals boom'. The manufacturing balance deteriorates, but the demand for domestically produced manufactures remains unchanged, as do manufacturing output and employment. This is not what is normally referred to as the 'Dutch disease'.

Consider, next, a strategy for general reflation. Assume that there is spare capacity in the 'non-minerals' sector of the economy. General reflation will result in an increase in domestic consumption and/or investment and, hence, in a rise in the level of activity in the 'non-minerals' sector of the economy. If reflation prevents the exchange rate from appreciating, then manufacturing experiences no induced loss of international competitiveness. However, as a result of the increased level of activity, the manufacturing balance deteriorates, either because of a fall in manufactured exports and/or a rise in imports. What happens to manufacturing output and employment depends on the size of the increase in total demand for manufactures, resulting from general reflation, relative to the size of the deterioration in the manufacturing balance. On the other hand, what happens to manufacturing's *share* in total employment depends on the country's stage of development, but it may even increase in a country at an early stage of development. Thus, if the 'minerals boom' is used to sustain a general reflation, then, so long as there is spare capacity in the 'non-minerals' sector of the economy, manufacturing output and employment will expand. This is not what is generally meant by the 'Dutch disease' either.

Finally, suppose that the level of output in the 'non-minerals' sector of the economy is *given*, either because capacity is fully utilized or for reasons of policy. What happens when income from the 'minerals boom' is used to increase domestic expenditure? Part of the increase will be spent on non-traded goods and services and part on tradeables – which, under our assumption, consist of manufactures. Since total output in the 'non-mining' sector is given, the increase in demand for non-tradeables can only be satisfied if resources are switched out of production of tradeables and into the production of non-traded goods and services. The mechanism for effecting this transfer is a reduction in returns to the production of tradeables, resulting from either demand-induced rises in costs and/or an appreciation of the exchange rate due to the 'minerals boom'. Thus, the 'minerals boom' gives rise to an induced loss of manufacturing competitiveness, and, as a result, there is a deterioration in the manufacturing balance of trade. As a consequence, both manufacturing output and employment are lower than they would have been in the absence of the 'minerals boom'.

This induced loss of manufacturing competitiveness appears to be at the root of what is known as the 'Dutch disease'. Of course, where there is scope for an expansion of output in the non-minerals sector of the economy, manufacturing output may expand, despite the induced loss of competitiveness; however, the 'Dutch disease' focusses on the fact that the induced loss of competitiveness may cause manufacturing output to stagnate or even contract. The same may happen to manufacturing employment.

The induced loss of competitiveness in the tradeables sector (which, under our assumption, is the manufacturing sector) may give rise to two kinds of employment problem. First, suppose manufacturing employment declines absolutely; in this case, those who lose their jobs may lack the necessary skills or mobility to take up employment opportunities in the non-tradeables sector, and there may be a severe 'structural' unemployment problem. Second, the 'minerals boom' may trigger such a wave of enthusiasm in the foreign exchange market that the real rate of exchange may appreciate relative to what is needed to ensure full employment. Such exchange rate 'overshooting' destroys too many jobs in the manufacturing sector relative to the growth of employment opportunities elsewhere in the economy arising from the 'minerals boom': as a result, people lose their jobs in manufacturing and join the dole queue. Both types of unemployment – structural and 'overshooting' – have been treated as symptoms of the 'Dutch disease'. A third type of unemployment, often coinciding with a 'minerals boom', occurs when governments, fearing the inflationary consequences of the 'minerals boom', pursue off-setting contractionary fiscal and monetary policies. As a result, the negative employment effects of any appreciation of the exchange rate due to the 'minerals boom' are exaggerated by restrictive fiscal and monetary policies. As a consequence, jobs are lost in the tradeables sector, but not enough new jobs are created in the non-tradeable sector. This third type of unemployment should probably be ascribed to government policy and not to the effects of the 'Dutch disease'.

Despite this induced loss of competitiveness, the non-tradeables sector may succeed in absorbing all of the labour shed by the tradeables sector, and unemployment may be kept to a minimum. If full employment can be maintained, and national income kept growing at a reasonable rate, there is little reason to be concerned at the induced loss of competitiveness in the tradeables sector of the economy – unless one attaches some special significance to the manufacturing sector compared with other parts of the economy.

Unless a country wishes to dispense with all the real income benefits of the 'minerals boom' e.g. by increasing foreign aid, the only valid reason for foregoing structural change is if the 'minerals boom' is thought to be a temporary phenomenon. In this case, once the 'minerals' have been depleted, it will be necessary to reconstruct part of the tradeables sector (the so-called 're-entry' problem). Thus, if the minerals boom is 'temporary', attempts ought to be made to maintain the competitiveness of the 'tradeables' sector during the course of the 'minerals boom' – either through a modernization programme (the *investment strategy*) or through improving the skills of the labour force. Except for this important proviso, we strongly suspect that there has been a tendency to exaggerate the dangers of the Dutch disease for a country's underlying economic performance.

Let us now turn to the specific case of Holland and try to answer the question: did Dutch manufacturing industry suffer as a result of the successful development of the country's indigenous natural gas resources? And, if so, to what extent?

First, it must be borne in mind that Holland's natural gas resources were not a temporary windfall. Extraction began in 1963, and it took 10 years of steadily increasing production before Holland arrived at a point where it was virtually self-sufficient in fuel and more or less in balance in fuel trade. In the late 1970s, more conservative depletion policies were adopted, and Dutch gas reserves are now forecast to last until the year 2010.[3] By then, Holland will have enjoyed its natural gas reserves for a period of 40 years. Since Dutch natural gas reserves can hardly be treated as a *temporary* windfall, it is hard to accept that Holland's non-gas tradeable sector should experience no loss of competitiveness during this period.

Second, it should also be borne in mind that the value of Dutch natural gas output is quite small relative to Dutch GDP.[4] Thus, we should not expect the economic effects of Dutch natural gas, either positive or negative, to be very large. The major expansion in Dutch natural gas production was concentrated in the period from 1963/4 to 1973/4 – i.e. prior to the oil price rises of the mid-1970s – and, during this period, Holland's balance of trade in fuel improved by no more than about 1% of GDP (see Table A13.1). Since the mid-1970s, Holland has been more or less in balance in fuel trade. Since the expansion of natural gas production had such a small effect on Holland's balance of trade in fuel, its adverse effect on the country's manufacturing balance and, hence, on manufacturing output, could not have been very great either. In fact, the main economic effect of gaining access to substantial indigenous supplies of natural gas was that it insulated the Dutch economy from the substantial degree of structural change which the fuel price increases of the mid-1970s induced

Table A13.1. *Statistics on the Netherlands*

	1963/64	1973/4	1978/9	1981/2
Trade balances				
Energy	−1.1	−0.3	−0.1	−0.3
Manufactures	−4.0	−0.1	−1.9	+0.3
Food and raw materials	+1.4	+2.6	+2.4	+3.6
Commercial services and transfers	+3.1	+1.6	+0.1	+0.4
Commercial account	−0.6	+3.7	+0.5	+4.0
Unemployment (as % of civilian labour force)	0.8	2.8	4.6	10.7
Growth rates (% p.a.)	1963/4–1973/4		1973/4–1978/9	
Manufacturing output	6.1		1.4	
Manufacturing productivity	7.4		4.3	
Real national income (p.c.)	4.0		1.6	

Source: OECD, *Main Economic Indicators: Historical Series, 1960–79*; OECD, *National Accounts Statistics*

in countries which were more dependent on net fuel imports. In such countries, increases in the price of oil necessitated an improvement in the manufacturing balance if external balance was to be maintained.

How did other areas of Dutch trade adjust to this rather minor improvement in the country's balance of trade in fuel? Consider, first, the period 1963–4.

In interpreting trade data for this period, we must bear in mind that the Dutch government clearly failed to utilize all the potential for increasing output and stemming the rise in unemployment which, on the balance of payments front at least, clearly seems to have existed between 1963/4 and 1973/4; unemployment rose from 0.8% to 2.8% of the labour force, whilst the commercial account balance improved by 4.3% of GDP and by 1973/4 the surplus on commercial account stood at 3.7% of GDP. Thus, trade data for this period need to be adjusted in order to take into account the trend rise in unemployment.

The improvement in fuel trade of 1% of GDP was accompanied by an *improvement* in manufacturing trade (amounting to +3.9% of GDP) and an *improvement* in trade in food and raw materials (amounting to +1.2% of GDP). The only adverse development was in 'non-government services and private transfers' (amounting to −1.5% of GDP). This was mainly caused by the rapid growth of Dutch tourist spending abroad, as well as growing migrant worker remittances.

Thus, on the trade data as they stand, changes in Holland's manufacturing balance during the period of greatest expansion of natural gas production had a *positive* impact on Dutch manufacturing output and employment, and much the greater part of the adjustment to the improvement in fuel trade took the form of a deterioration in 'non-government services and private transfers'.

In the subsequent period, from 1973/4 to 1978/9, there was little further change in Holland's fuel balance; however, the commercial account surplus dwindled, while unemployment continued to rise. There was a further deterioration in 'non-government services and private transfers' account, and the manufacturing balance also worsened during this period, probably as a consequence of the appreciation of the guilder: although Holland's fuel balance hardly changed, Holland's relatively high degree of fuel self-sufficiency resulted in the revaluation of the Dutch guilder, and this was responsible for some loss of manufacturing competitiveness. Holland could, nevertheless, have avoided rising unemployment and, possibly, a deterioration in her manufacturing balance if the Dutch government had been willing to pursue a more active exchange rate policy and more expansionary monetary and fiscal policies.

During the period from 1978/9 to 1982/3, Dutch unemployment worsened dramatically. However, in accounting for the rise in unemployment during this period, the specific contribution of any further erosion in the competitiveness of the country's 'tradeable' sector is impossible to identify, simply because of the world-wide character of the recession. What can be said, however, is that

Dutch monetary and fiscal policies were unduly restrictive at this time, given the scope for reflation presented by the country's large commercial account surpluses (+4% of GDP in 1981/2).

Since natural gas seems to have had so little impact on Holland's manufacturing balance, we would not expect it to have had much effect on Dutch manufacturing output either. In fact, there is no evidence whatsoever that Dutch industrial output stagnated as a result of the expansion of natural gas production. Between 1963/4 and 1973/4, namely the period in which the major expansion in Dutch natural gas production took place, manufacturing output grew by 6.1% p.a. and per capita real income by 4.0% p.a. For comparison, West German manufacturing output grew by 4.7% p.a. over the same period. Meanwhile, Dutch manufacturing employment declined by 11.1% during this period, giving rise to widespread concern about 'de-industrialization'. However, given that there was virtually no scope for any further contraction of agricultural employment in Holland, 'de-industrialization' of the manufacturing labour force was inevitable, given the rapid growth of per capita income in the economy – and rapid manufacturing productivity growth was the means used to achieve this. Between 1963–4 and 1973–4, Dutch manufacturing labour productivity grew at the exceptional rate of 7.4% p.a., and one result of this is that the ratio of labour productivity in the manufacturing sector to that in the rest of the economy is higher in Holland than in any other country in Western Europe. Thus, Dutch manufacturing certainly shed labour during this period; however, this was hardly the consequence of industrial stagnation. On the contrary, the sector's exceptional productivity performance was the key to the country's unusually strong industrial and economic performance and was responsible for the fact that Holland's manufacturing balance of trade remaining virtually unchanged at a time when – given the expansion of natural gas production – exactly the opposite might have been expected.

Between 1973/4 and 1978/9, the growth of both manufacturing output and real national income slowed quite dramatically to 1.4% p.a. and 1.6% p.a., respectively. This deceleration was partly due to the effect of the appreciation of the guilder on the international competitiveness of Dutch manufacturing industry, as well as the economy as a whole. Of course, Holland's relative strength in fuel trade was partly responsible for the appreciation, but so were restrictive monetary and fiscal policies, which were also directly responsible for the deceleration in growth. Nor was Holland immune from the effects of the international crisis. For comparison, the growth of West German manufacturing output was only slightly higher (at 1.6% p.a.) during the same period.

To conclude: in the case of Holland, the characteristic symptoms of the Dutch disease can hardly be diagnosed at all: during the period of maximum expansion of gas production, Dutch industrial performance was unusually strong in output terms, and the country's manufacturing balance of trade even registered an improvement. Whilst there has certainly been a rapid rise in Dutch unemployment, this has mainly been the consequence of rather restrictive monetary and fiscal policies, as well as the effects of the international recession. Rising unemployment has had relatively little to do with Holland's comparative strength in fuel supply. It is, therefore, extremely difficult to understand how the expression 'Dutch disease' ever entered our vocabulary.

Appendix 14

Notes on Chapter 13

Derivation of Table 13.1

Official projections for UK population assume that net outward migration is equal to 27.3 thousand per year over the period 1983–2023 [see OPCS (1985)]. Taking into account the effects of migration on births and deaths in the UK, the result is estimated to be a net loss of population equal to 1374 thousand over this period, of which the majority are males of working age. In deriving Table 13.1 we assume that net migration is equal to zero. This assumption allows for the fact that because of the additional demand for labour we envisage, fewer people would leave the UK in search of work, and more would enter the country than is assumed in official projections. Secondly, we assume that a strong demand for labour would lead to a large increase in female labour force participation, discourage premature retirement and encourage older people to seek work, possibly of a part-time nature. Taken as a whole, such changes in participation rates are assumed to increase the labour force by 70 thousand a year over the period 1985–2005, and 60 thousand a year over the period 2005–2025. Our calculations are summarized in Table A14.1.

Table A14.1. *Changes in UK population and labour force 1985–2025 (millions)*

	1985–2005	2005–2025	1985–2025
(1) Changes in total UK population[a]	2.1	1.5	3.6
(2) Changes in population of working age[b]	1.2	−0.5	0.7
(3) Effect of (2) on civilian labour force with constant participation rates[c]	0.9	−0.3	0.6
(4) Effect of increased labour force participation	1.4	1.2	2.6
(5) Change in civilian labour force [= (3) + (4)]	2.3	0.9	3.2

Notes: [a] Assumes net migration is zero
[b] Comprises males aged 16–64 years, females 16–59 years
[c] Assumes ratio of civilian labour force to population of working age is constant

Table A14.2(A). *UK primary energy balance 1983–2025 (variant A) MTOE*[a]

	Actual	Green Scenario		Growth Scenario		Super-growth Scenario	
	1983	2005	2025	2005	2025	2005	2025
				(a) Consumption			
Oil[b]	71	60	50	80	70	85	75
Natural gas	44	33	24	33	24	33	24
Coal	66	94	77	143	189	164	238
(MTCE)[c]	(111)	(160)	(131)	(243)	(321)	(279)	(405)
Renewables	1	5	12	5	12	5	12
Nuclear	11	—	—	—	—	—	—
Total	192	192	163	261	295	287	349
				(b) Production			
Oil	115	50	35	60	25	60	25
Natural gas	34	23	9	23	9	23	9
Coal	70	65	50	65	65	70	70
(MTCE)[c]	(119)	(111)	(85)	(111)	(111)	(119)	(119)
Renewables	1	5	12	5	12	5	12
Nuclear	11	—	—	—	—	—	—
Total	231	143	106	153	111	158	116
				(c) Production–consumption			
Oil	44	−10	−15	−20	−45	−25	−50
Natural gas	−10	−10	−15	−10	−15	−10	−15
Coal	5	−29	−27	−78	−124	−94	−168
(MTCE)	(8)	(−49)	(−46)	(−133)	(−211)	(−160)	(−286)
Renewables	—	—	—	—	—	—	—
Nuclear	—	—	—	—	—	—	—
Total	39	−49	−57	−108	−184	−129	−233

Notes: See end of table, p. 385

Hypothetical energy scenario

Tables A14.2(A)–(C) give detailed information about our assumptions covering energy production and consumption under each hypothetical scenario and variant thereof. All fuel prices are assumed to rise by the same amount, as shown in Table A14.3. In constructing these tables we have consulted a variety of sources and, where appropriate, have exercised our own subjective judgements. The figures for oil and gas production under the central B-variant of the Growth and Supergrowth Scenarios are derived, by interpolation, from Eden and Evans (1984); those for coal and nuclear production are derived from the same source, but with minor modification to allow for a somewhat different policy towards energy; in the case of renewables we assume a much larger increase than do

Table A14.2(B). *UK primary energy balance 1983–2025 (variant B) MTOE*

	Actual	Green Scenario		Growth Scenario		Super-growth Scenario	
	1983	2005	2025	2005	2025	2005	2025
				(a) Consumption			
Oil[b]	71	57	45	75	65	80	70
Natural gas	44	31	22	31	22	31	22
Coal	66	81	56	106	107	115	128
(MTCE)[c]	(111)	(138)	(95)	(180)	(182)	(196)	(218)
Renewables	1	7	15	7	15	7	15
Nuclear	11	—	—	20	40	30	60
Total	192	176	138	239	249	263	295
				(b) Production			
Oil[b]	115	55	40	65	30	65	30
Natural gas	34	25	11	25	11	25	11
Coal	70	70	55	70	70	75	80
(MTCE)[c]	(119)	(119)	(94)	(119)	(119)	(128)	(136)
Renewables	1	7	15	7	15	7	15
Nuclear	11	—	—	20	40	30	60
Total	231	157	121	187	166	202	196
				(c) Production–consumption			
Oil	44	−2	−5	−10	−35	15	−40
Natural gas	−10	−6	−11	−6	−11	−6	−11
Coal	5	−11	−1	−36	−37	−40	−48
(MTCE)	(8)	(−19)	(−2)	(−61)	(−63)	(−68)	(−82)
Renewables	—	—	—	—	—	—	—
Nuclear	—	—	—	—	—	—	—
Total	39	−19	−17	−52	−83	−61	−99

Notes: See end of table, p. 385

these authors. On the consumption side, we assume a somewhat smaller increase in oil demand and a considerably smaller increase in Total Primary Energy Requirements (TPER) than is implied by the figures given in Eden and Evans.[1] In each case, the difference is explained by a different government policy towards consumption, which we assume is successful in restraining the growth of energy demand. The demand for coal is the residual left after subtracting other forms of energy demand from TPER. Figures for energy production and consumption under variant-B of the Green Scenario are a compromise between what low energy enthusiasts, such as Oliver and Miall (1983) claim is possible, and orthodox opinion as represented by Eden and Evans (1984) or the International Energy Agency (1985). The A- and C-variants are derived by modifying upwards or

Table A14.2(C). *UK primary energy balance 1983–2025 (variant C) MTOE*

	Actual	Green Scenario		Growth Scenario		Super-growth Scenario	
	1983	2005	2025	2005	2025	2005	2025
			(a) Consumption				
Oil[b]	71	54	40	70	60	75	65
Natural gas	44	29	20	29	20	29	20
Coal	66	69	38	86	53	93	56
(MTCE)[c]	(111)	(117)	(65)	(146)	(90)	(158)	(95)
Renewables	1	9	18	9	18	9	18
Nuclear	11	—	—	25	60	35	90
Total	192	161	116	219	211	241	249
			(b) Production				
Oil[b]	115	60	45	70	35	70	35
Natural gas	34	27	13	27	13	27	13
Coal	70	75	60	75	75	80	90
(MTCE)[c]	(119)	(128)	(102)	(128)	(128)	(136)	(153)
Renewables	1	9	18	9	18	9	18
Nuclear	11	—	—	25	60	35	90
Total	231	171	136	206	201	221	246
			(c) Production–consumption				
Oil	44	6	5	—	−25	−5	−30
Natural gas	10	−2	−7	−2	−7	−2	−7
Coal	5	6	22	−11	22	−13	34
(MTCE)	(8)	(10)	(37)	(−19)	(37)	(−22)	(58)
Renewables	—	—	—	—	—	—	—
Nuclear	—	—	—	—	—	—	—
Total	39	10	20	−13	−10	−20	−3

Notes: [a] MTOE = million tonnes of oil or coal equivalent
[b] Includes petroleum for non-energy use
[c] MTCE = million tonnes of coal or coal equivalent

Table A14.3. *Index of fuel prices 1983–2025*

	Actual	Hypothetical:	all scenarios
	1983	2005	2025
Variant A	100	120	190
Variant B	100	110	155
Variant C	100	100	125

downwards, as appropriate, the figures for consumption and production which are assumed under the central B-variants.

Services, food and materials

Services: the A-variants shown in Table 13.9 are derived from Table 13.8 as follows: positive (negative) items are divided (multiplied) by 1.2 in 2005 and 1.4 in 2025. The C-variants are derived by reversing this procedure; thus, the positive (negative) items in Table 13.8 are multiplied (divided) by 1.2 in 2005 and 1.4 in 2025.

Food and materials: the A-variants shown in Table 13.9 are derived from the B-variants shown in the same table by multiplying the negative items by 1.2 in 2005 and 1.4 in 2025 (there are no positive items); the C-variants are derived by reversing this procedure.

Notes

Introduction

1 *National Institute Economic Review*, August 1982, p. 11, updated with *National Institute Economic Review*, 2/1986.
2 Either directly *via* increased home sales and/or indirectly *via* increased exports.
3 Just before this book went to press, the House of Lords Select Committee on Overseas Trade (House of Lords [1985]) published a report which covered much the same set of issues as we do and had a considerable impact on public opinion. We are in complete agreement with the Report's principal conclusion, namely that the prospective decline in North Sea fuel production may well give rise to an economic, political and social crisis of unprecedented proportions. We also agree with the Report's call for urgent and dramatic action to improve the competitive position of British manufacturing industry. Nevertheless, as will become clear during the course of this book, we are highly critical of certain passages in the Report – in particular, those dealing with the question of long-term trends in UK manufacturing trade.
4 See note 2.
5 Of course, countries in surplus in non-manufacturing trade will be able to resort to overseas suppliers (on a net basis) to meet part of their domestic demand for manufactures.

1 The structure of employment and its evolution: the theory of de-industrialization

1 For a discussion of how the role of women changes during the course of industrialization see Pinchbeck (1931), Boserup (1970), Richards (1974) and McBride (1977).
2 Agriculture includes forestry and fishing, whilst industry covers mining, public utilities (gas, electricity and water) and construction, in addition to manufacturing. The services includes transport, communication, distribution and finance, as well as community and personal services. Whilst there is some scope for disagreement concerning the precise allocation of individual activities in any tripartite classification of this sort, this is not something which affects the main thrust of our argument.
3 Conventional statistics give a rather misleading picture of pre-industrial society. They exaggerate the importance of agricultural employment and conceal the amount of time devoted to industrial and service activities. As a result, they exaggerate the extent to which the pattern of economic activity changes in the early stages of modern economic growth. The reason for this is as follows. In pre-industrial society there is relatively little specialization and many different tasks are performed by the same person. A large fraction of the population are peasants who, in addition to their main occupation of farming, spend much of their time on subsidiary activities such as transport, selling, construction, weaving, furniture-making and other handicrafts. The subsidiary activities

are ignored in conventional statistics which record only a person's main occupation. Peasants are treated as if they were full-time farmers and their contribution to industry and the services is thereby concealed. Thus, much of the apparent increase in industrial and service employment in the transition to modern society is merely the replacement of unspecialized peasant labour in these areas by the labour of specialized professionals.

4 For one of the few general studies on this topic see McBride (1976).

5 Good historical statistics on domestic service are hard to come by. Clark (1957), pp. 510–20 estimates the percentage of the labour force employed in domestic service in various countries as follows: Australia 6.9 (1891), Germany 9.1 (1882), Switzerland 7.8 (1880), USA 7.4 (1870). These are the earliest international figures available.

6 In late-industrializing countries, such as Japan and many contemporary newly industrializing countries, both the level and rate of growth of manufacturing productivity are higher relative to the rest of the economy than in the first industrial nations during an equivalent stage of development. This is partly because late-industrializing countries are highly dependent on imports of capital goods from already developed countries. As a result, in the typical late-industrializing country, neither the share of manufacturing in total employment nor the increase in manufacturing's share are anything like as large as in the case of the first industrial nations. This seems to be an unavoidable consequence of technological borrowing to establish a high productivity manufacturing sector in an otherwise low productivity economy (see model presented in Appendix 1). However, whilst the share of the labour force employed in manufacturing and public utilities is low in the typical late-industrializing country and may not increase very much during the initial phase of development ('industrialization'), the share of industry as a whole, as well as its rate of increase, are boosted by employment in the construction sector. The rudimentary nature of techniques of production used in the construction industry means that it is a relatively low productivity sector. As a result, urbanization gives rise to a rapid expansion of jobs in the construction industry, and employment in the industrial sector as a whole is thereby given a boost.

7 This argument is presented in a slightly different form in Lengelle (1966).

8 The employment shares shown in Appendix 1 and Fig. 1.4 are derived from data contained in Bairoch (1968) and in the OECD *Labour Force Statistics*. Real income per capita is estimated from data contained in Maddison (1982) and the OECD *National Accounts*. Per capita income is expressed in constant 1975 US dollars using purchasing power parity exchange rates; these have been estimated either from the OECD *National Accounts* or from information given in Kravis (1976).

9 This argument is to be found in Fisher (1935) and Clark (1957).

10 To our knowledge, the argument we are making here was first put forward in detail by Fuchs (1968). Since then, his ideas have been confirmed by a number of studies.

11 This argument is explored in more detail in the mathematical model given in Appendix 2. The model draws heavily on Baumol (1967).

12 The question of productivity in the services is covered in general terms by, amongst others, Fuchs (1968), Hill (1971), Stanback (1979) and Gershuny and Miles (1983). For a detailed discussion of individual sectors see Fuchs (ed.) (1969) and Mark (1980).

13 Note that Fig. 1.2b is merely a simplified and rearranged version of Fig. 1.1.

14 The formulae used for computing shares are as follows:

1. Intertemporal

Let S_{it} and $\bar{S}_{it}$ denote respectively the current and constant price share of item i at time t in output (expenditure). Then:

$$S_{it} = \frac{P_{it}Q_{it}}{\sum_i P_{it}Q_{it}}$$

and

$$\bar{S}_{it} = \frac{\bar{P}_{ito}Q_{it}}{\sum_i \bar{P}_{ito}Q_{it}}$$

where Q_{it} is the quantity of output (expenditure) of type i at time t, P_{it} is the price of this item at time t, and $\bar{P}_{ito}$ is the price in base year t_0.

2. Interspatial
Let S_{ia} and $\bar{S}_{ia}$ denote respectively the current (i.e. local) and constant (i.e. common) price share of item i in country a in output (expenditure). Then:

$$S_{ia} = \frac{P_{ia}Q_{ia}}{\sum_i P_{ia}Q_{ia}}$$

and

$$\bar{S}_{ia} = \frac{\bar{P}_i Q_{ia}}{\sum_i \bar{P}_i Q_{ia}}$$

where Q_{ia} is the quantity of output (expenditure) of type i in country a, P_{ia} is the price of this item in country a, and $\bar{P}_i$ is the hypothetical 'common' price which is the same for all countries.

15 Given the length of the current recession, the term 'cyclical' may be something of a misnomer to describe what seems to be a deep-seated and persistent inability to achieve full employment. However, we shall ignore this objection and treat the current recession as a cyclical phenomenon, even though no end is yet in sight.

16 For evidence on the impact of the business cycle on employment structure see Urquhart (1981).

17 This qualification is especially relevant in the case of the UK. For example, as argued elsewhere, the Thatcher government completely failed to use the opportunities provided by North Sea oil for economic expansion and, instead, pursued policies which made the situation even worse (see Chapters 4 and 12).

18 Note that we have been considering a mature economy, in which sustained growth is usually accompanied by a reduction in manufacturing's share in total employment. By contrast, in a less developed, sustained growth is usually accompanied by an increase in manufacturing's share. Hence, in a less developed economy, a strong trade performance, if it results in sustained growth, leads to an increase in manufacturing's share in total employment in both the short and the long term.

19 Throughout this book the index of 'specialization' we use is based on *net* exports of a particular item (i.e. exports minus imports). A country is described as specializing in a particular item (e.g. manufactures) if its net exports of this item are large in relation to GDP.

20 In this context, the term 'otherwise similar' denotes similarity in such areas as economic efficiency, per capita income and the internal structure of demand.

21 Clark (1957) hints at this proposition (p. 502), but it is not very clearly stated.

22 Over the past thirty years West Germany has enjoyed a surplus on manufacturing trade averaging around 10% of GDP, whilst Norway's manufacturing trade has been in deficit by about the same proportion of GDP. See Chapters 3 and 7 for a more detailed discussion of the differences in specialization amongst the OECD countries.

23 See Chapter 4 for a longer discussion of this topic.

24 The relationship between employment structure and income is specified in a logarithmic form in, for example, Fuchs (1968), Chenery (1960) and Chenery and Syrquin (1975). We also tried other functional forms, but these yielded virtually the same results as the logarithmic form used in the text.

25 Information on the values taken by the different variables has been derived from the following sources.

M: OECD *Labour Force Statistics*.

Y: OECD *National Accounts* and Maddison (1982). The exchange rates used to convert real income into dollars are based on purchasing power parity: these give a more accurate picture than official exchange rates. These purchasing power parity exchange rates have been estimated from information given in the OECD *National Accounts* and in Kravis *et al.* (1978).

U: Maddison (1982) and OECD *Main Economic Indicators*. These figures are standardized by the OECD to a common definition of unemployment.

B_m: UN, *Yearbook of International Trade Statistics* and Eurostat, *Monthly External Trade Bulletin.*

26 In Japan, the share of manufacturing in total employment is about one-third below that of other countries with similar levels of per capita income, unemployment and trade structure. This is because the productivity differential between industry and the services is so much greater in Japan than elsewhere. For a discussion of this point and its implications, see Appendix 2. However, as a check, we also did some regressions including Japan in the sample of countries. The estimated coefficients were similar to those shown in Table 1.6, although their statistical significance was somewhat lower.

27 In equations (1), (2), (7), (9), (11), (12) and (13).

28 For a numerical example, which yields a coefficient of exactly −0.57, see Appendix 4.

29 The *ceteris paribus* assumptions are as follows: (a) the domestic pattern of final demand does not change, (b) the level of economic activity does not alter, and (c) there are constant returns to scale in all industries. The range of variation in the estimates is explained by the fact that different assumptions can be made about what happens to non-manufacturing trade when net manufactured exports increase. The lowest estimate of 0.62 assumes there is no change at all in the volume and composition of net exports of non-manufactures, whilst the highest of 0.78 assumes that service exports fall by exactly the same amount as net manufactured exports increase.

2 Economic development and the structure of foreign trade

1 Throughout this book the term 'primary producer' is used to refer to a country which is a net exporter of primary products, whilst the term 'specialist manufacturing exporter' or, alternatively, 'manufacturing specialist', refers to a country which is a net exporter of manufactures.

2 Countries possessing an exceptionally favourable endowment of natural resources are an important exception to this rule.

3 See Cassen (1976), p. 786 and Rostow (1978), Chaps, 1–4.

4 See Fields (1980), Chap. 4.

5 See Fields (1980), Chap. 5 and Wells (1983).

6 The terms 'inferior' and 'superior' are used here in their economic sense only. Indeed, informed opinion now suggests that many aspects of the 'superior' diet, widely consumed in the developed countries, are quite harmful to health (*viz* excessively high levels of consumption of highly refined cereals, sugar and animal fats); see the *Observer*, 3 February 1985.

7 Lappé (1978), Chart 2, p. 11.

8 *Rates of growth of population (% p.a.)*

	1950–60	1960–70	1970–80	1975–80	1980–83
Western Europe	1.0	0.9	0.3	0.1	0.0
Northern Europe	0.5	0.5	0.2	0.1	0.0
Southern Europe	0.8	0.8	0.8	0.7	0.5
North America	1.8	1.3	0.9	1.0	0.9

Source: UN *Demographic Yearbook*

9 See UN (1982), p. 19.

10 *Daily per capita calorie availability (kcals): selected countries*

	Pre-war	1960–67	1979–81
US	3360	3204	3455
West Germany	3218	3116	3047
UK	3110	3258	3040
France	2837	3033	3260
Sweden	3120	2975	3005
Denmark	3462	3306	3306
Norway	3278	3009	3301
Australia	3273	3109	2876

Source: FAO *The State of Food and Agriculture* and FAO *Food Balance Sheets*

11 See Buckwell *et al.* (1982), Chap. 8.

12 Such trends are clearly visible in Latin America's recent experience.

Latin America: food trade data (at constant 1975 prices)

	Exports US$b	Imports US$b	Net exports US$b	As a % of GDP
1961–62	12.02	2.82	9.21	5.9
1965–66	13.38	3.21	10.17	5.3
1970–71	15.69	3.91	11.78	4.6
1975–76	16.69	5.50	11.18	3.2
1980–81	20.06	11.12	8.94	2.0

Sources and Notes: Data on food (SITC 0 + 1) export and import values from UN, *Yearbook of International Trade Statistics*. Extrapolated to other years, using index numbers on food import and export volumes for Latin America from FAO, *Trade Yearbook*. GDP data from CEPAL *Series Historicas del Crecimiento de America Latina.*

Note that the rate of growth of Latin America's net food exports has also been adversely affected by unfavourable trends in the growth of world demand for the region's principal commodity exports.

13 In some advanced countries (e.g. the UK), import-substitution has been the main source of improvements in the food balance (see Chap. 6); in others (e.g. West Germany and Austria), the improvement has been mainly due to increased exports.

14 *US and France: balance of trade in food as a % of GDP (at current prices)*

	US	France
1952–55	−0.3	−1.0
1961–65	+0.0	−0.2
1971–75	+0.2	+0.8
1981–82	+0.4	+0.9

Note: Constant price data on food trade not available for the US and France

Sources: See Appendix 5

15 *Annual % rate of growth of real value added, 1960–83*

	Agriculture	Manufacturing
United States	0.7	3.1
Japan	1.0	10.2
West Germany	1.2	3.2
France	1.2	5.0
United Kingdom	2.4	0.9
Italy	1.6	4.9
Canada	2.6	4.0
Austria	1.7	4.0
Belgium	0.6	4.2
Denmark	1.1	3.6
Netherlands	3.6	5.0
Norway	1.3	2.4
Sweden	1.4	2.9

Source: OECD, *Historical Statistics, 1960–83*, pp. 45–6.

16 Moreover, there is little reason to expect any strong relationship between the two at this stage of development. On the one hand, a relatively strong industrial performance has relatively little effect on the rate of growth of agricultural output. On the other, the set of policy instruments (trade protection and subsidies) which have been partly responsible for fostering such rapid agricultural output growth in the advanced countries have both harmful and beneficial effects, as far as industrial performance is concerned. In so far as such policies absorb resources which might otherwise have been devoted to supporting industry, they have harmful effects on industrial performance. However, to the extent that agricultural support policies succeed in relaxing the foreign exchange constraint on growth, they have a beneficial effect on industrial output growth. On balance, it is not clear whether agricultural support policies are harmful or beneficial, as far as industrial performance is concerned.

17 The reasons for this predominance are obvious enough. Given the relatively low level of per capita income at this stage of development, the size of the domestic market for basic manufactures is larger than that for more sophisticated products, such as durable consumers' goods and capital goods. Furthermore, for a country at an early stage of industrial development, the technology required to produce manufactures is both easier to acquire and to master.

18 Simple aggregate measures of the input of raw materials per unit of manufacturing output are difficult to obtain. However, the following indices of the volume of net raw materials imports per unit of manufacturing output for West Germany and Japan, neither of whom has experienced a significant increase in domestic production of raw materials, provide indirect evidence of this development.

Indices of the volume of net raw material imports per unit of manufacturing output, 1975 = 100

	West Germany	Japan
1961–62	125.2	131.7
1967–68	108.3	116.4
1971–72	104.3	103.7
1977–78	96.0	91.5
1981–82	93.3	75.6
1983–84	97.4	71.8

Sources and Notes: Export and import volume indices for raw materials (SITC 2 + 4) from OECD, *Historical Statistics of Foreign Trade*, updated with OECD, *Main Economic Indicators*. Net imports computed using trade values for 1975 from UN, *Yearbook of International Trade Statistics*, with imports c.i.f. adjusted to imports f.o.b. using adjustment coefficients in IMF, *International Financial Statistics: Yearbook*. Data on manufacturing output from OECD, *Industrial Production: Historical Statistics*, updated with OECD, *Main Economic Indicators*.

19 The main factors responsible for this are:
(1) Changes in the structure of final demand: as per capita income rises, domestic consumers devote a smaller proportion of their expenditure to basic manufactures and spend relatively more on durable manufactured goods. In addition, advanced industrial countries tend to specialize in exporting capital goods, partly because of their favourable demand characteristics (income-elastic and price-inelastic).
(2) Recent modifications in the international division of labour: advanced countries are now able to satisfy an ever-growing proportion of their requirements for basic manufactures by resorting to suppliers in newly industrializing countries.

20 The Latin American 'structuralist' economist, Raul Prebisch, was one of the first to emphasize the importance of this development; see e.g. Prebisch (1950).

21 Statistics from the advanced countries (the only ones for which data are available) confirm that there is no systematic relationship between economic performance and the rate of growth of minerals production. (The same applies to the rate of growth of energy production.)

Growth rates at constant prices, 1963–80 (% p.a.)

	GDP	Minerals plus energy	Minerals	Energy
United States	3.5	2.4	2.2	2.4
Japan	7.2	3.2	na	na
Austria	4.2	0.0	na	na
Belgium	4.0	1.0	na	na
Finland	4.1	3.5	3.5	0.0
France	3.7	−3.0	1.3	−9.4
West Germany	3.7	−3.9	na	na
Greece	5.9	7.3	na	na
Netherlands	3.9	7.1	na	na
Norway	4.5	22.6	na	na
Portugal	5.7	7.7	9.4	−5.9
Spain	5.5	3.3	4.1	2.5
Sweden	2.5	3.1	1.2	3.1

Source: OECD, *National Accounts*

22 Latin America's recent experience illustrates such adverse trends in the case of a net exporting region.

Latin America: trade in raw materials (at constant 1975 prices)

	Exports		Imports		Trade balance	
	At 1975 US$b	As a % of GDP	At 1975 US$b	As a % of GDP	At 1975 US$b	As a % of GDP
1961–62	4.3	2.8	1.1	0.7	3.2	2.0
1967–68	4.9	2.3	1.4	0.7	3.5	1.7
1971–72	5.4	1.9	1.7	0.6	3.7	1.3
1975–76	5.7	1.6	2.2	0.6	3.6	1.0
1977–78	6.5	1.7	2.9	0.7	3.6	0.9
1981	7.1	1.5	4.1	0.9	3.0	0.7

Sources and Notes: Raw materials (SITC 2 + 4) export and import values for 1975 from UN, *Yearbook of International Trade Statistics.* Extrapolated using export and import volume indices from FAO, *Trade Yearbook.* GDP data from CEPAL, *Series Historicas del Crecimiento de America Latina.* Note that the FAO export and import volume series are not ideal, since they refer to exports and imports of raw materials *and* food, originating in the agricultural sector only.

23 *Volume index of net raw materials imports (1975 = 100)*

	West Germany	Japan
1961–62	74.2	41.5
1967–68	83.7	75.4
1971–72	104.3	101.7
1977–78	107.5	109.2
1981–82	106.6	109.3
1983–84	112.5	113.3

Sources: Import and export volume series from OECD, *Historical Statistics of Foreign Trade,* updated with OECD, *Main Economic Indicators.* Net import volume series computed using data on import and export values for 1975 from UN, *Yearbook of International Trade Statistics.*

24 Of course, countries which are significant producers, in world terms, of some of the materials which they export might well suffer a deterioration in their raw materials balance of trade (relative to GDP), due to the unfavourable evolution of world demand for their exports. This issue is discussed more fully in Chapter 3.

25 See Eden *et al.* (1981), Chap. 2, 'Economic Growth and Energy Demand'.

26 See *Ibid.*

27 Note, however, that estimates of the fuel-intensity of GDP, based on data on the consumption of commercial fuel alone, exaggerate the extent of the rise in fuel-intensity at this stage of development, because of the substitution of commercial for non-commercial sources of fuel (e.g. wood, farm waste, etc.).

28 *Index of aggregate commercial energy input per unit of GDP (1975 = 100)*

	Italy	Japan	Spain
1952–55	47.4	89.7	—
1956–60	58.0	89.0	78.7
1961–65	74.6	92.9	71.8
1966–70	92.5	100.3	78.7
1971–75	99.2	105.0	93.2
1976–80	94.9	89.4	98.6

Source: Energy statistics from UN, *World Energy Supplies*, UN, *Yearbook of World Energy Statistics*. GDP data (at constant producers' values) from OECD, *World Energy Statistics, National Accounts*.

29 This coefficient differs from the income-elasticity of demand for fuel, because it incorporates the effect of relative price changes as well as changes in income.

30 *Commercial fuel coefficients for a number of newly industrializing countries*

	1950–60	1960–70	1970–80
Argentina	0.9	1.4	1.4
Malaysia	—	1.7	1.1
		(1.4)	(0.9)
		1965–72	1972–79
Mexico		1.08	1.61
			1971–79
Indonesia			1.8
			(1.1)
		1967–77	
Brazil		1.02	
		(0.90)	

( ) = including non-commercial fuel
Sources: Everson, Eden and Hope (1981); Eden and Jannuzzi (1981); Ang (1981); Ang (1982); Eden and Hope (1982).

31 This second factor appears to be of relatively minor importance. See Eden *et al.* (1981), Chap. 2.

32 *Index of commercial fuel consumption per unit of GDP (1975 = 100)*

	West Germany	UK
1952–55	132.5	130.1
1956–60	115.9	122.9
1961–65	107.9	116.4
1966–70	105.9	111.5
1971–75	104.7	105.7
1976–80	95.2	96.4

Sources: For West Germany, energy statistics from UN, *World Energy Statistics*, UN, *World Energy Supplies* and UN, *Yearbook of World Energy Statistics* and GDP statistics from OECD, *National Accounts*. For UK, HMSO, *Digest of UK Energy Statistics*.

33 OECD (1983).

34 In Eastern Europe and the Soviet Union, by contrast, there was an extremely rapid expansion of coal production in the post-war period as part and parcel of the general development effort.

35 One possible link between fuel output and the level of economic development (leaving aside the case of countries which are richly endowed in fuel resources) is that the more advanced a country, the greater its capacity to generate nuclear energy.

36 See note 24.

37 See UN, *World Energy Statistics* and UN, *Yearbook of World Energy Statistics*.

38 See Griffiths (1975), P. 76.

39 There are, of course, some notable exceptions. Norway, Greece and Liberia have all been net exporters of shipping services during the early stages of their development; see Delegations for the Promotion of Economic Cooperation between the Northern Countries (1937).

40 See e.g. UNCTAD (1971) and Sapir and Lutz (1981).

41 See Griffiths (1975), p. 11, Committee on Invisible Exports (1982), Woolley (1966). p. 42 and Sapir and Lutz (1980).

42 Committee on Invisible Exports (1967), p. 31 and Lutz and Sapir (1980).

43 *Balance of trade in non-government services as a % of GDP at market prices*

	1952–55	1981–82	Change
Holland	+3.9	+0.5	−3.4
West Germany	−0.5	−2.7	−2.2

Source: See Appendix 5

44 The principal exceptions being countries in possession of an exceptional endowment of natural resources.

45 Chapter 4 contains an exhaustive discussion of the various ways in which a country can adjust to an autonomous improvement in its non-manufacturing balance.

3 Trade and industry in developed economies

1 For details of sources and methods, see Appendix 5.

2 I.e. the balance of trade in primary products (food [SITC 0 + 1], raw materials [SITC 2 + 4] and fuel [SITC 3]) *plus* the balance in non-government services (excluding interest, profits and dividends) and private transfers.

3 I.e. SITC 5–8.

4 These four countries were the four net food-exporting countries in our sample at the beginning of the 1950s.

5 These four countries were four of the five net raw material-exporting countries in our sample in the early 1950s.

6 The deterioration in the food and raw materials balances of these primary producing countries was mainly due to the fact that primary product prices were much lower in the early eighties than in the early fifties.

7 This proposition is explored in greater detail in Chapters 5–7.

8 The mechanism responsible for this is fully explored in Chapter 4.

9 Although we couch the argument in terms of the need for a high per capita output of manufactures to attain a high level of development, it can also be presented in terms of the need for a rapid *growth* of manufacturing output in order to achieve a rapid *growth* of GDP.
10 E.g. small island economies possessing exceptional tourist potential.
11 Although import-substitution industrialization (i.e. reducing the share of imported manufactures in total supply) may well play an important role during the early stages of industrial growth.
12 Of course, such an economy can resort to an increased inflow of foreign savings (net) in order to meet its rapidly growing import needs. However, some increase in net manufactured exports is nevertheless necessary, not only to satisfy the country's creditors concerning its capacity to service its debts, but also to avoid running the risk of falling into the Debt Trap (see Chapter 4).
13 Even so, it would perhaps be more accurate to characterize such growth experiences as examples of 'growth-led manufactured exports', thereby emphasizing that the rapid expansion of manufactured exports is more often than not an *induced* response to the country's voracious import requirements rather than a crucial *autonomous* element in the growth process. Confirmation for this can be found in the fact that in many, though by no means all, 'young' workshop economies, manufactured exports are a relatively small proportion of total manufacturing output.
14 See the discussion in Chapter 2.
15 For example, Brazil's share of world coffee exports is so large that the country has frequently been unable to increase the purchasing power of its net coffee exports in terms of imported manufactures. Similarly, the USA kept a substantial proportion of it cultivable agricultural land idle in the post-war period, because a large increase in US net food exports represents quite a considerable addition to world trade in temperate foodstuffs and would, therefore, have had an adverse impact on US terms of trade.
16 This argument has much less force in the case of a 'small' primary producer, because the latter, if faced with an income-inelastic demand for its commodity exports, always has the option of increasing its market share – and since it is 'small', it runs less of a risk of triggering a deterioration in its own terms of trade.
17 In particular, if the growth of world demand for its commodity exports is income-inelastic, then the rate of growth of its export receipts will be less than that of world income. Thus, unless the 'large' primary producer can reduce its income-elasticity of demand for imported manufactures, it will be condemned to grow at a rate which is slower than that for the rest of the world.

4 The commercial account and why it tends to balance

1 It should be noted that the component parts of the *basic balance*, namely the *commercial balance* and the *residual balance* (to be defined shortly), are generally opposite to one another in sign: this is true in the case of 59 of the 78 separate observations for all three balances shown in Table 4.1. This is one of the reasons why any surpluses and deficits, recorded on basic balance, are so small relative to GDP.
2 The fact that the US dollar and the £ sterling were international reserve assets during this period undoubtedly made it easier for the US and the UK to incur deficits on basic balance.
3 This does not mean, of course, that all has been well in, for example, the UK's international transactions. The figures shown in Table 4.1 are *ex post* magnitudes and, in themselves, tell us nothing about the means by which a zero basic balance has been maintained or about the costs involved in achieving it. Since the Second World War, almost all British governments have been concerned with the balance of payments, and most have had occasion to restrain domestic growth and thereby reduce the demand

for imports, in order to strengthen the basic balance. And it is widely, if not universally, believed that such deflationary policies have been harmful to Britain's long-term economic development. Thus, Britain has only managed to achieve a more or less zero basic balance at the cost of deflationary economic policies and slower economic growth.

4 The reasons why West Germany accumulated such large reserves are relatively well known. First, the huge expansion in West Germany's foreign trade in the post-war period necessitated some increase in the country's gold and foreign exchange reserves. Second, West Germany made repeated attempts to restrict the extent of DM appreciation, so as not to endanger the country's extremely successful manufacturing export drive, and this resulted in reserve accumulation.

5 The additional items are as follows:
(1) non-government receipts from US military forces in the UK and (2) expenditure in the UK by overseas governments and non-territorial organizations. Since 1964, the first year for which information on these items is available, their combined value has fluctuated between 0.2% and 0.4% of GDP. Appendix 6 contains a complete description of our approach to measuring 'government services' in the UK.

6 The behaviour of each of these balances is examined in much greater detail in Chapter 5.

7 However, as we shall argue below, if the underlying circumstances responsible for the surplus on basic balance do not change, then foreign investment provides only a temporary respite from the continued accumulation of foreign exchange reserves. This is because the assets acquired as a result of foreign investment yield an income, some of which is bound to be repatriated.

8 It should be noted that a 'growth strategy' is more likely to be adopted under a regime of relatively fixed nominal rates of exchange than under one of more flexible rates since, under the latter, government may be tempted to use the improvement in non-manufacturing trade to strengthen the real rate of exchange, even in a situation of widespread under-utilization of domestic resources.

9 The case considered here is that of a net primary product importer, but the argument also applies, with suitable modifications, to the case of a primary producer.

10 This will happen either under a regime of flexible nominal rates of exchange or under one in which nominal rates of exchange are somewhat more fixed. Under a flexible regime, an improvement in non-manufacturing trade will give rise to an appreciation of the nominal and, hence, real rate of exchange. Under a regime of somewhat more fixed nominal rates, the real rate of exchange tends to appreciate for the following reasons: the improvement in non-manufacturing trade causes domestic absorption to increase, either because the value of non-manufactured exports increases and/or because expenditure on non-manufactured imports falls. However, if domestic absorption increases, whilst domestic output is fixed, then prices must rise. As a result, the real rate of exchange is likely to appreciate even under a regime of fixed nominal rates of exchange.

11 Any increase in the demand for primary products, following revaluation, is likely to be relatively modest in the typical OECD country, for reasons given earlier; in fact, because revaluation causes manufacturing output to be lower than it would otherwise have been, there may even be a fall in net primary product imports.

12 Suppose, for example, that the government were to distribute vouchers, which could only be spent on foreign holidays.

13 Appendix 7 contains a simple model illustrating how foreign investment influences the balance of payments.

14 The so-called 'Debt Trap', in which many less developed countries find themselves, is more familiar. Recent LDC borrowing from the international capital market can be used to illustrate the nature of the 'Debt Trap'. During the 1970s, many developing countries found that they could borrow large sums on the international private capital market and, as a result, were able to run quite significant deficits on their commercial

accounts. In this way, they received a transfer of resources (net) from the rest of the world. In many cases, their debts grew faster than GDP; however, since real rates of interest were often negative, interest payments grew quite slowly relative to GDP and could, in many cases, be financed by new loans. However, in the early 1980s, the real costs of debt-service rose dramatically (as a result of higher nominal interest rates, falling commodity prices and an appreciating US $); in addition, there was a sharp reduction in new capital inflow. As a result, many less developed countries quickly found themselves in a situation in which payment of debt interest exceeded net capital inflow so that, in order to maintain external balance, they had to generate surpluses on their commercial account. Thus, by 1982–3, many less developed countries were actually making a net transfer of resources to the rest of the world. Meanwhile, their foreign debts continued to rise, because net capital inflow, which covered some of their interest payments, remained positive. This 'Debt Trap' situation is the counterpart to the 'Wealth Trap' described in the text.

15 The UK's experience in the nineteenth century illustrates this point. Britain embarked on her career as a significant foreign investor during the 1850s and 1860s. At this time, her commercial account was in surplus and, as a result, she was making a net transfer of resources to the rest of the world. Meanwhile, on the residual account, net capital outflow exceeded foreign investment income. However, as early as the 1870s, investment income exceeded net capital outflow, and the UK went into deficit on her commercial account: the UK had already become a 'rentier' nation, in receipt of a net transfer of resources from the rest of the world. Even so, the UK continued to build up an ever-increasing portfolio of overseas assets, financed out of her huge investment income.

5 UK trade since the Second World War: an overview

1 In the 1980s the net gain to Britain's balance of payments from domestic oil and gas production has been equivalent to around 5.0% of GDP.

2 See for example, the influential book on de-industrialization published by the National Institute (ed. Cairncross, 1979). Apart from a passing reference by Cairncross himself, there is virtually no mention in this book of what has happened to the UK's trade in food and raw materials or of the implications of such changes for the internal structure of the British economy.

6 UK trade in non-manufactures

1 On the use of the terms 'inferior' and 'superior' see Chapter 2.

2 On this point, see Chapter 2 for a description of the 'gastronomic transition' which occurs almost universally in the course of economic development.

3 Pollard (1969), p. 138.

4 Centre for Agricultural Strategy (1980), p. 53. Engledow and Amey (1980), p. 55.

5 Mellanby (1975), p. 48.

6 See Engledow and Amey (1980), p. 155 for a rough break-down of energy use by sector.

7 Body (1984), p. 37. The figure cited here is at 1984 prices. Another estimate is given by Buckwell *et al.* (1982), p. 168. They estimate that the net cost of the CAP to the UK was 2664m EUA in 1980. At 1984 prices this is equivalent to roughly 2100 million per year.

8 The classic reference on this topic in Harrison (1964).

9 Buckwell *et al.* (1980), p. 130.

10 This index, like other volume indices in this book, was calculated for 1938 and all post-war years. The weights are based on prices in 1963. Note that the figures given here refer only to food; they exclude drink and tobacco.

11 In the years prior to the First World War, the highest figure recorded for net fuel exports was 1.7% of GDP. In the inter-war period, the figure never exceeded 1.6% and was normally considerably lower.

12 The trend towards the use of coal in electricity generation was reversed during the 1984–5 miners' strike, when oil was widely used in power stations in place of coal. However, this was a temporary phenomenon and, with the strike over, coal is once again the main fuel used in electricity generation.

13 For a concise discussion of North Sea oil and gas see Bending and Eden (1984), Chapter 12. See also Chapter 12 of the present work.

14 MTOE = million tonnes of oil or oil equivalent.

15 The output of North Sea oil in 1983 was 115 MTOE.

16 Note that all of the statistics for energy consumption in Table 6.7, and most of those in Table 6.8, are on a heat supplied basis. They are not directly comparable to those used in the rest of this chapter, which refer to consumption of primary fuels.

17 In another context, Andrew Glyn has used a cricketing analogy to describe this kind of 'improvement'. Any captain can improve the batting average of his cricket team by refusing to field his worst batsmen. The total score of the team will fall, but the average score of those who actually play will rise.

18 In their recent study of UK manufacturing industry, Jenne and Cattell (1983) conclude that the pace of energy saving was slower after 1973 than before. However, the period covered by their study ends in 1978; it therefore excludes more recent years, in which the pace of energy saving has accelerated.

19 Since this section was written, a good survey of the UK service sector has appeared in the *Bank of England Quarterly Bulletin* [Key (1985)].

20 See Appendix 6 for a full description of the way we measure government services and how our approach differs from that used in official statistics.

21 See Strange (1971) for a discussion of how the fortunes of the City of London revived during the 1960s.

22 The following are official figures for net service income:

	£ Million							
	1977	1978	1979	1980	1981	1982	1983	1984
Construction work overseas	757	929	900	891	995	1090	1102	1128 (est)
Insurance	585	628	562	435	599	602	715	672
Banking	311	349	406	475	564	709	810	950

Source: HMSO, *UK Balance of Payments*, 1984 and 1985 editions

Note that the above figures refer only to income resulting from the provision of services; they do not include interest, profits and dividends on the overseas assets of British financial institutions.

23 The turnaround in the travel account in 1985 is partly due to the gross overvaluation of the US dollar, which led to a massive inflow of high-spending American tourists; it also discouraged UK travellers from visiting the United States. With the devaluation of the dollar in autumn 1985, this factor is no longer operative and its beneficial impact on the travel account will soon be reversed.

24 Some of the decline shown in Table 6.14 may be illusory. The figures shown in this table refer to UK-registered ships and include foreign-owned vessels operating under the British flag. However, they exclude British-owned ships operating under foreign flags. Thus, part of the decline may reflect mere changes in registration without any corresponding change in ownership. Some British owners may have 'flagged-out' their ships and left the UK register, so as to take advantage of cheap labour from low-wage

countries in Asia and elsewhere. At the same time some foreign owners, previously registered in the UK, may have switched to other flags for a variety of reasons. But this is only part of the story, and even allowing for such errors, the figures shown in Table 6.14 indicate a genuine and massive decline in the British fleet since 1977.

25 Colvin and Marks (1984).

26 National Union of Seamen (1982).

27 For a general survey of barriers to invisible trade see Griffiths [1975]. For a more comprehensive discussion of barriers in the insurance sector see OECD (1984).

28 For a fuller discussion of how government policy has influenced the exchange rate see Chapter 12.

7 UK trade and economic growth: a quantitative assessment

1 The econometric models consulted were those of the Cambridge Growth Project, the London Business School, the National Institute and the Treasury.

2 The most comprehensive treatment of services is contained in the Treasury Model, which distinguishes two export categories and four import categories. However even this is not very useful for our purposes. Many of the long-term coefficients are imposed, and most of the econometrics is concerned with the estimation of lag structures and short-term variations.

3 The energy coefficient is defined as follows:

$$\text{Energy coefficient} = \frac{\%\ \text{change in energy consumption}}{\%\ \text{change in GDP}}$$

Under the hypothetical scenarios GDP is 40% higher than its actual level in 1983. Since the energy coefficient is assumed to lie between 0.8 and 1.0, the rise in energy consumption lies between $0.8 \times 40\ (=32)\%$ and $1.0 \times 40\ (=40)\%$.

4 For the years 1951 to 1982 the hypothetical figures are derived using a simple formula which is described in Appendix 8.

8 The UK trade structure in an international perspective

1 The classification of countries used in the present chapter is the same as that used in Chapter 3.

2 Details of the behaviour of per capita food consumption and of the striking advances in food self-sufficiency in all the member countries of the EEC (with the exception of Italy) can be found in EC (1975), Tables 1/8.3 and 1/9.1, which can be updated with the aid of EC (1982).

3 Consumption standards were lower on the Continent than in the UK in the 1950s, partly because per capita incomes were lower and partly because continental agriculture was still suffering from the effects of war-time devastation.

4 The exceptional experience of both Japan and Italy in food trade requires a brief mention. For much of the post-war period, both Japan and Italy were in the full flood of their gastronomic transitions (see Chapter 2). In neither country did the growth of domestic agricultural output keep pace with the enormous changes taking place in both the level and composition of food demand. As a result, both countries experienced a decline in food self-sufficiency during the 1960s and early 1970s, as well as growing deficits in food trade. However, by the late 1970s, both Japan and Italy were probably on the verge of completing their gastronomic transitions. The evidence in favour of this is that Italian per capita consumption of cereals and beef stabilized in the 1970s (see EC (1975, 1982)), whilst Japanese per capita food consumption, after virtually doubling between 1950 and 1970, appears to have stabilized during the late 1970s. (Index No. (1953 = 100): 1973 = 195.8; 1982: 195.6. See Statistics Bureau, *Monthly Statistics of Japan*, and Statistics Bureau, *Japan Statistical Yearbook*.)

9 The changing geography of UK trade since the Second World War

1 This chapter is a thoroughly revised and more fully developed version of ideas first presented in Rowthorn (1982).
2 This chapter is only concerned with changes in the direction of UK *visible* trade; this is because the available data on the direction of UK trade in non-government services are not adequate for a proper discussion. Thus, the expression 'UK trade' refers, throughout this chapter, to UK *visible* trade only.
3 For definitions, see notes to Table 9.1.
4 I.e. the majority of developing countries, who are neither members of OPEC nor have been included in our category of NICs (newly industrializing countries) (see Table 9.1).
5 Throughout this discussion, EEC refers to the original EEC6: West Germany, France, Italy, the Netherlands, Belgium and Luxembourg.
6 It should be noted that this process of increasing integration in trade with Western Europe was already extremely well advanced even before Britain's entry into the European Community in 1972. Membership of the EEC mainly served to formalize a process which had already been under way for a considerable period of time. Though trading relations between the UK and other members of the EEC certainly became closer after UK membership, there is little sign sign of any really marked acceleration in the pace of integration.
7 *Index number of UK terms of trade (Px/Pm) (1963 = 100)* (constructed from export (*Px*) and import (*Pm*) unit value indices for total trade (see Tables 9.2 and 9.8)).

1947	94.2	1956	86.7	1965	100.9	1974	81.7
1948	92.2	1957	89.0	1966	102.7	1975	88.1
1949	94.2	1958	95.4	1967	104.3	1976	86.3
1950	86.3	1959	95.4	1968	101.4	1977	88.5
1951	76.0	1960	96.2	1969	100.6	1978	94.3
1952	81.2	1961	99.1	1970	102.3	1979	94.8
1953	85.9	1962	101.0	1971	103.1	1980	93.2
1954	85.8	1963	100.0	1972	104.6	1981	94.2
1955	85.0	1964	98.1	1973	92.8	1982	93.1
						1983	92.3

8 Even so, between 1950 and 1973 (i.e. for much of the post-war period), UK imports of food and raw materials increased steadily in terms of volume, reaching their maximim in 1968 and 1973 respectively.
9 Note that between 1948 and 1973, there was a somewhat disproportionate increase in the share of UK imports accounted for by 'Other Western Europe' (see Table 9.3). This was largely a reflection of UK membership of EFTA, which resulted in a margin of preference being extended to manufactured imports from EFTA countries – partly at the expense of suppliers in the EEC. The decline in importance of 'Other Western Europe', following the UK's entry into the EEC in 1973, reflected the subsequent unravelling of this EFTA-related preferential trade in manufactures.
10 *UK import volume indices (1963 = 100)*

	All food	Sugar	Beef
1956–59	98.3	102.9	122.9
1980–83	92.1	68.6	72.3

Source: computed from HMSO, *Overseas Trade Statistics of the U.K.* and HMSO, *Annual Report on U.K. Agriculture.*

11 *UK import volume indices (1963 = 100)*

	All raw materials	Raw cotton	Jute and other vegetable fibres
1938	106.1	159.9	111.2
1950–59	98.0	111.2	93.0
1975–80	103.2	42.1	30.1
1981–83	87.9	29.0	18.1

Sources: computed from HMSO, *Trade and Navigation Accounts for the U.K.* and HMSO, *Overseas Trade Statistics for the U.K.*

12 *Share of the EEC and the White Dominions in UK food imports (%)*

	1962	1972	1982
EEC	26.1	32.7	52.0
White Dominions	30.5	30.0	16.2

Source: HMSO, *Trade and Navigation Accounts of the U.K.*, and HMSO, *Overseas Trade Statistics of the U.K.*

13 *EEC as a source of supply of UK primary product imports 1962, 1972, 1982 (%)*

	1962	1972	1982
Food	25.2	32.7	52.0
Beverages	7.4	13.1	15.5
Drink	77.0	74.2	78.9
Tobacco	2.6	9.9	23.1
Raw materials	8.2	11.0	22.2
Fuel	11.3	18.0	20.9
Total primary products	16.9	23.2	32.5

Sources: HMSO, *Trade and Navigation Accounts of the U.K.* and HMSO, *Overseas Trade Statistics of the U.K.*

14 *Import volume indices (1963 = 100)*

	Food	Non-alcoholic beverages	Alcoholic beverages	Tobacco
1938	108.0	82.6	56.7	106.2
1946–49	78.6	70.5	59.3	100.7
1950–59	89.5	86.1	70.1	95.5
1960–69	100.3	97.1	112.1	95.5
1970–73	96.2	99.3	194.8	91.8
1974–79	91.5	94.5	255.8	121.7
1980–81	92.9	86.3	293.8	98.2
1982–83	91.4	89.8	312.0	96.7

Sources: HMSO, *Trade and Navigation Accounts for the U.K.* and HMSO, *Overseas Trade Statistics of the U.K.*
cf. Table 9.2 for aggregate index for food, beverages and tobacco.

15 As noted previously, a large proportion of the increase in UK demand for the manufactured products of US business enterprise was met by the overseas subsidiaries of these companies operating in Continental Europe, as well as in the UK itself.
16 This issue has recently been examined by the House of Lords, Select Committee on the European Communities (1983). The conclusions reached by this Committee are similar to our own, but the Report is entirely lacking in any sort of analytical framework of the kind developed here.
17 The share of 'Other Western Europe' in UK manufactured imports increased between 1951 and 1973 from 12.3% to 21.5% (see Table 9.6).
18 The share of UK manufactured exports destined for the 'other LDCs' declined, between 1961 and 1973, from 26.0% to 10.7% (see Table 9.9).
19 Note that the EEC was the largest single market for British manufactured exports even before Britain entered the Community.
20 *UK primary product export volume indices, 1963 = 100*

	Food	Non-alcoholic beverages	Alcoholic beverages	Tobacco	Raw materials	Fuel
1938	112.9	129.4	28.9	159.8	91.1	124.6
1946–49	68.8	88.4	25.1	163.4	57.8	38.9
1950–59	99.5	117.2	50.7	150.9	75.9	62.4
1960–69	116.0	111.8	118.4	119.6	98.7	87.4
1970–73	147.8	150.6	n.a.	174.3	115.2	126.4
1974–79	268.9	229.6	268.2	402.3	146.7	183.9
1980–81	462.3	212.4	235.3	377.9	191.1	360.7
1982–83	602.3	210.5	229.3	407.7	190.2	458.6

Sources: Cols. (1)–(4) constructed from HMSO, *Trade and Navigation Accounts of the U.K.* and HMSO, *Overseas Trade Statistics of the U.K.* For Cols, (5)–(6), see Table 9.8.
21 *EEC's share in UK primary product exports (%)*

	1962	1972	1983
Food	36.1	47.5	59.5
Non-alcoholic beverages	31.6	25.5	35.2
Alcoholic beverages	13.2	18.1	26.1
Tobacco	18.4	26.1	33.9
Raw materials	38.3	51.3	54.3
Fuel	53.5	51.3	62.0
Total	37.1	41.1	56.7

Sources: HMSO, *Trade and Navigation Accounts of the U.K.* and HMSO, *Overseas Trade Statistics of the U.K.*
22 Due to factors mentioned earlier – loss of Imperial preference and mounting competitive pressures.
23 This group includes the NICs in addition to the industrialized countries (Western Europe, Japan and the USA – see Table 9.11).
24 Note that we are describing the situation as it existed in the early to mid-1980s. The prospective decline in UK fuel production, together with a possible expansion in fuel consumption – if and when there is a sustained rise in GDP – means that such a situation is unlikely to persist into the late 1980s. See Chapter 13 for a discussion of these issues.
25 This issue has received the attention of the House of Commons, Select Committee

on Trade and Industry (1984). However, the conclusions reached by this committee are largely erroneous, although certain witnesses, in particular, the Secretary of State for Trade and Industry, demonstrated a keen appreciation of some of the consequences of the increased triangularity of British trade described above. This issue has also been considered by the House of Lords, Select Committee on the European Communities (1983). In general, the conclusions reached by this latter committee are similar to our own, although the Committee's Report is entirely lacking in any kind of analytical framework of the sort developed here.

10 De-industrialization in the UK: three theses

1 For example, in the USA, the number of people employed in manufacturing rose by 5.2% between 1970 and 1981. However, total employment rose by 27.6% over the same period, so the share of manufacturing fell considerably, despite an increase in the absolute number employed in this sector. The USA is unusual in this respect. In most other countries a falling share of manufacturing in total employment has been accompanied by a decline in its absolute number of people working in this sector.
2 An exception to this is Denmark, which belongs to group A but has also experienced a big fall in the share of industry (see Table A9.1 in Appendix 9).
3 The principal exception in this group is Germany, where the industry's share hardly changed at all between 1955 and 1981.
4 In Fig. 10.3 the base year is 1955 because this is the year in which the share of manufacturing in total employment began to fall in the UK. In Fig. 10.4 the base year is 1966 because this is the year in which the absolute number of people employed in UK manufacturing begun to fall.
5 As always, in the present work, the term 'non-manufactures' includes services.
6 The six major OECD countries referred to here are: the USA, Canada, Japan, France, Germany and Italy.
7 Amongst the exceptions are agriculture, coal-mining and the railways. In none of these activities would a stronger manufacturing performance have created additional employment. On the contrary, by improving job opportunities elsewhere, it might have accelerated the long exodus of labour from these activities.

11 Towards a better past

1 The hiatus in employment growth in the late 1960s occurs both in the actual economy and under the hypothetical scenarios. It is caused by a hiatus in the growth of labour supply due partly to demographic factors and partly to a sharp fall in the proportion of young people leaving school at the age of 15 years.
2 Singh (1977) p. 128.
3 We take the term 'socially acceptable exchange rate' to be a reference to the distribution of income associated with a particular real rate of exchange.
4 See Chapter 1 for a definition of this term.
5 See p. 271 above.
6 'Support' in the sense of providing the manufactured inputs and manufactured consumer goods used by those working in the service sectors and/or the manufactured exports used to pay for imported inputs or wage goods.

12 Oil and the UK economy

1 Note that the scenarios labelled 40B, 40I and 40W in the present chapter are identical to those labelled simply B, I and W in Chapter 7.
2 This is the same scenario for which detailed estimates of non-manufacturing trade were provided in Chapter 7.

3 As it is used here, the term 'structural' refers only to changes in the pattern of employment which arise at a *given* level of economic activity. It does not include those changes in the pattern of employment which are induced by variations in the level of activity. Throughout this book, such changes in the pattern of employment are classified as macro-economic effects. For further discussion of this point see Chapter 1.

4 In one of the scenarios considered by Barker and Fairclough (1983), North Sea oil has a positive impact on total employment. However, these authors also consider other scenarios, in which the opposite is the case. For a theoretical justification for the view that North Sea oil may have stimulated the non-oil economy see Eastwood and Venables (1982).

5 Buiter and Miller (1981b) take a similar position, and theoretical support for this view is provided by Buiter and Purvis (1980). The arguments of Buiter and Purvis are also developed by Neary and Wijnbergen (1984).

6 Kaldor (1983). The same view is expressed more moderately by Bond and Knobl (1982) and in a muted form in Bank of England Quarterly Bulletin (March 1982).

7 Minford (1981) also argues that North Sea oil had had a minor effect on total employment.

8 Atkinson *et al.* (1983), p. 43.

9 Barker and Fairclough consider a number of different scenarios. Our discussion here refers to their Scenario 2, which they themselves consider to be the most realistic. It is also closest to the scenario used in the National Institute simulation.

10 See, for example, Nigel Lawson.

11 One obvious stress would arise from the fact that the 5 million unemployed would have to be supported by social security without the benefit of the revenue from oil.

12 A notable exception is the team from the London Business School. Despite claims to the contrary, their approach is similar to that of Buiter and Purvis, and they recognize that a more expansionary monetary policy could avoid some of the harmful consequences of oil. However, they reject such an option on what seem to be purely ideological grounds – they certainly provide no analytical justification for their hostility to the more expansionary monetary policy required to prevent crowding-out (Beenstock *et al.*, 1981).

13 For a survey of UK monetary policy since the early 1970s see Fforde (1983).

14 This is implicitly recognized by Buiter in a joint article with Miller (1981b) where they quote, with approval, the following passage by Dornbusch on the lasting effects of a tight monetary policy: 'If pursued over any period of time, the (high real exchange rate) policy will lead to a contraction of industry, reduced investment, shutdowns, declining productivity, loss of established markets and a deterioration of commercial position' (p. 146).

15 In a House of Lords speech on the subject, Kaldor (1983) had this to say:

It was a national misfortune that Mrs Thatcher and North Sea oil came on stream more or less at the same time. For North Sea oil meant a resource boom, involving a sudden fall in oil imports and a sudden increase in oil exports – a turn-round of 10 billion in three years – and unless this is accompanied by an expansion of domestic demand of the same order of magnitude, either by a large increase in public investment or a large remission of tax, or both, the gain from this valuable new source of wealth will be lost since it will lead to a corresponding diminution of existing sources of wealth, which give the same value-added but provide many times the number of jobs provided by the new source of wealth by which they are replaced. In other words, unless this is combined with an expansionary policy – if I may use the dreaded word, unless it is combined with reflation – the new wealth from oil does not enrich the nation because it destroys existing sources of wealth to the same extent. In Britain it meant a 15 to 20 percent fall in manufacturing output and a two million loss in civilian employment, four-fifths of which was in manufacturing.

16 For a clear statement of this position see Bond and Knobl (1982), especially pp. 380–1.

17 For an exposition of this argument see Eastwood and Venables (1982).
18 Bond and Knobl (1982), p. 378. Note that the authors themselves do not directly estimate what has been the impact of North Sea oil. However, they do estimate that a 10% rise in North Sea oil production would lead to a permanent reduction of 0.8% in real income. Since their model is linear, it follows mathematically that complete cessation of oil production (i.e. a 100% fall in output) would lead to an 8% rise in real income. This gives some indication of how much North Sea oil has harmed the non-oil economy and is the basis for our statement in the text.
19 Beenstock *et al.* (1981) p. 106.
20 For estimates of the long-term impact of North Sea oil on the real exchange rate see: Beenstock *et al.* (1981), Byatt *et al.* (1982), Hall and Atkinson (1983), Buiter and Miller (1983). All of these authors consider this impact to be in the range of 10–15%. One exception is Minford (1981), who says it is 'probably about 10%'.
21 See Bank of England, *Bank of England Quarterly Bulletin* (1980) and (1982). For a clear exposition of the same argument see Byatt *et al.* (1982) or Hall and Atkinson (1983).

13 Towards a better future

1 For a description of how the future labour force is estimated see Appendix 14.
2 See Andreassen *et al.* (1983). These authors predict that total employment in the USA will rise at an annual rate of 1.5 to 1.8% over the period 1982–95.
3 Civilian employment in the countries listed in the text has grown at the following annual percentage rates:

	USA	Japan	Canada	Australia	New Zealand	Norway
1962–73	2.1	1.3	3.1	2.7	2.1	n.a.
1973–84	1.9	0.9	2.1	1.0	1.1	1.5
1962–84	2.0	1.1	2.6	1.8	1.6	n.a.

4 The proviso that *hourly* wage rates are constant is important here. If hourly wage rates rise when hours of work are cut, then older or less efficient techniques of production may be driven out of use. As a result, output per hour may increase so much that output per worker remains unchanged despite the fall in hours of work. Under these conditions, a reduction in hours of work will have no effect at all on total employment (assuming total output is given).
5 According to the official definition a part-timer is someone who works less than 30 hours a week. With this definition, virtually all workers would be classified as part-timers by the year 2025 under the Green Scenario.
6 *Confederation of British Industries* (1985).
7 The following section has been influenced by the writings of the Cambridge Energy Research Group, in particular the following works: Evans (1983), Bending and Eden (1984), Eden and Evans (1984) and Eden, Evans and Catell (1985). However, some of the groups' assumptions have been modified, on occasion quite radically, to allow for different policies towards energy production and use. In considering energy use under the Green Scenario we have been influenced by: Olivier and Miall (1983), Hillman (1984) and Ray (1985).
8 For predictions of future oil prices made before the 1986 collapse see International Energy Agency (1985), p. 60.
9 See Appendix 14 for more details. Note that throughout our discussion of the balance of payments 1983 is taken as base year. This year is chosen because it is the last full year in which UK trade is unaffected by the miners' strike of 1984–5.
10 In 1983, the Total Primary Energy Requirement (TPER) per unit of GDP was as

follows: UK: 0.74; W. Germany: 0.51; Japan: 0.49; Denmark: 0.37. In this comparision TPER is measured in tonnes of oil equivalent and GDP in thousands of US dollars at 1975 prices and exchange rates. The figures are taken from International Energy Agency (1985), National Tables.

11 See International Energy Agency (1985) p. 254.

12 MTOE = million tonnes of oil or oil equivalent.

13 For a detailed breakdown of energy production and consumption under the various scenarios see Appendix 14.

14 Evans (1983) p. 7 predicts that France will have a nuclear capacity of between 95 and 130 GW by the year 2020 (= approximately 200–250 MTOE). This is over twice the figure assumed for the UK even under variant C of the Supergrowth Scenario. For Japan, Evans predicts an even larger nuclear capacity in the range 170–250 GW by 2025.

15 This is about what is currently forecast for the UK. For example, under their 'central trend' Eden and Evans (1984) assume that nuclear power will generate 49 MTOE of electricity by the year 2020.

16 In their consideration of different scenarios, Bending and Eden (1984) and Turner (1984) both take 140 million tonnes as their highest figure for coal output. Marshall and Robinson (1984) put coal production in 2020 in the range 69–105 million tonnes.

17 Most long-term projections of economic growth in the UK are based on the Cambridge Growth Model. However, the analysis of trade in services in this model is unsatisfactory for several reasons. It uses an industrial classification which is quite different from that employed in balance of payments statistics, and the results are therefore difficult to interpret. Moreover, the model predicts a massive growth in what are called 'distribution exports', the exact meaning of which is obscure. The term *seems* to refer to the revenue earned from the distribution of goods imported into the UK, although this is not certain. In view of these difficulties, we have not used the Cambridge Growth Model in analysing the future behaviour of UK trade in services. Even so, it is interesting to note that in aggregate our informal predictions for net earnings from service exports are broadly similar to those formally derived using the Cambridge Growth Model.

18 For a description of what has been happening to international finance and the City of London see: Bank of England (1985) and Plender and Wallace (1985).

19 The reason for the slower growth of earnings from both financial and other services under the Green Scenario is as follows. Under this scenario we assume that other advanced countries also pursue a green policy and expand very slowly. As a result, the market for UK service exports grows less rapidly than under the remaining scenarios which envisage a much higher rate of world economic growth.

20 See note 19.

21 Over the periods 1964–72 and 1973–85 the commercial balance averaged £416 million and £583 million respectively (at 1983 prices). In each case, this represents around 0.2% of GDP.

22 Using the Cambridge Growth Model, Dr Michael Landesmann of the DAE has obtained the following predictions for domestic expenditure in the UK. The figures refer to annual percentage growth rates over the period 1984 to 2000, and results are given for two slightly different scenarios.

	Scenario 1	Scenario 2
(1) Expenditure on manufactures	1.90	2.11
(2) Total expenditure	2.01	2.19
Ratio (1):(2)	0.95	0.96

23 The US Bureau of Labor Statistics has made the following projections of output growth

in the US over the period 1979–95 [Andreassen *et al.* (1983)]. The figures refer to annual percentage growth rates, and the results are for three:

	Low growth	Moderate growth	High growth
(1) Output of manufactures	2.36	2.51	2.78
(2) GNP	2.33	2.39	2.72
Ratio (1) : (2)	1.01	1.05	1.02

The relevant figures on expenditure are not given. However, if the above figures on output are any guide, it seems that expenditure on manufactures will rise at about the same rate as total expenditure.

24 The reduction in North Sea oil and gas production over the period 1985–2025 represents a loss of potential revenue equal to £18–20 billion, depending on the scenario concerned. Over the same period net manufactured exports increase by £2 billion under the Green Scenario, £10 billion under the Growth Scenario and £23 billion under the Supergrowth Scenario. These figures refer to the B-variant of each scenario and are measured at 1980 prices.

25 Andreassen *et al.* (1983).

Appendix 2 The simple mathematics of structural change

1 The model presented here has been strongly influenced by the ideas contained in Baumol (1967).

2 This is obvious from the fact that, in the long run, P_i converges to zero. The sign of dP_i/dt can be found by differentiating equation (20).

3 For a discussion of dynamic economies of scale see Kaldor (1966) and Cripps *et al.* (1973).

Appendix 3 Empirical evidence on output and expenditure data at constant and current prices

1 For a description of their method and basic results see Kravis *et al.* (1982). And for a specific discussion of services and their evolution in the course of development see Kravis *et al.* (1983) and Summers (1982).

2 See, for example, Kravis *et al.* (1983) for time-series evidence on the evaluation of expenditure patterns.

3 For a definition see Chapter 1, note 14.

4 For the exact formulae used to compute shares see Chapter 1, note 14.

5 The UK is excluded from the table because it is a special case. Unlike the countries included in the table, the UK experienced a radical change in trade specialization over the period 1962–81, which had a profound effect on her internal economic structure.

6 For a detailed comparison of pre- and post-1973 experience, see Mittelstadt and Correira (1985).

7 This statement ignores the impact of changing trade specialization, which in exceptional cases may have a large and permanent effect on economic structure. The effects of trade specialization are discussed below.

Appendix 7 Overseas investment and the balance of payments

1 Remember we are assuming in this section that $\frac{s}{k}\pi > g > s\pi$.

Appendix 8 Trade and economic growth: the intermediate scenario

1 These variables are smoothed by taking three-year moving averages for the years 1951–82 inclusive.

Appendix 12 North Sea oil

1 Note that, as we explain in Chapter 1, variations in the level of activity may also cause the pattern of employment to change. Thus, macro-economic effects may have implications for the pattern of employment. These are of minor importance in the present context and are ignored.

Appendix 13 Holland and the Dutch disease: a case of severe hypochondria

1 Two of the principal contributions to this discussion (in English) are Ellman (1977, 1982).
2 This discussion draws on the following: Byatt *et al.* (1982); Forsyth and Kay (1980); Forsyth and Kay (1981); Gregory (1976); Atkinson and Hall (1983), and Barker and Brailovsky (1981).
3 See Barker and Brailovsky (1981), Table 2, p. 15.
4 Government receipts from natural gas (the government takes 80% of net income from this sector) were estimated to be worth 1.4% of national income in 1974: see Ellman (1981) p. 154.

Appendix 14 Notes on Chapter 13

1 The scenarios considered by these authors cover slightly different time periods from ours and assume slower rates of output growth than under our Growth and Supergrowth Scenarios. An exact comparison is not therefore possible.

Bibliography

Andreassen, A. J., Saunders, N. C. and Su, B. W. (1983), 'Economic Outlook for the 1990s: three scenarios for economic growth', *Monthly Labor Review*, November.

Ang, B. W. (1981), *Malaysia: The Energy Outlook* (Cambridge, Energy Research Group, Cavendish Laboratory).

— (1982), *Indonesia: The Energy Outlook* (Cambridge, Energy Research Group, Cavendish Laboratory).

Astor, Viscount and Seebohm Rowntree, B. (1939), *British Agriculture: The Principles of Future Policy* (London, Penguin).

Atkinson, F. J. and Hall, S. G. (1983), *Oil and The British Economy* (London, Croon Helm).

Atkinson, F. J., Brooke, S. J. and Hall, S. G. F. (1983), 'The Economic Effects of North Sea Oil', *National Institute Economic Review*, May.

Bacon, R. and Eltis, W. (1976), *Britain's Economic Problem: Too Few Producers* (London, Macmillan Press).

Bairoch, P. *et al.* (1968), *La Population active et sa structure* (Brussels, Free University).

Bank of England (1980), 'The North Sea and the United Kingdom Economy', *Bank of England Quarterly Bulletin*, Vol. 20, December.

Bank of England (1982), 'North Sea Oil and Gas: Costs and Benefits', *Bank of England Quarterly Bulletin*, Vol. 22, March.

Barker, T. and Brailovsky, V. (1981), *Oil or Industry?* (London, Academic Press).

Barker, T. S. and Fairclough, I (1983), 'North Sea Oil and the UK Economy 1974–81', Paper presented to the 10th EARIE Conference in Bergen, Norway.

Baumol, W. J. (1967), 'Macroeconomics of Unbalanced Growth: The Anatomy of the Urban Crisis', *American Economic Review*, June, pp. 415–26.

Beenstock, M., Budd, A. and Warburton, P. (1981), 'Monetary Policy, Expectations and Real Exchange Rate Dynamics', *Oxford Economic Papers*, Vol. 33, July Special Supplement.

Bending, R. and Eden, R. (1984), *UK Energy* (Cambridge, Cambridge University Press).

Blackaby, F. (ed.) (1979), *De-industrialization* (London, Heinemann).

Body, R. (1984), *Farming in the Clouds* (London, Temple Smith).

Bond, M. E. and Knobl, A. (1982), 'Some Implications of North Sea Oil for the UK Economy', *IMF Staff Papers* (29), No. 3.

Boserup, E. (1970), *Women's Role in Economic Development* (London, G. Allen and Unwin).

Buckwell, A. E., Harvey, D. R., Thomson, K. J. and Parton, K. A. (1982), *The Costs of the Common Agricultural Policy* (London, Croom Helm).

Buiter, W. H. and Purvis, D. D. (1980), 'Oil, Disinflation and Export Competitiveness: A Model of the Dutch Disease', *Warwick Economic Research Papers*, No. 85.

Buiter, W. H. and Miller, M. (1981a), 'The Thatcher Experiment: Two Years On', *Brookings Papers on Economic Activity*, 2.

— (1981b), 'Monetary Policy and International Competitiveness: The Problems of Adjustment', *Oxford Economic Papers*, Vol. 33, July Supplement.

— (1983), 'Changing the Rules: Economic Consequences of the Thatcher Regime', *Brookings Papers on Economic Activity*, 2.

Byatt, I., Hartley, N., Lomax, R., Powell, S. and Spencer, P. (1982), 'North Sea Oil and Structural Adjustment', *Treasury Working Paper*, No. 22.

Cairncross, A. (1979), 'What is De-industrialization?' in F. Blackaby (ed.), *De-industrialization.*

Cassen, R. H. (1976), 'Population and Development: A Survey', *World Development*, 1976, Vol. 4, Nos. 10/11, pp. 785–830.

Centre for Agricultural Strategy (1980), *The Efficiency of British Agriculture*, (Reading).

CEPAL (1978), *Series Historicas del Crecimiento de America Latina*, (Santiago, CEPAL).

Chenery, H. B. (1960), 'Patterns of Industrial Growth', *American Economic Review*, 50 (September), pp. 624–54.

Chenery, H. B. and Syrquin, M. (1975), *Patterns of Development* (London, Oxford University Press).

Clark, C. (1957), *The Conditions of Economic Progress*, 3rd edition (London, Macmillan).

Colvin, M. and Marks, J. (1984), *British Shipping: The Right Course* (London, Centre for Policy Studies).

Committee on Invisible Exports (1967), *Britain's Invisible Earnings* (London, British National Export Council).

Committee on Invisible Exports (1982), *World Invisible Trade* (London).

Confederation of British Industry (1985), *Change to Succeed* (London).

Cripps, T. F. and Tarling, R. J. (1973), *Growth in Advanced Capitalist Countries* (Cambridge, Cambridge University Press).

Cuddy, J. D. A. (1976), *International Price Indexation* (Farnborough, Saxon House).

Deane, P. and Cole, W. A. (1967), *British Economic Growth 1688–1959*, 2nd edition (Cambridge, Cambridge University Press).

Delegations for the Promotion of Economic Cooperation Between the Northern Countries (1937), *The Northern Countries in the World Economy* (Finland, Otava Printing Office).

Dornbusch, R. (1976), 'Expectations and Exchange Rate Dynamics', *Journal of Political Economy*, Vol. 84, December.

Eastwood, R. K. and Venables, A. J. (1982), 'The Macroeconomic Implications of a Resource Discovery in an Open Economy', *Economic Journal*, Vol. 92, June.

EC (European Commission) (1975), *The Agricultural Situation in the Community: 1975 Report* (Brussels).

EC (1982), *The Agricultural Situation in the Community: 1982 Report* (Brussels).
ECLA (UN Economic Commission for Latin America) (1951), 'Economic Survey of Latin America 1949' (New York: UN).
Eden, R. and Jannuzzi, G. (1981), *Brazil: The Energy Outlook* (Cambridge, Energy Research Group, Cavendish Laboratory).
Eden, R., Posner, M., Bending, R., Crouch, E. and Stanislaw, J. (1981), *Energy Economics* (Cambridge, Cambridge University Press).
Eden, R. and Hope, C. (1982), *Mexico: Energy Outlook* (Cambridge, Energy Research Group, Cavendish Laboratory).
Eden, R. and Evans, N. (1984), *Electricity's Contribution to UK Self-Sufficiency* (London, Heinemann).
Ellman, M. (1977), 'Report fron Holland: The Economics of North Sea Hydro-carbons', *Cambridge Journal of Economics*, September, pp. 281–90.
— (1981), 'Natural Gas, Restructuring and Re-industrialization: The Dutch Experience of Industrial Policy' in T. Barker and V. Brailovsky (eds.) *Oil or Industry?* (London, Academic Press).
Engledow, F. and Amey L. (1980), *Britain's Future in Farming* (Berkhampstead, Geographical Publication).
Eurostat, *Balance of Payments: Global Data, 1969–80* (Luxembourg, Statistical Office of the European Communities).
Eurostat, *Monthly External Trade Bulletin, 1958–80* (1981) (Special number) (Luxembourg, Statistical Office of the European Communities).
Evans, N. (1983), *Nuclear Power in the Eastern World to 2020*, Energy Discussion Paper No. 29, (Cambridge, Energy Research Group, Cavendish Laboratory).
Everson, C., Eden R. and Hope, C. (1981), *Argentina: The Energy Outlook*, July (Cambridge, Energy Research Group, Cavendish Laboratory).
FAO, *Food Balance Sheets* (Rome), various years.
FAO, *Trade Year Book* (Rome), various years.
FAO, *The State of Food and Agriculture* (Rome), various years.
Fforde, J. S. (1983), 'Setting Monetary Objectives', *Bank of England Quarterly Bulletin*, Vol. 23, June.
Fields, G. S. (1980), *Poverty, Inequality, and Development* (Cambridge, Cambridge University Press).
Fisher, A. G. B. (1935), *The Clash of Progress and Security* (London, Macmillan).
Forsyth, P. J. and Kay, J. A. (1980), 'North Sea Oil and Revaluation', *Fiscal Studies*, Vol. 1, No. 3.
— (1981), 'Oil Revenues and Manufacturing Output', *Fiscal Studies*, Vol. 2, No. 2, July, pp. 9–17.
Fuchs, V. R. (1968), *The Service Economy* (New York, NBER).
Fuchs, V. R. (ed.) (1969), *Production and Productivity in the Service Industries* (New York, NBER).
Gershuny, J. I. and Miles, I. D. (1983), *The New Service Economy* (London, F. Pinter).
Griffiths, B. (1975), *Invisible Barriers to Invisible Trade* (London, Macmillan).
Hall, S. G. and Atkinson, F. (1983), *Oil and the British Economy* (London, Croom Helm).

Harrison, R. (1964), *Animal Machines: The New Factory Farming Industry* (London, Vincent Stuart).

Hill, T. P. (1971), *The Measurement of Real Product* (Paris, OECD).

Hillman, M. (1984), *Conservation's Contribution to UK Self-Sufficiency* (London, Policy Studies Institute).

HMSO, *Accounts Relating to Trade and Navigation of the United Kingdom* (London), various years.

HMSO, *Annual Abstract of Statistics* (London), various years.

HMSO, *Annual Review of Agriculture* (formerly *Annual Review and Determination of Guarantees*) (London), various years.

HMSO, *Digest of UK Energy Statistics* (London), 1984.

HMSO, *Economic Trends Annual Supplement* (London), various years.

HMSO, *Overseas Trade Statistics of the UK* (London), various years.

HMSO, *Trade and Navigation Accounts of the UK* (London), various years.

HMSO, *United Kingdom Balance of Payments* (London), various years.

House of Lords, Select Committee on the European Communities (1983), *Trade Patterns: The UK's Changing Trade Pattern Subsequent to Membership of the European Community*, London, HMSO, 7th Report, Session 1983–4.

House of Lords (1985), *Report from the Select Committee on Overseas Trade* (London, HMSO).

House of Commons, Select Committee on Trade and Industry (1984), *The Growth in the Imbalance of Trade in Manufactured Goods between the UK and Existing and Prospective Members of the EEC* (London, HMSO), 2nd Report, Session 1983–4.

IMF, *International Financial Statistics: Yearbook* (Washington D.C.), various years.

IMF, *Yearbook of Balance of Payments Statistics* (Washington D.C.), various years.

International Energy Agency (1985), *Energy Policies and Programmes of IEA Countries: 1984 Review* (Paris, OECD).

Jenne, C. and Cattel, R. A. (1983), 'Structural Change and Energy Efficiency in Industry', *Energy Economics*, Vol. 5, No. 2.

Kaldor, N. (1966), *Causes of the Slow Rate of Economic Growth in the United Kingdom* (Cambridge, Cambridge University Press).

— (1981), 'The Energy Issues', in T. Barker and V. Brailovsky (eds.) *Oil or Industry?* (London, Academic Press).

— (1983), 'Oil and the Decline of Manufacturing', House of Lords Speech, 29 June.

Key, T. S. (1985), 'Services in the UK Economy', *Bank of England Quarterly Bulletin*, September, pp. 404–14.

Kravis, I. B., Heston, A. W. and Summers, R. (1978), 'Real GDP per Capita for More Than One Hundred Countries', *Economic Journal*, vol. 88, pp. 215–42.

— (1982), *World Product and Income*, UN International Comparison Project, Phase III, London.

— (1983), 'The Share of Services in Economic Growth' in Adams, F. G. and Hickman, B. G. (eds.) *Global Econometrics* (London).

Lappé, F. M. (1978), *Diet for a Small Planet* (New York, Ballantine).

Lengelle, M. (1966), *The Growing Importance of the Service Sector in Member Countries* (Paris, OECD).

Leontief, W. and Duchu, F. (1985), *The Future Impact of Automation on Workers* (Oxford, Oxford University Press).

Mark, J. (1980), 'Productivity Measurement in the Public Sector', in Bailey, D. and Hubert, T. (eds.), *Productivity Measurement* (Farnborough, Gower).

Marshall, E. and Robinson, C. (1984), *The Economics of Energy Self-Sufficiency* (London, Heinemann).

Matthews, R. C. O., Feinstein, C. H. and Odling-Smee, J. C. (1982), *British Economic Growth* (Oxford, Clarendon Press).

McBride, T. (1976), *The Domestic Revolution 1820–1920* (London, Croom Helm).

Mellanby, K. (1975), *Can Britain Feed Itself?* (London, Merlin).

Minford, P. (1981), 'The Exchange Rate and Monetary Policy', *Oxford Economic Papers*, Vol. 33, July Supplement.

Mittelstadt, A. and Correira, F. (1985), 'Changes in the Composition of Output and Employment', *OECD, Working Papers, No. 23* (Paris, OECD).

National Institute Economic Review, various issues.

National Union of Seamen (1982), *British Shipping Heading for the Rocks* (London).

Neary, J. P. and Van Wijnbergen, S. (1984), 'Can an Oil Discovery Lead to a Recession?', *Economic Journal*, 94, June.

OECD, *Balance of Payments Statistics, 1950–61* (Paris) 1964.

OECD, *Balance of Payments, 1960–77* (Paris), 1979.

OECD, (1983), *Economic Outlook*, 33, July. 'The Effects of Changes in Energy Prices', pp. 75–80.

OECD, *Historical Statistics, 1960–83*, (Paris), 1985.

OECD, *Historical Statistics of Foreign Trade, 1965–80* (Paris), 1982.

OECD, *Industrial Production: Historical Statistics* (Paris), various years.

OECD, *International Trade in Services: Insurance* (Paris) 1984.

OECD, *Main Economic Indicators* (Paris), various years.

OECD, *Main Economic Indicators: Historical Statistics, 1960–75* (Paris), 1976.

OECD, *Main Economic Indicators: Historical Statistics, 1964–83* (Paris), 1984.

OECD, *Main Accounts*, Vol. 1, Main Aggregates (Paris), various years.

OECD, *Quarterly National Accounts*, No. 1, (Paris), 1985.

Olivier, D. and Miall, H. (1983), *Energy Efficient Futures: Opening the Solar Option* (London, Earth Resources Research).

OPCS (1985), *Population Projections, 1983–2023*, Series Papers, No. 13 (London, HMSO).

Petit, P. (1986), *Slow Growth and the Service Economy* (London, Frances Printer).

Pinchbeck, I. (1931), *Women Workers and the Industrial Revolution* (London).

Plender, J. and Wallace, P. (1985), *The Square Mile* (London, Hutchinson).

Pollard, S. (1969), *The Development of the British Economy, 1914–1967*, 2nd edition (London, E. Arnold).

Prebisch, R. (1959), *Economic Development of Latin America and its Principal Problems* (New York, UN).

— (1951), *Theoretical and Practical Problems of Economic Growth* (Santiago, ECLA).

Ray, G. F. (1985), *Energy Management: Can We Learn From Others?* (Aldershot, Gower).

Richards, E. (1974), 'Women in the British Economy since about 1700: An Interpretation', *History*, LIX, October.

Robinson, C. and Marshall, E. (1984), *Oil's Contribution to UK Self-Sufficiency* (London, Heinemann).
Rostow, W. W. (1978), *The World Economy: History and Prospect* (London, Macmillan).
Rowthorn (1982), 'Britain and Western Europe', *Marxism Today*, April.
Sapir, A. and Lutz, E. (1980), *Trade in Non-factor Services: Past Trends and Current Issues*, World Bank Staff Working Paper, No. 410 (Washington D.C.).
— (1981), *Trade in Services: Economic Determinants and Development Related Issues*, World Bank Staff Working Paper, No. 480 (Washington D.C.).
Shelp, R. K. (1982), *Beyond Industrialization* (New York, Praeger).
Singh, A. (1977), 'UK Industry and the World Economy: a Case of De-industrialization', *Cambridge Journal of Economics*, Vol. 1, No. 2, 113–36.
Stanback, T. M. (1979), *Understanding the Service Economy* (Baltimore, John Hopkins).
Statistics Bureau, *Monthly Statistics of Japan* (Tokyo, Prime Minister's Office), various issues.
Statistics Bureau, *Japan Statistical Yearbook* (Tokyo, Prime Minister's Office), various years.
Strange, S. (1971), *Sterling and British Policy* (London, Oxford University Press).
Summers, R. (1982), *Services in the International Economy*, Wharton, Conference Paper, Wharton Business School.
Thirlwall, A. P. (1982), 'De-industrialization in the United Kingdom', *Lloyd's Bank Review*.
Turner, L. (1985), *Coal's Contribution to UK Self-Sufficiency* (Aldershot, Gower).
UN, *Monthly Bulletin of Statistics* (New York), various issues.
UN, *Demographic Yearbook* (New York), various years.
UN, *World Energy Statistics 1950–74* (New York), various issues.
UN, *World Energy Supplies 1973–78* (New York), 1979.
UN, *Yearbook of International Trade Statistics* (New York), various years.
UN, *Yearbook of World Energy Statistics 1980* (New York) 1981.
UN, *Population Prospects as Assessed in 1980* (New York), 1982.
UNCTAD (1971), Committee on Invisibles and Financing Related to Trade Insurance, TD/B/C.3/99 (Geneva).
Urquhart, M. (1981), 'Are Services Recession Proof?' *Monthly Labour Review*, October.
Vines, D., Maciejowski, J. and Meade, J. E. (1983), *Stagflation. Vol. 2: Demand Management* (London, Allen and Unwin).
Wells, J. R. (1983), 'Industrial Accumulation and Living-Standards in the long-run: The São Paulo Industrial Working Class, 1930–75', Parts I and II, *Journal of Development Studies*, Vol. 19, Nos. 2 + 3, pp. 145–69, 297–328, January and April.
Woolley, H. B. (1966), *Measuring Transactions Between World Areas* (New York, Columbia University Press).

Index